D0368222

Carolean Coventree

Making Face, Making Soul

H A C I E N D O   C A R A S

Other books by Gloria Anzaldúa:

Borderlands/La Frontera: The New Mestiza

This Bridge Called My Back:
Writings by Radical Women of Color (co-editor)

Making Face, Making Soul

HACIENDO CARAS

Creative and Critical Perspectives by Women of Color

edited by Gloria Anzaldúa

an aunt lute foundation book
SAN FRANCISCO

Copyright © 1990 by Gloria Anzaldúa

All rights reserved

First Edition
10-9-8-7-6-5-4-3-2

Aunt Lute Foundation Books
P.O. Box 410687
San Francisco, CA 94141

Cover and Text Design: Pamela Wilson Design Studio

Cover Art: Judy Baca's "Triumph of the Heart," from her participatory mural project, The World Wall: A Vision of the Future Without Fear

Typesetting: Debra DeBondt

Production:

Eileen Anderson	Tawnya Keedy
Daniel Bao	Cynthia Lamb
Martha Davɪ	Moire Martin
Nancy Fishman	Joan Meyers
Rosana Francescato	Camille Pronger
Sharon Franklet	Kathleen Wilkinson
Laura Jiménez	Kathy Zumski

Cover color separation donated by Henrietta Boberg

Printed in the U.S.A. on acid-free paper

Library of Congress Cataloging-in-Publication Data

Making face, making soul = Haciendo caras : creative and critical perspectives by feminists
    of color / edited by Gloria Anzaldúa. —
    1st ed.
        p.   cm.
    ISBN 0-933216-74-2 : $24.95. — ISBN 0-933216-73-4 pbk.) : $14.95
    1. Feminism—United States—Literary collections. 2. Minority women—United
States—Literary collections. 3. Feminism and literature—United States. 4. American
literature—Minority authors. 5. American literature—Women authors. 6. American
literature—20th century. 7. American literature—California.
    I. Anzaldúa, Gloria. II. Title: Haciendo caras.
PS509.F44M35   1990
810.8'09287—dc20
                                                                    90-9428
                                                                    CIP

The editor gratefully acknowledges the following authors, presses and publications for their kind permission to reprint the works noted below. All effort has been made to cite the correct bibliographic data. Apologies are made for any errors or omissions.

"What The Gypsy Said To Her Children" from *Woman Of Her Word: Hispanic Women Write, Revista Chicano-Riqueña*, vol. xi, nos. 3-4, 1983, ed. Evangelina Vigil, Houston, TX: Arte Público Press. © 1983 by Judith Ortiz Cofer. By permission of the publisher. "Poem For The Young White Man Who Asked Me How I, An Intelligent, Well-Read Person, Could Believe In The War Between Races" from *Emplumada*, Pittsburgh, PA: University of Pittsburgh Press. © 1981 by Lorna Dee Cervantes. By permission of the author and publisher. "Punto Final" from *That's What She Said: Contemporary Poetry and Fiction by Native American Women*, ed. Rayna Green, Bloomington, IN: Indiana University Press. © 1984 by Shirley Hill Witt. By permission of the publisher. "We Exist" from *Naming the Waves: Contemporary Lesbian Poetry*, ed. Christian McEwen, Freedom, CA: Crossing Press, 1989; London: Virago Press, 1988. © 1988, 1989 by Janice Gould. By permission of the author. "Desert Run" and "Masks of Woman" from *Desert Run, Poems and Stories*, © 1988 by Mitsuye Yamada. By permission of the author and Kitchen Table: Women of Color Press, P.O. Box 908, Latham, NY 12110. "Generations of Women," "Suicide Note" and "Prisons of Silence" from *Shedding Silence*, © 1987 by Janice Mirikitani. By permission of the author and Celestial Arts, P.O. Box 7327, Berkeley, CA 94707. "Something About the Subject Makes It Hard to Name" from *Changing Our Power*, ed. Cochran et al, Dubuque, IA: Kendall-Hunt Publishers. © 1987 by Gloria Yamato. By permission of the author. "Racism and Women's Studies" from *All The Women Are White, All The Blacks Are Men, But Some of Us Are Brave*, eds. Gloria T. Hull, Patricia Bell Scott and Barbara Smith, Old Westbury, NY: The Feminist Press. © 1982 by Barbara Smith. By permission of the author. "The Costs of Exclusionary Practices in Women's Studies" from *Signs*. © 1986 by The University of Chicago Press. By permission of the authors and the publisher. "Feminism and Racism: A Report on the 1981 National Women's Studies Association Conference," Oakland, CA: The Center for Third World Organizing. © 1982 by Chela Sandoval.

"A Woman Cutting Celery" from *My Wicked Wicked Ways*, Bloomington, IN: Third Woman Press. © 1987 by Sandra Cisneros. By permission of the publisher. "Turtle Gal" from *Canadian Fiction Magazine 60—The Native Issue*, ed. Thomas King. © 1987 by Beth Brant. By permission of the author. "La Dulce Culpa" from *Loving in the War Years: Lo que nunca pasó por sus labios*, Boston, MA: South End Press. © 1983 by Cherríe Moraga. By permission of the author. "Notes from a Chicana 'Coed'" from *Caracol* vol. 3, no. 9. © 1977 by Bernice Zamora. By permission of the author. "Between Ourselves" from *The Black Unicorn*, New York: W.W. Norton & Co. © 1978 by Audre Lorde. By permission of the publisher. "En rapport, In Opposition: Cobrando cuentas a las nuestras" from *Sinister Wisdom* 33. © 1987 by Gloria Anzaldúa. By permission of the author.

"I Give You Back" and "For Alva Benson, And For Those Who Have Learned To Speak" from *She Had Some Horses* by Joy Harjo, New York: Thunder's Mouth Press. © 1983 by Thunder's Mouth Press. By permission of the publisher. "Journeys of the Mind" from *Living the Spirit: A Gay American Indian Anthology*, compiled by Gay American Indians; ed. Will Roscoe, New York: St. Martin's Press. © 1988 by Anne Waters. By permission of the author. "You're Short, Besides!" from *Making Waves: An Anthology of Writings By and About Asian American Women*, Boston, MA: Beacon Press. © 1989 by Asian Women United of California. By permission of the publisher. "Notes on Oppression and Violence" from *Compañeras: Latina Lesbians: An Anthology* ed. Juanita Ramos, New York: Latina Lesbian History Project. © 1987 by Aletícia Tijerina.

By permission of the author. "Where Is The Love?" from *Essence*, September, 1978. © 1978 by June Jordan. By permission of the author.

"Periquita" from *Revista mujeres*, vol. 4, no. 1. © 1987 by Carmen Morones. By permission of the author. "Refugee Ship" from *Revista Chicano-Riqueña* vol. 3, no. 1. © 1975 by Lorna Dee Cervantes. By permission of the author and publisher. "The Eskimos" from *Past, Present and Future Passions*, available for women only from Her Books, P.O. Box 7467, Santa Cruz, CA 94061. © 1987 by Barbara Ruth. By permission of the author. "Elena" and "Legal Alien" from *Chants*, Houston, TX: Arte Público Press. © 1984 by Pat Mora. By permission of the publisher. "Unnatural Speech" from *Borders*, Houston, TX: Arte Público Press. © 1986 by Pat Mora. By permission of the publisher. "The Three Tongues" from *Sinister Wisdom* 34. © 1988 by Catalina Ríos. By permission of the author. "I Lost It at the Movies" from *Testimonies: A Collection of Lesbian Coming Out Stories*, ed. Sarah Holmes, Boston, MA: Alyson Publications. © 1988 by Jewelle Gomez. By permission of the publisher. "Talking Back" from *Talking Back: Thinking Feminist, Thinking Black*, © 1988 by bell hooks. By permission of South End Press, 116 St. Botolph St., Boston, MA 02115.

"Madness Disguises Sanity" from *Morena*, February, 1988. © 1988 by Opal Palmer Adisa. By permission of the author. "A Julia de Burgos" from *Obra Poética*, Río Piedras, Puerto Rico: Ediciones Huracán. © 1961 by Julia de Burgos. By permission of the publisher. "To Julia de Burgos," trans. William M. Davis, from *The Defiant Muse: Hispanic Feminist Poems from the Middle Ages to the Present: A Bilingual Anthology*, ed. Angel Flores and Kate Flores, New York: The Feminist Press at CUNY. © 1986 by Angel Flores and Kate Flores. By permission of the publisher. "Commitment from the Mirror-Writing Box" excerpted from *Woman Native Other: Writing Postcoloniality and Feminism*, Bloomington, IN: Indiana University Press. © 1989 by Trinh T. Minh-ha. By permission of the publisher. "Judy Baca: Our People Are The Internal Exiles" from *Cultures in Contention*, ed. Douglas Kahn and Diane Neumaier, Seattle, WA: The Real Comet Press. © 1985 by The Real Comet Press. By permission of the publisher. "Object Into Subject: Some Thoughts On The Work Of Black Women Artists" from *Heresies* 15: "Racism Is the Issue." © 1982 by Michelle Cliff. By permission of the author. "Nopalitos: The Making of Fiction (Testimonio)" from *Breaking Boundaries: Latina Writing and Critical Readings*, ed. Asunción Horno-Delgado, Eliana Ortega, Nina M. Scott and Nancy Saporta Sternbach, Amherst, MA: University of Massachusetts Press. © 1989 by The University of Massachusetts Press. By permission of the publisher.

"For the white person who wants to know how to be my friend" from *Movement In Black*, Ithaca, NY: Firebrand Books, 1990. Earlier editions by The Crossing Press, 1983 and Diana Press, 1978. © 1978 by Pat Parker. By permission of the publisher. "Some Like Indians Endure" from *Living the Spirit: A Gay American Indian Anthology*, compiled by Gay American Indians, ed. Will Roscoe, New York: St. Martin's Press, 1988. Previously in *Common Lives, Lesbian Lives*, 1982. © 1982 by Paula Gunn Allen. By permission of the author. "Girlfriends" from *Feminary* 13. © 1984 by Andrea Canaan. By permission of the author. "I Am Your Sister: Black Women Organizing Across Sexualities" from *A Burst of Light*, Ithaca, NY: Firebrand Books. © 1988 by Audre Lorde. By permission of the publisher.

"The Race for Theory" from *Cultural Critique* 6. © 1989 by Barbara Christian. By permission of the author. "The Politics of Poetics: Or, What Am I, A Critic, Doing in This Text Anyhow?" from *Chicana Creativity and Criticism: Charting New Frontiers in American Literature*, ed. María Herrera-Sobek and Helena María Viramontes, Houston, TX: Arte Público Press. © 1988 by Tey Diana Rebolledo. By permission of the author and publisher. "Definition of Womanist" from *In Search of Our Mothers' Gardens*, New York: Harcourt Brace Jovanovich, Inc. © 1983 by Alice Walker. By permission of the publisher. "Not You/ Like You: Post-Colonial Women and the Interlocking Questions of Identity and Difference" from *Inscriptions* 3/4. © 1988 by Trinh T. Minh-ha. By permission of the author. "La conciencia de la mestiza: Towards a New Consciousness" from *Borderlands/La Frontera: The New Mestiza*, San Francisco,

CA: Spinsters/Aunt Lute Book Company. © 1987 by Gloria Anzaldúa. By permission of the publisher. "Playfulness, 'World'-Travelling, and Loving Perception" from *Hypatia: A Journal of Feminist Philosophy*, vol. 2, no. 2. © 1987 by María Lugones. By permission of the author.

Many of the pieces in this anthology have not previously been published. Each author is respectfully acknowledged for agreeing to have her work printed here.

"Inclusion Without Influence: The Continuing Tokenism of Women of Color" © 1990 by Lynet Uttal; "*Hablando cara a cara*/Speaking Face to Face: An Exploration of Ethnocentric Racism" © 1990 by María Lugones; "Postscript" © 1990 by Canéla Jaramillo; "Notes from a Fragmented Daughter" © 1990 by Elena Tajima Creef; "Light Skinned-ded Naps" © 1990 by Kristal Brent Zook; "The Visit Home" © 1990 by Rosemary Cho Leyson; "Corrosion" © 1990 by Gisele L. Fong; "Sessions" © 1990 by Nora O. Cobb; "On Passing" © 1990 by Laura Munter-Orabona; "Corazón de una anciana" © 1990 by Edna Escamill; "To Omoni, In Korea" © 1990 by Anne Mi Ok Bruining; "A Letter to My Daughter" © 1990 by Siu Wai Anderson; "In Magazines (I Found Specimens of the Beautiful)" © 1990 by Ekua Omosupe. "Her Rites of Passage" © 1990 by Lynda Marin; "*Palabra de mujer*" © 1990 by Elba Rosario Sánchez; "The Girl Who Wouldn't Sing" © 1990 by Kit Yuen Quan; "Not Editable" © 1990 by Chrystos; "Grace" © 1990 by Carmen Morones; "Developing Unity Among Women of Color: Crossing the Barriers of Internalized Racism and Cross-Racial Hostility" © 1990 by Virginia R. Harris and Trinity A. Ordoña; "Nods That Silence" © 1990 by Lynet Uttal. "Recognizing, Accepting and Celebrating Our Differences" © 1990 by Papusa Molina. "The Theoretical Subject(s) of *This Bridge Called My Back* and Anglo-American Feminism" © 1990 by Norma Alarcón.

Quiero darles las gracias a mis estudiantes
in the Women of Color in the U.S. class
who first "tried out" the reader on which this anthology is based,
to all the contributers especially those *carnalas* who faithfully revised their pieces,
to Helene Moglen and Nicolette Czarrunchick of Women's Studies at UCSC,
the F.R.A. (Feminist Research and Action) for their financial contribution,
to my writing interns/literary assistants:
Audrey Berlowitz, Rosalinda Ramirez and Claire Ricardi
for their dedicated and unstinting support.

To Chela Sandoval, Lynda Marín, Irena Klepfisz, Carolyn Woodward, Kit Quan,
Jeffner Allen, Melanie Kaye-Kantrowitz, Kristal Zook, Jamie Lee Evans,
Donna Haraway, Marge Franz, Bettina Aptheker *y otras amigas*
who in various ways incited, encouraged and/or critiqued my labor,
listened to my list of woes
and put up with my cancellations of lunch and dinner dates, my absences
when I closeted myself with the manusript.

Most especially to Joan Pinkvoss, publisher, editor and kindred spirit
whose unrelenting faith in my work sustained me through all the various stages,
crises and crazies I went through constructing this book.
To the extraordinarily dedicated, capable and loyal staff at Spinsters:
Debra DeBondt, Martha Davis, Eileen Anderson, sharon franklet,
Joan Meyers, Kathy Zumski and Sherry Thomas
who produced this reader with loving labor and generous overtime.

And lastly to all the Virgen de Guadalupe candles,
the *copa*/incence that burned nightly
and Amigita and Manzanita Mordida, the computers that hummed
to my repeated curses when things got out of control
and to the stress reduction tapes I played and the gallons of stress tea I drank
to stay sane—well almost sane.

This book is dedicated to all *mujeres-de-color*
to the memory of Rosa Villafañe-Sisolak
and to the memory of Pat Parker.

Haciendo caras, una entrada

An introduction by Gloria Anzaldúa

Masks and Interfaces/*Caras y máscaras*. Among Chicanas/*méxicanas*, *haciendo caras*, "making faces," means to put on a face, express feelings by distorting the face—frowning, grimacing, looking sad, glum or disapproving. For me, *haciendo caras* has the added connotation of making *gestos subversivos*, political subversive gestures, the piercing look that questions or challenges, the look that says, "Don't walk all over me," the one that says, "Get out of my face." "Face" is the surface of the body that is the most noticeably inscribed by social structures, marked with instructions on how to be *mujer, macho*, working class, Chicana. As mestizas—biologically and/or culturally mixed—we have different surfaces for each aspect of identity, each inscribed by a particular subculture. We are "written" all over, or should I say, carved and tattooed with the sharp needles of experience.

The world knows us by our faces, the most naked, most vulnerable, exposed and significant topography of the body. When our *caras* do not live up to the "image" that the family or community wants us to wear and when we rebel against the engraving of our bodies, we experience ostracism, alienation, isolation and shame. Since white AngloAmericans' racist ideology cannot take in our faces, it, too, covers them up, "blanks" them out of its reality. To become less vulnerable to all these oppressors, we have had to "change" faces, *hemos tenido que cambiar caras "como el cambio de color en el camaleón—cuando los peligros son muchos y las opciones son pocas."*[1] Some of us are forced to acquire the ability, like a chameleon, to change color when the dangers are many and the options few. Some of us who already "wear many changes/inside of our skin" (Audre Lorde)[2] have been forced to adopt a face that would pass.

The masks, *las máscaras*, we are compelled to wear, drive a wedge between our intersubjective personhood and the *persona* we present to the world. "Over my mask/is your mask of me." (Mitsuye Yamada) These masking roles exact a toll. "My mask is control/concealment/endurance/my mask is escape/from my/self." (Mitsuye Yamada) "We are all bleeding, rubbed raw behind our masks."[3] After years of wearing masks we may become just a series of roles, the constellated self limping along with its broken limbs.

In sewing terms, "interfacing" means sewing a piece of material between two pieces of fabric to provide support and stability to collar, cuff, yoke. Between the masks we've internalized, one on top of another, are our interfaces. The masks are already steeped with self-hatred and other internalized oppressions. However, it is the place—the interface—be-

xv

tween the masks that provides the space from which we can thrust out and crack the masks.

In this anthology and in our daily lives, we women of color strip off the *máscaras* others have imposed on us, see through the disguises we hide behind and drop our *personas* so that we may become subjects in our own discourses. We rip out the stitches, expose the multi-layered "inner faces," attempting to confront and oust the internalized oppression embedded in them, and remake anew both inner and outer faces. We begin to displace the white and colored male typographers and become, ourselves, typographers, printing our own words on the surfaces, the plates, of our bodies. We begin to acquire the agency of making our own *caras*. "Making faces" is my metaphor for constructing one's identity. *"[U]sted es el modeador de su carne tanto como el de su alma."*[4] You are the shaper of your flesh as well as of your soul. According to the ancient *nahuas*, one was put on earth to create one's "face" (body) and "heart" (soul). To them, the soul was a speaker of words and the body a doer of deeds. Soul and body, words and actions are embodied in Moyocoyani, one of the names of the Creator in the Aztec framework, "the one who invents himself/herself...the Builder Kachina himself/herself."[5] In our self-reflectivity and in our active participation with the issues that confront us, whether it be through writing, front-line activism, or individual self-development, we are also uncovering the inter-faces, the very spaces and places where our multiple-surfaced, colored, racially gendered bodies intersect and interconnect. This book aims to make accessible to others our struggle with all our identities, our linkage-making strategies and our healing of broken limbs.

How the Book Was Made and Why

Comienzos/**Origins.** For years I waited for someone to compile a book that would continue where *This Bridge Called My Back* left off. A book that would confront the Racism in the white women's movement in a more thorough, personal, direct, empirical and theoretical way. A book that would deepen the dialogue between all women and that would take on the various issues—hindrances and possibilities—in alliance-building. A book that would explode the neat boundaries of the half dozen categories of marginality that define us and one that would unflinchingly bring us *cara a cara* with our own *historias*. A book that would bear unmistakable witness. I got tired of hearing students say that *Bridge* was required in two or three of their women's studies courses; tired of being a resource for teachers and students who asked me what texts by women of color they should read or teach and where they could get these writings. I had grown frustrated that the same few women-of-color were asked to read or lecture in universities and classrooms, or to submit work to anthologies and quarterlies. Why weren't other women-of-color being asked? Repeatedly tokenizing the same half dozen *mujeres* was stymieing our literary/political movement. Drained of our energy, we few tokens had little left to deploy into the development of our own literary and political movements.

The urge to anthologize, to bring more voices to the foreground, grew stronger. Then, in the spring of 1988, when I came to Santa Cruz to teach for U.C. Santa Cruz's Women's Studies, I realized there were no recent anthologies of women-of-color writings. I stopped waiting. In the midst of my unpacking, I worked around the clock frantically locating, reading, copying, compiling and organizing material for a class reader which I titled *Haciendo caras.* On the last day of this whirlwind task, Chela Sandoval and I sat down on my living room floor and together we looked at my six piles of papers. What was left after discarding and rearranging became a framework for this book.

Section one focuses on the degradations and horrors that Racism inflicts, the various ways we are wounded and scarred by its corrosive legacy. Section two focuses on how we combat Racism and sexism and how we "work through" internalized violence, how we attempt to decolonize ourselves and to find ways to survive personally, culturally and racially. Love, humor and optimism are the feelings that permeate the third section. The silencing strategies of the privileged, the repression of our voices and our painful passage from psychic numbing into utterance and creation of our own *paroles*—how we learn to (in Kit Quan's words) metaphorically "sing" our songs—is the gist of section four. Section five focuses on the woman-of-color as writer/artist, intellectual. Section six, on debates about alliances and how we work within our own communities, with other ethnic groups and with marginalized whites. The last section focuses on the intellectual, critic and theorist, and on our critical theories and theories of consciousness as well as the intellectual spaces we are beginning to occupy. It is about other ways, including traditional ethnic modes, of perceiving and knowing.

Originally, I had intended the anthology to consist entirely of previously published historical documents, but as I worked on it, I found myself (as we had with *This Bridge*) wanting to include the unknown, little published or unpublished writers. Because there is little publication support for our writings, I've made a special effort to work with women who do not consider themselves writers, or at least not yet. The book provides space for some ethnic mestizas who have been silenced before uttering a word, or, having spoken, have not been heard. A few pieces give fresh, immediate voice to the issues facing women who, in university surroundings, are often thrown into confusion about their ethnic and/or racial identity.

Montage and fragmented discourse. Let the reader beware—I here and now issue a *caveat perusor:* s/he must do the work of piecing this text together. The categories in this work reflect our fragmented and interrupted dialogue which is said to be a discontinued and incomplete discourse. The method of organizing the book was largely that of poetic association, another way of organizing experience, one that reflects our lives and the ways our minds work. As the perspective and focus shift,

xvii

as the topics shift, the listener/reader is forced into participating in the making of meaning—she is forced to connect the dots, to connect the fragments.

The anthology is meant to engage the reader's total person. I do not believe that "distance" and "objectivity" alone help us come to terms with our issues. Distancing cannot be a major strategy—only a temporary breather. Total feeling and emotional immersion, the shocking drench of guilt or anger or frustration, wakes us up to some of our realities. The pieces in this book awaken the emotions—our emotional bodies "take in" and process the whole spectrum of states of consciousness from waking to dreaming. The intellect needs the guts and adrenaline that horrific suffering and anger, evoked by some of the pieces, catapult us into. Only when all the charged feelings are unearthed can we get down to "the work," *la tarea, nuestro trabajo*—changing culture and all its oppressive interlocking machinations. These pieces are not only *about* survival strategies, they *are* survival strategies—maps, blueprints, guidebooks that we need to exchange in order to feel sane, in order to make sense of our lives.

Besides being a testimonial of survival, I wanted a book which would teach ourselves and whites to read in nonwhite narrative traditions—traditions which, in the very act of writing, we try to recoup and to invent. In addition to the task of writing, or perhaps included in the task of writing, we've had to create a readership and teach it how to "read" our work. Like many of the women in this anthology, I am acutely conscious of the politics of address. *Haciendo caras* addresses a feminist readership of all ethnicities and both genders—yes, men too. Contrary to the norm, it does not address itself *primarily* to whites, but invites them to "listen in" to women-of-color talking to each other and, in some instances, to and "against" white people. It attempts to explore our realities and identities (since academic institutions omit, erase, distort and falsify them) and to unbuild and rebuild them. We have always known that our lives and identities are simultaneously mediated, marked and influenced by race, class, gender and vocation. Our writings and scholarship, built on earlier waves of feminism, continue to critique and to directly address dominant culture and white feminism. But that is not all we do; these pieces attest to the fact that more and more we are concentrating on our own projects, our own agendas, our own theories.

Everything About Racism Evades Direct Confrontation

> I am from an island whose history is steeped in the abuses of Western imperialism, whose people still suffer the deformities caused by Euro-American colonialism, old and new. Unlike many third world liberationists, however, I cannot claim to be a descendent of any particular strain, noble or ignoble. I am, however, "purely bred," descendent of all the parties involved in that cataclysmic

epoch. I despair, for the various parts of me cry out for retribution at having been brutally uprooted and transplanted to fulfill the profit-cry of "white" righteousness and dominance. My soul moans that part of me that was destroyed by that callous instrument...the gun, the whip, the book. My mind echos with the screams of disruption, desecration, destruction.

—ROSA VILLAFAÑE-SISOLAK [6]

Racism, the word nobody likes. Whites who don't want to confront Racism and who don't name themselves white recoil in horror from it, shun it like the plague. To mention the word in their company disrupts their comfortable complacency. To call a text or methodology under discussion in a classroom or conference "racist," or to call a white person on her or his Racism, is to let loose a stink bomb. Like a tenacious weed, Racism crops up everywhere—it has a stranglehold on everyone. It is cultivated and produced in families, churches, temples and state institutions. The psychological effects of Racism have been greatly underestimated.

The people who practice Racism—everyone who is white in the U.S.—are victims of their own white ideology and are empoverished by it. But we who are oppressed by Racism internalize its deadly pollen along with the air we breathe. Make no mistake about it, the fruits of this weed are dysfunctional lifestyles which mutilate our physical bodies, stunt our intellects and make emotional wrecks of us. Racism sucks out the life blood from our bodies, our souls. As survivors of Racism, women-of-color suffer chronic stress and continual "post-traumatic stress syndrome" (suffered by survivors of wars). We are at high risk, and not just from AIDS.

Racism is a slippery subject, one which evades confrontation, yet one which overshadows every aspect of our lives. And because so few (white) people are directly and honestly talking about it, we in the book have once again had to take on the task. Making others "uncomfortable" in their Racism is one way of "encouraging" them to take a stance against it.

A Classic Example. Racism is especially rampant in places and people that produce knowledge. I want to describe the dynamics in the U.S. Women-of-Color class I taught at U.C. Santa Cruz because it may help prepare teachers who will use this text in similar courses. Two of the goals I had were for the 120 students to identify and interpret instances of Racism ("internalized dominance"[7]) and to both recognize their internalized Racism and oppression and to develop strategies against them. I wanted students-of-color to become aware of, and get out from under, conditioned subservience; I wanted to call attention to the dynamic of avoidance among us, of not acknowledging each other—an act of dehumanizing people like ourselves. Yet another goal was to encourage them to emerge from "blank-outness" and openly combat the dominant groups' denial and erasure of ethnic subjectivity by allowing the students a relatively safe space (there is no completely safe space) to speak up and "expose" their feelings.

At first, what erupted in class was anger—anger from *mujeres*-of-color, anger and guilt from whites, anger, frustration and mixed feelings by Jewish women who were caught in the middle (being white but often sympathizing with colored), and anger and frustration on my part from having to mediate between all these groups. Soon my body became a vessel for all the tensions and anger, and I dreaded going to class. Some of my students dreaded going to class. But gradually the *mujeres-de-color* became more assertive in confronting and holding whites accountable for their unaware, "blocked" and chronically oppressive ways. They "agitated" other students into actively demanding that the school system address their needs. When whitewomen or Jewishwomen attempted to subvert the focus from women-of-color's feelings to their own feelings of confusion, helplessness, anger, guilt, fear of change and other insecurities, the women-of-color again and again redirected the focus back to *mujeres-de-color*. When several whitewomen stood up in class and either asked politely, pleaded or passionately demanded (one had tears streaming down her face) that women-of-color teach them, when whitewomen wanted to engage women-of-color in time-consuming dialogues, *las mujeres-de-color* expressed their hundred years weariness of trying to teach whites about Racism. They were eloquent in expressing their skepticism about making alliances with whites when most whitewomen focused exclusively on their own feelings and needed reassurance, acceptance and validation from *mujeres-de-color*.

Many whitewomen did not acknowledge that they were agents of oppression, while others became more aware of their racial "blank spots," stating in class how Racism undermined the integrity of their personhood and how guilt had a debilitating effect in their lives. Most of the white Jewishwomen in the class did not want to identify as white (I'm not referring to the Jewish women-of-color). Some declared they felt they "belonged" more to the women-of-color group than they did to the white group. Because they felt isolated and excluded, they felt that their oppressions were the same or similar to those of women-of-color. Some *mujeres-de-color* questioned the concept of "same" oppressions and claimed that all oppressions were being collapsed into one. The problem was that whitewomen and white Jewishwomen, while seeming to listen, were not really "hearing" women-of-color and could not get it into their heads that this was a space and class on and about women-of-color. As one student-of-color wrote: "I think the hardest thing for me was having to understand that the white students in class... [could not] understand the experiences that we have lived."[8] Though there were important lessons learned, the inability to listen and hear, along with the confusion, anger and doubts about ever being able to work together almost tore our class apart.

"Selective Reality" and "Blank Spots." Failure to empathize with (empathy may open the door to understanding) another's experience is due, in part, to what I call "selective reality," the narrow spectrum of reality that human beings select or choose to perceive and/or what their culture "selects" for them to "see." Perception is an interpretive process conditioned by education.[9] That which is outside of the range of consensus perception is "blanked out." Lorna Dee Cervantes' piece, "Poem for the Young White Man Who Asked Me How I, An Intelligent, Well-Read Person, Could Believe in the War Between Races," is a perfect example of the young man's "selective reality." Racism and internalized oppression result from this "editing" of reality. "You do not see me because you do not see yourself and you do not see yourself because you declare yourself outside of culture," writes María Lugones. According to Lugones, dis-engagement is a sanctioned ethnocentric racist strategy. Whites not naming themselves white presume their universality; an unmarked race is a sign of Racism unaware of itself, a "blanked-out" Racism.

Diversity and Difference: Tactics to Avoid Confronting Racism

"Diversity" and "difference" are vague, ambiguous terms, defined differently by whitefeminists and feminists-of-color. Often whitefeminists want to minimize racial difference by taking comfort in the fact that we are all women and/or lesbians and suffer similar sexual-gender oppressions. They are usually annoyed with the actuality (though not the concept) of "differences," want to blur racial difference, want to smooth things out—they seem to want a complete, totalizing identity. Yet in their eager attempt to highlight similarities, they create or accentuate "other" differences such as class. These unacknowledged or unarticulated differences further widen the gap between white and colored. In the act of pinpointing and dissecting racial, sexual or class "differences" of women-of-color, whitewomen not only objectify these differences, but also change those differences with their own white, racialized, scrutinizing and alienating gaze. Some white people who take up multicultural and cultural plurality issues mean well, but often they push to the fringes once more the very cultures and ethnic groups about whom they want to disseminate knowledge. For example, the white writing about Native peoples or cultures displaces the Native writer and often appropriates the culture instead of proliferating information about it. The difference between appropriation and proliferation is that the first steals and harms; the second helps heal breaches of knowledge. (The author Lynn Andrews is a prime example of a white woman who "rips off" people of color, examining Native spirituality and myth with a white collector's mentality. She passes off fiction as fact and distorts the true picture of native peoples in a way they, as writers, would not. Tony Hillerman, on the other hand, is an example of a white man who, through his fiction and reference to works by Native writers, spreads factual information that widens our knowledge of the Hopi and Navajo cultures.)

xxi

In June, 1989, I was asked to speak at the Texas Lesbian Conference in Houston, Texas, where "diversity" was stressed. Many different groups belonging to Chicana, Latina, German, Italian and other white ethnic Texan groups attended. There was an assumption that all these groups were in the same boat—after all, all the women were lesbians. But ethnic colored people in this country are *not* on an equal footing with other ethnic American groups. We're never just "one of the guys." The pull to believe we can "belong," that we can blend in, that we can be accepted like any other "American" can seduce us into putting our energies into the wrong battles and into picking allies who marginalize us further. Dwelling on "diversity" and multiculturalism (a euphemism for the imperializing and now defunct "melting pot") is a way of avoiding seriously dismantling Racism—by both whitewomen and women-of-color. We want so badly to move beyond Racism to a "postracist" space, a more comfortable space, but we are only prolonging the pain and leaving unfinished a business that could liberate some of our energies.

In Which Voice/With Which Voice

The Silence That Hollows Us. For silence to transform into speech, sounds and words, it must first traverse through our female bodies. For the body to give birth to utterance, the human entity must recognize itself as carnal—skin, muscles, entrails, brain, belly. Because our bodies have been stolen, brutalized or numbed, it is difficult to speak from/through them. *No hables de esas cosas, de eso no se habia. No hables, no hables. ¡Cállate! Estate quieta.* Seal your lips, woman! When she transforms silence into language, a woman transgresses. Women-of-color in the U.S. must not only transform silence into our native speech, but as immigrants, Chicanas/Latinas and speakers of Black or different varieties of Asian English as well as other dialects, we must learn a foreign tongue—standard American English, a language laden with alien ideologies which are often in direct opposition to those in our own cultures. To speak English is to think in that language, to adopt the ideology of the people whose language it is and to be "inhabited" by their discourses. *Mujeres-de-color* speak and write not just against traditional white ways and texts but against a prevailing mode of being, against a white frame of reference. Those of us who are bilingual, or use working-class English and English in dialects, are under constant pressure to speak and write in standard English. Linguistic code-switching, which goes against language laws and norms, is not approved of.

We cross or fall or are shoved into abysses whether we speak or remain silent. And when we do speak from the cracked spaces, it is *con voz del fondo del abismo,* a voice drowned out by white noise, distance and the distancing by others who don't want to hear. We are besieged by a "silence that hollows us."[10] As "present" beings, though ones who have been "blanked out" and whose voices are heard as static, women-of-color have difficulty speaking within a discourse and within a group of speakers who (be they white or colored) exclude her. And, in the case of Kit Quan, a discourse whose speakers take pleasure in disdaining and belittling her as a triply marginalized woman-of-color and do so in the name of feminist or leftist politics.

A Chicana graduate student talked to me about not knowing how to argue against the professors who were trying to shove their methods and theories down her throat. "I don't have the language, the vocabulary," she said, sobbing. Like many *mujeres*-of-color in graduate school, she felt oppressed and violated by the rhetoric of dominant ideology, a rhetoric disguised as good "scholarship" by teachers who are unaware of its race, class and gender "blank spots." It is a rhetoric that presents its conjectures as universal truths while concealing its patriarchal privilege and posture. It is a rhetoric riddled with ideologies of Racism which hush our voices so that we cannot articulate our victimization.

While Kit Quan and the Chicana graduate student are not permitted a voice, Lynda Marín's protagonist in "Her Rites of Passage" cannot speak in first person. She is in that place where there is no language. So thoroughly has she been made to identify with the position of object to someone else's subject that she seems doomed to silence until her young daughter, struggling against the same silencing forces, evokes in her mother a claim to her own subjecthood. Her "rites of passage" locate her outside the patriarchal system of language, but corporeally in charge of her resistance to that system, her body finally responding to what she could not earlier allow herself to be fully aware of. "Silence. It breaks with all the force of a tidal wave. You may be deafened in the ending of silence. You may be crushed under its power."[11]

¿En qué voz? When we do acquire a voice, we often become *periquitas* (parrots), as in Carmen Morones' poem, imitators, loquacious in a foreign tongue. Untied, our tongues run away from themselves. When we come into possession of a voice, we sometimes have to choose with which voice (the voice of the dyke, the Chicana, the professor, the master), in which voice (first person, third, vernacular, formal) or in which language (Black English, Tex-Mex, Spanish, academese) to speak and write in. When we, the objects, become the subjects, and look at and analyze our own experiences, a danger arises that we may look through the master's gaze, speak through his tongue, use his methodology—in Audre Lorde's words, use the "master's tools." Some feminist theorists-of-color write jargonistically and abstractly, in a hard-to-access language that blocks communication, makes the general listener/reader feel bewildered and stupid. These theorists often mistakenly divide theory and lived experience and are more off-putting than many of the masters they ape. Operating here may be defense mechanisms that an intellectually colonized person adopts. I too am seduced by academic language, its theoretical babble insinuates itself into my speech and is hard to weed out. At the same time I feel that there is a place for us to use specialized language addressed to a select, professional, vocational or scholarly group—doctors, carpenters and seamsters use language that only those in their own particular work

can understand. We should not give up these "languages" just because they are not accessible to the general public.

Creativity is a Coping Strategy

A woman-of-color who writes poetry or paints or dances or makes movies knows there is no escape from race or gender when she is writing or painting. She can't take off her color and sex and leave them at the door of her study or studio. Nor can she leave behind her history. Art is about identity, among other things, and her creativity is political.

Remember again the Nahuatl concept: the soul speaks, the body acts. The hand is an extension of our will, it holds the pen, the brush, the lump of clay. It is both a symbol and a vehicle of communication. Without the hand the voice is helpless. *"La lengua necesita la mano para dar vida a los pensamientos,"* writes Margo Glantz. The tongue needs the hand to give thoughts life. *"La lengua se monta sobre la mano y produce la escritura."*[12] The tongue mounts the hand and produces writing. When tongue and hand work together, they unite art and politics and attack the dominant ideology. For many of us the acts of writing, painting, performing and filming are acts of deliberate and desperate determination to subvert the status quo. Creative acts are forms of political activism employing definite aesthetic strategies for resisting dominant cultural norms and are not merely aesthetic exercises. We build culture as we inscribe in these various forms.

Inherent in the creative act is a spiritual, psychic component—one of spiritual excavation, of (ad)venturing into the inner void, extrapolating meaning from it and sending it out into the world. To do this kind of work requires the total person—body, soul, mind and spirit. Ultimately alone with only the hum of the computer, accompanied by all my faces (and often yours as well), the monitor's screen reflects back the dialogue among "us." I talk to myself. That's what writers do, we carry on a constant dialogue between language and hands and images, one or another of our identities trying desperately to get in a word, an image, a sound.

But language, fine arts and literature do not belong to women-of-color, and culture and the social system enslave our hands in clerical, factory, field or secretarial work to service it. We are forced to steal a bit of visual, oral or written language, to escape and hide out long enough so that with half a hand we can struggle to rearrange or create "new" patterns that will contribute to building, creating and being an integral part of the molding we are encased in. Art is a struggle between the personal voice and language, with its apparatuses of culture and ideologies, and art mediums with their genre laws—the human voice trying to outshout a roaring waterfall. Art is a sneak attack while the giant sleeps, a sleight of hands when the giant is awake, moving so quick they can do their deed before the giant swats them. Our survival depends on being creative.

Even when our bodies have been battered by life, these artistic "languages," spoken from the body, by the body, are still laden with aspirations, are still coded in hope and *"un desarme ensangretado,"* a bloodied truce.[13] By sending our voices, visuals and visions outward into the world, we alter the walls and make them a framework for new windows and doors. We transform the *posos*, apertures, *barrancas*, *abismos* that we are forced to speak from. Only then can we make a home out of the cracks.

Haciendo teorías

Theory originally meant a mental viewing, an idea or mental plan of the way to do something, and a formulation of apparent relationships or underlying principles of certain observed phenomena which had been verified to some degree. To have theory meant to hold considerable evidence in support of a formulated general principle explaining the operation of certain phenomena.[14] Theory, then, is a set of knowledges. Some of these knowledges have been kept from us—entry into some professions and academia denied us. Because we are not allowed to enter discourse, because we are often disqualified and excluded from it, because what passes for theory these days is forbidden territory for us, it is *vital* that we occupy theorizing space, that we not allow whitemen and women solely to occupy it. By bringing in our own approaches and methodologies, we transform that theorizing space.

What does being a thinking subject, an intellectual, mean for women-of-color from working-class origins? It means not fulfilling our parents' expectations, it means often going against their expectations *by exceeding them*. It means being in alien territory and suspicious of the laws and walls. It means being concerned about the ways knowledges are invented. It means continually challenging institutionalized discourses. It means being suspicious of the dominant culture's interpretation of "our" experience, of the way they "read" us. It means being what Judy Baca terms "internal exiles."

What is considered theory in the dominant academic community is not necessarily what counts as theory for women-of-color. Theory produces effects that change people and the way they perceive the world. Thus we need *teorías* that will enable us to interpret what happens in the world, that will explain how and why we relate to certain people in specific ways, that will reflect what goes on between inner, outer and peripheral "I"s within a person and between the personal "I"'s and the collective "we" of our ethnic communities. *Necesitamos teorías* that will rewrite history using race, class, gender and ethnicity as categories of analysis, theories that cross borders, that blur boundaries—new kinds of theories with new theorizing methods. We need theories that will point out ways to maneuver between our particular experiences and the necessity of forming our own categories and theoretical models for the patterns we uncover. We need theories that examine the implications of situations and look at what's behind them. And we need to find practical application for those theories. We need to de-academize theory and to connect the community to the academy. "High" theory does not translate well when one's intention is to communicate to masses of people made up of different audiences. We need to give up the notion that there is a "correct" way to write theory.

Theorists-of-color are in the process of trying to formulate "marginal" theories that are partially outside and partially inside the Western frame of reference (if that is possible), theories that overlap many "worlds." We are articulating new positions in these "in-between," Borderland worlds of ethnic communities and academies, feminist and job worlds. In our literature, social issues such as race, class and sexual difference are intertwined with the narrative and poetic elements of a text, elements in which theory is embedded. In our *mestizaje* theories we create new categories for those of us left out or pushed out of the existing ones. We recover and examine non-Western aesthetics while critiquing Western aesthetics; recover and examine non-rational modes and "blanked-out" realities while critiquing rational, consensual reality; recover and examine indigenous languages while critiquing the "languages" of the dominant culture. And we simultaneously combat the tokenization and appropriation of our literatures and our writers/artists.

Some of the tasks ahead of us then: to go beyond explaining why women-of-color aren't writing more theory, why our work isn't being published or distributed, and, instead, to strategize about ways to get our work out; to change the focus from the topic of whitewomen's exclusionary practices to address the quality of what has been included and the nature of this inclusion. If we have been gagged and disempowered by theories, we can also be loosened and empowered by theories.

La tarea que nos queda por delante

Left-Handed Guardians. Looking at how far we've come and what we've had to endure to maintain what little space we've managed to wrest from the dominant culture, I see incredible hard work and amazing results. We are busy beavers (and like them also an endangered species), doers, determined and willing to work at building our arts and our theories and actualizing our dreams. Though we've accomplished much, for us it is *never enough*. In the midst of our laboring, we've had to watch our backsides, we've had to develop very sharp teeth to protect our creations. Because we've had to be cautious, we've often mistrusted each other. Wherever we are, we make sure there are several entrances and exits, that our homes have alternate escape routes, and we don't let ourselves get painted into corners. In spite of all this, we have a sense of teamwork and honor and respect for the abilities of other women, and we work hard at building community. In trying to settle our differences, we look for alternative solutions. This makes us visionaries, people with vision, with new things to say and new perspectives to say them from.

Our strength lies in shifting perspectives, in our capacity to shift, in our "seeing through" the membrane of the past superimposed on the present, in looking at our shadows and dealing with them. A medicine story tells of Crow's fascination with her own shadow. "She kept looking at it, scratching it, pecking at it, until her shadow woke up and became alive. Then Crow's shadow ate her. Crow is Dead Crow now...."[15] Crow is the Left-Handed Guardian who does not let the past eat us up. *Encrucijadas*, haunted by voices and images that violated us, bearing the pains of the past, we are slowly acquiring the tools to change the disabling images and memories, to replace them with self-affirming ones, to recreate our pasts and alter them—for the past can be as malleable as the present. So, throwing caution to the wind, *rechazamos esas falsas imágenes*, we refute those false images, *quebramos los falsos espegos para descubrir las desconocidas sombras*, we break the false mirrors in order to discover the unfamiliar shadows, the inner faces, *las caras por dentro*. To make face is to have face—dignity and self-respect.

Among the strengths working for us is the ability to see through our self-sabotaging behaviors. Our inner *payasa*, clown-face, is always aware of what's going on and uses humor to volley back the racial slurs. We have the ability to enter other levels, to listen to our gut knowledge and acknowledge that some of us do know where we are in particular stages of our lives. We are cultivating our ability to affirm our knowing. Jauntily we step into new terrains where we make up the guidelines as we go.

We are in the present, with both feet on the ground and one eye to the future. Chela Sandoval wrote: "We had each tasted the shards of 'difference' until they had carved up our insides; now we were asking ourselves what shapes our healing would take." Our healings take many forms: our ability to laugh at ourselves, to see through our own foolishness, our pride, hope, love. We are continuing in the direction of honoring others' ways, of sharing knowledge and personal power through writing (art) and activism, of injecting into our cultures new ways, feminist ways, mestiza ways. Adaptability, when we forget to stand firm on some issue or when we allow others to choose the terms of our relationships, can be our biggest weakness. But adaptability is also our biggest strength.

We have not one movement but many. Our political, literary and artistic movements are discarding the patriarchal model of the hero/leader leading the rank and file. Ours are individual and small group *movidas*, unpublicized *movimientos*—movements not of media stars or popular authors but of small groups or single *mujeres*, many of whom have not written books or spoken at national conferences. Though unnoticed, right now in small towns women are organizing, attending meetings, setting up retreats or demonstrations. Our movements, like the wind, sweep through the sea of grass in California, cut swaths in Texas, take root in Maine, sway public opinion in North Dakota, stir the dust in New Mexico. Now here, now there, *aquí y alla*, we and our *movimientos* are firmly committed to transforming all our cultures.

Notes

1. Rosario Castellaños, "*Apuntes:* Para una declaración de fe," *Poesía No Eres Tú* (my translation). (Mexico: Secretaría de Educación Pública, Colección Séptima Setentas 83, 1975), 25.

2. Subsequent unfootnoted references refer to pieces in this book.

3. Chrystos, from a letter to me.

4. Rosario Castellaños, "El Mar," *Poesía No Eres Tú*, 92.

5. Inés Hernandez, "Triumph is a sweet song—the one you know': The Voices of Gloria Anzaldúa, Wendy Rose and Joy Harjo," presentation at MLA Conference, December, 1988.

6. Rosa Villafañe-Sisolak, from an unpublished paper.

7. This is a phrase used by Gail Pheterson. I have slightly modified her definition. See "Alliances Between Women: Overcoming Internalized Oppression and Internalized Domination" *Signs: Journal of Women in Culture and Society* vol. 12, no. 1 (1986).

8. Jodi Stephens, *Women-of-Color Class Anthology*, 7. Segments from that anthology are presently being used in core courses at UCSC and the editors are now seeking a publisher.

9. T.S. Kuhn, *The Structure of Scientific Revolutions*, (Chicago: Chicago University Press, 1970), 198.

10. Amber Coverdale Sumrall, "Coming Home," *Porter Gulch Review* 9 (Fall/Winter, 1989), 74.

11. Amethyst Uchida, *Women-of-Color Class Anthology*, 8.

12. Margo Glantz, *La lengua en la mano* (Puebla, Mexico: Premia Editora Tlahuapan, 1983), 9.

13. Ixok Amargo, *Central American Women's Poetry for Peace*, ed. Zoe Anglesey (Penobscot: Granite Press, 1987), 205.

14. *Webster's New World Dictionary of American Language*, College Edition, 1959.

15. Jamie Sams and David Carson, *Medicine Cards*, illus. Angela C. Werneke (Santa Fe: Bear and Company, 1988), 133.

*"Triumph of the Heart" from
Judith F. Baca's participatory
mural project the WORLD
WALL: "A Vision of the Future
Without Fear"*

Table of Contents

Section 3 (De)Colonized Selves: Finding Hope Through Horror
Turning the Pain Around: Strategies for Growth

Section 4 In Silence, Giving Tongue
The Transformation of Silence Into (An)other Alphabet

Section 7 "Doing" Theory in Other Modes of Consciousness

Making Face, Making Soul
HACIENDO CARAS

1 Still Trembles Our Rage in the Face of Racism

There Is War:
Some Losses
Can't Be Counted

What The Gypsy Said To Her Children

Judith Ortiz Cofer

We are like the dead
invisible to those who do not
want to see,
and color is our only protection against
the killing silence of their eyes,
the crimson of our tents pitched
like a scream
in the fields of our foes,
the amber warmth of our fires
where we gather to lift our voices
in the purple lament of our songs,
And beyond the scope of their senses
where all colors blend into one
we will build our cities of light,
we will carve them
out of the granite of their hatred,
with our own brown hands.

From *Woman of Her Word: Hispanic Women Write*

Poem For The Young White Man Who Asked Me How I, An Intelligent, Well-Read Person, Could Believe In The War Between Races

Lorna Dee Cervantes

In my land there are no distinctions.
The barbed wire politics of oppression
have been torn down long ago. The only reminder
of past battles, lost or won, is a slight
rutting in the fertile fields.

In my land
people write poems about love,
full of nothing but contented childlike syllables.
Everyone reads Russian short stories and weeps.
There are no boundaries.
There is no hunger, no
complicated famine or greed.

I am not a revolutionary.
I don't even like political poems.
Do you think I can believe in a war between races?
I can deny it. I can forget about it
when I'm safe,
living on my own continent of harmony
and home, but I am not
there.

I believe in revolution
because everywhere the crosses are burning,
sharp-shooting goose-steppers round every corner,
there are snipers in the schools...
(I know you don't believe this.
You think this is nothing
but faddish exaggeration. But they
are not shooting at you.)

I'm marked by the color of my skin.
The bullets are discrete and designed to kill slowly.
They are aiming at my children.
These are facts.
Let me show you my wounds: my stumbling mind, my
"excuse me" tongue, and this
nagging preoccupation
with the feeling of not being good enough.

These bullets bury deeper than logic.

Outside my door
there is a real enemy
who hates me.

I am a poet
who yearns to dance on rooftops,
to whisper delicate lines about joy
and the blessings of human understanding.
I try. I go to my land, my tower of words and
bolt the door, but the typewriter doesn't fade out
the sounds of blasting and muffled outrage.
My own days bring me slaps on the face.
Every day I am deluged with reminders
that this is not
my land

and this is my land

I do not believe in the war between races

but in this country
there is war.

From *Emplumada*

Punto Final

Shirley Hill Witt

You Spaniards. You evil ones
Of the golden tongues and
Miraculous dreamweaving!
Once again a believing Malinche
Finds herself with amputated
Hands, feet, heart—like Acoma.

You never have enough, do you?
There are always the Seven Cities
Of adventure beckoning
For you to plunder, loot and rape
Always upon the horizon
Awaiting for your deflowering.

And Malinches like me,
We always surrender, don't we?
No matter how proud we be
Always we capitulate
In the darkest night
To your cobra persuasion.

This Malinche yet stands
While the joy that had grown
Inside her bronzen body
Melts away searing her limbs
With molten streams of shame,
Of humiliation.

Someday soon I will be
Old and ugly and wear a wig
And live in a foreign hotel
Eating my meals alone.
And I too will mouth my thoughts,
No one to hear me.

It must be the daiquiri
But they all look like Navajos
And I keep dropping my bread.
I want to weep for La Vieja
Two booths away,
But I can't: she is me.

From *That's What She Said: Contemporary Poetry and Fiction by Native American Women*

We Exist

Janice Gould

You write to me: 'Indians must be
the loneliest people on Earth.
Loneliness
          from our histories,
our losses,
even things we cannot name
             which are inside us.

We write to counteract a history
that says we are a dead,
          a conquered people.

It is like a shout in a blizzard.
We shout
      to prove we exist.'

In snow that December
At Wounded Knee, Sioux people
lay dead, dying
        their mouths frozen open.
Soldiers dug a ditch,
          dumped the bodies in.
Soil crumbled over them, then
their hearts fed on roots and stones,
their mouths filled with dust.

It is dawn.
The daughter lies on her bed,
legs drawn up,
her fist in her mouth.
I am poisoned, she thinks,
beneath my heart, I feel it.
This is what it means
        to be Indian.
My mother is not here.
They mined her
      for her grief,
they followed each vein,
invading every space,
removing, they said, the last
vestige of pain.

                    At dawn,
this time of prayer,
the daughter
in a voice mined

                    from a sickness of soul,
tries to name,
                    to make words
which say
                    we exist.

_____

From *Naming the Waves*: *Contemporary Lesbian Poetry*

Desert Run

Mitsuye Yamada

I.

I return to the desert
where criminals
were abandoned to wander
away to their deaths
where scorpions
spiders
snakes
lizards
and rats
live in outcast harmony
where the sculptor's wreck
was reclaimed
by the gentle drifting sands.

We approach the dunes while
the insistent flies bother our ears
the sound of crunching gravel under
our shoes cracks the desolate stillness
and opens our way.

Everything is done in silence here:
the wind fingers fluted stripes
over mounds and mounds of sand
the swinging grasses sweep
patterns on the slopes
the sidewinder passes out of sight.
I was too young to hear silence before.

II.

I spent 547 sulking days here
in my own dreams
there was not much to marvel at
I thought
only miles of sagebrush and
lifeless sand.

I watched the most beautiful
sunsets in the world and saw nothing
forty years ago
I wrote my will here
my fingers moved slowly in the
hot sand the texture of whole wheat flour
three words: I died here
the winds filed them away.

I am back to claim my body
my carcass lies
between the spiny branches
of two creosote bushes
it looks strangely like a small calf
left to graze and die
half of its bones are gone
after all these years

but no matter
I am satisfied
I take a dry stick
and give myself
a ritual burial.

III.

Like the bull snakes brought
into this desert by the soldiers
we were transported here
to drive away rattlers
in your nightmares
we were part of some one's plan
to spirit away spies
in your peripheral vision.

My skin turned pink brown
in the bright desert light
I slithered in the matching sand
doing what you put me here to do
we were predators at your service
I put your mind at ease.

I am that odd creature
the female bull snake
I flick my tongue in your face
an image trapped in your mirror.
You will use me or
you will honor me in a shrine
to keep me pure.

IV.

At night the outerstellar darkness
above is only an arm's length away
I am pressed by the silence around me
the stars are bold as big as quarters
against the velvet blue sky
their beams search for the marrow
of my bones
I shiver as I stumble my way to
the outhouse.

In the morning we find
kangaroo rats
have built mounds of messy homes
out of dry sticks and leavings
behind our wagon
They have accepted our alien presence.
The night creatures keep a discreet
distance.

V.

The desert is the lungs of the world.
This land of sudden lizards and nappy ants
is only useful when not used
We must leave before we feel we can
change it.

When we leave the dirt roads
my body is thankful for the
paved ride the rest of the way
home.
Rows of yucca trees with spiked crowns
wave stiffly at us
Some watch us arms akimbo.

I cannot stay in the desert
where you will have me nor
will I be brought back in a cage
to grace your need for exotica.
I write these words at night
for I am still a night creature
but I will not keep a discreet distance
If you must fit me to your needs
I will die
and so will you.

From *Desert Run: Poems and Stories*

Generations of Women

Janice Mirikitani

I.

She rests,
rocking to ritual,
the same sun fades
the same blue dress
covering her knees
turned inward
from weariness.
The day is like the work
she shoulders,
sacks of meal, corn, barley.
But her sorrow wears
like steady rain.
She buried him yesterday.
Incense still gathered
in her knuckles knotted
from the rubbings
the massage with nameless
oils, on his swollen gouted feet,
his steel girded back
muscled from carrying calves,
turning brutal rock,
building fields of promises,
gardens alive with camellias,
peaches, clover.

> *Time has sucked my body.*
> *He is buried*
> *in his one black suit*
> *we kept in mothballs*
> *for that day.*
> *I want to lay next to him*
> *in my goldthreaded wedding*
> *kimono, grandly purple*
> *with white cranes in flight,*
> *drape my bones with*
> *wisteria.*

I want to shed the century
of incense resting in my pores
like sweat or dirt.
I want to fly with the birds
in this eternal silk,
heading sunward
for warm matings.
I want this soil
that wraps him
to sleep in the smell
of my work.

Obachan
walked to the store
wearing respectable
shoes, leather
hard like a wall
against her sole.
She carefully fingered her coins
in the pocket of her thinning
blue dress,
saved for sugar, salt and yellow onions.
The clerk's single syllable spit
out a white wall—
JAP.
She turned to the door
with shopping bag empty as the sound
of her feet in
respectable shoes.
There are no tears
for moments as these.

II.

Her body speaks,
arms long,
thin as a mantis.

I am afraid
to leave this room
of myself, imprisoned
by walls of cloth.
Only the man clocks
my moments
as he fingers the
corners of my fabric,

empty buttonholes,
my muslin,
sandy as a desert.
I wait.
I wait for his presence,
my flesh like
sheets drying in the wind.
I wait,
weaving chains of flowers
to scent my hands,
color my skin,
mourn my loss.
I wait
for him to open
the bloom
hidden in the folds
of flannel.
I do not remember
being beautiful or proud.

Some losses
can't be counted:
departures to desert camps
and barracks,
men leaving to separate
camps or wars
and finally to houses
walled white full with women
in silk dresses,
wilted flowers and rhinestones
around their necks,
fast drinking, quick joking
women with red lipstick
sleek
and slippery as satin.
Her thin arms
chained by wringing
and worry
and barbed wire
slashing her youth,
her neck bowed to history
and past pain that haunts
her like a slain woman-child.

I watched as they
let her die—seventh sister
born like a blue fish into
that dry orange day.
No more women, they prayed,
a son. A son to carry on the name.

Some losses can't be counted:
abandonments left her
frightened, hungry,
made her count the grains
of rice,
wrinkles in her cheek,
pieces of rock in the desert
sand, shadows of guardtower
soldiers, mornings without
waking men,
the syllables of her name.
Some imprisonments are permanent:
white walls encaged her
with a single syllable:
JAP.
Her lips puckered
from humiliations
that made her feel like mildewed cloth,
smelling with neglect.
Her body a room
helpless to the exit of men.
The day he left her for the
red-lipped woman,
she, damp, wringing,
stood between desert camps
and bedrooms,
brooding for unburied female infants,
her thin arms dripping chains
of flowers
weighted with tears.

III.

Two generations
spit me out
like phlegm,
uncooked rice
one syllable words,
a woman foetus.

There are few places
that are mine.
I claim them,
this ground,
this silent piece of sky
where embroidered cranes keep vigil,
this purple silk smelling of mothballs,
this open cage,
this broken wood from Tule Lake.
I keep these like a rock
in my shoe
to remind me not to weep,
to mend my own body,
to wait not for the entry of men
or ghosts.
I claim
my place
in this line of
generations of women,
lean with work,
soft as tea,
open as the tunnels of the sea
driven as the heels of freedom's feet.
Taut fisted with reparations.

Mother, grandmother
speak in me.
I claim their strong fingers
of patience, their knees
bruised with humiliation,
their hurt, longing,
the sinews of their survival.
Generations of yellow women
gather in me
to crush the white wall
not with the wearing of sorrow
not with the mildew of waiting,
not with brooding or bitterness or regret,
not with wilted flowers or red lipstick.
We crush
the white wall
with a word, a glance,
a garden new with nimosa bamboo,
juniper with barbed wire at their root,
splinters from barracks.

We will come like autumn shedding sleep
a sky about to open with rage,
thunder on high rocks.
I crush
the white wall
with my name.

From *Shedding Silence*

Something About the Subject Makes It Hard to Name

Gloria Yamato

Racism—simple enough in structure, yet difficult to eliminate. Racism—pervasive in the U.S. culture to the point that it deeply affects all the local town folk and spills over, negatively influencing the fortunes of folk around the world. Racism is pervasive to the point that we take many of its manifestations for granted, believing "that's life." Many believe that racism can be dealt with effectively in one hellifying workshop, or one hour-long heated discussion. Many actually believe this monster, racism, that has had at least a few hundred years to take root, grow, invade our space and develop subtle variations…this mind-funk that distorts thought and action, can be merely wished away. I've run into folks who really think that we can beat this devil, kick this habit, be healed of this disease in a snap. In a sincere blink of a well-intentioned eye, presto—poof—racism disappears. "I've dealt with my racism…(envision a laying on of hands)…Hallelujah! Now I can go to the beach." Well, fine. Go to the beach. In fact, why don't we all go to the beach and continue to work on the sucker over there? Cuz you can't even shave a little piece off this thing called racism in a day, or a weekend, or a workshop.

When I speak of *oppression*, I'm talking about the systematic, institutionalized mistreatment of one group of people by another for whatever reason. The oppressors are purported to have an innate ability to access economic resources, information, respect, etc., while the oppressed are believed to have a corresponding negative innate ability. The flip side of oppression is *internalized oppression*. Members of the target group are emotionally, physically, and spiritually battered to the point that they begin to actually believe that their oppression is deserved, is their lot in life, is natural and right, and that it doesn't even exist. The oppression begins to feel comfortable, familiar enough that when mean ol' Massa lay down de whip, we got's to pick up and whack ourselves and each other. Like a virus, it's hard to beat racism, because by the time you come up with a cure it's mutated to a "new cure-resistant" form. One shot just won't get it. Racism must be attacked from many angles.

The forms of racism that I pick up on these days are 1) aware/blatant racism, 2) aware/covert racism, 3) unaware/unintentional racism, and 4) unaware/self-righteous racism. I can't say that I prefer any one form of racism over the others, because they all look like an itch needing a scratch. I've heard it said (and understandably so) that the aware/blatant form of racism is preferable if one must suffer it. Outright racists will, without apology or confusion, tell us that because of our color we don't appeal to them. If we so choose, we can attempt to get the hell out of their way before we get the sweat knocked out of us. Growing up, aware/covert racism is what I heard many of my elders bemoaning "up north," after having escaped the overt racism "down south." Apartments were suddenly no longer vacant or rents were outrageously high, when black, brown, red, or yellow persons went to inquire about them. Job vacancies were suddenly filled, or we were fired for very vague reasons. It still happens, though the perpetrators really take care to cover their tracks these days. They don't want to get gummed to death or slobbered on by the toothless laws that supposedly protect us from such inequities.

Unaware/unintentional racism drives usually tranquil white liberals wild when they get called on it, and confirms the suspicions of many people of color who feel that white folks are just plain crazy. It has led white people to believe that it's just fine to ask if they can touch my hair (while reaching). They then exclaim over how soft it is, how it does not scratch their hand. It has led whites to assume that bending over backwards and speaking to me in high-pitched (terrified), condescending tones would make up for all the racist wrongs that distort our lives. This type of racism has led whites right to my doorstep, talking 'bout, "We're sorry/we love you and want to make things right," which is fine, and further, "We're gonna give you the opportunity to fix it while we sleep. Just tell us what you need. 'Bye!!"—which *ain't* fine. With the best of intentions, the best of educations, and the greatest generosity of heart, whites, operating on the misinformation fed to them from day one, will behave in ways that are racist, will perpetuate racism by being "nice" the way we're taught to be nice. You can just "nice" somebody to death with naïveté and lack of awareness of privilege. Then there's guilt and the desire to end racism and how the two get all tangled up to the point that people, morbidly fascinated with their guilt, are immobilized. Rather than deal with ending racism, they sit and ponder their guilt and hope nobody notices how awful they are. Meanwhile, racism picks up momentum and keeps on keepin' on.

Now, the newest form of racism that I'm hip to is unaware/self-righteous racism. The "good white" racist attempts to shame Blacks into being blacker, scorns Japanese-Americans who don't speak Japanese, and knows more about the Chicano/a community than the folks who make up the community. They assign themselves as the "good whites," as opposed to the "bad whites," and are often so busy telling people of color what the issues in the Black, Asian, Indian, Latino/a communities should be that they don't have time to deal with their errant sisters and brothers in the white community. Which means that people of color are still left to deal with what the "good whites" don't want to...racism.

Internalized racism is what really gets in my way as a Black woman. It influences the way I see or don't see myself, limits what I expect of myself or others like me. It results in my acceptance of mistreatment, leads me to believe that being treated with less than absolute respect, at least this once, is to be expected because I am Black, because I am not white. "Because I am (*you fill in the color*)," you think, "life is going to be hard." The fact is life may be hard, but the color of your skin is not the cause of the hardship. The color of your skin may be used as an excuse to mistreat you, but there is no reason or logic involved in the mistreatment. If it seems that your color is the reason, if it seems that your ethnic heritage is the cause of the woe, it's because you've been deliberately beaten down by agents of a greedy system until you swallowed the garbage. That is the internalization of racism.

Racism is the systematic, institutionalized mistreatment of one group of people by another based on racial heritage. Like every other oppression, racism can be internalized. People of color come to believe misinformation about their particular ethnic group and thus believe that their mistreatment is justified. With that basic vocabulary, let's take a look at how the whole thing works together. Meet "the Ism Family," racism, classism, ageism, adultism, elitism, sexism, heterosexism, physicalism, etc. All these ism's are systemic, that is, not only are these parasites feeding off our lives, they are also dependent on one another for foundation. Racism is supported and reinforced by classism, which is given a foothold and a boost by adultism, which also feeds sexism, which is validated by heterosexism, and so it goes on. You cannot have the "ism" functioning without first effectively installing its flip-side, the internalized version of the ism. Like twins, as one particular form of the ism grows in potency, there is a corresponding increasing in its internalized form within the population. Before oppression becomes a specific ism like racism, usually all hell breaks loose. War. People fight attempts to enslave them, or to subvert their will, or to take what they consider theirs, whether that is territory or dignity. It's true that the various elements of racism, while repugnant, would not be able to do very much damage, but for one generally overlooked key piece: power/privilege.

While in one sense we all have power, we have to look at the fact that, in our society, people are stratified into various classes and some of these classes have more privilege than others. The owning class has enough power and privilege to not have to give a good whinney what the rest of the folks have on their minds. The power and privilege of the owning class provides the ability to pay off enough of the working class and offer that paid-off group, the middle class, just enough privilege to make it agreeable to do various and sundry oppressive things to other working-class and outright disenfranchised folk, keeping the lid on explosive inequities, at least for a minute. If you're at the bottom of this heap, and you believe the line that says you're there because that's all you're worth, it is at least some small solace to believe that there are others more worthless than you, because of their gender, race, sexual preference-...whatever. The specific form of power that runs the show here is the power to intimidate. The power to take away the most lives the quickest, and back it up with legal and "divine" sanction, is the very bottom line. It makes the difference between who's holding the racism end of the stick and who's getting beat with it (or beating others as vulnerable as they are) on the internalized racism end of the stick. What I am saying is, while people of color are welcome to tear up their own neighborhoods and each other, everybody knows that you cannot do that to white folks without hell to pay. People of color can be prejudiced against one another and whites but do not have an ice-cube's chance in hell of passing laws that will get whites sent to relocation camps "for their own protection and the security of the nation." People who have not thought about or refuse to acknowledge this imbalance of power/privilege often want to talk about the racism of people of color. But then that is one of the ways racism is able to continue to function. You look for someone to blame and you blame the victim, who will nine times out of ten accept the blame out of habit.

So, what can we do? Acknowledge racism for a start, even though and especially when we've struggled to be kind and fair, or struggled to rise above it all. It is hard to acknowledge the fact that racism circumscribes and pervades our lives. Racism must be dealt with on two levels, personal and societal, emotional and institutional. It is possible—and most effec-tive—to do both at the same time. We must reclaim whatever delight we have lost in our own ethnic heritage or heritages. This so-called melting pot has only succeeded in turning us into fast food-gobbling "generics" (as in generic "white folks" who were once Irish, Polish, Russian, English, etc., and "black folks," who were once Ashanti, Bambara, Baule, Yoruba, etc.). Find or create safe places to actually *feel* what we've been forced to repress each time we were a victim of, witness to or perpetrator of racism, so that we do not continue, like puppets, to act out the past in the present and future. Challenge oppression. Take a stand against it. When you are aware of something oppressive going down, stop the show. At least call it. We become so numbed to racism that we don't even think twice about it, unless it is immediately life-threatening.

Whites who want to be allies to people of color: You can educate yourselves via research and observation rather than rigidly, arrogantly relying solely on interrogating people of color. Do not expect that people of color should teach you how to behave non-oppressively. Do not give into the pull to be lazy. Think, hard. Do not blame people of color for your frustration about racism, but do appreciate the fact that people of color will often help you get in touch with that frustration. Assume that your effort to be a good friend is appreciated, but don't expect or accept gratitude from people of color. Work on racism for your sake, not "their" sake. Assume that you are needed and capable of being a good ally. Know that you'll make mistakes and commit yourself to correcting them and continuing on as an ally, no matter what. Don't give up.

People of color, working through internalized racism: Remember always that you and others like you are completely worthy of respect, completely capable of achieving whatever you take a notion to do. Remember that the term "people of color" refers to a variety of ethnic and cultural backgrounds. These various groups have been oppressed in a variety of ways. Educate yourself about the ways different peoples have been oppressed and how they've resisted that oppression. Expect and insist that whites are capable of being good allies against racism. Don't give up. Resist the pull to give out the "people of color seal of approval" to aspiring white allies. A moment of appreciation is fine, but more than that tends to be less than helpful. Celebrate yourself. Celebrate yourself. Celebrate the inevitable end of racism.

From *Changing Our Power*

Racism and Women's Studies

Barbara Smith

Although my proposed topic is Black women's studies, I've decided to focus my remarks in a different way. Given that this is a gathering of predominantly white women, and given what has occurred during this Convention, it makes much more sense to discuss the issue of racism: racism in women's studies and racism in the women's movement generally.

"Oh no," I can hear some of you groaning inwardly. "Not that again. That's all we've talked about since we got here." This, of course, is not true. If it had been all we had all talked about since we got here, we might be at a point of radical transformation on the last day of this Convention that we clearly are not. For those of you who are tired of hearing about racism, imagine how much more tired *we* are of constantly experiencing it, second by literal second, how much more exhausted we are to see it constantly in your eyes. The degree to which it is hard or uncomfortable for you to have the issue raised is the degree to which you know inside of yourself that you aren't dealing with the issue, the degree to which you are hiding from the oppression that undermines Third World women's lives. I want to say right here that this is not a "guilt trip." It's a fact trip. The assessment of what's actually going on.

Why is racism being viewed and taken up as a pressing feminist issue at this time, and why is it being talked about in the context of women's studies? As usual, the impetus comes from the grassroots, activist women's movement. In my six years of being an avowed Black feminist, I have seen much change in how white women take responsibility for their racism, particularly within the last year. The formation of consciousness-raising groups to deal solely with this issue, study groups, and community meetings and workshops; the appearance of articles in our publications and letters in newspapers; and the beginning of real and equal coalitions between Third World and white women are all phenomena that have really begun to happen, and I feel confident that there will be no turning back.

The reason racism is a feminist issue is easily explained by the inherent definition of feminism. Feminism is the political theory and practice that struggles to free *all* women: women of color, working-class women, poor women, disabled women, lesbians, old women—as well as white, economically privileged, heterosexual women. Anything less than this vision of total freedom is not feminism, but merely female self-aggrandizement.

Let me make quite clear at this point, before going any further, something you must understand. White women don't work on racism to do a favor for someone else, solely to benefit Third World women. You have to comprehend how racism distorts and lessens your own lives as white women—that racism affects your chances for survival, too, and that it is very definitely your issue. Until you understand this, no fundamental change will come about.

Racism is being talked about in the context of women's studies because of its being raised in the women's movement generally, but also because women's studies is a context in which white and Third World women actually come together, a context that should be about studying and learning about all of our lives. I feel at this point that it is not only about getting Third World women's materials into the curriculum, although this must be done. This has been happening, and it is clear that racism still thrives, just as the inclusion of women's materials in a college curriculum does not prevent sexism from thriving. The stage we are at now is having to decide to change fundamental attitudes and behavior— the way people treat each other. In other words, we are at a stage of having to take some frightening risks.

I am sure that many women here are telling themselves they aren't racist because they are capable of being civil to Black women, having been raised by their parents to be anything but. It's not about merely being polite: "I'm not racist because I do not snarl and snap at Black people." It's much more subtle than that. It's not white women's fault that they have been raised, for the most part, not knowing how to talk to Black women, not knowing how to look us in the eye and laugh *with* us. Racism and racist behavior are our white patriarchal legacy. What is your fault is making no serious effort to change old patterns of contempt—to look at how you still believe yourselves to be superior to Third World women and how you communicate these attitudes in blatant and subtle ways.

A major roadblock for women involved in women's studies to changing their individual racism and challenging it institutionally is the pernicious ideology of professionalism. That word "professionalism" covers such a multitude of sins. I always cringe when I hear *anyone* describe herself as "professional," because what usually follows is an excuse for inaction, an excuse for ethical irresponsibility. It's a word and concept we don't need, because it is ultimately a way of dividing ourselves from others and escaping from reality. I think the way to be "successful" is to do work with integrity and work that is good. Not to play cutthroat tricks and insist on being called "Doctor." When I got involved in women's studies six years ago, and particularly during my three and a half years as the first Third World woman on the Modern Language Association Commission on the Status of Women, I began to recognize what I call women's studies or academic feminists: women who teach, research, and publish about women, but who are not involved in any way in making radical social and political change; women who are not involved in making the lives of living, breathing women more viable. The grass-roots/community women's movement has given women's studies its life. How do we relate to it? How do we bring our gifts and our educational privilege back to it? Do we realize also how very much there is to learn in doing this essential work? Ask yourself what the women's movement is working on in your town or city. Are you a part of it? Ask yourself which women are living in the worst conditions in your town and how your work positively affects and directly touches their lives. If it doesn't, why not?

The question has been raised here whether this should be an activist association or an academic one. In many ways, this is an immoral question, an immoral and false dichotomy. The answer lies in the emphasis and the kinds of work that will lift oppression off of not only women, but all oppressed people: poor and working-class people, people of color in this country and in the colonized Third World. If lifting this oppression is not a priority to you, then it's problematic whether you are a part of the actual feminist movement.

There are two other roadblocks to our making feminism real which I'll mention briefly. First, there is Third World women's antifeminism, which I sometimes sense gets mixed up with opposition to white women's racism and is fueled by a history of justified distrust. To me, racist white women cannot be said to be actually feminist, at least not in the way I think and feel about the word. Feminism in and of itself would be fine. The problems arise with the mortals who practice it. As Third World women we must define a responsible and radical feminism for ourselves and not assume that bourgeois female self-aggrandizement is all that feminism is and therefore attack feminism wholesale.

The other roadblock is homophobia, that is, antilesbianism, an issue that both white and Third World women still have to deal with. Need I explicate in 1979 how enforced heterosexuality is the extreme manifestation of male domination and patriarchal rule and that women must not collude in the oppression of women who have chosen each other, that is, lesbians? I wish I had time here to speak also about the connections between the lesbian-feminist movement, being woman-identified, and the effective antiracist work that is being done by many, though not all, lesbians.

In conclusion, I'll say that I don't consider my talk today to be in any way conclusive or exhaustive. It has merely scratched the surface. I don't know exactly what's going on in your schools or in your lives. I can only talk about those qualities and skills that will help you to bring about change: integrity, awareness, courage, and redefining your own success.

I also feel that the women's movement will deal with racism in a way that it has not been dealt with before in any other movement: fundamentally, organically, and nonrhetorically. White women have a materially different relationship to the system of racism than white men. They get less out of it and often function as its pawns, whether they recognize this or not. It is something that living under white-male rule has imposed on us; and overthrowing racism is the inherent work of feminism and by extension feminist studies.

From *All The Women Are White, All The Blacks Are Men, But Some of Us Are Brave*

The Costs of Exclusionary Practices in Women's Studies

Maxine Baca Zinn, Lynn Weber Cannon, Elizabeth Higginbotham, and Bonnie Thornton Dill

As women who came to maturity during the social upheavals of the late sixties and early seventies, we entered academia to continue—in a different arena—the struggles that our foreparents had begun centuries earlier. We sought to reveal untold tales and unearth hidden images, and we believed (or at least hoped) that, once illuminated, the truths of the lives of our people—Black, brown, and working-class white—would combat the myths and stereotypes that haunted us. We were, in that sense, scholars with a special mission. In the tradition of W.E.B. DuBois, Oliver Cox, Joyce Ladner, and other pioneers, we sought to use the tools of history and social science and the media of literature and the arts to improve our people's future and more accurately portray their past.

We each had developed critical perspectives on society and sought theoretical explanations for the continued poverty and oppression of our people. We had different but related foci for our research: on Chicanos and the impact of outside resources on family structure and ethnicity; on working-class consciousness and class conflict; on Black women achieving a college education; and on the relationship of work and family for Black women private household workers. In the process of conducting it, we became acutely aware of the limitations of traditional social science with regard to working-class women and women of color.[1] More profoundly, however, we realized that the experiences of these groups of women were virtually excluded from consideration as vital building blocks in feminist theory.

In the past, many working-class women and women of color have been critical of women's studies for the lack of attention given "their" women.[2] This "Viewpoint" draws from those arguments and adds our own perspectives. Our effort is not only to voice discontent but also to elaborate on some of the implications of the exclusionary nature of women's studies. There are many issues that must be addressed regarding the need for attention to race and class in women's studies. This "Viewpoint" can only attend to some of them. If dialogue is reopened in these or related areas, our goal will have been realized.

The Institutionalization of Privilege

Many recent studies have documented organizational barriers to women's full and equal participation in society. Institutions are organized to facilitate white middle-class men's smooth entry into and mobility in positions of power. These men establish criteria for the entry of others into similar positions, defining success, the reward system, the distribution of resources, and institutional goals and priorities in a way that perpetuates their power. In higher education, as in other areas, women— even white middle-class women—have been excluded from many of these activities. They continue to struggle to move out of token positions of authority and into the true centers of power as presidents, administrators, trustees, members of state governing boards, officers of professional associations, editors of prestigious journals, and members on policy-making boards and on review panels of granting agencies. Over the past decade, women have made gains in approaching those centers of power, but the institutional barriers have been formidable, and the fight to break them down has left many women scarred.

The obstacles white middle-class women face are compounded many times over for women of color and working-class women. For these two groups, completing college and graduate education itself poses financial, emotional, and intellectual challenges.[3] As students, they are more likely than middle-class white women to attend public institutions—community colleges and state universities—or, in the case of Blacks, traditionally Black institutions. As faculty, they are more likely to be employed in public institutions and in those that do not grant doctorates. A 1970 study estimated that Blacks made up only 0.9 percent of faculty in universities and 5.4 percent in four-year colleges. This number drops to only 2.0 percent when traditionally Black institutions are eliminated.[4] Among these less prestigious schools, few have the financial and other resources necessary to facilitate and encourage research and scholarship. In fact, these settings are characterized by high teaching loads, heavy demand for institutional service, and limited dollars for travel, computer facilities, research libraries, secretarial support, or research assistance.

Most of the scholarly research and writing that take place in the United States are conducted at a relatively small number of institutions. To a large extent, research and other scholarly production in women's studies have also been closely tied to the resources and prestige of these academic centers. Indeed, women's studies, partly because of its marginal position in the academy, has sought to validate the field through association with prestigious institutions of higher education. In these schools, there are very few women of color, and while we cannot know how many of the women faculty at these institutions are from working-class backgrounds, it is safe to assume that their numbers also are relatively small.[5]

The result is that women of color and women from working-class backgrounds have few opportunities to become part of the networks that produce or monitor knowledge in women's studies. In addition, those who have the advantage of being researchers and gatekeepers are primarily located at privileged institutions, where they get little exposure to working-class and ethnically diverse students. As a result, they tend to develop and teach concepts divorced from the realities of women of color and working-class women's lives.

For example, a concept such as the "positive effect of the multiple negative" could not have survived the scrutiny of professional Black women or Black women students. The theory suggests that the negative status of being Black combines with the negative status of being female to give professional Black women an advantage in the labor market.[6] Although this may have appeared to be the case for the researcher isolated from significant numbers of Black women as colleagues or students, Blacks' life experiences would have suggested many alternate interpretations. Such cases clearly illustrate that the current organization of the academy perpetuates the production and distribution of knowledge that is both Anglo and middle-class centered.

To explore further the institutional structures that limit the contributions of women of color and women from working-class backgrounds to the field of women's studies, we engaged in a simple exercise. We looked at the published information about the official gatekeepers of two leading interdisciplinary journals in the field of women's studies: *Signs* and *Feminist Studies*. These groups of editors, associate editors, and consultants make important decisions about which individual pieces of scholarship will be contained in the journals' pages and what special issues will be undertaken, officially sanctioning and defining important concerns and critical scholarship in the field. We asked, "Where are women of color located within these publications generated out of the women's movement and its accompanying scholarship?"

Despite white, middle-class feminists' frequent expressions of interest and concern over the plight of minority and working-class women, those holding the gatekeeping positions at these journals are as white as are those at any mainstream social science or humanities publication. The most important groups within the hierarchies of the two journals—that is, the groups most involved in policy decisions—are the eleven editors of *Feminist Studies* and the editor and eight associate editors of *Signs*. Among those twenty women, in 1983-84, there was not a single Black woman, there were no Hispanic women, no Native American women, and no Chinese American women. The only woman of color was a Japanese American woman, an associate editor of *Signs*.*

---

* The new group of associate editors for *Signs*, when it moves to Duke University, will include three Black women, one of whom is a faculty member at a traditionally Black

As reported in table 1, token representation also occurs at positions below those of the editors themselves. The primary function of those in these groups is to review articles and on occasion to give advice to the editors. *Feminist Studies* has fifty-nine whites and five women of color serving as associate editors and consultants, whereas *Signs* has thirty-eight whites and three women of color in those categories. Regardless of position, the total number of editors and consultants for both journals combined shows that there are 119 whites, six Blacks, one Hispanic, and two Asian Americans.

Table 1: Representation of Minorities on Signs and Feminist Studies Editorial Boards, 1983-84

	Editor(s)		Associate Editor(s)		Consultants		Total	
	Minority	White	Minority	White	Minority	White	Minority	White
Feminist Studies . .	0	11	2	13	3	46	5	70
Signs	1	8	...	...	3	38	4	46
Both Journals . .	1	19	2	13	6	84	9	116

NOTE—*Sign's* associate editors were included under the heading of "Editors" because their functions match more closely those perfomed by editors of *Feminist Studies*. The data were obtained from the lists published in recent issues of these journals.

It is much easier to designate the ways that women of color have been excluded than it is to show the ways that white working-class women have been kept out of the mainstream. Furthermore, it is more difficult to delineate the ways that classism excludes both whites and women of color who are from the working class. The information that *Signs* gives about the institutional affiliations of its editors and consultants, however, can be used to illustrate other biases in the gatekeeping positions. None of the fifty women in these positions represents a traditionally Black institution; only about six represent schools whose student bodies are primarily constituted of working-class students (i.e., the first in their families to attend college); and only three are from the South—where the highest concentrations of minorities continue to live.

The major implication of these figures is that women of color are rarely sitting around the table when problems are defined and strategies suggested. They are not in positions to engage in the theoretical discourse behind specific decisions on what will be published. Thus, even when white feminists attempt to include women of color, there are often difficulties because women of color reject the dominant paradigms and approach problems from divergent perspectives. Typically, women of

institution. *Feminist Studies* reports that their current (1985) group of editors and consultants includes two women of color as editors (out of twelve), one woman of color as an associate editor (out of fifteen), and fifteen women of color as consultants (out of a total of sixty-four).

color then find their work rejected on the grounds that it does not conform to the established ways of thinking. This clash of paradigms resounds through the following example.

In 1981, the planners of a conference on communities of women asked Elizabeth Higginbotham to submit an abstract for a paper.[7] The expectation communicated in the letter of invitation was that her research would demonstrate the applicability to Black women of a concept of women's communities set forth by white feminists. Instead of attempting to alter her work to fit such a model, Higginbotham wrote to the organizers and challenged their narrow definition of communities of women.

Higginbotham noted that, unlike their white sisters who are often excluded from male-dominated spheres or retreat from them, the majority of Black women are ordinarily full participants in mixed-sex spheres and make unique contributions both to the definitions of problems and to solutions. Typically, Black women's vision of their situation leads them not to seek solace from Black males but to create spheres where men, women, and children are relatively protected from racist cultural and physical assaults. Historically, white people, male and female, have rarely validated the humanness of Black people; therefore, it was and is critical for Black people and other people of color to nurture each other. This is a primary fact about the communities of racially oppressed peoples. Thus, as white feminists defined the focus of the conference, only the research of a few Black scholars seemed appropriate—and that research did not necessarily capture the most typical and common experiences of Black women.

The Limitations of Popular Feminist Theory

Practices that exclude women of color and working-class women from the mainstream of women's studies have important consequences for feminist theory. Ultimately, they prevent a full understanding of gender and society. The failure to explore fully the interplay of race, class, and gender has cost the field the ability to provide a broad and truly complex analysis of women's lives and of social organization. It has rendered feminist theory incomplete and incorrect.

Until the past few years, women of color have been virtually hidden in feminist scholarship, made invisible by the erroneous notion of universal womanhood. In an effort to emphasize the shared experiences of sexism, scholars passed over the differences in women's situations.[8] Knowledge assumed to be "universal" was actually based for the most part on the experiences of women who were white and primarily middle class. Feminist scholarship, a center of a developing critical intellectual tradition, increasingly came under fire for this myopia from other critical scholarships, namely, the scholarship on people of color and on the working class. As a result, there now exists in women's studies an increased awareness of the variability of womanhood. Women's studies journals and classroom texts are more likely at present to contain material about minority women. Still, such work is often tacked on, its significance for feminist knowledge still unrecognized and unregarded.

A close look at feminist social science reveals three common approaches to race and class. The first treats race and class as secondary features in social organization with primacy given to universal female subordination. Such thinking establishes what is taken to be a common feminist ground and labels any divergence from it, in Phyllis Palmer's phrase, a "diversionary special interest."[9] To make gender relations primary is to assume that they create a set of universal experiences more important than those of other inequalities.

A second approach acknowledges that inequalities of race, class, and gender generate different experiences and that women have a race-specific and a class-specific relation to the sex-gender system. However, it then sets race and class inequalities aside on the grounds that, while they are important, we lack information that would allow us to incorporate them in the analysis. As Bonnie Thornton Dill puts it, inequalities other than sex and gender are recognized, but they are not explicated.[10] After a perfunctory acknowledgement of differences, those taking this position make no further attempt to incorporate the insights generated by critical scholarship on race and class into a framework that would deal with women generally.[11]

The third approach, often found in conjunction with the first two, focuses on descriptive aspects of the ways of life, values, customs, and problems of women in subordinate race and class categories. Here differences are detailed with little attempt to explain their source or their broader meaning. Such discussions of women are "confined to a pretheoretical presentation of concrete problems."[12]

Each of these conceptualizations is inadequate for the development of feminist theory. They create an illusion of comprehensiveness and thereby stifle the development of scholarship about women of color. Moreover, when race and class are set aside, even the analysis of white middle-class women's lives is incomplete. A woman's "place" in society, her opportunities and her experiences, must be understood in relation to the societal placement of men as well as of other classes and races of people.

An approach to the study of women in culture and society should begin at the level of social organization. From this vantage point one can appreciate the complex web of hierarchical social arrangements that generate different experiences for women. For example, Denise Segura has recently documented the ways in which gender and race produce distinctive consequences in the labor force experiences of Chicanas. Using a four-way comparison, she examines the occupational profiles of

Chicanas, Chicanos, white women, and white men. Her findings reveal that while Chicanas are triply oppressed, the dynamics of class, race and gender oppression are different. Racial barriers impede access to professional and managerial occupations, whereas gender produces an earnings gap at all occupation levels.[13]

The integration of race and class into the study of gender creates different questions and new conceptualizations of many problems. For instance, in the last few years, there has been a great deal of attention to the entrance of women into professional and managerial occupations. In fact, the levels of female professional and managerial employment are often the standard used to evaluate women's success. In such conceptualizations, Black women are frequently held up as exemplars because they are more concentrated in professional employment than Black males. White women, in contrast, are less concentrated than white males in such positions and are viewed as less "successful" than their Black sisters.[14]

Black professional women understand such seemingly favorable comparisons differently. The analysis behind them lacks a sense of Black history and of racial stratification and thus ignores a number of underlying factors: the racial barriers that limit educational attainment for Black men; a history of limited employment options for Black women who have only a high school education; and the high concentration of Black professional and managerial women in the public sector and in traditionally female occupations. Each of these realities suggests that professional or managerial work will have a different meaning to Black women.[15] In short, an analysis of gender and occupation that also incorporates race would have raised a variety of other issues and avoided the narrow focus on Black women's "success."

Classism, Racism, and Privileged Groups of Women

We recognize that there are significant reasons behind the fact that a synthesis of class, race and gender perspectives into a holistic and inclusive feminist theory and practice has not yet taken place. Some derive from both the short- and long-term costs of struggling to overcome institutionally supported and historically reproduced hierarchies of inequality. Others have to do with the benefits that accrue to those in a group with relative power.

White middle-class women profit in several ways from the exclusion of upwardly mobile women and women of color from the ranks of academic equals in their universities, from the pages of women's studies journals, from positions of power in our professional associations, and from a central place in feminist theories. Foremost among these advantages is the elimination of direct competition for the few "women's jobs" in universities; for the limited number of tenure-track and tenured jobs;

for the small number of places for women among the higher professorial ranks; for the meager number of pages devoted to research and writing on women in the mainstream professional journals; and for the precious, limited space in women's studies journals. White women, struggling for acceptance by male peers, a secure job, and a living wage in the academy—especially since many are forced to work part-time or on a series of one-year appointments—may not "feel" that they are in a privileged position. Indeed, in many ways and in many cases there is little privilege. However, their relative disadvantage in comparison with white men should not obscure the advantages of race and class that remain.

Despite the benefits to some that derive from exclusionary practices, there are also costs to feminist theory and to women's lives—even to the lives of privileged groups of women. Scholarship that overlooks the diversity of women's experiences cannot reveal the magnitude, complexity, or interdependence of systems of oppression. Such work underestimates the obstacles to be confronted and helps little in developing practical strategies to overcome the sexist barriers that even privileged women inevitably confront.

As women in academia, we are obliged to compete for rewards individually in a system where we are not among the power brokers. Individual competition in a hierarchical scheme based on "merit" may work well to explain the experiences and structure of the lives of middle- or upper-class white men. As a theoretical perspective or guiding principle, it does not explain the life experiences of groups—including that of white middle-class women—who lack power. In this situation, the merit, motivation, and work of an individual who suffers discrimination are not relevant, since discrimination, like all other forms of oppression, operates against a whole group. Thus, as a group, women find themselves up against barriers to success.

Relatively privileged groups of women are nonetheless shielded from awareness of the institutional barriers that their working-class and minority sisters come to recognize early. Many middle-class white women "buy into" the system and assume that it will work for them. Linda Nielsen's comments on her tenure battle show her recognition that she had made just this error: "During those beginning years I was not seriously worried about my future, since I had been exceptionally successful at publishing and teaching, and I believed that this guaranteed my professional security. It did not." She was denied reappointment even though she met objective university criteria.

The experience, she came to realize, found her unprepared for the reality and consequences of sexism and ready, furthermore, to blame herself for the serious blow she had received. "Women continue to look for the enemy as though it were only in themselves, I was no exception."[16] While Nielsen's generalization may be true of many women, the literature shows that minority women are much more likely to blame the system when things go wrong than are white women.[17]

Nielsen also describes herself as experiencing the need for white male approval so common among white women: "I feel my colleagues' lack of support would have been far less painful and less detrimental to my self-esteem had I not learned to define my worth so exclusively by men's judgments." After a brief look at some research and at autobiographical accounts, she draws some conclusions about the special difficulties that women have to overcome as a minority group. The characteristics are "over-reliance on male approval, passivity or non-assertiveness, ambivalence and anxiety over contradictory female roles, inclination toward self-blame and guilt, affiliative needs which interfere with achievement, motivation, and discrimination from other females."[18]

Unfortunately, although Nielsen's courageous account is a useful analysis of a white middle-class woman's experience, there is not a single reference in her bibliography to a work by a woman of color. Familiarity with research on minority groups immediately reveals that the reactions Nielsen lists contain responses that do not apply *uniquely* to women. Some, such as discrimination from members of one's own group, are common among other minorities, and others—such as overreliance on male approval, ambivalence and anxiety over contradictory female roles, and passivity or nonassertiveness—do not apply to many women of color. For example, numerous Black working-class women have not employed passivity as a survival mechanism—indeed, their aggressive actions in comparison with those of white middle-class women are often viewed antagonistically by whites as "unfeminine."

Thus, Nielsen's conclusions, while somewhat instructive to white middle-class women, actually shed little light on the circumstances and experiences of upwardly mobile women and women of color. Because she does not look at the latter's situations to understand the nature of all women's oppression, her observations and conclusions are incorrect. Nielsen rightly identifies some responses to discrimination as they are manifested in her own life and the lives of other middle-class white women. Yet from this narrow perspective she can only partially glimpse even her own plight, and her observations do little to recognize hers as part of a wider struggle shared with women who are different from her.

Some Goals and Strategies for Change

We seek to build a more diverse women's studies and an integrative feminist theory. Achievement of these goals requires many structural changes in the practices and policies of academic communities. In the present political climate, we cannot expect leadership in these areas to come from government or university administrations. Instead, we must ourselves make an effort at every level to build alliances, set priorities, and work in whatever ways we can to create more diverse academic communities and a field of women's studies open to wide participation.

First, we need to establish and maintain heterogeneous college faculties. Frequently, feminists are ready to fight for women colleagues but do not extend such support to minorities and people from working-class backgrounds. We must learn about each other and appreciate our differences in order to form the types of alliances that will transform the composition of faculties at our institutions. Without such alliances, any group can be isolated and eliminated without much controversy on any particular campus. Above all, we must withstand the temptation to secure our individual futures by accommodating to the "principles" of the institution.

Second, we should actively encourage dialogue among academic centers, especially in local areas, by forming close links with faculty in different types of institutions. Faculty in elite schools particularly must reach out beyond their campuses to faculty and students in less prestigious centers of higher education. Faculty with low teaching loads, large research funds, and frequent opportunities to travel are indeed privileged; those without such "perks" are no less worthy of respect. In fact, scholars who are struggling to conduct research in institutions where the primary emphasis is on teaching merit our encouragement. Faculty are not distributed among colleges solely by talent and ability; racism, classism, and sexism all function to shape academic careers. Consequently, we have to reject the elitism so prevalent in academe, visit other campuses and learning centers, make friends with new colleagues, and share resources. There are reasons behind the pattern whereby faculty in research institutions conduct and produce research while faculty in teaching institutions fail to publish. The current structure of academia is indeed designed to produce that outcome, and strategies should be designed to change it.* The number of women and minorities hired in second-tier, four-year colleges and community colleges makes it imperative that we do everything possible to pull down the structural barriers that block their careers.

Third, efforts should continue to open up the gatekeeping positions in women's studies to include a broad representation of women. Editorial

---

*The Center for Research on Women, Memphis State University; the Women's Studies Research Center, Duke University—University of North Carolina; and the Women's Research and Resource Center, Spelman College, are developing a series of working papers on Southern women. To achieve this goal, we are identifying scholars of Southern women outside our institutions, bringing them into a network, providing feedback on their work, and publishing their articles as working papers. We also encourage them to submit their products to journals for publication. We are helping a small but isolated group of researchers to produce work and to participate in the growth of this new area of scholarship.

boards need to reject the tokenism that has characterized them so far, and they must strive to solicit and publish feminist scholarship from all corners. Committees and organizations that plan conferences need diverse membership—members who will seriously address issues of age, race, class, and sexual preference in the definition and formation of programs and in the means used to recruit participants. Dill's comments on the "Common Differences" conference cosponsored by Duke University, the University of North Carolina, and North Carolina Central Universities are illustrative of this point and the positive consequences of such planning: "The most outstanding thing about this conference was...the commitment to an honest, frank, and equal exchange among black and white women.... It pervaded the entire organization of the conference from the planning committee through the workshops, films, lectures, and presentations. Workshops were led by a team consisting of one black and one white woman. The leaders played an important role in facilitating discussions of the commonalities in black and white women's lives, and presented approaches to the teaching of women's experiences that initiated the process of transforming curriculum to be more inclusive of racial differences."[19]

In everything we attempt, we must strive to welcome diversity rather than gather around us what is comforting and familiar. Without serious structural efforts to combat the racism and classism so prevalent in our society, women's studies will continue to replicate its biases and thus contribute to the persistence of inequality. We must commit ourselves to learning about each other so that we may accomplish our goals without paternalism, maternalism, or guilt. This requires a willingness to explore histories, novels, biographies, and other readings that will help us grasp the realities of class, race, and other dimensions of inequality.* At the same time, we must take the personal and professional risks involved in building alliances, listening to and respecting people who have firsthand knowledge of how to cope with oppression, and overcoming the institutionalized barriers that divide us. Within this context, our efforts to develop common goals have the potential to produce a truly diverse community of people who study women and who understand their

---

* It is important that reading and learning about the diversity of women's experiences is integrated into our lives. You cannot take one week and learn this field, nor does it come from reading one novel. To assist people in this endeavor, the Center for Research on Women at Memphis State University has developed an extensive bibliography on women of color. It has also developed a research clearinghouse on women of color and Southern women. This clearinghouse is a computer-based resource containing up-to-date information on researchers working in these fields and their latest projects, as well as bibliographic references to relevant social science works published in the last ten years on these groups of women. For more information, write to: Research Clearinghouse, Center for Research on Women, Memphis State University, Memphis, Tenn. 38152.

scholarship as part of the broader quest to arrest all forms of social inequality.

From *Signs* 11:2

The authors wish to thank Barrie Thorne and an anonymous reviewer for their encouragement and helpful suggestions on this piece.

University of Michigan—Flint (Baca Zinn), Memphis State University (Cannon, Higginbotham, and Dill)

Notes

1. Maxine Baca Zinn, "Review Essay: Mexican American Women in the Social Sciences," *Signs: Journal of Women in Culture and Society* 8, no. 2 (Winter 1982): 259–72, "Social Research on Chicanos: Its Development and Directions," *Social Science Journal* 19, no. 2 (April 1982): 1–7, "Sociological Theory in Emergent Chicano Perspectives," *Pacific Sociological Review* 24, no. 2 (April 1981): 255–69, and "Field Research in Minority Communities: Ethical, Methodological, and Political Observations by an Insider," *Social Problems* 27, no. 2 (December 1979): 209–19; Lynn Weber Cannon, "Trends in Class Identification among Black Americans from 1952 to 1978," *Social Science Quarterly* 65 (March 1984): 112–26; Reeve Vanneman and Lynn Weber Cannon, "The American Perception of Class" (Memphis State University, Center for Research on Women, 1985, typescript); Elizabeth Higginbotham, "Race and Class Barriers to Black Women's College Attendance," *Journal of Ethnic Studies* (in press), "Issues in Contemporary Sociological Work on Black Women," *Humanity and Society* 4, no. 3 (November 1980): 226–42, and "Educated Black Women: An Exploration into Life Chance and Choices" (Ph.D. diss., Brandeis University, 1980); Bonnie Thornton Dill, "We Must Redefine Feminism," *Sojourner, the Women's Forum* (September 1984): 10–11, "Race, Class, and Gender: Prospects for an All-inclusive Sisterhood," *Feminist Studies* 9 (Spring 1983): 131–50, and "On the Hem of Life: Race, Class, and the Prospects for Sisterhood," in *Class, Race, and Sex*, ed. Amy Swerdlow and Hanna Lessingler (Boston: G.K. Hall & Co., 1983), 173–88.

2. See, e.g., Audre Lorde, *Sister Outsider* (Trumansburg, N.Y.: Crossing Press, 1984); Angela Y. Davis, *Women, Race and Class* (New York: Random House, 1981).

3. Higginbotham, "Educated Black Women."

4. William H. Exum, "Climbing the Crystal Stair: Values, Affirmative Action and Minority Faculty," *Social Problems* 30, no. 4 (April 1983): 383–97.

5. For a discussion of the experiences of scholars from working-class backgrounds in the academy, see Jake Ryan and Charles Sackrey, *Strangers in Paradise* (Boston: South End Press, 1984); and Carol Sternhell, "The Women Who Won't Disappear," *Ms.* (October 1984): 94–98.

6. Cynthia Epstein, "The Positive Effects of the Multiple Negative: Explaining the Success of Black Professional Women," *American Journal of Sociology* 78, no. 4 (January 1973): 912–33. Although this article serves as a useful example of failure in the applicability of a theory to reality, we single it out as one among many that could demonstrate the same phenomenon. See below for further discussion of this point in a related context.

7. This conference was held in February 1982. The proceedings can be found in *Signs*, vol. 10, no. 4 (Summer 1985).

8. Margaret A. Simons, "Racism and Feminism," *Feminist Studies* 4, no. 2 (1979): 384–401, esp. 388.

9. Phyllis Marvnick Palmer, "White Women/Black Women: The Dualism of Female Identity and Experience in the United States," *Feminist Studies* 9 (Spring 1983): 151–70, esp. 152.

10. Dill (n. 1 above), "On the Hem of Life," 179.

11. For a recent popular example, see Carol Gilligan, *In a Different Voice: Psychological Theory and Women's Development* (Cambridge: Harvard University Press, 1982). The problem of the exclusion of race and class from this work is discussed in a review by Maxine Baca Zinn in *Newsletter of the Center for Research on Women* (Memphis State University, Tenn.), vol. 2, no. 1 (November 1983).

12. Simons, 388.

13. Denise Segura, "Labor Market Stratification: The Chicana Experience," *Berkeley Journal of Sociology* 29 (Spring 1984): 57–91.

14. Marion Kilson, "Black Women in the Professions," *Monthly Labor Review* 100 (May 1977): 38–41. Relevant also is Epstein (n. 6 above).

15. Sharon M. Collins, "The Making of the Black Middle Class," *Social Problems* 30, no. 4 (April 1983): 369–82; Elizabeth Higginbotham, "Employment for Professional Black Women in the Twentieth Century" (paper delivered at the Ingredients for Women's Employment Policy Conference, State University of New York at Albany, 1985).

16. Linda L. Nielsen, "Sexism and Self-Healing in the University," *Harvard Educational Review* 49, no. 4 (November 1979): 467–76, esp. 467. Again this account is singled out as only one among many possible examples, useful because it is so forthright.

17. Patricia Gurin, Arthur Miller, and Gerald Gurin, "Stratum Identification and Consciousness," *Social Psychological Quarterly* 43, no. 1 (1980): 30–47.

18. Nielsen, 474.

19. Bonnie Thornton Dill, "Director's Comments," *Newsletter of the Center for Research on Women* (Memphis State University, Tenn.) vol. 2, no. 2 (May 1984).

Inclusion Without Influence: The Continuing Tokenism of Women of Color

Lynet Uttal

Feminist scholarship needs to move beyond addressing the lack of information about women of color as merely the result of the absence of women of color scholars in academic discussions. In recent years, the number of feminist publications and activities consciously including information by and about women of color has proliferated. We are no longer dealing with only a problem of exclusion. We must readdress our attention to assessing the quality of what has been included and the nature of this inclusion in predominantly Anglo middle class feminist frameworks (such as published anthologies, conference agendas and discussion groups). The lack of representation of women of color perspectives in these frameworks is a much more complex issue than simple omission.

Women of color scholars have lamented the absence of women of color scholars, political activists and artists in discussions that have focused on women's issues and have assessed why these absences occur. We have been much less adamant in pointing out the significance of including women of color perspectives and less successful in getting published articles demonstrating how the inclusion of our perspectives revolutionizes social analyses.[1] So much attention has been paid to analyses of why dominant feminist discourses have been inattentive to women of color that we have yet to see analyses which include these neglected perspectives. Most Anglo feminists have been more responsive to hearing the call for diversity in membership than they have been to hearing the call for the analytic inclusion of race, class and gender.

In response to the call for diversity, Anglo feminists have sought out, recruited, promoted and supported women of color. The Ford Foundation has provided enormous financial support to Anglo feminist research institutes specifically for these efforts. Most feminist anthologies include at least one chapter on women of color. Women of color are being included both as researchers and as subjects in research projects. This would seem to negate any evidence of exclusionary practices.

Yet I am discouraged by the nature of this inclusion. Well-intended Anglo feminists are developing support networks for women of color and including women of color as subjects/objects of their research without actually modifying their own academic practices to reflect the significance of race and class dynamics. By not doing so, they continue to deny the significance of representing the varied perspectives of women of color in their own work. These practices limit the quality of *all* scholarship as well as information about women of color. In other words, business goes on as usual with the only change being the inclusion of token women of color in the feminist group, a token women of color issue in an anthology, or token women of color in research samples.

Misunderstandings arise because we are not clear why we are working so hard to achieve multicultural diversity in our feminist groups. I had a recent experience that illustrates this problem. At the University of California, Santa Cruz, some Anglo feminists formed a subgroup of the Feminist Studies Formal Research Activity allegedly to study race, class and gender. It is only in hindsight that I realize that their desire to get more women of color actively involved in the larger group (rather than a desire to look more closely at race, class and gender) motivated this strategy. This short-sighted goal of some Anglo feminists sabotaged the attempt of other Anglo feminists and feminists of color to jointly think about the analytic intersection of race, class and gender.

At the first organizational meeting, one woman of color suggested the need for a subgroup to discuss, theorize and analyze the intersection of race, class and gender from the perspectives of women of color. Her suggestion was erroneously redirected by a few Anglo feminists as a need for a separate support group for women of color. We ended up only discussing what kinds of support women of color would want—computer support, research assistantships, special speakers, etc.

This discussion disturbed me because many of us (both Anglo and women of color) had come to the group to discuss the analytic inter-linkages between race, class and gender. Instead we were faced only with discussion about the personal needs of women of color, and not about our research interests. This experience suggests to me that while many Anglo feminists are very actively trying to provide support for women of color, many have not altered their own core concerns to really see the relevancy of the dynamics of race, class and gender to their own work or how they might benefit from incorporating varied perspectives into their own work. Instead, in current feminist usage, the concept of "race, class and gender" is applied only to "women of color." This usage fails to take into account that "gender," "race" and "class" are not static categories, but rather dynamic social processes in which everyone is located. Therefore, an Anglo middle-class feminist also has a raced, classed and gendered position in society.

Because a concern for diversity has not impacted upon the personal work of most feminists, an array of problems has been created. In classrooms, students continue to point out that though their Anglo feminist teachers are supportive, they are not prepared to be resources for learning about women of color and/or working class women. Another problem is the way in which women of color are perceived in a pre-dominantly Anglo feminist group. When a woman of color appears, her presence and comments are objectified as a representation of an entire racial/ethnic group, and her personal research interests are subordinated to this understanding of her. The reclaiming of subjectivity that is so central to feminist scholarship is not granted to women of color.

The problem of inclusion without influence is further illustrated by a recent study in which the researcher interviewed a sample of racially/ethnically diverse women without altering her intellectual agenda. My intent is not to discredit her work, but to challenge the limits of collecting diverse samples which are not analyzed with race and ethnicity in mind. Her sample was composed of 39% African American women, 23% Anglo American women, 18% "Hispanic" women and 20% American Indian women. Not only was her sample racially diverse, but the majority of her sample were women of color. When I discovered her sample, I was exhilarated by it and eager to read her analysis.

But for the most part, race was not included in her analysis except as a marker to describe the race of a respondent. In only a brief section was the women's awareness of culture and racism examined. By neglecting to deal with the issue of racism more thoroughly, the researcher failed to examine how cultural and racial consciousness might vary for each racial/ethnic group represented in her sample. Instead, she conflated racism into a monolithic experience that all women of color experience. She left me wondering what her raw information really looked like. Had race been an integral part of her analytic agenda, she could have gone much further with her analysis.

Because of these problems, Anglo feminists and feminists of color who are concerned about women of color from different racial/ethnic groups than their own need to more actively seek out information about women of color and relate it to their particular interest. To become better informed can be such an easy matter. I have gone to the library and have browsed through periodicals, journals, magazines and books for anything on Mexican American women. The bookshelves are not as bare as they were prior to 1975, and computerized searches make this exercise even easier. After only a few afternoons, I am much more aware of the variety of issues and this has influenced my own personal research agenda. We need to do this homework on our own topics before we begin recruiting women of color onto our faculties, as graduate students and members in our groups. Being better informed about different groups and their critiques not only will make the process of inclusion more fruitful, but the personal work of each recruiter will benefit and may even be radically modified.

Anglo feminists who are politically supportive of feminists of color are not convinced of the urgency to include the perspectives of women of color in their own academic work. They are well aware of the absence of women of color in their groups and they are actively trying to correct this problem. But I contend that this limited interpretation of inclusion results in a new kind of exclusion of women of color of which we need to be aware. Editors perpetuate this problem by publishing essays on the processes of absence, instead of about the lives of women of color. Editors also perpetuate the problem by considering a non-integrated chapter on women of color as sufficient inclusion. Concerned Anglo feminists perpetuate the problem by providing professional support without actually modifying their own topics and interests to take into account the perspectives of women of color. We must continue working on issues of inclusion, but we must realize that diverse inclusion is not enough if these token voices have no impact and influence on all our ways of thinking.

Notes

1. Two recent articles by Patricia Hill Collins, "Learning From The Outsider Within: The Sociological Significance of Black Feminist Thought," *Social Problems* 33, and "Black Women's Ways of Knowing," *Signs* vol. 14, no. 4, are two exceptions.

Hablando cara a cara/ Speaking Face to Face: An Exploration of Ethnocentric Racism

María Lugones

Esta es escritura hablada cara a cara. This is writing spoken face to face. *Escritura solitaria por falta de compañía que busca solaz en el dialogo.* Writing that is solitary for lack of company and looks for solace in dialogue. *Monólogo extendido hacia afuera y hablado en muchas lenguas.* Monologue spoken outwardly and in tongues.*

Empazaré monologándoles en mi lengua ancestral para hacerle honor, para prepararme y prepararlas a hablar con comprensión** de las dificultades de nuestros diálogos y para recrearlas con el precioso son de una de las lenguas vivas de este país.

La soledad de mi escritura me pesa en la multitud de sus significados. Por eso, porque no quiero estar sola, invocaré a dos hermanas poetizas que me han guiado y acompañado en esta tarea. Marina Rivera, poetiza de Arizona, y Margarita Cota-Cárdenas, poetiza de California, me espantaron la soledad de lejos.

Dice Marina:[1]

> *Quedo solamente yo*
> *persona de en medio*
> *que luché en vida color de café*
> *luché en vida color blanco*

---

*Inglés and several varieties of Spanish. If you do not read Spanish, see footnote below.

***Porque si compartes mis lenguas, entonces comprendes todos los niveles de mi intención.* And if you do not understand my many tongues, you begin to understand why I speak them. It is truly not just to be understood by you. I speak them because I want to point to the possibility of becoming playful in the use of different voices and because I want to point to the possibility of coming to appreciate this playfulness. Here I exercise this playful practice. The appreciation of my playfulness and its meaning may be realized when the possibility of becoming playful in this way has been collectively realized, when it has become realized by us. It is here to be appreciated or missed and both the appreciation and the missing are significant. The more fully this playfulness is appreciated, the less broken I am to you, the more dimensional I am to you. But I want to exercise my multidimensionality even if you do not appreciate it. To do otherwise would be to engage in self-mutilation, to come to be just the person that you see. To play in this way is then an act of resistance as well as an act of self-affirmation.

> *y me hice fuerte*
> *bastante para decir*
> *no me llamen por la chicana*
> *ni por el chicano*
> *ni por las mujeres*
> *llámenme por mi misma*

y Margarita:[2]

> *Todas aguantaron*
> *...y yo*
> > *yo no quise*
>
> *no acepté*
> *...no quería que una débil tarde*
> *vieras tus antiguas penas bordadas en mi cara*
> *...yo quise*
> *...volar altísimo*
> *definir mis entrañas*
> *...yo ya no pude*
> *que mis hijas y sus hijas y sus hijas no*
> *dolorosa...*
> *di que comprendes*
> > *resucita conmigo*
>
> *ya era tiempo*
> *de abortar los mitos*
> *de un solo sentido*

¡Qué bonita la coincidencia que no es azarosa! La relación íntima entre el abortar los mitos de un solo sentido y el romper espejos que nos muestran rotas, despedazadas. We want to be seen unbroken, we want to break cracked mirrors that show us in many separate, *unconnected* fragments.

Soy de la gente de colores, soy mestiza, latina, porteña, indita, mora criollita, negra. Soy de piel morena y labios color ciruela. Soy vata, mujer, esa. To know me unbroken requires the kind of devotion that makes empathetic and sympathetic thinking possible. I think it is possible for White/Anglo women to think empathetically and sympathetically about those who are harmed seriously by racism and about their lives held in communities where culture flourishes through struggle. But I do think that this takes the devotion of friendship. In becoming conscious and critical of the ways of thinking about racism and ethnocentrism, I thought it realistic to reserve sympathetic and empathetic thinking for the rarity of deep friendship. But anyone who is not self-deceiving about racist ethnocentrism can begin to see us unbroken through engaged thinking that takes seriously her own participation in an ethnocentric culture in a racial state. Such thinking requires that she become and think as a self-conscious critical practitioner of her culture and a self-conscious and critical member of the racial state. Furthermore, such thinking is possible because she is a participant in both.

Resucita conmigo y llámame por mi misma.[3] Come back to life with me and call me for myself, or don't call me at all.

Racism and ethnocentrism

To speak another language and another culture are not the same as being racialized. One can be ethnocentric without being racist. The existence of races as the products of racialization presupposes the presence of racism, but the existence of different ethnicities does not presuppose ethnocentrism, even if ethnocentrism is universal. So we should conclude that ethnicity is not the same as race and ethnocentrism is not the same as racism.

> *Ethnocentrism*: the explicit and arrogantly held action-guiding belief that one's culture and cultural ways are superior to others'; or the disrespectful, lazy, arrogant indifference to other cultures that devalues them through not seeing appreciatively *any* culture or cultural ways except one's own when one could do otherwise; or the disrespectful, lazy, arrogant indifference that devalues other cultures through stereotyping of them or through non-reflective, self-satisfied acceptance of such stereotypes.

Thus if I lead you to recognize your own and my ethnicity, I would not yet have led you to recognize that we are differently racialized, that we occupy very different positions in the racial state and that our ethnicities may be contaminated to some small or maximal degree with racism. But, on the other hand, unless there is a very high degree of assimilation, racism always seems to be accompanied and in part expressed by ethnocentrism.

Investigating collectively one's ethnocentrism and its roots may lead one to locate it in one's racism.

> *Racism*: one's affirmation of or acquiescence to or lack of recognition of the structures and mechanisms of the racial state; one's lack of awareness of or blindness or indifference to one's being racialized; one's affirmation

of, indifference or blindness to the harm that the racial state inflicts on some of its members.*

Racist ethnocentrism: ethnocentrism that is expressive of racism.

Hablando cara a cara/speaking face to face: Muting and disengagement

I am thinking about cracked mirrors that reflect us falsely because I want to lead you into the spaces where I explore racist ethnocentrism with White/Anglas or with White-assimilated-to-Anglo women.** In this context bi-lingualism and bi-culturalism or multiculturalism are very hard to express because they, as well as the racialization of everyone in the learning space, are muted: our ethnicities and races are muted. Since these mutings are not heard, they are not heard as related. This three-fold muting is a central feature of the context of inquiry, one which needs to be overcome collectively simply because so long as it is present, we cannot really hear or speak about what is muted. Within this silence White/Anglo

---

*We need to produce a theory of the racial state and its mechanisms. So far, the following seems to me true of the racial state:

i. It produces a classification of people that gives rise to race.

ii. The classification is not a rational ordering based on any 'natural' phenomena.

iii. The classification is historically variable.

iv. The classification has a strong normative force in the form of custom or in the form of positive law.

v. The classification is presupposed (explicitly or not) by many other legal and customary norms.

vi. The classification imposes on people a false identity and arrogates the power of self-definition, even though the history of the classification may include the search and the hegemonical struggle for identity and self-definition by particular groups.

vii. The classification is given meaning by particular organizations of social, political and economic interaction that regulate relations among people who are differently classified.

viii. The racial state also produces ideologies that create the illusion that both the classification and the organization of life that accompany and give meaning to it are justified. (These claims about the racial state were provoked by Michael Omi's and Howard Winant's "By the Rivers of Babylon: Race in the United States," *Socialist Review* 71 and 72. I think that Omi and Winant would find fault in my formulation of (vi) because it does not give enough attention to competing racially defined political projects. My intent in formulating (vi) is to take these competing projects into account, but I am uncomfortable with the lack of clarity of this formulation on this particular point.)

**I have in mind the institutional academic classroom and other intellectual contexts that are predominantly White/Anglo. I also discuss racism and ethnocentrism in predominantly raza contexts, and in contexts that are predominantly peopled by Third World interlocutors. But this paper is not located in the latter contexts. The understanding of racism and ethnocentrism in the latter contexts proceeds in a very different manner than the one delineated in this essay.

women can see themselves as simply human or simply women. I can bring you to your senses *con el tono de mi voz*, with the sound of my—to you—alien voice.

Precisely because thinking about this feature of the context of inquiry collectively presupposes a recognition of it and because I cannot assume this recognition, I speak to you in tongues. But as I speak in tongues, *me siento separada como por una pared en el presentarme frente a los demás*. As I speak to you in the many incarnations of my native tongue, one of the live tongues of this country, I feel isolated from you as if by a thick wall. *Pero no lo hago para romper la pared, lo hago tan solo para reconocerla.* My intention is not to break the wall down, just to recognize it. This recognition is *a* first step to an honest understanding of ethnocentric racism and of the connections between the two.

So the central and painful questions for *me* in this encounter become questions of speech: *¿En qué voz* with which voice, *anclada en qué lugar* anchored in which place, *para qué y porqué* why and to what purpose, do I trust myself to you...*o acaso juego un juego de* cat and mouse just for your entertainment...*o por el mio?* I ask these questions out loud because they need to be asked. Asking them in this way *demands* recognition and places the burden (?) of answering them *actively* on your and not just on my shoulders.

So we can see that *si pudiera decir todo "derecho viejo"* if I could say everything straighforwardly *lo diría mal* I would be saying it falsely, so I can't, *porque me hace mal* because it harms me. It harms me to be clean and easy when it is a pretense, a pretense imposed on me because double talk is supposed to be more efficient and more educational than bi-lingual talk. So, for "our" sake, for the sheer possibility *de un "nosotras,"* I will swallow my tongue *"a medias,"* half-way.

We have begun to see that one cannot think well about racism and ethnocentrism or challenge and reconstruct the racial state or the ethnocentrism in one's culture and in oneself without an awareness of one's ethnicity, or one's being racialized as well as of the ties between the two. It is one's competence and the competence of the other investigators as inquirers that is at stake. Being unaware of one's own ethnicity and racialization commits the inquirer to adopt a disengaged stance, one from outside the racial state and the ethnocentric culture looking in. *But it is one's culture and one's society that one is looking at.* Such a disengaged inquirer is committed either to dishonest study or to ignoring deep meanings and connections to which she has access only as a self-conscious member of the racial state and as a sophisticated practitioner of the culture: she is committed to ethnocentric racism.

Everyone who is racialized is a member of and participant in at least one culture. One's position in the racial state may be maintained by beliefs of cultural superiority or by either active or passive devaluation, erasure or stereotyping of cultures other than one's own.* That is, ethnocentrism may be one of the mechanisms of the racial state. Ethnocentrism may be part of the *ideology* of the racial state. Dis-engagement as a sanctioned ethnocentric racist strategy works as follows: you do not see me because you do not see yourself and you do not see yourself because you declare yourself outside of culture. But declaring yourself outside of culture is self-deceiving. The deception hides your seeing only through the eyes of your culture. So dis-engagement is a radical form of passivity toward the ideology of the ethnocentric racial state which privileges the dominant culture as the only culture to "see with" and conceives this seeing as to be done non-self-consciously.

Reading *Drylongso*,[4] *White Over Black*,[5] *I Know Why the Caged Bird Sings*,[6] *They Called Them Greasers*,[7] *The Woman Warrior*,[8] *Invisible Man*,[9] etc. is not helpful in exploring racism and ethnocentrism *unless* these works are read from this engaged position. When read from the engaged position, these works can help the White/Angla become self-consciously White/Anglo in the racial and ethnic senses of the words: they can help her unravel the connections between racism, ethnocentrism, White/Anglo self-esteem, polite arrogance, polite condescension and a troubled sense of responsibility in the face of people of color.

> *Para interrupción, un son:*
>
> *Todo cada cual con su cada cuala*
> *doblando la espalda o volviendo la cara.*
> *Miras en mis ojos y te ves mirada,*
> *me tocas la mano y ya estás tocada.*
> *Si no miras, vata, nunca verás nada.*

Lo nuestro

Thinking back about the claim that ethnocentrism may be universal, as it is sometimes claimed, I think it is worth making a distinction between two phenomena which, because they are expressed similarly, are often taken to exemplify ethnocentrism. I think one of them does not.

"*¡Ay qué linda mi gente (o mi cultura, o mi comunidad, o mi tierra), qué suave, si, la más suave!*" "Ah, how beautiful my people (or my culture, or my community, or my land), how beautiful, the most beautiful!" I think this claim is made many times non-comparatively. It is

---

*When one's position in the racial state is that of a victim of racism, then that position may be partially maintained by beliefs of cultural inferiority or by either active or passive devaluation, erasure or stereotyping of one's own culture.

expressive of the centrality that one's people, culture, community or language have to the subject's sense of self and her web of connections. It expresses her fondness for them. In these cases, the claim does not mean "better than other people's," but "dearer to me than other people's communities, etc., are to me." It is like a mother saying "*¡Qué bella mi niña, la más bella!*" "How beautiful my child, the most beautiful!" and expressing the centrality of this child in her affection. Similar claims are made many times comparatively and invidiously and I think that *only then* are they ethnocentric.

It is worth noticing that rarely have I heard White/Anglos make such claims in the first way, though I have heard similar claims used by White/Anglos to convey the second meaning. Many White/Anglos seem to me disaffected from, or indifferent to, or unaware of, or chauvinistically proud of their culture, people, communities.

In making this distinction I do not mean to imply that one cannot make judgements about a people, culture, etc., that are not chauvinistic, not ethnocentric, and yet critical. Indeed, becoming aware of racism through an understanding of one's own ethnicity and the extent to which it is expressive of racism presupposes the possibility of making non-ethnocentric critical judgements about one's own culture.

But sometimes Third World peoples in this country are accused of ethnocentrism and chauvinism when we are expressing our fundamental ties to "lo nuestro." Keeping this distinction in mind may result in an undermining of the claim that ethnocentrism is universal. It may also help White/Anglos in exploring their ethnicity. In this exploration it may be helpful to see the extent to which White/Anglos do or can make the first kind of claim. One may be too quick to assume an ethnocentric interpretation of one's claims and too quick to see the whole of one's culture and cultural ways as tainted with ethnocentrism. This distinction should be helpful in keeping that tendency in check.

Infantilization of judgement

I think it is essential that in exploring racism and ethnocentrism, the White/Angla challenge and be challenged in her own sense of incompetence. So far I have directed my attention to the particular incompetence that results from the three-fold muting mentioned at the beginning of this essay and which leads the inquirer, when the muting is not heard, to a disengaged position in the inquiry. I would like to conclude by addressing another source of incompetence in the White/Anglo exploration of racism and ethnocentrism: infantilization of judgement.

I have encountered this phenomenon so many times and in so many people of good judgement in other matters, that it is frequently disconcerting: *Se han vuelto como niños, incapaces de juzgar, evitando el compromiso, paralizados en tantos seres responsables*. They have turned into children, incapable of judgement, avoiding all commitment except against racism in the abstract, paralyzed as responsible beings, afraid of hostility and hostile in their fear, wedded to their ignorance and arrogant in their guilty purity of heart.

Infantilization of judgement is a dulling of the ability to read critically, and with maturity of judgement, those texts and situations in which race and ethnicity are salient. It appears to me as a flight into a state in which one cannot be critical or responsible: a flight into those characteristics of childhood* that excuse ignorance and confusion, and that appeal to authority. If the description "child" is an appropriate description of White/Anglas in the context of racism and ethnocentrism, then to ascribe responsibility to them for the understanding and undoing of these phenomena is inappropriate. If a child, the White/Angla can be guilty of racism and ethnocentrism innocently, unmarked and untouched in her goodness, confused with good reason, a passive learner because she cannot exercise her judgement with maturity. But, of course, she is not a child. She is an ethnocentric racist.

Infantilization of judgement is a form of ethnocentric racism precisely because it is a self-indulgent denial of one's understanding of one's culture and its expressing racism. One of the features of this denial is the denial that racism is a two-party affair, an interactive phenomenon. In infantilization of judgement the racist attempts to hide that she understands racism as a participant.

Infantilization is broken if one squarely and respectfully sets the White/Anglo inquirer in the position of seeing herself as a competent practitioner of her culture and a racialized member of the racial state and if one also blocks the possibility of escape into lack of engagement. She cannot then take refuge into incompetence, for this presupposes that racialization and the having of a culture are what happens to others who are not her people and whom she can know only abstractly. One cannot disown one's culture. One can reconstruct it in struggle.

One's experience of time, of movement through space, one's sense of others and of oneself are all culturally formed and informed:

Siempre hay tiempo para los amigos.
> I'll see you next Tuesday
> at 5:15.

---

*I use the word "child" here not because I think that young human beings are incapable of judgement, but because young human beings are *alleged* to be incapable of judgement *and* because women have been thought to be like children in this respect. Any woman who rejects this attribution but falls into infantilization with respect to racism should be struck by the inconsistency of her stance. (Thanks to Sarah Hoagland for eliciting this note from me with her criticism of my use of the word "child" to make my point.)

Vente y tomamos un café y charlamos
mientras plancho la ropa.

I'll call you Monday
evening to let you know for sure
that I am coming.

Ay mujer, te ves triste,
¿te sientes bien?
Me duele mucho la cabeza y
estoy un poco sola y cansada.
Dura la vida, ¿no?

Hi, how are you? Fine, and you?
Fine, thank you.

My suggestions here are directed to the breaking down of traits in the inquirer that make the inquiry pointless, an exercise in self-deception or an exercise in further domination, and adorns the inquirer with dishonesty.

Ya era tiempo
de abortar los mitos
de un solo sentido.[10]

Notes

1. Marina Rivera, "Mestiza: poema en cinco partes," *Mestiza* (Tucson: Grilled Flowers, 1977).

2. Margarita Cota-Cárdenas, "A una Madre de Nuestros Tiempos," *Noches Despertando Inconciencias* (Tucson: Scorpion Press, 1977).

3. Marina Rivera, ibid.

4. I chose these texts because they are and should be examples of classics in the contemporary White/Angla bibliography on racism. J. Gwaltney, *Drylongso: A Self Portrait of Black America* (New York: Random House, Vintage Books, 1980).

5. Winthrop D. Jordan, *White Over Black* (Chapel Hill: University of North Carolina Press, 1968; Baltimore: Penguin Books, 1971).

6. Maya Angelou, *I Know Why The Caged Bird Sings* (New York: Bantam Books, 1969).

7. Arnoldo de Leon, *They Called Them Greasers* (Austin: University of Texas Press, 1983).

8. Maxine Hong Kingston, *The Woman Warrior* (New York: Vintage Books, 1976).

9. Ralph Ellison, *Invisible Man* (New York: Vintage Books, 1963).

10. Margarita Cota-Cárdenas, ibid.

Feminism and Racism: A Report on the 1981 National Women's Studies Association Conference

Chela Sandoval,

as Secretary to The National Third World Women's Alliance

The Beginning

> "My kinswomen, with a good heart and sturdy hands, I greet you."
>
> —BEA MEDICINE, LAKOTA TRIBE,
> AT THE BEGINNING OF THE CONFERENCE

The contemporary women's movement was constructed with the best of intentions. But underlying contradictions began to emerge as U.S. feminists of color denounced the racism and classism inherent in a "unified women's movement" which could only be "unified" within the perimeters of white women's values. Ideological differences divided and helped to dissipate the movement from within between the years 1972 and 1980, so that now white feminists are confusing straws and tools in a desperate attempt at its revitalization. This is the context within which one of the most powerful organizations born of the "white" women's movement, the National Women's Studies Association (NWSA) held its Third Annual Conference in June of 1981. The theme and title of the conference, "Women Respond to Racism," was already fraught with ambiguities and contradictions. Who are the "women" represented in this title? Should we assume that these women are some homogeneous group that will act and can "respond" in concert? Is there a unified racism outside of most of our experiences which we can identify and courageously confront?

It was with a mixture of irony, hope, fear and anger that women from throughout the United States and abroad made their way to Storrs, Connecticut. For many the time had come: to examine the women's liberation movement as it had never been examined before; to enable a now over-due critique which would allow feminist activists of every ideological persuasion the opportunity to confront the kind of movement which had been constructed so far; to identify and pool their various skills in order to map out the contours of a new kind of "women's" movement; and ultimately, to further the development of "Women's Studies" as an academic discipline. Many felt that the issue of "racism" would make these goals achievable. Examining racism in all its complexities, defining its many meanings and challenging its resiliency within movements for egalitarian change, opens the possibility of identifying new theory and methods for action which can re-shape and revitalize the current U.S. version of the women's movement. Yet as important as this movement is in the feminist history of consciousness, it is exactly at this juncture that the movement is stuck. For even one year later the question posed by Audre Lorde in her opening speech lingers on: "Do the women of the Academy really *want* to confront racism?"

Women of color who attended felt that a report of the conference would be of historical significance to the on-going commitments of feminism and of Women's Studies. To this end, they elected a Secretariat-General, a Treasurer, a Secretary, and commissioned the writing of this report. More than anything else the group wanted to document the work they had accomplished and the stands that they made during their difficult and painful meetings. However, it was agreed that such a report would be more meaningful if written within the context of the conference at large—the conference structure that surrounded and determined our activities. This document is divided into four parts: part one is this introduction; part two is a report on the conference structure and its problems; part three, the heart of the report, is a hard look at the coming together of third world feminism including its theoretical underpinnings; and part four is the conclusion in which I discuss the possibility of creating a feminist movement whose central concerns are those of egalitarian gender, race, class and culture relations. My hope is that this four-part structure provides a map (charted and dictated by the U.S. third world feminists who attended the conference) of the structures of consciousness which typify both the dominant women's movement and U.S. third world feminism.

The pilgrimage from California to Storrs, Connecticut is over 3,000 miles—women came from that far away, and further. The route there was difficult, a maze of a journey through obscure airports, bus-stations, and taxi-rides. The difficulty of the journey and the suggested unpopularity of the theme "racism" whittled down the number of conference participants from approximately 1,800 in 1980, to 1,300 in 1981. Feminists of color reported that the impetus for completing such a journey lay in the yearning (created by years of educational, political and community work) to confront the "women's" liberation movement with the anger, frustration, cynicism, and hope that those years had inspired.

In contrast to the diversity of our expectations, the conference program greeted us all alike, with what seemed to be a conflict-free agenda. It listed a week-long cornucopia of workshops and panels to choose from, their titles and descriptions expertly detailing every conceivable topic. It was difficult to tell if the program was a promise of where we would be at the end of the conference or a serious mis-reading of where we were beginning. Still, most of us were willing to accept the spirit of the program agenda with optimism and proceeded to tightly schedule in our activities for the next five days. Many were momentarily lulled into accepting the program's abundance as a signal of problems already resolved.

NWSA president, Elaine Reubin, opened the conference by announcing, "The situation is precarious—there are groups within the women's movement and the NWSA who feel not heard or represented." She pointed out that "Women's Studies realizes its obvious limitations...its racism." She hoped the conference would provide a landmark opportunity to "dialogue," to somehow find "the skills and tools to reach across difference." Despite these best of intentions the grave difficulties which bespeak the condition of racism kept even these, the boldest and the brightest of U.S. women, from overcoming the blocks and barriers intrinsic to self examination and hoped for change. The conference divided women into one of two oppositional categories: "third world" and "white." This report documents how those divisions were given life, and how they are challenged by U.S. third world feminism.

The Hegemonic Structure of the Conference

> "Anger is what we know best, we know it, we cut our teeth on it."
>
> —AUDRE LORDE, FROM HER OPENING SPEECH

Social separations between women were exacerbated by the very structure of the conference. Morning Consciousness Raising Groups (CR Groups) were followed by a profusion of workshops, panels and presentations promising the fine-tooth-approach of the academic probe while in effect exhibiting the watered-down-propensity of capitalist overabundance...the typical conference shopping mall effect. Choosing among presentations became an arbitrary procedure for it was difficult to gauge the presenter's expertise or the presentation's content or orientation despite its description in the program. Women of color often found themselves frustrated as the sole representatives of "third world" opinion at a conference workshop, while at the same time missing those few presentations which were able to identify and dissect racism at its roots. More importantly, the overabundance of presentations and their often misleading descriptions resulted in the inability of the larger conference to advance any collective discussion and understanding of racism in the women's movement. This shortcoming was not simply the fault of the presenters; they, after all, were drawn together from separate locations throughout the world and in most cases had little sense of how to connect their own individual work with the larger social, cultural and political issues seething just below the surface of the conference structure.* The first day, ironically enough, the only place where "racism" was directly confronted and heatedly debated was in the workshop on the "Unacknowledged Racism:....Anti-Semitism." Efforts to confront other kinds of racism were dissipated in the apparent abundance of opportunities to do so.

Thinkers such as Audre Lorde, the women in "Sweet Honey in the Rock," Adrienne Rich, the contributors to *This Bridge Called My Back* and other excellent workshop presenters provided the conference with the raw materials needed to create an intensely powerful five-day learning experience. But the conference schedule did not allow time for the development of their ideas. Furthermore, the well-known or "special" workshop presenters often did not participate in the day-to-day work of the conference, which included the CR groups, workshops and political and other social groups. Meanwhile the individual presenters continued to demand our attention and support, while the unfortunate structure of the conference divided us into fragmented interest groups. In all of these ways, then, any sense of continuity was broken down, as was any opportunity for a cumulative dialogue to develop.

Perhaps the most crucial feature missing from the conference was the kind of flexibility that would allow the structure to be overturned in order to better meet the needs of the participants, even as those needs were in the process of being discovered. The busy conference program had everything scheduled in except the critical time to evaluate its progress. Meanwhile, the strategy of accepting every proposal submitted for presentation hid the poverty of our understanding under the flamboyant disguise of overabundance: what seemed a generous conference format became a maze in which participants played hide-and-seek games of knowledge and which ultimately led conference participants to blame themselves if they failed to extricate the maximum amount of knowledge from the situation. In the future, the third world feminist CR group suggests: that conferences be structured in a manner which makes them responsible to the historical importance of the topic discussed; that we attend, en mass, a daily general session to ensure a common denominator to our intellectual and political development; and that we hold daily collective evaluation sessions.

In theory, the function of the conference was to permit women to "respond to racism." However, the structure of the conference (represented not only by the atomized presentations following one another in

---

*This dynamic has resulted in most post-conference evaluations analyzing it solely in terms of its "most interesting" workshops. Critics have not been able to access the larger meanings of the overall conference. For an example of this phenomenon, see *off our backs* July, 1981.

lock-step formation, but by the speeches presented by the NWSA officials themselves) controlled and undermined the attainment of this goal. These speeches moderated and restrained the discussions of racism by invoking the imperatives of a higher order, the "survival" of the organization itself: a new chairperson had to be found, the constitution had to be revised, and the inevitable financial problems had to be solved. The official response to racism soon became: "Remember, the NWSA *is* dealing with racism by sponsoring this conference: what would it be like if the NWSA were not around?"; "The NWSA, after all, can't be everything to everybody"; "Is separatism within the NWSA a luxury we can afford?" Such messages oversaw and guided the imagination of the meanings of racism into permitable arenas.

This conference was the first sponsored by the women's movement to confront the idea of "racism" and over three hundred feminists of color attended from all over the country, the largest number of third world women to ever assemble under the banner of the women's movement. Of these women, several important theorists and writers who could not afford to pay the registration fee were not permitted to present their work. In the name of the NWSA's "survival," "no exceptions" were "permitted." Instead, the organization developed a hard-line response to any request to make a more constructive and positive interpretation of the rules. Like the women's movement itself, the organization of the NWSA was beginning to fray around the edges...the official response to this inevitable condition was to tighten rules and regulations. Officials, following the letter rather than the spirit of NWSA regulations, prioritized the values of the dominant order over and above the conference theme itself, "Women Respond to Racism." Or perhaps this theme *was* adequately interpreted. Perhaps the conference structure and the strategy of its organizers *is* an accurate rendering of how white women respond when faced with the issues of "racism." Perhaps the conference overall, like the dominant women's movement itself, was being shaped by the precision instruments which are the values of white women.

In the months since the conference has ended feminist activists all over the world have asked how this first movement conference on racism could have inspired the charge of "racist." But we have seen how, hidden within the very structure of the conference, the supports were already in place for such an accusation.

The Conference Within the Conference: U.S. Third World Feminism

> "Shall we, as Third World women, decide to 'join' the 'movement'?"
> "We can't join the movement...because we *are* the movement!"
>
> —FROM A CONFERENCE DIALOGUE

"Consciousness-Raising" (CR) groups were scheduled for two hours every morning and were required of every conference participant. Women of color on the NWSA conference organizing committee had designated one specific CR group for "Third World" women only. This isolation of three hundred conference participants had repercussions that plunged all conference participants into storms of controversy. The most immediate effect was on the conference structure—it created a smaller conference within the larger one. What follows is a report on the U.S. third world feminism which emerged from the activities within that smaller conference.

Conference participants were initially introduced to the CR groups at the moment of registration. While paying our fees and obtaining a room assignment we were also asked to choose a CR group which would "best fit our needs." In examining the lists registrants discovered one single title designated "women of color," while "white" women were offered a series of lists signifying their diversity and emphasizing their choices: "white/immigrant," "white/upper-class," "white/working-class," "middle-class," "educated," "Jewish," "experienced in CR groups," and so on.

While many "white" women were unhappy with being separated from women "of color," many of the women of color felt immediately suspicious of a conference structure which would place them under one, seemingly homogeneous category. However unintentional, this segregation reflected the way in which women of color are positioned in the dominant culture and within the women's movement itself. The questions raised by this seeming isolation of women of color at this early juncture of the conference were superseded only by their anger. Were women of color to be segregated for the safety of white women? Were women of color expendable to this conference on racism? Or was the separation in their own interests? Did conference participants have a choice? How would these initial categorizations cast the kinds of roles that "white women" and "women of color" could assume for the rest of the conference? In spite of good intentions the lists became another reminder of the multi-dimensionality of white women, while three hundred women of color found themselves seemingly without choice, classified and sorted into one room...eyeing one another in anger.

In the face of that anger the feminists of color who had been instrumental in organizing the one large CR group offered well-articulated explanations for the structure we confronted. Yet even after hearing them out, the first questions raised for intense deliberation remained the same: "Shall we continue to meet together in this single, supposedly homogeneous group? If so, what KIND of group are we? Shall we separate into smaller groups that more closely reflect our identities?" For two hours we struggled to overcome our disappointment and anger at both the conference and each other.

The questions that plagued us during that initial meeting eventually evoked a plethora of positions which forced us to examine not only the women's movement and our own separate ethnic liberation movements, but the idea of a united third world women's standpoint. Even though we understood the many levels of the "logic of separatism" we felt its imposition as a "ghettoization," especially within the context of a predominantly "white" conference. Our discussions led us to question the very nature of separatism...perhaps this on-the-surface repugnant condition was, after all, the most liberating category in the situation within which we found ourselves. The heated discussions that ensued included looking at all forms of categorization including the logic of separatism as a long-term political tactic.

In time we recognized that many of our concerns were motivated by shared experiences. Each of us had experienced both the oppression and the empowerment that the processes of categorization, re-naming and re-categorizing can mean. Now we wished to use such lessons self-consciously in the re-construction of a liberatory movement better suited to our needs. Somehow during this, at times, heartwrenching process of examination and change, we grew into a single congregation. These initial discussions, however volatile and time-consuming, provided the group the opportunity to hammer out shared standards with which to work together—working standards which were to serve us well in the struggles that followed.

As diverse as we were, we realized that we would have to hammer out (as part of our community building) issues as basic as finding the common ground for our "unity"—aside from the shared oppressions we had experienced within the movement and the society at large. A major stumbling block in our discussions was an undeveloped, if not racist, use of discourses on race. Many women of color complained about the tendency of white women to interpret a discussion of "racism in the women's movement" as an opportunity to discuss the personal relationship between themselves and Black women alone. This tendency to understand racism in its most dualistic of terms not only relegated the experiences of other women of color to invisibility, but also served to keep conference participants from understanding the nuanced and subtle processes which characterize racism. Meanwhile, within our own miniconference, we had to acknowledge and confront our own internalized stereotypes in order to begin to talk with one another. The difficulties of these discussions were eased by our collective efforts to imagine a new, affirming movement, one which would lighten the shadows engulfing so many peoples. Our debates uncovered and encouraged a diversity of communications and we found strength in their expression without forcing them into any kind of unity. Many of these differences centered around the problem of naming the kind of sisterhood that we might share.

Do the classifications recognized by the U.S. Census Bureau offer us a useful way of understanding our cultural experiences? Are we solely "Native American," "Black," "Asian," "Hispanic?" If so, then too many of our identities become excluded. Is it possible that our similarities and differences be named a single name? Given the institutionalization of power in the U.S., some women argued that a single name would, in fact, have the most strategic political effect. We decided to explore this possibility further by imagining the repercussions such a naming might have. During these discussions there were those who argued that it is the color of a woman's skin which marks her as closer or further away from any center of power. For this reason, they suggested that the title "Women of Color" was one which would point out both the nature of our oppression and the basis of our political solidarity. But many objected on the grounds that the designation was one which held insulting connotations. Still others objected to its use on the grounds that they did not wear their "color" in the form or color of their bodies. Other women called for the title "Third World," arguing in its favor on the grounds that we had originally been constituted as a group by the dominant powers, which needed us defined in particular ways in order to define themselves in another. For these women then, to be "Third World" meant three things: first, to have been de-centered from any point of power in order to be used as the negative pole against which the dominant powers can then define themselves; second, to be working politically to challenge the systems that keep power moving in its current patterns, thus shifting it onto new terrains; and third, such a name would work to underline the similarity between our oppression in the U.S. and that of our international sisters in Third World countries. Other voices opposed these positions with the fear that the title "Third World" would diffuse the naming of our *particular* oppressions as Americans too much, while arguing that the title was one more appropriate to International Third World women. So would our potential unity be designated "Third World," or "Colored," or neither? The group came up with no final resolutions—these questions would await another moment in history for their answers. Finally, there were many heterosexual women of color who had never before met other women of color who were also open lesbians. In the process of discussing these issues the hidden was revealed, the fears clarified, the stereotypes confronted and the mutual pains and visions shared. These were the processes necessary for helping us understand who we were together, the current status of our similarities and differences, and what our tactics might be for the creation of a healthier "feminism."

As the idea of a new feminist movement grew, we became concerned with the pitfalls that have confronted liberation movements in the past.

We remembered arrogance disguised as leadership. We recalled the kind of "unity" which had been offered by previous movements for liberation and remembered how our lives had been erased under the edicts of that unity. We wondered if we could create a new flexible movement capable of listening, hearing and transforming with difference. Would our group be able to embrace those who have been shaped by a multitude of forces—those who have experienced a combination of culture, race, color, gender and/or language oppressions and who have become un-categorizable? Would we be capable of shifting the categories? Would we understand our lessons and could we teach them? What did we desire that was different from what we had known within other previous liberation movements?

As the days of the conference slipped away, so too did the initial suspicions we had of one another. The morning CR times seemed to become more and more precious and all too brief as participants felt a working collectivity evolve. In spite of, and then *because* of our differen-ces, a solidarity amongst the group grew slowly. The larger conference, however, was suffering from the dispersion of its energies caused partially by the prolific but superficial shopping mall nature of its structure which precluded the time or space for collective effort. Within a few days it became clear that the most effective place to work; to challenge "racism;" to discuss what it has been, is, and what it might become; to discuss the previous "women's" movement and the kinds of liberatory movements possible in the future, was in this so-called "CR" group for women of color. As we worked we could not help but recognize that our activities belonged to the participants, witnesses, and midwives of a newly emerging movement.

The Common Ground

Many ideas were set forth in the attempt to define the "common ground" of our unity, although one particular vision prevailed over all the others—a vision which translates into a shared understanding of the workings of power. This "shared understanding" becomes a theoretical model which identifies the boundaries within which human subjectivity is constituted. Further, this theoretical model has the capability of allowing connections to be forged across class, race, culture, and gender differences, and it is a model which does not privilege any one of those categories. However, this conception of human subjectivity is only valid given the social and cultural dynamics at work within the United States. At some moment or other during our discussions, every woman had to position herself in relation to the meanings generated by the theoretical model which we had created. It is important to make its construction clear so that we can more self-consciously determine its usefulness, choose our own relationships to it, and clarify the consequences to which our choices will lead. This model can be presented as a typology with four categories. All four categories can be viewed as signifying "nodules" in the currents of power as they flow within the U.S. In the pages which follow, I summarize the strengths of this model, the predicaments it creates for women of color and the possibilities which emerge from its dissolution.

This theoretical four-part model begins with the idea that most definitions of "freedom" in the U.S. are activated in relation to a primary category most easily embodied by the white, capitalist and male reality. White males who move into this power nodule do so by defining themselves in opposition to white women and to third world women and men who are cast as "others." White women inhabit the second category in this hierarchy through the very definition of a primary white male position. Interestingly, even though white women experience the pain of oppression they also experience the will-to-power. For while white women are "othered" by men and feel the pain of objectification, within this secondary category they can only construct a solid sense of "self" through the objectification of people of color. Within the dialectic of this power construct no one can deny the oppression of third world men. However, men of color can call upon the circuits which charge the primary category with the gendered aspect of its privileges and powers, even without the benefit of race or class privileges. This kind of identification with the powerful stratum/caste of "male" for the construction of a solid sense of self has been utilized as an effective weapon for confronting the oppressions they experience. Ironically, however, women of color are cast into the critical category against which third world "male" subjectivity becomes constituted. The final and fourth category belongs to women of color who become survivors in a dynamic which places them as the final "other" in a complex of power moves. Social relations in the U.S. are overlaid by this dialectic of interlinking categories, a pattern which relegates women of color to the crucial category against which all the other categories are provided their particular meanings and privileges.

This four-part typology and its content do not exhaust the many routes through which power might move. What is important is that this pattern has served as a major sieve through which power works to charge life in the U.S. with meaning. The recognition of this four-part model provided the third world feminist CR participants at the conference a shared conceptual framework through which to understand the position we occupy as women of color. However, if power works in these ways to create a unique cultural category for the women of color to occupy, then it not only hurtles its occupants through the destructiveness of sexism, racism and classism, but also provides them visions, intuitions and values which work to charge the definitions of "liberation" and of "feminism" with new and different meanings. It was the voices of these women which were raised in anger and in prophecy as this common ground which comprises a unique sisterhood was recognized.

Danger—And the Production of U.S. Third World Feminism

The utilization of this four-part theoretical model can also create political dangers. First, because it tends to categorize and then freeze our understandings of power into place and second, because this kind of "freezing" tends to limit the kinds of political responses available to us for creating change. Power centers can perhaps be best visualized as clusters of choices on an electromagnetic field—a field that is capable of movement and change into ever new and different designs. However empowering our recognitions of the present design, the dangers in thinking of it as a frozen four-part model is that we simplify and freeze what must be seen as a process of complicated and ever-changing dynamics. One false advantage of conceptualizing power as frozen into such categories is that it then becomes too easy for us to identify who our friends and who our enemies might be. Though empowered as a unity of women of color, the cost is that we find it easy to objectify the occupants of every other category. The dangers in creating a new heroine, a political "unity" of third world women who together take the power to create new kinds of "others," is that our unity becomes forged at the cost of nurturing a world of "enemies." And in the enthusiasm of our empowered sisterhood, perhaps a greater cost lies in the erasure of our many differences. However, if one attribute of power is its mobile nature, there can be no simple way of identifying our enemies or our friends...and no simple unity for feminists of color.

I consider these understandings hard won lessons born out of our struggles within other liberation movements. For example, the previous (white) women's movement had attempted to create an empowered sisterhood through erasing our differences as women of color under the "unifying" category of "women," a category which was given its particular meanings in opposition to the category "men." The privileging of this binary opposition, however, made invisible important differences within each of these categories. Thus racism was unthinkingly perpetuated in the name of liberation. The "common ground" which was to comprise the sisterhood of the women's movement was constructed so that it forced a false unity of women, a unity which worked to erase and thus oppress the lives of many women. To demand the recognition of differences from the inside of this unity signified disloyalty—the division of the movement from within. There is no denying that the construction of a unity as a political tactic has been an effective political move. This position, however, was not seen as only *one* tactic among many, it was privileged as the only legitimate strategy—an all encompassing ideology. Most efforts to deconstruct the unity of women from within in order to recognize other tactics for challenging power were either ignored or seen as acts of betrayal. Thus the ideological differences which emerged from within the women's side of the binary opposition women/men could not be utilized as sources of strength but served instead to weaken the movement. Eventually, the dominant women's movement began to falter under a proliferating multitude of ideological differences with unexpected "enemies" and "friends" emerging from every side.

We third world feminists do not take this lesson lightly, as we realize that for us there will be no simple, utopian route to sisterhood. We will not naively repeat the same mistakes as the women's movement by erasing our own internal differences through gathering them up into one single unity which will then stand against all other categories—though we can tactically use this kind of "unity" to temporarily force power relations into new positions. Although the four-part model of power is one which has largely constituted the kind of sisterhood we presently share, we cannot depend upon this construct to remain stable, nor to provide our empowered unity with the same meanings over time. The meanings of our sisterhood will change. If society's powers are ever mobile and in flux, as they are, then our oppositional moves must not be ideologically limited to one, single, frozen, "correct" response.

As women of color who are looking to find new ways of creating a better world, we are looking to the dissolution of the four categories in order to free the movement of power once again, while working to re-define the terms upon which it will be re-constituted. In this effort we must imagine the categories which now constitute the relations both between one another and between differing social groups (such as "white man," "white woman," "Third World man" and "Third World woman") dissolving and reforming to become charged with new and different meanings. To accomplish these goals, U.S. third world feminists must recognize that our learned sensitivity to the mobile webs of power is a skill that, once developed, can become a sophisticated form of oppositional consciousness. This is a form of oppositional consciousness which creates the opportunity for flexible, dynamic and tactical responses, it is another critical theory for political action which allows us no *single* conceptualization of our position in society. Rather, it focuses us instead upon the process of the circulation of power, on the skill of reading its moves, and on the recognition that a new morality and effective opposition resides in a self-conscious flexibility of identity and of political action which is capable, above all else, of tactically intervening in the moves of power in the name of egalitarian social relations.

If we as third world feminists decide it will be counter productive to act as a single entity (which must deny its differences for the sake of unity) then we free ourselves to explore a different kind of community building. The oppressions we had experienced in the women's liberation movement taught us how easily one's humanity can be erased under the

edicts of liberation. In order to avoid this kind of liberation we realized
that we must develop new definitions of community based on the strength
of our diversities. During the conference's five days of discussion and
debate we explored these diversities, with any final attempts at creating
a single, homogeneous unity dissolving before the undeniability of our
varying physiognomies, religions, classes, cultures, nations, languages,
perceptions and sexual experiences. What emerged from that dissolution
was the deluge of differences which mark the separate worlds of our
experiences and which can no longer be erased, ignored, or made
invisible, for it is these differences which lie at the source of a new kind
of political movement.

Our differing opinions seemed to place us in opposition to one another.
We managed this seeming conflict by considering our differences, not as
idiosyncratic and personal, but as a rich source of tactical and strategic
responses to power. This positive perception of difference is not divisive,
so there is no need to deny our differences or make them invisible. Instead
these once personal responses to racism and oppression can be recognized
as new weaponry in the ideological warfare necessitated by power
struggle. Through the compassionate inclusion of our differences and the
self-conscious understanding that each difference is valid in its context,
we are awakened to a new realm of methodological, theoretical, political,
and feminist activity—with a pool of differences, born of survival and
resistance, at our disposal. These differences give us access to ever new
and dynamic tactics for intervening in the systems which oppress us—
tactics which are capable of changing to confront the ever-changing
movements of power. And if we are courageous enough to legitimate this
multiplicity of tactical approaches as valid, our movement will be less
likely to oppress its own people through the forcing of certain "correct"
political lines. What U.S. third world feminists are calling for is a new
subjectivity, a political revision that denies any *one* perspective as the
only answer, but instead posits a shifting tactical and strategic subjectivity that has the capacity to re-center depending upon the forms of
oppression to be confronted.

Our group recognized that the most important contribution U.S. third
world feminists can offer to the organization of social order is the
development of a subjective, ideological and political process which is
organized to end the form of destructive "othering" from which we have
all suffered. This effort will break new ground. It will mean no longer
relying upon the ancient categories and power moves which have characterized the West. It will mean that we construct a liberation movement
from a vantage point that enables us to map the geographies of new social
worlds. It is at this turning point in Western history that U.S. third world
feminism will play a pivotal role. In self-consciously recognizing this
moment, we must wholeheartedly engage in the development of skills to

make us more capable of the tasks before us...no simple, easy sisterhood for U.S. third world feminists.

Coalitions On New Psychic Terrains

"We will not obey racism
We will not tolerate injustice
We will not bow down to exploitation
I'm gonna stand,
I'm gonna stand,
I'm gonna stand."

—SWEET HONEY IN THE ROCK, THE LAST EVENING

Globally, women are becoming conscious of their positions inside of the sexual-caste system within which they live. Their responses to this realization are multi-form. "Feminist" responses to this realization are as varied as the women who create them. U.S. third world feminists are positing new forms of political response. Their visions depend upon the alternatives inherent in the recognition of difference—these visions generate new theoretical models which have the potential to reshape the discipline known as "Women's Studies." The third world feminist CR group provided us time to identify some of the tools necessary for the construction of these models. We became frustrated, however, by an imposed two hour working limit and angered by a larger conference structure which did not permit the opportunity to make our discoveries public. By the time we agreed on challenging the conference structure, the third day of the conference had passed.

Outside of the third world CR group the rest of the conference was trapped in a structure which did not create any new sense of community. Although an abundance of presentations on "racism" were available, few were able to advance our understandings of racism and engender unity among us. Mounting frustration or numbness were the result of being herded from one workshop to another while missing the most meaningful presentations. Instead of undermining racism, the conference structure itself divided rather than unified, rekindling and reinforcing racist feelings between ethnic groups.

For these reasons, some of the third world feminists proposed to their morning CR group that the conference be "stopped and reorganized" so that we might intervene and share the discoveries we had made. This position, however, was countered by other third world feminists who argued that our discoveries would be received more positively if we tried to present them within the current conference structure. These women suggested that we call a "coalition meeting" between the "third world" CR group and all interested "white" women. They hoped such a meeting would provide both sides the opportunity to communicate our mutual discoveries, listen to each other's positions, evaluate the conference, and collectively decide upon a plan of action. By late afternoon of the conference's fourth day the first successful coalition meeting between third world and white women was adjourned. The approximately two hundred women who attended (comprised equally of women of color and white women) became an energetic and committed gathering which provided its participants an opportunity to heal the blistering divisions. Through hard work these women were able to forge their varying positions into a set of resolutions which they presented at the NWSA Delegate Assembly the next and final day of the conference. The most important of these resolutions follows:

> •Because the conference structure has alienated people from each other and from the topic;
>
> •Because the conference has not allowed for a cumulative understanding of the issues, and a working definition of "racism" has not yet been achieved;
>
> •Because the conference participants have yet to directly address the issue of "racism in the women's movement;"
>
> •Because separations between women are being frozen into place;
>
> •Because the conference is being held in a rural area, an area difficult for urban, working or poor women to reach;
>
> it is agreed that:
>
> This has been a racist conference in its structure, organization, and individual interaction despite its theme. Be it resolved that...next year's conference be organized around the same theme, with the leadership of Third World women, in cooperation with NWSA organizers, and that the location of the next conference be changed from another rural area, Humboldt, California, to a place more accessible to Third World women, such as Los Angeles.

Eight women were elected from the Third World Caucus to present this and other resolutions to the Delegate Assembly on the last day of the conference. But despite the best of intentions, conflicts arose which should have been foreseen given all that had come before. The coalition's resolutions were met with a great deal of irritation by the majority of white Delegates to the Assembly. Many of the white Delegates had spent a week of boredom and alienation sitting through too many lectures on women of color—they had "put in their time." For them, the issue of racism was worn to the bone. By the last Assembly meeting most delegates were ready to move onto, as they called it, "more pressing issues." The continued "haranguing" by the third world delegates was seen as "idiosyncratic," "selfish," and as "unnecessarily divisive to the movement." The resolution was not passed. In spite of the one successful coalition meeting, by the end of the conference the division between third world and white women had become intensified and cemented with antagonism. It was an ironic ending to a movement conference on racism.

Almost one year has passed and the NWSA continues to experience financial and membership difficulties. The atmosphere which allows issues to go unaddressed still survives. As long as we live in a society guided by the unexamined imperatives of capitalism and the values of white racial superiority, the webs of power that permit the lives we lead will also work to suppress the expression of U.S. third world feminism. This is at a great cost to the advancement of global egalitarian social relations, i.e., feminism. Despite the surfacing of "racism" as an issue in the white women's movement, Audre Lorde's question "Do the women of the Academy really *want* to confront racism?" is a question yet to be answered in the affirmative.

For U.S. third world feminists, the 1981 Storrs conference provided the setting to shape and clarify visions which represent a new way of seeing, a new method for approaching feminist political change and a new theory of oppositional consciousness. Unfortunately these visions have found no "official public" expression until the publication of this report. The three hundred women of color who attended the conference, however, have organized into a "National Alliance for American Third World Women" and are in the process of publishing a monthly newsletter. This Alliance (along with the publication of books like *This Bridge Called My Back*[1]) is an accomplishment signifying a major turning point—a moment of transformation which is coalescing into new kinds of liberatory activities. After ten years of struggle the issue of racism has finally surfaced within the white women's movement and the continuing publication of academic books on the topic is demanding certain forms of wary recognition. Still, such limited recognition does little to help affect the radical transformations necessary to create a coalition of U.S. women through their differences. What is necessary is that the new model for political action and consciousness proposed here, and represented by U.S. third world feminism, be recognized by both white feminists and women of color alike.

Human consciousness is rapidly changing on a global level. U.S. third world feminism is a world-view expressed in the emergence of a new citizen-subject. Lost histories are once again being made visible through the works of women like Gloria Anzaldúa, Yvonne Irvin, Carol Lee Sanchez, Gwena Johnson, Nellie Wong, Azizah al-Hibri, Lisa Lowe, Ruby Nell Johnson, Lucia Ortiz and Rosa Maria Villafañe-Sisolak. Across distances, time, and differences, these names and many others are becoming the landmarks of a new psychic territory. In order for the new academic discipline of Women's Studies to understand, clarify, present strategy and provide a basis for political action which will end domination and subordination, it must incorporate the discoveries being made by *all* women. U.S. third world feminists are in the process of presenting what must be recognized as a new model for thought and action. This model is crucial for the continuing effectiveness of any U.S. oppositional and de-colonial liberation movement which is working toward egalitarian social relations, for the theory and method outlined in this report can provide the ground upon which oppositional actors can stand together. This ground is constituted by a form of political consciousness which can make of us Countrywomen and men in a shared psychic terrain. We cannot afford to ignore our differences any longer, they provide us the keys to new tactics for confronting oppression. We must face the Medusa, the unfaceable in ourselves, in order to have access to the powers we require. Mistakes must be forgiven. Every day repeats an opportunity for beginning anew.

Published in 1982 by The Center for Third World Organizing, Oakland, CA and Washington, DC.

I want to thank the Center for Third World Organizing for publishing and distributing this report in 1982. I sincerely hope that this effort will find its other authors, and that this tactical intervention into oppositional politics will meet with their approval. For editorial assistance I am grateful to Rosa (Ro) Villafañe-Sisolak, Janet Sandoval, Ruth Frankenberg and Gloria Anzaldúa. Thanks also to Donna Haraway, who recognized the purpose of this pamphlet, and used it among her many Women's Studies students to encourage the development of feminist, anti-racist and egalitarian principles.

Notes

1. Cherríe Moraga, Gloria Anzaldúa, eds., *This Bridge Called My Back: Writings by Radical Women of Color* (Watertown, MA: Persephone Press, 1981).

2 Denial and Betrayal

*...An Asian American college student was
reported to have jumped to her death from her
dormitory window. Her body was found two days
later under a deep cover of snow. Her suicide
note contained an apology to her parents for
having received less than a perfect four point
grade average...*

Suicide Note

Janice Mirikitani

How many notes written...
ink smeared like birdprints in snow.

    not good enough   not pretty enough not smart enough
dear mother and father.
I apologize
for disappointing you.
I've worked very hard,
                 not good enough
harder, perhaps to please you.
If only I were a son, shoulders broad
as the sunset threading through pine,
I would see the light in my mother's
eyes, or the golden pride reflected
in my father's dream
of my wide, male hands worthy of work
and comfort.
I would swagger through life
muscled and bold and assured,
drawing praises to me
like currents in the bed of wind, virile
with confidence.
    not good enough not strong enough not good enough

I apologize.
Tasks do not come easily.
Each failure, a glacier.
Each disapproval, a bootprint.
Each disappointment,
ice above my river.

So I have worked hard.
                    not good enough
My sacrifice I will drop
bone by bone, perched
on the ledge of my womanhood,
fragile as wings.
                    not strong enough
It is snowing steadily
surely not good weather
for flying—this sparrow
sillied and dizzied by the wind
on the edge.
                    not smart enough
I make this ledge my altar
to offer penance.
This air will not hold me,
the snow burdens my crippled wings,
my tears drop like bitter cloth
softly into the gutter below.
        not good enough   not strong enough   not smart enough

                Choices thin as shaved
                ice. Notes shredded
                drift like snow

on my broken body,
covers me like whispers
of sorries
sorries.
Perhaps when they find me
they will bury
my bird bones beneath
a sturdy pine
and scatter my feathers like
unspoken song
over this white and cold and silent
breast of earth.

From *Shedding Silence*

Postscript

Canéla Jaramillo

12 October 1986

Postscript—

The subject of my own ethnicity has not been explored in this piece; it was, in truth, one of the reasons I was so long in preparing this manuscript for you. I troubled myself for several months over the significance of a Latina heritage in my life, and realized that it was a question with which I have been grappling for many years. Cherríe Moraga's thoughtful essay "*La Güera*" comes closer to defining some of my confusion/guilt than other literature (or party lines), yet Cherríe can at least claim her culture through immersion, if not "appearance," while I was separated from my Chicano father and his dark family when I was very young. My mother, under fire from her family to negate her low-life meanderings in East L.A.—especially her "dirty wetback" first husband—raised us up on thick bastardizations of our fluid Spanish names, pronouncing our surnames harshly in English and calling us Cindy and Bobby (my brother's name is Ernesto Roberto Jaramillo, after our father). I didn't know 'til I was a freshman in high school—coming out of eight years at a lily-white Catholic school—that our names were mispronounced.

Too, my mother took us to live with a brutal, angry white man when we were still quite young. This man was (is) ex-military, had gone from laborer to a desk job after twenty-some years in the same company, and had bought the first house in a tract which eventually (and ironically) sold only to black families, after his purchase.

Culturally, then, I am a "home girl" from Southeast San Diego, thoroughly shaped by black language and the street ethic. I didn't even begin to speak Spanish until I was in high school and, while it comes easily to me and is a source of great beauty in my life, I still return, almost unconsciously, to black "street talk" often—especially when I am angry. Yet, oddly, when I began college at fashionable and wealthy UCSD, black women were the first to scrutinize and avoid me, until they discovered I wasn't white! I have one friend who still insists on forewarning her guests, "she looks Anglo, but she's Chicana." Secret password.

Not long ago, I dreamed that I moved back to the barrio. As I was unpacking, the wheels of my car were stripped clean. I ran outside, angry and hurt, thinking, "They wouldn't have done this if they'd known I'm Chicana." Safety. Acceptance. Yet it's less a question of my ethnicity, I think, than of sharing a common background—of lower-class children struggling against or out of the ugliness of inferiority and discrimination;

of mostly uneducated, largely illiterate parents; of the terror and abuse within many of our homes, outside from territorial gangs from other barrios, and from a police force and legal system which despised us. And the women—my god. We were nothing unless we could stay off drugs and alcohol or away from pregnancy long enough to keep our only desirability: "beauty."

Most of us didn't. All of us—men and women alike—are scarred now, our faces marred, our teeth ugly, our voices brazen and somehow paranoid. And the fury. I got out of there early—left home at fourteen—because the violence was killing my spirit and because my mother's was already dead. A practicing alcoholic, she's been telling me since she was thirty, "My life is over." She's only forty-six and looks ten years older. Shit.

But I went out the wrong way, like most of us, at first, because we didn't have the tools to make a smooth transition from the coarseness of the streets to the unblemished facade of the universities, corporate structures, whatever. I used my body against the way my mother used hers: fucking but never cooking, cleaning or loving. Until I realized it was the same kind of poison. Later, I married a gentle white man, grew a garden, baked bread, had a baby. But neither rejecting nor "perfecting" my mother's lifestyle solved anything for me, and so.

So after one and a half years of marriage, I fell in love with a woman—first in a long string of "broken children" I began to collect, trying to nurse my own pain, to rock it to sleep. This first one was a painter, who allowed me to explore many of the symbols I'd used to get through, get on, get by. A very angry woman who had spent most of her childhood/adolescence in an institution, as a ward of the court, because her mother was also locked up, in an "insane" asylum, and her father couldn't manage her. Much of the violence and abuse of our pasts became integrated in our four-year relationship, and we unleashed a lot of fury and terror on each other, just trying to be vulnerable enough to love.

This is getting off-track. The point is, I think, that I can never (or haven't) just pinpoint any one event or series of circumstances or even emotions that I can label "Chicana." My mother's ferocious guilt for having the children of a "wetback," maybe. A way to find initial acceptance with my black friends, sisters of the same people I came up with, perhaps. But that's all so tangential. Doesn't it negate something? Yes, there is a commonality between me and the lower-class women of color I grew up with and continue to meet. And, coupled with my lesbianism, there is a fervent bond with all despised peoples. I just haven't been able to categorize it all...not yet. My lover now, the woman I married, is Filipino-Puerto Rican. Dark, dark, woman—black thick hair, black eyes, deep brown skin. Yet she is one of the most apolitical women I've ever met, raised by old world parents, now in their senior years (sixties and seventies), who wanted very badly to "Americanize" their children, and succeeded. She's only just beginning to understand, and is often shocked by, the implications of her heritage—as a Latina and a lesbian. (When we were stopped and searched at a border check near San Onofre, *la migra* harassed her so badly that when they asked her citizenship, she stammered, "Garden Grove"—where she was born, near L.A. She just didn't get it.)

I guess I don't get it either, not all of it. I hope this helps to explain the absence of that aspect in my work.

—Canéla

A Woman Cutting Celery

Sandra Cisneros

is savage
because a car door slams.
But he does not come home.

Miles after thoughts
have turned from worry,
have turned to rage,
a car door slams.

And she is cutting
celery and more celery,
but no familiar stumble

of the key. Nor
crooked tug and coy
apology. No blurred kiss
to comfort this cruel

hour and quit those
sometime fears to sleep. Surely
love has strayed before.

Love has come and love has gone
and love has been away
before but ultimately
stays. It must be

the errant lover of the girl
across the way who arrives
at such an independent hour,

whose rude feet
startle gravel beyond the borders
of begonias asleep under the back
porch light. Not here.

A thin blond vein
rises from the corner of her jaw
like a crack in a porcelain plate.

A car door slams.
But he does not come home.
This is how the story begins.

From *My Wicked Wicked Ways*

Notes from a Fragmented Daughter

Elena Tajima Creef

Some Personal Scenes

1. At an art gallery opening for local Asian American women artists, a tall white man in glasses, beard, and big hair bundled up into a ponytail hovers over a table full of sushi, chow mein, egg rolls, and teriyaki chicken. He looks at me awkwardly and attempts conversation. "Did you make any of the food? I notice you look kinda Asian."

2. Marion is half Chinese and half Japanese and I like the way his face looks. We sit and talk about what it means to have mixed backgrounds in a culture that can't tell Chinese apart from Japanese and where McDonald's still serves Shanghai Chicken McNuggets with teriyaki sauce.

3. I am fifteen and am sitting in the backseat of my best friend Doreen's Volkswagon Bug, when her uncle's new wife Clara climbs into the passenger seat and we are introduced. Clara speaks in tongues at the Ladies Prayer Meetings, and has seen angels in the sky through her Kodak Instamatic.
She turns to me and shouts in a thick New York accent,
"So what are you studying?"
I say, "English."
She says, "Gee, your English is very good.
How long have you been in this country?"
I say, "All of my life."
She shouts, "Are you Chinese?"
I say, "Japanese."
She says, "I admire your people very much!"
I smile and say, "Yes, and we are very good with our hands, too."

4. Katie Gonzales follows me around for one week at sixth grade summer camp, her left arm in a sling from a tetherball accident. "I'm gonna get you, you flat-faced chinaman." I want to tell her that I'm only half-Japanese, but the words stick in my mouth and instead, I call her a beaner and imagine I am twisting that left arm right off her brown skinny body.

5. Later, when I am thirteen, I bury my mother once and for all and decide to go Mexican. It makes a lot of sense. I am no longer Elena, I am now Elaina and I begin insisting I am Mexican wherever I go. With my

long black hair, my sun-darkened skin, and my new name, I can pass and I am safe. For the next year, I obsessively hide my Japanese mother and deny my Japanese roots. No one is allowed to meet her. I do not let her answer the phone if I can help it, or go near the door if I can get there first. I sabotage the PTA's efforts to get her to come to their monthly meetings, and I conveniently get dates mixed up for "Open House." I live in fear that someone will find out that my mother is Japanese and spread it around the classroom like a dirty rumor. I love it when people ask if I am Español, because it is safe, because it means I do not stand out.

6. My mother and I are getting out of the car at Builder's Emporium when a young, ugly, straw-haired man gets out of his truck and shouts that my mother has stolen his parking space. She says she doesn't know what he's talking about and he tells her to shut up her slant-eyed face. My heart is pounding as we shop for light fixtures and nails but we never say a thing.

7. It is a dark, wet, rainy Santa Cruz night, and I go to see "Tampopo"— your basic Japanese noodle western—by myself. I am in a very good mood and allow a balding middle-aged man with a burgundy plum scarf tied around his neck to make conversation with me in the lobby.

"I really love Japanese films, almost as much as I love Asian girls! I'm going to Taiwan next month to meet this woman I've been corresponding with. I really prefer Oriental women to American because (he whispers) there are so many 'feminists' in this town. You are Asian, aren't you? Don't tell me, let me guess. Japanese? Chinese? Hawaiian? Eurasian?"

Idiot. I am the daughter of a World War II Japanese war bride who met and married my North Carolinan hillbilly father one fine day in 1949 while she was hanging up the laundry to dry. Nine months out of the year, I pose as a doctoral student—a historian of consciousness; the rest of the time, I am your basic half-Japanese postmodernist gemini feminist, existentialist would-be writer of bad one-act comedy revues, avid cat trainer, and closet reader of mademoiselle, cosmo, signs, diacritics, elle, tv guide, cultural critique, representations, people magazine, critical inquiry, national enquirer, feminist issues, house beautiful, architectural digest, country living, cat fancy, bird talk, mother jones, covert action, vogue, glamour, the new yorker, l.a. times, l.a. weekly, and sometimes penthouse forum.

So how do you like them apples, bub? If you come near me one more time with your touch-me-feel-you New Age Bagwan male sensitivity, I just may strangle you with the burgundy plum scarf you have tied around your neck.

Deconstructing My Mother as the Other

The headlines blare: "They're Bringing Home Japanese Brides! Six thousand Americans in Japan have taken Japanese brides since 1945, and all the little Madam Butterflys are studying hamburgers, Hollywood and home on the range, before coming to live in the U.S.A."

Although she is not interviewed, my mother appears in one of the bright technicolor photographs in the January 19, 1952, issue of the *Saturday Evening Post*. She is the short one with the funny hairdo, hovering over an apple pie, smiling with her classmates in the American Red Cross "Brides' School" for Japanese Wives. While the article attempts to tell the postwar story of the Japanese war bride in general, it also tells the story of how my own American G.I. father met and married my Japanese mother in war-torn occupied Japan. It is, in essence, my own pictorial origin story.

There are over 45,000 Japanese women who married American servicemen after World War II and immigrated to the United States. I have been meeting and interviewing these women for the last few years for a collection of oral histories I hope to someday publish. I have been told over and over again by many of these women that they despise the name "war bride." There is something dirty and derogatory about this word, but rarely has anyone told me why. "Call us 'Shin Issei' (the New Immigrants)," they say. Or how about, "Japanese Wives of American Servicemen." Don't call us "war brides." They whisper, "It is not nice."

I am the daughter of a World War II Japanese war bride
who met and married my white North Carolinan hillbilly father
one fine day in 1949 while she was hanging up the laundry to dry.

There is no escaping this body made out of history,
war and peace,
two languages,
and two cultures.

My name is Elena June,
I am the youngest daughter of Chiyohi,
who is the only surviving daughter of Iso,
who was the daughter of the Mayor of Yokoze
and was the Village Beauty
born in the last century to a Japanese woman
whose name is now forgotten,
but who lived in the Meiji era
and loved to tell ghost stories.

Light Skinned-ded Naps*

Kristal Brent Zook

> While traces of old color biases linger—largely affecting interpersonal relations and romantic entanglements...Blacks today have shed the bonds of the old 'lighter is better' philosophy that for generations separated much of the community into color-coded factions...
> —*EBONY* MAGAZINE[1]

Oh reeeaaaly?!?! Well, if it's not color, then what exactly *is* going on here?! What is it that's making my fuzzy blond/brown kinks so volatile? My fiery brown/red/yellowness glow, steadily simmering—explosive anger, threatening eruption every moment of every day? Silent detonation occuring, in fact, with each glimpse of flaming hazel green I catch in my own eyes.

If it's not about color and/or culture then why did my cousin and I—just fifteen years ago—eagerly play "Cathy and Susie" on an everyday basis? Often wearing scarves to pretend that our hair was longer (in the same way that Michele Wallace did when she was a girl)[2] we would reenact this imaginative game in which we became, magically, white career women. Suddenly we were carefree, with smooth professional voices and endless dinner engagements.

It seems to me that this is some terribly ancient garbage we're talking about and unfortunately, it doesn't go away as easily as the editors of *Ebony* might like to think. Although I would love to share their optimism, the little bit of experience I have accumulated in my 24 years of life does not allow it.

> What black women would be interested in, I think, is a consciously heightened awareness on the part of light black women that they are capable, often quite unconsciously, of inflicting pain upon them; and that unless the question of Colorism—in my definition, prejudicial or

---

*In traditional Black English, the adjective "light skinned" is often pronounced skinned-ded.

preferential treatment of same-race people based solely on their color—is addressed in our communities and definitely in our black "sisterhoods" we cannot, as a people, progress.

—ALICE WALKER[3]

I want to emphasize here that the anger of both my darker *and* my lighter skinned (ded) sisters is truly valid. In spite of rumors regarding the infinite privileges open to those of us with visible white ancestry, there is always, yes always, a great deal of pain that comes with this "privilege." Our sufferings as Black sisters of different shades are not identical, and they aren't even always equal, but they most certainly *are* mutual. And because my experience of racism as it is felt through this light skinned body is not the same as that experience which is felt through darker colored flesh does not mean that either of the two is any truer, more valid or authentic. Because the blows you received may have been overt, physical and/or apparent while mine were insidiously covert, psychological and internal does not mean that the ground we stand on isn't common.

"What Does That Yellow Bitch Know About Being Black Anyway?"

His historic fury/
righteous indignation
triggers instant dryness
of tongue, throat, lips
where words/sounds have died
and nausea gushes forth
putrid
I fight the urge to crawl
slumping rounded shoulders
and lowering silent lashes.

5 years or months ago
I might have remained
silent
a hopeless and helpless bundle
of paleness
ashamed of having ever presumed
to squeak/speak
much less
to sing

But it is now
and I am able
to concentrate on strength

cool Libra balance of
neck with spine
shoulders with hips
my gaze level and very squarely locked
with his

He blinks twice
and I realize there is much
red and brownness
in the "whites" of his eyes

My own eyes
tree and leaf colored
respond by blurring
moistly clouding and
flooding with memories

I relive the childish fear that gripped me
held me gazing into a same murkiness
of bright and darkness
just 5 years
or months ago
in my own grandmother's
precious
gaze

And I see us togetha
my brotha
and I
comfortably trapped
in our same oneness
one sameness
of outer inner beauty
ugliness

Finally
I am able to moisten throat
swallow
and reply:

Enough
my brothaman...

In fact much more

than enough.

> The thing that we have to see is what neither black nor white people want to face: that in this country we have developed and arrived at a point where our culture is neither black nor white but mulatto, a synthesis of the two. The white man and the black man are still fighting over their racial integrity or entity when it doesn't exist anymore. It's a terrible thing to say, but I have just as many white ancestors as I've got black. That as an American, I am no pure-blooded African. I am both continents.
>
> —MARGARET WALKER[4]

Let's talk about our anger first...the flaming rage around, between and within us. Yes, I *do* see the light skinned (ded) "pretty girls" on Video Soul, and yes, I realize that the first Black "Miss America" had to be light in order to win. Mmmm hmmm, I know how much money and time we're spending on giving ourselves longer, straighter, "better" hair. And yes girlfriend, it does make me as sad, angry and confused as you.

Speaking of hair—that o so explosive issue among us—I have a confession to make, as politically unpopular as it may be: the truth is that even I, after all these years, tears and chemical relaxers, am *still* annoyed by my own "good" hair at times and am perfectly willing to forcefully "tame" it for purposes of convenience and even *pleasure*. Highly atypical by both white and Black standards, its thickness is often noted and commented upon by both friends and strangers. At times it fascinates me and at other times it's just far too wild and kinky. Period.

I have, over the last few years, passed through various phases of 1) disgust—with any kind of process, relaxer, straightener, etc.; 2) evangelicism—attempts to convert my sistas with "oppressed hair"* (oftentimes much darker than I) by showing them the error of their ways; 3) isolation—feeling that I was the lone radical with funky hair on the smooth scene of L.A. nightlife; 4) compromise—a decision to wear my hair in the same way that I wear my clothes: according to mood, activity and environment. In an attempt to recognize and validate the complexities of who I am, I have been giving full reign to my own instinctive need for change and creativity regardless of what is deemed "P.C." or

---

*Alice Walker uses this term to describe hair that is processed or otherwise coerced into doing something it would not naturally do. (i.e. be more 'manageable,' 'straight,' 'curly,' (as opposed to kinky) etc.[5]

"politically correct" at the present moment.* By allowing myself to be that slick city woman with the wind-blown hair *when I feel the urge to do so*, I am defying preconceived notions of who I am or should be as a light skinned, somewhat politically conscious Black woman, aspiring to understand and embrace various feminist ideals. I am forever resisting unyielding definitions of my reality as they are imagined and presented by "others"—whoever they may be.

Although I have, for the moment, come to this tentative understanding of my own personal hair politics, I want to express my limitless admiration and even envy for those sistas and brothas around me who do not insult their natural kinks and dreads with chemicals and appliances. At the risk of sounding patronizing, I need to say that I have great respect for their confidence and courage. As anyone who has worn their hair dreaded, braided or just plain natural will tell you, an extra dose of self-esteem is needed just to get through the day, whether we are surrounded by white *or* Black colleagues, co-workers and friends.

So, it's all true. We are not hallucinating by any means. There is still a very strong rejection of boysenberry black beauty and nappy, nappy hair. This I see. And as long as the dominant culture continues to find people of my complexion "less offensive," I imagine that those of a darker hue will remain (understandably) bitter toward us *as well as* toward white people. As long as people who look like me continue to be "the right kind" of Blacks to be hired, promoted and allowed into the higher economic circles first, there will be resentment and even lawsuits between us, as Tracey Morrow has recently demonstrated with her lawsuit against a darker skinned supervisor she claimed discriminated against her for being light.[7] Without condoning any type of discrimination that may have taken place, it is important that the defendant's (Ms. Lewis) reality be recognized in all its multi-faceted complexity. As a darker skinned Black woman, any hostility or bitterness that she may have felt toward Ms. Morrow is predictable and even understandable, situated within proper historical context. As I imagine it, the pain of Ms. Lewis' existence is, and should be, unmistakably vivid and tangible for *all* Black women who understand this history and not just for those whom she resembles in appearance.

---

*In a recent talk which focused on Black hair, Kobena Mercer, a critic of film and popular culture, alerted me to the possibilities of conceptualizing the politics of hair within a framework other than that of Black cultural nationalism and the politically "correct" Afro of the 1960s and 1970s. The advantages of an alternative paradigm, such as the one presented by Mercer, is that it allows for a discussion of *creativity* and artistic expression as they pertain to the practices of hair transformation. Mercer also points to the probability that what has taken place between the dominant (white) cultures and people of African descent (both in the U.S. and Britain) is a kind of *mutual* appropriation of artistic styles rather than a narrowly defined, blind imitation of white, Eurocentric standards of beauty.[6]

In our private lives, those of us who are heterosexual will continue to be excessively competitive with each other for the few "available" Black men we see around us. Those who are lesbian may actually have greater stakes, both political and personal, in resolving some of this sooner than the rest of us and will, perhaps, be able to "lead on with the light" (as Gloria Naylor would say) in the very near future. Until then however, we will all be vulnerable to self-destructive behavior brought on by a fundamental sense that we are somehow deficient, lacking and/or incomplete.

Now, if this all sounds just too, too pessimistic, try reading it together with the overly optimistic *Ebony* article to find a more balanced perspective.

No.
I will not be defeated
will not weaken/shrivel up inside
although it does seem amazing
that a woman
(a Chicana-Mexican-Mestiza at that)
rightfully refers to me as 'Black'
and a sista
interjects
"well,
sort of..."

I will not return to the hell of exile
nor cry burning tears of desire
to know self

Even as I know that I have been struck
physically
psychically
smacked
with an older wiser palm
which demands and deserves respect

even as I know this
I also know
she is wrong
she

is

wrong.

I dreamt I was standing in the lobby of a large, marbled hotel watching as a line of glamorous African ambassadors dressed in brilliant scarlet, magenta and purple flowed down the staircase. My grandmother had told me that they would be there. She had me rush over to meet them, saying they were people that I should know. They seemed not to see me as they glided one by one out the front door. I was especially invisible to a much older, dignified man with a wild mane of beautiful gray hair who almost walked right through me as he swept by.

> It never ceases to amaze me that I am mistaken by my own. White people I can forgive their ignorance, but Blacks I cannot...I have been mistaken by my own on more than one occasion. Probably the most ridiculous one was the time Malcolm X mistook me...
>
> —CAROLE BROWN[8]

My anger is really a mixture of great confusion and sadness. I see so many of us in the streets today...on college campuses, driving buses, grocery shopping, at night clubs. We're part of a very unique, late 1960s biracial baby boom and now we're coming out, coming into our own, finding our way through this relatively new thing called adulthood. We're confused and in many ways still "tragically" torn as doors seem to open and close on us with unpredictable, malicious capriciousness. Other Blacks nod and greet us with a "How you doin today" or they don't. Only to explain later in whispering, secretive tones, "I really wasn't sure when I first saw you...." And when we openly identify African American, often overcompensating in an attempt to be finally and fully recognized, we're told to forget it. That we're not *really* Black, not authentic, down-home, jive-talkin, chitt'lin-eatin sistas. On the other hand, if we identify white (oh lord), we're "wanna be's" betraying the race, just another yellowassednigga tryin to pass.

To add to the bewilderment of it all, we've got both whites and Blacks up, down and around us, trying to get close to us for all the wrong reasons. To our right there are flashy blonde girls reassuring us that we're not really like "them" anyway...so grateful for our presence and our friendship, which serve as evidence of their own hipness and anti-racist stance. To our left we have uptight buppies, swarming to us, hoping to paste our faces into their portfolios, to boost their resumes and to show bossmen that they really are the "right" kind of Negroes for the job.

So I guess I'm mostly angry at myself. Looking back and remembering all the ways in which I was used; in fact, let myself be used, for someone else's fantasy. I become simultaneously shameful and irate. My tongue burns with the memory of shaping itself to speak in a way that would please another's ears. My body stings knowing that it moved and seduced not for its own pleasure, but for that of someone who wanted to shape, mold and possess it. And after the fury and confusion subside there's really not much left besides the deep, aching rawness of hurt, plain and simple.

> There were the fights home from school with the children who thought that because of my color, I thought I was better than they—little did they know how I suffered inside as I defended myself and beat them up... There was the time in Sunday school when a little girl called me a white bitch. I turned around and called her a black bitch—I was the one whom the Sunday-school teacher punished...
>
> —CAROL BROWN[9]

And so, feeling rejection all around us, we accept shelter when/wherever we find it. Due to a complex combination of socio-economic circumstances, I happened to find a kind of psychological shelter in Latino heritage and even grew to identify more with *it* than with my own culture(s). And believe me, that is not an easy confession to make.

I would describe this "attraction" as one which began during my contact with a Guatemalan family who lived next door to us many years ago. Through my eight-year-old eyes, their seemingly "whole" family unit, complete with mother, father, children and mother's sister had a profound effect, both positive and negative, on my life. Their acceptance of my cousin Lisa and me into their lives and their home must have seemed to me a piece of fantasy-land, as close to Brady Bunch utopia as I could get. So we visited, and ate black beans, and played with the baby (there was always a newly arrived baby it seemed). It wasn't until years later that I realized why I had such an obsessive drive to learn Spanish and why I felt so at ease, relaxed and at home in Spain, a country whose people had the *exact* same skin color as I did: I had simply been searching for a kind of psychic shelter, wherever I could find it.

There was a campus orientation for new students of color. A black woman slowly approached me and as she hesitated, I knew she was going to ask the inevitable question. After struggling with it for a few seconds, she finally blurted out, "What are you...? I mean, where do you come from?" Then instead of waiting for me to answer, she showed that she already knew and said, "Your mama is Black, right?" I nodded in agreement and then I realized that she had said everything in Spanish.

*A heavy log cabin door slams with the weight of an entire forest.
Silent midnight air and a cold, thin moon surround and illuminate
pale/tan Dutch/African mulatta flesh. Steamy tears scald frosty red-
dened cheeks while trembling hands and weary muscles betray stranded
hybrid bodies who simply yearn for shelter, and the light and warmth
of home.*

On Beauty and Color in Literature:

> Like black men, black women have been forced to play a
> precarious role in white America. However, in respect to
> not being able to measure up to popular Anglo-Saxon
> standards of beauty, Mary Helen Washington suggests
> that the black woman's oppression in this country has
> been more severe than the black male's. In her research,
> she did not find "a single piece of fiction written by a
> Black male in which he felt ugly or rejected because of
> the shade of his skin."
>
> —VASHTI LEWIS[10]

> And we also, rightly, fear that emphasizing this color
> contradiction will lead to a rejection of all but the most
> jet black and the kinkiest-headed as beauty symbols. A
> reversal. There is a clear and present danger that frank
> discussion of this contradiction can in fact be divisive.
>
> —ANN COOK[11]

Many of us have been working in our writing and in our lives to expose
and to correct color biases. Perhaps this is why the truly admirable
heroines of so many recent works of fiction by Black women writers are
decidedly *brown* skinned.[12] While this is ultimately a positive trend which
is necessary in order to begin to visualize self-loving role models, I would
warn against a kind of blind reversal of stereotypes that Ann Cook refers
to above. My fear is that these inversions of traditional Black female
characterizations are based on reaction instead of confident and affirming action.

> Black people, when asked to make judgements about
> complexions, tend to prefer something in the middle of
> the color range. They prefer brown. They tend to as-
> sociate some negative attributes with being light and
> others with being dark...
>
> —*EBONY* MAGAZINE[13]

In short, both extreme shades of the African American rainbow carry negative connotations today. As a result of various historical truths and mistruths, all of us but the most even-toned, chestnut-smooth browns are inevitably screwed in one way or another (and of course, even they are resented for their own particular coloring). In recent literature, Black women authors are constantly transposing and reshaping stereotypical images of light and darkness. Repudiating what was once the dainty and refined nineteenth century mulatta character while reifying her darker and poorer sister, they seek to invalidate old hierarchies of beauty and worthiness created and sustained by patriarchal and eurocentric world visions.

This desire to transform outmoded paradigms can become especially dangerous when it relies on dichotomies of dark, strong, "authentic" women versus light, helpless, devitalized sex objects. In our fictions, I've noticed that the biracial or light skinned Black woman is able to defend herself less and less against threats which come from outside her own community/home as well as those which come from within.[14] Whether we're represented as incompetent, whining or otherwise weakened 'ladies' or as stereotypically arrogant mulattas who call to mind elitist octoroon balls, these characterizations of the light Black woman are severely restrictive.

Toni Morrison, author of *The Bluest Eye* has, herself, recognized with compelling honesty that Maureen Peal was the only character that she never allowed herself to really become a part of.[15] By never going inside this haughty light skinned child to actually feel the pain as well as the privilege of her existence, Morrison was unable to present a living, breathing, multi-dimensional personification. While there are, of course, many exceptions to this pattern in current creative works by Black women writers, and the vast majority of our fiction *does* remains reassuringly productive, I point to the possibility of a destructive trend taking place as a warning: for what is manifested in our art inevitably appears in our lives.

We must look one another in the eye and risk connections that validate and affirm us all. This must be done on a constant basis and with a relentlessness that demonstrates our intolerance of both colorism and classism *as well as* of traditional racist, sexist and homophobic thought. I would like to see extended, honest, nitty-gritty conversations take place among us. For example: What do we think of Whitley, the sneering Southern Black woman on TV's "A Different World"? How do we understand her arrogance? her wealth? her beauty? and of course, her light skin? Why is it important that we address these questions in the first place?

Ultimately, we must learn to celebrate the deaths of Cathy and Susie in our imaginations and to rejoice in our own, authentic, vanilla, coffee, and boysenberry Black, beautiful selves.

There was a community fundraiser and every single Black person in town was involved. As I approached the group, I felt embarrassed and unsure of myself. I didn't know what I could do to help and I felt left out since no one had told me about the event earlier. I saw that people were sewing.... Finally an acquaintance of mine handed me a piece of cloth and a sewing kit and kindly told me I could either work on it there or at home—whenever I had time. I took the things that were offered to me.

I thank my sister-writers Gloria Anzaldúa, Gloria Hull, Margaret Daniel, Ekua Omosupe, Nanci Luna Jimenez and Paula Powell for reading earlier drafts of this work and for sharing their thoughts with me.

Notes

1. "Light vs. Dark: Why Skin Color No Longer Makes a Difference," *Ebony Magazine*, May 1988, 180.

2. See Michele Wallace, "A Black Feminist's Search for Sisterhood," in which the author recounts: "...my sister and I used to tie the short end of a scarf around our scrawny braids and let the rest of its silken mass trail to our waists. We'd pretend it was hair and that we were some lovely heroine we'd seen in the movies..." *All the Women Are White, All the Blacks Are Men, But Some of Us Are Brave*, eds. Gloria T. Hull, Patricia Bell Scott, and Barbara Smith (New York: The Feminist Press, 1982), 5.

3. Alice Walker, "If the Present Looks Like the Past, What Does the Future Look Like?" *In Search of Our Mothers' Gardens* (New York: Harcourt Brace Jovanovich, 1983), 290.

4. Margaret Walker, *A Poetic Equation: Conversations Between Nikki Giovanni and Margaret Walker* (Washington D.C.: Howard University Press, 1974), 130-31.

5. Alexis De Veaux, "Rebel With A Cause," *Essence*, September 1989, 56.

6. "Black Aesthetics and Postmodernism," University of California, Santa Cruz, March, 1989.

7. Peter Applebome, "Lawsuit Raises Issue of Color Bias Between Blacks," *New York Times* 23 May 1989, p. 1.

8. Carole Brown, "From the Family Notebook," *The Black Woman: An Anthology*, ed. Toni Cade (New York: Mentor Books, 1970), 234.

9. Brown, 232–33.

10. Vashti Lewis, "The Near-White Female in Frances Ellen Harper's *Iola Leroy*," *Phylon* vol. XLV, no. 4 (1984), 321.

11. Ann Cook, "Black Pride? Some Contradictions," *The Black Woman: An Anthology*, ed. Toni Cade (New York: Mentor Books, 1970), 152.

12. For a further discussion of this recent development see my "Representations of Mulatta Women in Literature: A Focus on Contrasting Portrayals of Light and Dark-Skinned Black Women," *Expressions* (University of California, Santa Barbara: 1986).

13. *Ebony*, 182.

14. Two examples that immediately come to mind are the characters of Squeak in *The Color Purple* by Alice Walker (New York: Harcourt Brace Jovanovich, 1982) and Lorraine in *The Women of Brewster Place* by Gloria Naylor (New York: Viking Press, 1982). In the history of U.S. fiction, the mulatta has always occupied a privileged space as an overly romanticized heroine and/or a tragically virtuous and beautiful victim. While these images have been presented far too often, we have, for the most part, been denied the opportunity of seeing light skinned Blacks as "fighters" or as figures who otherwise challenge stereotypical notions of the "ladylike mulatta." One exception to this overall trend may be seen in the novels and short stories of Kristin Hunter, a contemporary author who describes herself as coming from "a complex racial identity."

15. Toni Morrison, "A Conversation Between Toni Morrison and Gloria Naylor," *The Southern Review* 21, no. 3 (1985), 581.

The Visit Home

Rosemary Cho Leyson

Today the bus ride to her parents' house seems very long. Her body settles into her seat as if the seat is a part of her. It has been several months since she has gone to visit her family in the Mission. Today is special. It is time to celebrate the fall of Marcos and the first day of liberation in her home country.

Every time she visits her parents, it's as if she's going back into the past. A past filled with sorrow, shame and broken dreams, in a pit with no bottom or top. Her memories of growing up are a list of events poisoned and shot with indignities, malice and a feeling of nonexistence.

As she looks out the window her mind plays a flashback: Melinda is her name. A Puerto Rican girl who lived around the corner of the block. Didn't know why she wanted to be friends, and at that time, it didn't matter much. It just felt nice that someone wanted to be friends with me. She asked me to hold a watch for her. When I gave it back, she said it was broken and that if I didn't give her twenty bucks, she'd break my face and I'd be sorry I ever moved into the neighborhood.

Her body's reaction breaks the spell; the girl in this adult has surfaced. Her throat is dry and tight, her jaws clench and her body tenses from keeping in the tears. She has no hatred for Melinda—just confusion from trying to understand why she did it.

Pull yourself together, she interrupts herself. That was then. You're not going to let anyone push you around anymore. You have some power now, you've been here awhile. You're not the same girl who just came to the States from the Philippines. You can't change what happened then, but no one's gonna push you around and get away with it anymore.

She stands up, getting ready to hop off the bus, repeating to herself that no one had better mess with her and no one will. She carries her orange plastic bag and runs across the street looking straight ahead.

Everything looks the same. Same dirty streets, same kids who thought they were better than me. They say one stupid thing to me—I swear, I'll beat the shit out of them, she tells herself.

She finally reaches the steps to her parents' flat. Already she is upset. Nothing changes for the better around here, she thinks, as she observes the dried-out, split-up wood steps and the loose handrails attached to them. The stairs carry more meaning for her than what's in front of her. It's a reminder, another symbol of degradation that her parents have suffered while renting it as subsidized housing through the government.

She remembers it vividly through her ten-year-old eyes.

"Don't tell me you want to read it! I don't have time for this. Just sign the lease!"

Mom signed it without reading it or saying anything and I watched, trying to figure out what this lady was and then I knew what a devil must look like—tall, blonde, blue-eyed White woman from the Housing Authority. I vowed never to forget it, so that when I grow up I won't let them treat me or my parents that way. If mom knew English better, she wouldn't have let that bitch get away with it, she thinks to herself as she reaches the last step.

She knocks on the door, carefully listening to the footsteps approaching and guesses whose step patterns they are. Sounds like mom's, she thinks. Slowly, the door cracks open and a fair-skinned, short and stout woman appears at the door. Her face brightens to a modest smile. It's her mother. They both greet each other and then the daughter follows it with "It's me—Maree" in Korean. Her mom looks at her and replies "long time no see" in English.

By now, they've gone through the short, narrow hallway that serves as the kitchen and the daughter sets the bag on the cluttered kitchen table next to where her sister is sitting. They greet each other in English. Everything's the same, the same old gloomy way, she thinks. She tries to ignore it this time. She feels uneasy and disconnected speaking English in the house. Korean is her first language, even though her mom had banned it.

"How's things going?" she asks her mom and sister.

"Oh, the same."

"The usual."

They both reply simultaneously.

"That means it isn't good but it can't be worse than it already is. Is that what it means?" the visiting sister asks.

"You should know that by now," her little sister answers casually.

She is hoping maybe this one time it could be different.

"I brought roast duck and strawberry shortcake from Chinatown. Marcos is out—aren't you glad? Have to celebrate," she says, directing her words to no one in particular. It's no surprise to her that there is no response, or any sign of joy. After all, life is still the same miserable way it was and will be and what's the point of celebrating anything. In fact, she has no recollection of when they ever celebrated anything once they got to the States—except once. It was her mother's birthday and her mom's brother and sisters came. But that didn't turn out so well because they started to fight and that drove her mom to have a nervous breakdown on her birthday.

She walks over to the door of her dad's room. He's lying down watching television, an old black and white set he bought from Goodwill. The picture on the tube is so bad you can barely make out the faces. His room is cluttered, full of old bills. By his door is the dresser that he picked up from the street. There's a poster of a kitten next to the only window in the room.

"Hi, how are you feeling?" she asks her dad, concerned with his health since his drinking and smoking caught up to his heart and lungs, and his dishwashing job is aggravating the arthritis in his legs. The cataracts in his eyes, even after the surgery, have left him close to blind. He takes a couple of minutes to get his eyes focused and adjusted to the figure by the door.

He looks over at his daughter. "Oh, Maree, how are you?" he asks, his Filipino accent thick and his voice boisterous with joy for only a split second. His dark bushy eyebrows umbrella his deep-set eyes. His wrinkles are thick across his forehead but spread thin throughout his face.

"Aren't you glad Marcos left?" she asks gleefully.

"Oh—ya" he replies flatly. She frowns. If she was expecting anyone in the family to be a little happy, it was her dad. He's probably tired, she reasons. She tells him what she brought to celebrate and his only response is the terse chuckle he always gives when she mentions that she brought something. Almost always food.

He felt his guts twist and his heart sink into his bed. Why does she keep doing that? First she runs away from home, and now she keeps bringing food. What is she trying to tell me? I can't provide for my family? Was living here so bad she'd rather be with strangers in a runaway house? I kept warning her, don't go out. There are devils who want to hurt little girls. But she still didn't come home after what happened, he thinks as he shifts in his bed.

"Baby, get your mom to fix you something to eat."

She stares at him and thinks, is it too late for you to be happy about anything? She feels sad thinking about it.

"You don't want anything to eat, Dad?"

"You eat. Your mommy—she always yells at me if I ask her to do anything for me," he laughs. She can feel the pain in his voice.

"Okay, well I'll talk to you later," she says, opening the door.

"Okay, bye—call. I just want to know you're not dead, huh."

She walks back to the living room/kitchen area. Her mom is heating up the duck.

"Do you have any kimchee?" she asks in Korean.

"No, not for a long time," her mother answers in English. The visiting daughter sits down among the clutter, clearing up just enough space on the table to eat.

Even after all those times growing up when there was little to eat, there was something about eating at home. She reminisces about her early childhood in Manila, where except for her dad who was stateside, her family was together. They ate together and stuck up for each other. Nothing was ever the same after they came to the States.

The home her family made here is now a place saturated in painful and unhealed experiences of growing up in a country that didn't want her or her family. She was crushed between the constant hostility between her parents and the anger from each one not being what the other wanted them to be. They took the frustrations the world put upon them, swallowed them and turned them on themselves. They were unprepared and unable to cope with the reality of racism in a country they idealized as the great United States. They felt powerless in a country that ridiculed their accents and the color of their skin. Their presence handed them third class citizenship wherever they went. But her family, however disjointed they have become with each other from living in this country, is all she has to tell her who she is, what she is and where she was from.

The white, short-grained rice her mother scoops into her bowl never looked so precious sitting full along the top edge of the bowl ready to be eaten. She reaches for the pyrex bowl on the table and scoops a little bit of the content onto her bowl with her chopsticks. It is chut: salted baby shrimps, fermented Korean style with ferocious Korean chili powder, garlic and all sorts of other potent ingredients. Spread across a little bit of rice, it really hits the spot. She almost feels like crying as the sensation of the food sinks into her taste buds. It is an old familiar feeling, one too precious to ever take for granted. It is the only link she has to who she is and where she is from.

Silently, she eats with her sister as their mother cooks more rice. After she finishes eating, she takes her dishes to the sink and gets ready to leave. Her mother's face seems to get longer and more solemn each time she visits, though she never seems to age, a quality she knows her mother is proud of.

Reaching into her pocket, she hands her mom a bill and tells her it's pocket money, then she takes her jacket off the chair. She asks her mother if she wants to go to the Korean market. "When?" her mother asks, her eyes widening.

"Not this weekend, but I'll call you," the daughter replies. The mother helps her daughter with the jacket. My little girl is grown up. How did you ever go away from me? All my other children are here. Why did you feel you had to leave? her mother is thinking.

The daughter straightens out the collar on her jacket. Her mother carefully inspects her coat for unwanted objects and then picks a piece of lint off her right shoulder. The daughter feels an uneasiness in this ritual. Silence has taken over and it is about the only time she has stood so close to her mother that they can hear each other's breathing. For this reason she allows, and to an extent enjoys, this rare moment of her mother paying attention to her. The childhood feeling of neglect sends ripples into her heart. Her memories of girlhood consist of feelings of sorrow and anger and a helplessness that seemed devastating and eternal with no one by her side. But now, for a fleeting second, the sadness in her soul transforms into a healing glow.

She understands the damage to each of her family members and how it separates each one from the other. Even with this awareness, she still holds back from showing the love and understanding she has for her mother, the love that she wanted from her kin long ago when the only world around her was her family.

But she is no longer the little girl, the daughter is trying to convince herself. With that thought her body moves toward the door. She opens it and as she steps out, her breathing returns to normal. She thanks God she is able to keep from crying.

"Come again soon," her mother says.

She takes one last look at her mother. "Okay, bye. I'll call you about the market," she says as she jogs down the steps.

Turtle Gal

Beth Brant

SueLinn's mama was an Indian. She never knew from where, only that Dolores wore a beaded bracelet, yellow, blue and green beads woven into signs. Burnt out from alcohol and welfare, Dolores gave up one late afternoon, spoke to her daughter in a strange language, put the bracelet around her skinny girl's wrist where it flopped over her hand. She turned her face to the wall and died. November 4, 1968.

SueLinn watched her mother die. Knowing by an instinct that it was better this way. Better for Dolores; but her child mind, her nine-year-old mind, had not yet thought of the possibilities and penalties that lay in wait for little girls with no mama. She thought of her friend, James William Newton, who lived across the hall. She went and got him. He walked SueLinn back to the room where her mother lay dead.

'Lord, lord, lord, lord,' the old man chanted, as he paid his respects, covering the still, warm woman with the faded red spread. His tired eyes, weeping with moisture, looked down at the child standing close to him.

'Go get your things now, little gal. Bring everything you got. Your clothes, everything.'

With his help, she removed all the traces of herself from the darkening apartment. James William made a last, quick search, then told the child to say goodbye to her mama. He waited in the hall, his face wrinkled and yellow. His hand trembled as he reached into his pants pocket for the handkerchief, neatly folded. He shook the thin, white cloth and brought it to his eyes where he wiped the cry, then blew his nose.

SueLinn stood beside the bed she and her mother had shared for as long as the girl could remember. She pulled the spread from her mother's face. She looked intensely at Dolores. Dolores' face was quieter, younger looking. Her broad nose looked somehow more delicate. Her eyes were still closed, the dark lashes like ink marks against her reddish, smooth cheek. SueLinn felt a choking move from her stomach up through her heart, her lungs, her throat and mouth. With an intake of harsh breath, she took a lock of Dolores' black hair in her small fist. She held on, squeezing hard, as if to pull some last piece of life from her mama. She let go, turned away, and closed the door behind her. James William was waiting, his arms ready to hold the girl, ready to protect.

Together they opened his door, walked into the room that was welcoming and waiting. African violets sat in a row along the windowsill, their purple, white, and blue flowers shaking from the force of the door being closed. SueLinn went to touch the fuzzy heart leaves, wondering once again what magic the old man carried in him to grow these queer, exotic plants in the middle of a tired, dirty street.

James William put aside the sack filled with SueLinn's few belongings and told the child to sit in his chair while he went to call the ambulance.

'Don't answer the door. Don't make no sounds. Sit quiet, little gal, and I be back in a wink.'

SueLinn sat on James William's favorite chair, a gold brocade throne, with arms that curved into wide, high wings. She stared at the window. She looked past the violets, past the ivy hanging from a pot attached to threads dangling fresh and alive in front of the glass. She looked onto the street, the avenue that held similar apartment buildings, large and grey. Some had windows knocked out; some had windows made bright by plastic flowers. Some had windows decorated with crosses and 'Jesus is my Rock' painted on from the inside. The Harbor Lights complex of the Salvation Army stood low and squat, the lights beginning to be turned on, bringing a softening sheen to the beige cement. The air was cold, the people on the street pulling their coats and jackets closer to their bodies as they walked hunched over in the struggle past the Chinese restaurants, the grocery, the bars, the apartments. Cars made noises; the noises of rust, of exhaust pipes ready to fall off, the noises of horns applied with angry hands. Buses were unloading people, doors opening to expel faces and bodies of many shapes and colors. The avenue seemed to wander forever in a road of cement, tall buildings, people, machines, eventually stopping downtown, caught up in a tangle of other avenues, streets, and boulevards.

James William walked down the three flights of stairs to the pay phone in the lobby. He called the operator to report the dead woman, walked back up the three flights of stairs, his thoughts jumping and beating against his brain as his heart lurched and skipped from the climb. When he entered his room, the child turned to look at the man.

'They be here soon child. Now we not lettin' on you here with me. We be very quiet. We let them medical peoples take care of things. We don't say one word. Ummmhmmm, we don't say a word.'

He came to the window and watched for the ambulance that eventually came screaming to the curb. Two white men, their faces harried and nervous, got out of the ambulance and entered the building. A police car followed. The cops went inside the building, where the manager was arguing with the medics.

'I don't know nothing about a dead woman! Who called you? Who did you say she was?'

The officers hurried things along, the manager angrily getting out his keys.

'It's probably that Indian. She's all the time drinking and carrying on. Her and that sneaky, slant-eyed kid. Who did you say called in? Nobody let on to me.'

On the third floor, cops, medics and manager formed a phalanx around the door to 3D. Knocking and getting no answer, they unlocked the door and entered the room. Up and down the hall, doors were opened in cracks. Eyes looked out, gathering information that would be hoarded and thought about, then forgotten.

'Anybody know this woman?' the cops shouted in the hall.

Doors closed. Silence answered. One of the officers pounded on a door. A very old woman opened it, a sliver of light behind her.

'Do you know this woman in 3D? When was the last time you saw her?' Her dark brown face resettled its lines as she spoke.

'I don't know her. I hear she was a Injun lady. One a them Injuns from out west. I don't know nothin'.'

The cop waved his hand in disgust. He and his partner started down the stairs, their heavy black shoes scratching the steps, the leather of their holsters squeaking as it rubbed against their guns.

James William stood, his ear pressed to the door panel. SueLinn continued to look past the glass. There were sounds of feet moving away, sounds of hard breathing as the body of Dolores was carried down the three flights of stairs and out into the cold November twilight.

Children were massed on the sidewalks, faces sharp and excited. Mothers called to them, the air moving with words of Chinese, English, other languages tumbling together to make one sound. Together, SueLinn and James William watched the white truck back up, turn around, and head for uptown and the morgue. The cops followed.

James William Newton was 70 years old. Singer of the blues, Prince of Georgia Blues, Sweet William, he moved from the window, went to the kitchenette, and put the kettle on to boil. He moved slowly to the icebox, then to the cupboard, taking out a pot and settling it on the hotplate. Everything surrounding James William was small and tiny like him. The table, covered in blue oilcloth, was just big enough for two. Little wood chairs were drawn tight up to the edge of the table, waiting for Sweet William's hands to arrange the seating. The one window in the kitchenette was hung with starched white curtains trimmed in royal-blue rick-rack. A single wall was papered in teapots and kettles, red and blue splashed on a yellow background. The wall was faded from age but still looked cheerful and surprising. A cupboard painted white held the thick dishes and the food. Rice, red beans, spices, cornmeal, salt, honey, and sugar. A cardboard box placed on the cracked yellow linoleum held potatoes and onions, the papery skins sometimes falling to the floor, coming to rest by the broom and dustpan leaning against the teapot wall.

On the first night of SueLinn's new life, she watched James William work in the kitchen, her eyes not moving from his round body as he walked the few steps across the linoleum, taking leaves out of the tin box, placing them in a brown pot, pouring the whistling water over the tea. He replaced the lid on the pot, removed a tea cozy from a hook, and placed this over the teapot. The child, ever fascinated by Sweet William's routine, his fussy kitchen work, his hands dusting and straightening, felt comforted by the familiar activity. Often Sweet William had made supper for the girl. Cooking up the rice, a towel wrapped around his fat waist, mashing the potatoes, adding canned milk and butter. Sometimes, there were pork hocks or chitlins. The hot, pungent dishes were magic, made from the air and a little salt.

James William sang quietly as he busied himself with the pot of soup. His eyes grabbed quick looks toward the chair and the thin, gold child who watched him with blank eyes. Little folds of flesh covered her eyelids, which she rapidly opened and closed. Sitting like that, so still, her eyes blinking, blinking, she reminded the old man of a turtle he'd seen a long time ago, home in Georgia.

Poking around in the marsh, he and his friends had found a spotted turtle, upside down, struggling to put itself right. He had picked up the turtle and looked at its head, pulling in, eyefolds closing over the eyes in panic, then opening, staring at him. He had set the turtle on its legs where it continued on. The boys had watched and laughed at the creature's slow journey. James remembered the turtle, remembered his friends; the sweetness of them. Memories like this came often in a haze. When they came to his mind, he clutched them, holding on to each minute of them, afraid never to see them again. He recalled the day. So hot and lush, you could hold the air in your hand and feel it wet on your skin. He recalled the smell of the swamp, a green smell, a salty smell. He recalled the reeds pulled from the mud, stuck between their lips. The taste of bitter grass mingling with another taste of sweet, almost like the stick of licorice his daddy had brought him from town. He tried to recall his friends, their names, the colors of brown and tan, but the memory was going. Yet, he remembered the black skin of Isaac, his best friend of all. Remembered, when Isaac held his arm, the thin fingers spread out looked like molasses spilled against his own yellowish, almost white-looking arm. Isaac?

Stirring the soup, he sang bits of song culled from memories of his mama, church, and memories of the band, Big Bill and the Brown Boys. Tunes spun from his lips. Notes and chords played in his throat, starting somewhere in his mind, trickling down through his scratchy voice box, coming out, round, weeping and full. Sweet William sang, his face shifting as he wove the music in and out, in and out of his body. His head moved and dipped, his shoulders shrugged and jerked to emphasize a word, a phrase. To SueLinn, it was as pleasurable to watch Sweet William sing, as it was to listen. His words and music were almost always the same. Sad and lonely words, words that came from heartache, a home with no furniture.

'Lord, what I gonna do with this here child. Now listen up girl. You gonna be my little gal. We be mama and little gal. We be a family. Mmmmhmmm, anybody ask you, you be mine. It ain't gonna be easy.

Old James William here, he gots to think of some heavy talkin' to fool them peoples be snoopin' round here. Them government types. Yes mam, James William got to think of some serious talkin'. Lord! Old man like myself with a child. A baby! I tells you, you know I never bes married. Least-wise, not no marriage like the government peoples thinks is right. Just me and Big Bill, movin' with that band. Me bein' a fool many a time over some sweet boy what talks with lots of sugar and no sense. But that Big Bill, he were some man. Always take me back, like I never did no wrong. Yes mam, I be a fool many a time. But I always got a little work. Workin' on them cars sometime. Child, I swear the metal in my blood! I can still hear that noise. Whoo, it like to kill me! That noise, them cars hurryin' along the line, waitin' for a screw here, a jab there. But I worked it! I worked it! Yes I did, and me and Big Bill, we make a home. Yes we did. We did. And before the sugar and the high bloods get him, we was a family, that fine man and me. Mmmmhmmm. Now look at her sit there with them turtle eyes. She can't talk! Now listen here baby, you mama at rest now, bless her sorry little life. You got you another kind a mama now. I take care of my baby. You mama so peaceful now. With the angels and the Indians. She make that transition over, mmhmm. She be happy. Now I gots to make this here turtle gal happy. You gots to cry sometime child. Honey lamb, you gots to cry. If you don't grieve and wail, it get all caught up in you, start to twistin' your inside so bad. Girl! It hurt not to cry. You listen to this old man. Sweet William, he know what he talkin' bout.'

> *Precious lord, take my hand*
> *Lead me to that promise land*
> *In that Kingdom grace is nigh*
> *In that Kingdom way on high.*

The old man began his song in a whisper. As he ladled out the soup into bowls, he switched from hymn to blues, the two fitting together like verse and chorus. He nodded his head toward the child, inviting her to sing with him. SueLinn's thin voice joined James William's fat one.

> *Heaven's cryin', seem like the rain keep comin' down*
> *Heaven's cryin', seem like the rain keep comin' down*
> *That heaven don't let up*
> *Since my baby left this mean ole town.*

They sang together. They sang for Dolores. They sang for Big Bill. They sang for each other. Blues about being poor, being colored, being out of pocket. Blues about home. And home was a hot, sweet, green and brown place. Home was a place where your mama was, waiting on a porch, or cooking up the greens. Home was where you were somebody. Your name was real, and the people knew your name and called you by that name. It was when you got to the city that your name became an invisible thing, next to the other names you were called, familiar names all the same. *Nigger, bitch, whore, shine, boy*. It was when you got to the city that you started to choke on your name and your breath, and a new kind of blues was sung. SueLinn often asked about home. And Sweet William sang and sang.

Precious lord take my hand
Lead me to that promise land
In your kingdom grace is nigh
In your kingdom way on high.

The man came from the kitchen and picked the child up in his arms, set her on his lap in the brocade chair, covered them with his special afghan, and the two rocked and swayed.

'She like a bird, no weight on her at all. I *do* likes a rock in this old chair. It help a person to think and study on things what ails us. Yes mam, just a rockin' and a studyin' on those things.'

SueLinn's tears began. She sobbed, the wails moving across the room, coming back as an echo. James William sang, crooned, wiped her eyes and his own with the dry palms of his hands.

'My baby. My turtle gal. Lord, I remember my own mama's passin'. It hurt so bad! She were a good woman, raisin' us ten kids. My daddy workin' his body to a early grave. It hurt when a mama die! Seem like they should always just go on bein' our mama. Yellin' to be good, bein' proud when we deserves it. You mama, she try her best. She were a sad woman. She love you, little gal. And I loves you. We be a family now. Big Bill! You hear that? A family! SueLinn Longhorse and James William Newton. Now ain't they gonna look twice at this here family? I tell you. I tell *you!* It be all right, my baby girl. It be all right.'

SueLinn stopped crying as suddenly as she had started. Her thin face with its slanted eyes, small nose, and full lips subdued itself.

'But James William! I hear people talk about heaven. My mom didn't believe in it, but where will she go now? I don't know where she is! And sometimes...Sometimes, she said she wished I was never born.'

The girl stared into the old man's face, trusting him to give her the answers. Trusting him to let her know why she ached so much, why she always felt alone and like a being who didn't belong on this earth. His skin was smooth, except for the cracks around his eyes and down his cheeks, ending at the corners of his mouth. His eyes were brown and yellow, matching the color of his skin, like mottled corn, covered with hundreds of freckles. He had few teeth except for a startlingly white stump here and there. When he opened his mouth to sing, it looked like stars on a black map. His lips were wide and dark brown. His nose was flat, the nostrils deep.

'Baby, I don't know bout no heaven. My mama truly believed it. But I thinks this here story bout pearly gates and all is just a trick. Seem like there ain't nothin' wrong with this here earth. The dirt gonna cover her and that be right with her. She miss the sky and the wind and the land. Told me plenty a time. Seem like, compared to that heaven where the peoples hang playing harps and talkin' sweet, this here earth ain't so bad. You mama, she be mighty unhappy in a place where they ain't no party or good lovin' goin' on! Seem like that heaven talk is just a way to get the peoples satisfied with the misery they has to bear in this here world. Once you gets to thinkin' that a reward waitin' on you for bein' poor and colored, why it just beat you down more. You don't gets to think about doin' somethin' about it right here, right now. Mmmmhmmm, them white peoples, they thinks of everything. But there be a lot they don't know. Everything don't always mean *every thing!* I do believe Dolores be more at rest in the brown dirt. And lord, child, from jump every mama wish her children never be born sometime! That's a fact. Mmmmhmmm. Honey, she love you. She just too full a pain to remember to *tell* you. It just like me and Big Bill. Why, they be days go by we forgets to say, Big Bill you my onliest one. James William, you sure one fine man. Then you gets to thinkin', hey, this man don't love me no more! And you gets afraid to ask, because you thinkin' that's *his* duty to remember. Then you gets mad and sad all together, and then you speakin' in shortness and evil kinda ways. You forgets that everybody be carryin' his own pain and bad things. The disrememberin' be a thing that happen though. We be foolish, us peoples. Ain't no way gettin' round that! Seem like, if we be perfect, we be white peoples up there in that heaven they thinks so special! Yes, yes, we be in that white heaven, with the white pearly gates and the white robes and the white slippers. Child! Lord child! Whooo!'

And he laughed and laughed, hugging SueLinn tight, his chest rumbling in her ear. She laughed too, even though she wasn't sure she knew the joke. But it made her feel better, to be sitting in Sweet William's lap, her head pressed to his heart, the afghan of bright colors covering her coldness and fright. She had laughed with Dolores. Mostly over Dolores' mimicry of the people in the street or in the bars. She almost became those people, so good was she at capturing a gesture, a voice, a way of holding her body. There was no meanness in the foolery; just fun, just a laugh, a present for SueLinn.

'Now my turtle gal, this old colored man be talkin' more than his due. I says, after a song and a good cry, they ain't nothin' better than hot soup and peppermint tea. I thinks I even gots a little banana cake saved for you.'

They unfolded from the brocade chair and went to the table. The tiny Black man with light skin. The tiny girl of gold skin and Indian hair, her body wrapped in the afghan crocheted by Sweet William's hands. The colors moved across her back, the ends trailing on the floor. As Sweet William poured the tea, his white shirt dazzled the girl's eyes. She watched his short legs walk slowly to the stove, his small feet wearing the felt slippers he never seemed to take off. He was wearing his favorite pants, grey flannel with handsome pleats in the front and small cuffs at the bottom. And his favorite belt, a wide alligator strip weaving in and out of the grey wool belt loops. The buckle was of solid silver, round and etched with the words *Florida Everglades*. It had been a gift from Big Bill, so many years ago the date and reason for the gift were lost in James William's memory. He only remembered Big Bill's face as he handed the belt to Sweet William. The dark beige of his skin flushing and reddening as he pushed the tissue-wrapped gift toward James William, saying, 'Here honey. For you. A gift.'

James William's starched, white shirt had cuffs turned back, fastened with silver-colored links, a red stone gleaming in the center of each piece of metal. She looked at the stones that seemed to signal on—off—stop— red means stop.

She had learned that in school when she had started kindergarten. That was four years ago. She was in third grade now, a big girl. She liked school. At least, she liked it when she went. When her mom remembered to send her. When SueLinn remembered to wash out her T-shirt so she could be clean. When she felt safe to ask Dolores to braid her long hair without making the woman cry. When Dolores was in a good mood from having extra money and bought SueLinn plaid dresses and white socks and shoes that were shiny and had buckles instead of laces. Dolores talked loud these times, talked about how her baby was just as good as anybody, and, anyway, she was the prettiest kid in school by far. SueLinn had a hard time understanding this talk. Everybody in school wore old clothes and shoes with laces. It didn't make sense. Maybe it had to do with the picture magazines that showed up around the apartment. The people on the shiny pages were always white and stood in funny poses. They wore fancy clothes and coats made from animals. They looked as if they were playing statues, which SueLinn had played once with the kids at school. It was a scary feeling to stop and stand so still until the boss kid said you could move. She liked it though. It made her feel invisible. If she were really a statue, she'd be made out of stone or wood, something hard. Sort of like the statues at the place her teacher, Miss Terrell, had taken them. Miss Terrell had called the giant building a museum and called the statues sculptures. She had pointed out the one made by a colored man. She took them to the Chinese room. The Chinese kids had stood around self-consciously, denying any link to a people who wrote on silk and made bowls of green, so thin and fine one could see through to the other side. She took them to see a display case that had Indian jewelry resting on pieces of wood, only Miss Terrell had called it Native American art. The Indian kids had smirked and poked each other and hung back shyly as they all looked at the bead work and silver work so fantastic no human could have been remotely connected to the wearing of it. SueLinn had remembered her mother's beaded bracelet and stared at the glass case. It made her want to cry for a reason she couldn't begin to think about. She remembered the Chinese room and the Indian case for a long time after that. She told her mom about them. Dolores said it would be nice to go there, she had gone there once, she thought. But they never talked about it again. SueLinn was not a statue, but bony and covered with soft gold skin and coarse black hair that reached beyond her shoulder blades. She practiced statues at home, standing on the worn, green couch, trying to see herself in the wavy mirror on the opposite wall.

'Getting stuck on yourself, honey? That's how I started. A grain of salt. That's what we should take ourselves with. We're just bones and skin, honey. Bones and skin.'

The child thought her mother much more than bones and skin and salt. She thought Dolores was beautiful and was proud to walk with her on the avenue. The day they got the food stamps was one of the best days. Dolores was sober on those days. She sat at the card table, making lists and menus. Dolores labored hard on those days. Looking through her magazines, cutting out recipes for 'tasty, nutritional meals within your budget.' SueLinn stayed close to her mother on those days, fascinated by Dolores' activity.

'How would you like chicken vegetable casserole on Monday? Then on Tuesday we could have Hawaiian chicken. I found a recipe for peanut butter cookies. It says that peanut butter is a good source of protein. Would you like Dolores to make you cookies, baby? Maybe we could make them together.' SueLinn shook her head yes and stood even closer to her mother. Shiny paper with bright colors of food lay emblazoned on the table. SueLinn was caught by Dolores' words. Her magic talk of casseroles and cookies. Writing down words that came back as food. Food was something real, yet mysterious. Food was something there never was enough of. And she knew there were people in the world who always had enough to eat, who could even choose the food they ate. People who went into stores and restaurants and read the labels and the columns and maybe glanced at prices, but often paid no attention to such details. SueLinn didn't know how she knew this was so, but she knew all the same. She ate a free lunch at school. Always hungry, eating too fast, not remembering what she ate, just eating, then being hungry again. Miss Terrell asked each morning if anyone had forgotten to eat breakfast, because she just happened to bring orange juice and graham

crackers from home. There was always enough for everyone. Miss Terrell was a magic teacher. Her whole being was magic. Her skin was darker than any colored person SueLinn had ever known. Almost a pure black, like the stone set in the school door, proclaiming when it was built (1910) and whose name it was built to honor (Jeremy Comstock). Marble, yes that's what Miss Terrell called it. Black marble, that was Miss Terrell's skin. Her hair was cut close to her head. It curled tight against her scalp. James William's hair was like this, but somehow not so tightly curled and his hair was white, while Miss Terrell's was as black as her skin. She wore red lipstick, sometimes a purple color to match her dress with the white and pink dots on the sash. Her clothes were a marvel to see. Blue skirt and red jackets. Green dresses with gold buttons. Her shoes, a red or black shining material with pointy, pointy toes and little wood heels. Miss Terrell was tall and big. Some of the boys whispered and laughed about Miss Terrell's 'boobs.' SueLinn saw nothing to laugh at, only knowing that boys giggled about sex things. She thought Miss Terrell's chest was very beautiful. It stuck out far and looked proud in a way. When she had mentioned this to James William, he had said, 'Child, that Alveeta Terrell be a regular proud woman. Why wouldn't her chest be as proud as the rest of her? She mighty good-lookin' and one smart lady. You know you just as lucky as can be to have proud Alveeta Terrell be your teacher!'

One time, and it was the best time, Miss Terrell had come to school in a yellow dress over which she wore a length of material made from multi-colored threads of green, red, purple, yellow and black. She had called it Kente cloth and told the class it had been woven in Africa and the people, even the men, wore it every day. It was a day the Black people celebrated being African, and, even though they might live in all kinds of places, they had still come from Africa at one time. Then she had shown them a map of Africa, then traced lines running from that continent to America, to the West Indies, to South America, to just about everywhere. Amos asked if Africa was so good, why did the people leave? Miss Terrell said the people didn't leave because they wanted to, but because these other people, Spanish, British, American, French had wanted slaves to work on their land and make things grow for them so they could get rich. And these same people had killed Indians and stolen land, had lied and cheated to get more land from the people who were the original owners. And these same people, these white people, needed labor that didn't cost anything so they could get richer and richer. They had captured Black people as if they were herds of animals and put them in chains and imported them to countries where their labor was needed. The children pondered on this for minutes, before raising their hands and asking questions. The whole school day was like that, the kids questioning and pondering, Miss Terrell answering in her clear, sure voice. It seemed as though she knew everything. She told them about

Denmark Vesey, Nat Turner, Chrispus Attucks whose last name meant deer, because his mama was a Choctaw Indian. She told them about Touissant L'Overture, about the Maroons in Jamaica, she told them about the Seminoles and Africans in Florida creating an army to fight the U.S. *soldiers and how they won the fight. SueLinn's mind was so filled with these wondrous facts, she even dreamed about them that night. And it came to her that Miss Terrell was a food-giver. Her thoughts and facts were like the graham crackers she laid out on her desk each morning. They were free to take; to eat right at that moment, or to save up for when one got real hungry. SueLinn copied down her realization in the little notebook she carried with her everywhere. 'Miss Terrell is a food-giver.' She told James William, who agreed.*

Food-stamp day. Dolores making something out of nothing. What did it mean? Everything meant something. This she had learned on her own; from the streets, from the people who surrounded her, from being a kid. SueLinn wanted to ask Dolores about it, but was too shy.

Dolores was ready. SueLinn puttered at the card table, stalling for time, prolonging the intimacy with her mother. SueLinn was not ready for the store. It happened every time. Dolores got sad. The store defeated her. It was a battle to see how far down the aisles she could get before giving up. The limp vegetables, the greenish-brown meat, the lack of anything resembling the good food in the magazines. SueLinn sensed it before it came. The faint shrug of Dolores' shoulders, the shake of her head as if clearing it from a fog or a dream. Then they proceeded fast, Dolores grabbing at things that were cheap and filling, if only for a few hours. The little girl tried calling her mama's attention to funny people in the store or some fancy-packaged box of air and starch. Anything, please, please, that would take that look off Dolores' face. That look of fury and contempt. That look of losing. They would end up coming home with a few things like bread and canned corn and maybe hamburger sometimes, cereal in a box and a bottle of milk. Dolores would put the pitiful groceries away, go out and not return until the next day.

Dolores picked up her lists and stamps, placed them in her purse, a beige plastic bag with her initials stamped in gold lettering. D.L. Dolores Longhorse. She went to the wavy mirror and with her little finger applied blue eye shadow because, 'You never know who we'll meet.' She brushed her black hair until it crackled with sparks and life across her wide back. Dressed in blue jeans too tight, a pink sweater frayed and unravelling at the bottom, her gold-tone earrings swinging and dancing, she defied anyone or anything to say she didn't exist. 'Let's go.'

Her daughter took hold of her mother's hand and stared up at Dolores, as if to burn the image of her mama into her brain, to keep the smell of lily-of-the-valley cologne in her nose. The brown eyes ringed in blue looked down at her child. Dark eye watched dark eye. Two females locked in an embrace of color, blood and bewildering love. Dolores broke the intensity of the moment, cast her eyes around the apartment, committing to memory what she had come home to, tightening her hold on SueLinn's hand, and said, once again, 'Let's go.' She set the lock, and the two went out onto the street.

SueLinn's eyes closed with this last memory. Her head nodded above the soup. James William rose from the table and pulled the bed down from the wall. Straightening the covers and fluffing the pillows, he made it ready for the child's tired body. He picked her up and carried her the few feet to the bed. Taking off her shoes, he gently placed the girl under the blankets and tucked the pillow under her head. He placed the afghan at the foot of the bed, folded and neat.

James William Newton went to his chair and sat in the night-time light. He could see a piece of the moon through a crack between the two buildings across the street.

'Ole moon, what you think? I got this here child now. Them government peoples be wantin' to know where this child be. Or is they? Seem like the whereabouts of a little gal ain't gonna concern too many of them. Now I ain't worryin' bout raisin' this here turtle gal. It one of them things I be prepared to do. Moon, we gots to have a plan. I an old man. This here baby needs me, yes she does. There gots to be some providin' to do. Big Bill? Is you laughin' at me? It be a fix we in. Mmmmhmmm, a regular fix. Big Bill? I needs a little a them words you always so ready with. Honey, it ever be a wonder how a man could talk so much and *still* make sense like you done! I sittin' here waitin' on you. Yes sir, I sittin' and waitin' on you.'

He sat through the night, refilling his cup many times. His memories came and went like the peppermint tea he drank. Sometime before dawn, he drank his last cup, rinsed it and set it upside down in the sink. He settled his body on the blue davenport, the afghan pulled up to his shoulders. He looked one more time at the child, her dark hair half-hiding her face in sleep.

'Child, sleep on and dream. Sweet William, he here. You be all right. Yes mam, you be all right.'

He closed his eyes and slept.

From *Canadian Fiction*

Masks of Woman

Mitsuye Yamada

I.

This is my daily mask
daughter, sister
wife, mother
poet, teacher
grandmother.

My mask is control
concealment
endurance
my mask is escape
from my
self.

II. (Noh mask of benign woman)

Over my mask
is your mask
of me
an Asian woman
grateful
gentle
in the pupils of your eyes
as I gesture with each
new play of
light
and shadow
this mask be
comes you.

But here
I shall remove
your mask
of me and
my daily mask
of me
like the used skin
of a growing reptile
it peels away
and releases

III. (Mask of Daruma, weighted toy-god)

Daruma
my mouth is a funnel
words implode within and
burst forth through an
inverted megaphone
my bulging eyes command
your attention
I am Daruma
push me
I will not stay
stare me down
I will not look away
dare me to laugh
it off
I will not wince
a smile.

Daruma moves
me to resist
Daruma defies me
to act and
I become

IV. (Mask of Onibaba, old witch)

Onibaba
old woman hag
watch Onibaba's
streaks of light
ages of my sorrows
glow through each
lentigo
my infrared rays
will pierce your
mask.

V. (Noh mask of benign woman)

This is my daily mask
daughter, sister
wife, mother
poet, teacher
grandmother
My mask is control
concealment
endurance
my mask is escape
from my
self.

From *Desert Run: Poems and Stories*

Corrosion

Gisele Fong

Ashamed of you
    woman pushing her way rudely to the snowpeas
    Loud restaurants and the slurpings, accents,
        the strange animal parts
        that show up in your soup
    Old man sitting on a corner
        slowly rocking, slowly rocking,
        ranting of old days,
        as the pigeons
            clutter
            by his feet
You are not a part of me.

I am
    a normal teenager
    eat pizza, go roller skating, listen to top 40
    flirt with boys, go to the beach;
    fit in.

"Are you Chinese, Japanese, Korean, Filipino, Hawaiian?
    Do you eat lice...Do you know Bruce?
    Oh AAAAH So, Sukiyaki!
        Sahlee, Chalee!"
You are not a part of me.

Immigrant, sweatshop woman,
    kung fu man, laundry worker,
    Chinese waiter, computer nerd.
You are not a part of me.

Eyes, tongue,
   leg, breast,
    heart
You are not a part of me.

La Dulce Culpa

Cherríe Moraga

What kind of lover have you made me, mother
who drew me into bed with you at six/at sixteen
oh, even at sixty-six you do still
lifting up the blanket with one arm
lining out the space for my body with the other

    as if our bodies still beat
    inside the same skin
    as if you never noticed
    when they cut me
    out
    from you.

What kind of lover have you made me, mother
who took belts to wipe this memory from me

    the memory of your passion
    dark & starving, spilling
    out of rooms, driving
    into my skin, cracking
    & cussing in spanish

    the think dark *f* sounds
    hard *c*'s splitting
    the air like blows

    you would *get a rise out of me*
    you knew it in our blood
    the vision   of my rebellion

What kind of lover have you made me, mother
who put your passion on a plate for me
nearly digestible. Still trying to swallow
the fact that we lived most of our lives
with the death of a man
whose touch ran
across the surface of your skin

never landing nightly
when you begged it
to fall

>   to hold your desire
>   in the palm of his hand
>
>   for you to rest there
>   for you to continue.

What kind of lover have you made me, mother
so in love

with what is left

unrequited.

_____

From *Loving in the War Years: lo que nunca pasó por sus labios*

Sessions

Nora Cobb

Nah, I don't hate her—I mean, she's my mom. The only thing I hold against her is that she fed me regurgitated kimchee and rice. I was only three, you see, and had no conception of gross. We were flying to Hawaii for the first time, me and my mom, to meet her new boyfriend—now my ole stepdad. In one arm she carried me, and in the other arm she smuggled a bottle of kimchee, a small pot of rice, chopsticks and a spoon, all wrapped in an old K-Mart sack and stuffed into a plastic Pan Am bag.

Once we settled into our seats and the flight settled into a comfortable monotony, she opened up the lunch pouch. "This Korean Sauerkraut," I'm sure she must have giggled to the screwed-up faces and surprised eyes which sought the source of the smell and found her. She took a bite of rice, a bite of kimchee, and—switching chopsticks for spoon—spit everything back out for me. Later she explained that I wouldn't eat it without the added mother flavor, that I'd cry if she gave it to me straight. But I imagine fellow passengers, even those who had said, "Cute kid," even those who could still smile after having been assaulted by the smell of garlic and fermented cabbage, must have turned away too embarrassed to look anymore, too polite to comment on our eating habits. Even the gentle man who sat next to us in his soft blue suit, briefcase on lap, must have hurriedly shuffled through papers and studied his documents with unwavering concentration and straightforward eyes.

Sometimes when people stare at me funny, I wonder if it's 'cause they recognize me as that weird girl on the plane, the one who would only eat spit-up food.

But that's all I'd be mad at her for, not that I'm mad. I don't even hold it against her that she married Jack; she just believed his lies.

"I love you. I'll take care of you," he said to my mom. What did she know?

After they got married, we moved into the Ala Wai Plaza. All I remember from that place is: I couldn't keep a pony there, or a dog or a cat, only a fish which I tried to train to come to the top of the aquarium when I tapped on the glass. I tried to pet it, my hand chasing the red and yellow tail around till water overflowed, but it got some skin disease and died. Its name was Herman Hoopster, but I don't know why.

Also, I remember that a woman jumped off the roof and my mom wouldn't let me go out to see what was left of her.

Oh, and I remember the time I wet my pants. I was in the second grade and my favorite book was "The Little Black Pony." That ties in 'cause one day after school I rushed to the library to borrow this book and—even though I had to pee really bad—I ran right home to read it. When I got to 12E, the door was locked. Mom used to be there all the time, but I guess she'd already started working at the restaurant by then. I didn't have a key, so I waited in front of the door thinking someone would come home any minute. I sat on my Josie and the Pussycats lunch box and twisted my legs together. I sang, "I'm a little teapot," to get my mind off my bladder. But I ended up crying and squatting. Yellow water trickled from our welcome mat down to that little gutter opening rainwater drains out of. Raindrops of pee must have dripped right down to the parking lot. I sat there crying and that's how Jack found me.

"What happened here?" he said.

And I told him: "I fell in that puddle. I hurt my butt."

Jack stood me up and rubbed my butt, his hands sliding right up to my crotch. His eyes were closed. "Hmm...I see," he said and he opened the door. Jack led me to my bedroom and laid out dry panties and a dress for me. The panties and the dress matched—white cotton with pink polka dots and pink lace. Jack liked lace. Whenever he bought me panties they had lace edged around them.

"Change," Jack said. He sat down on my bed.

I changed with my back facing him, but I know he watched me 'cause I felt it.

"We won't tell your mama what you did today," he said. "As if she'd understand, anyway."

I felt his eye, but he didn't touch me.

Then.

The first time? There was no first time, really. Hands creeping to touch mine when mom fell asleep at the TV, fingers wrestle-tickling me and then brushing against my chest, brushing "down there." Once he came home with groceries and asked me to scratch through his jeans for him: "My hands are full, can you...?" Once when I was taking a bath he unlocked the door with a butter knife. He came in to use the bathroom, he said, but then he couldn't pee.

Yeah, he came into my room sometimes, late at night when the crickets are real loud, the only thing you can hear above the growling of the refrigerator. Sometimes he'd watch me when I pretended to sleep—I know how to make my breaths so even and smooth, and how to make my lips smack together like people sometimes do in their sleep.

Sometimes he'd get into bed with me.

Those times I'd make him small—smaller and smaller than the palm of my hand. I'd make him so tiny that in my dreams he turned into a tiny white mouse that scurried all over my legs and up and down my arms. A little mouse that I could pick up by the tail and put into a cage.

Jack told me a joke one night. I breathed deep and even, eyes closed, but he told it to me anyway: "I had a China-girl once, but how disappointing...I was horny again an hour later."

My mom—she cried a lot and was tired and sick a lot. Jack took care of her during the days when she was off from work, massaging her feet, giving her medicine: "Let her sleep," he'd say. And he didn't like her to wear glasses or contacts 'cause of her disease called "astingementism," or something like that. She could have gone completely blind. Once when she bought contacts, I saw him dump them into the bathroom sink. When she tried to ask him about it, he scolded her for being stupid and absent-minded, but she got mad. So then he just sweet-talked her.
"Now, now, hon, what exactly do you want from me?" Jack asked her, even though he knew.
"You have contak?" Mom was holding her hand out to the side of him, palm up, like she was gonna hit him. I was hoping she would.
"Contact? Contact? Oh, you mean like that allergy pill I give you, that sneezing pill?"
"No, contak contak." Mom pointed to her eyes. "No see good."
"You mean contacts, don't you. Contacts." Jack made a real long ssss sound. "Now you know that's a no-no, honey. Bad, bad for you."
"No, no bad," Mom said. "You have? Gib me right now, this min."
Jack made clucking and shhing noises. "Calm down," he said. "You people have bad tempers...let me give you something to relax." Jack stroked Mom's head, her cheeks, and her forehead. "I'm your man, sugar pie," he clucked. "I take care of you, don't I?" And mom was led away to the bedroom saying, "You right, you right." She always said that in the end.
It was hard to talk to her, anyway. 'Cause she'd be so tired most of the time her words would drool together, or she'd forget where she was and start to speak in Korean, which was forbidden in the house. Jack said that those "ching-chong" words made him nervous. Besides, he said, mom had to learn better English for her own good.
So, no, I never did tell on him.

I have to wash my hands a lot because it got harder and harder for me to change Jack into a mouse. He'd change into animals I couldn't handle: a wolf, a giant worm, a man.
Finally, I managed to turn him into a squirrel, but only by making myself into a tree for him to hide in. When he became a squirrel, bark creeped and caked over my skin, and my blood would turn into sap, making my body stiff and strong and very heavy. My hair became autumn leaves falling around my head, blinding me with gold, red, brown cracklings when I turned this way or that.

At first I just washed it off once in the mornings so the bark wouldn't root down for good. I'd scrub and scrub till my own skin showed itself again, pink and raw. But then I noticed I had to wash more often. One day at lunch one of my fingers—my left littlest one—sprouted a twig. I washed it off quickly. I don't think anyone noticed.

But you know something? I'm tired of taking baths.

I had a pet fish once. I named him Herman Hoopster, I don't know why. It died because I petted him to death. And I had a pet squirrel once, too. I named him Jack, I don't know why. It died. One day I made it get smaller and smaller till it was a small little ant crawling around way high in my branches. When I shook my leaves, the squirrel fell all the way down. If you ever wondered if animals could scream, they can.

Hey, I don't think I'll wash anymore. It's only been a day, but look at how rough and brown my skin is already. And see how dry and crackly my hair is? My toes are even getting longer and are starting to curl downwards.

Hurry, can you plant me in the country?

You don't have to take care of me anymore, my mom can do that. She can dig around me with a spade and ivory chopsticks. She can take a sip of water from her green watering can and spit it onto my roots.

On Passing

Laura Munter-
Orabona

"*No lo creo, no lo creo....*" As they lowered the casket into the ground, her words came back to me in hot whispers, "*¡no lo creo!*" "Stay with me, Mami," I answered half aloud. My head jerked. I shifted in the chair, aware of others sitting quietly around me. I turned my gaze and let the grief slide from my face as I focused on the well-trimmed grass and the thin metal pole of the tent surrounding us.

Familia...my father, my brother, titi Chelin, Abuelito, Lena, *la gente de mami....* Nearly strangers to me. Tio Luis had broken into tears when he entered the hospital and got a last look at my mother. I wasn't used to so much emotion in men—in anyone. His sobs caught him in the middle. They took his breath and bent him in two next to her bed. Now at the funeral I felt their sideways glances. Their questioning looks. I could throw myself at the side of her grave like on TV. Would they understand then? How my tears lay deep beneath each layer of skin like buried cities...each with a woven tale.... This was my grief when they took me from you *mis tias*...snatched me from your arms...your music, the warmth *de mi tierra...la lengua de mi corazón*...and this is the grief as they took you mami. How could they understand? I hadn't lived with them in so many years and in my new home I did not cry before strangers...especially family.

I did times tables in my head, like in Catholic school. Soon the familiar band of steel locked around my forehead like a tight hat. I had regained control.

"Thank you for the sparse gathering," I said to myself, relieved that my parents had quit their teaching jobs a year earlier and moved to this small Florida town. There were no neighbors, no teachers. At her gravesite, my anger would have sliced those people in two. Only the closest *familia* stood by. Tio Tonio...he looks just like my brother Kerry, I thought. In twenty years in small Michigan towns I had never seen a person who looked like my family. We moved so often. We were always the new family in town. In those towns everyone was related to each other. Three last names would take up half of the population. Isolation is an odd thing. It shows its face only as it's leaving, but takes your guts with it. There was one sobbing woman whom I did not recognize. I welcomed her hysteria. The absurdity of a woman I had never seen before wailing at my mother's funeral tamed the hysteria within me.

"Gastritis," the doctor had said, and kept saying. Later they corrected their diagnosis, as though they'd merely forgotten a comma in the sentence "Cancer of the lower intestines." It had spread. It kept spreading. After the third surgery, I heard the doctor tell my father, "If it comes back, we'll just open her up and take it out again. All the lesions, looks like somebody took a bottle of glue and spread it all over her insides." The glasses sat straight on his angular nose, his hands were shoved deep in the pockets of a starched white coat. She was just another body to him, a woman and a Puerto Rican at that. Just another spic. "You don't know her," I wanted to scream. "She studied medicine just like you, at better schools than you, she's fluent in five languages, her father and the Governor called each other by nickname."

But here it didn't matter. It hadn't mattered. She'd tried to pack her lineage with the baggage and two small children as she left the island to rejoin her American husband, my father. But her aristocracy was of a crumbling class and did not survive the journey. It was lost in the translation and thrived only in the mind of my mother. The grandeur was recaptured in my daydreams, nurtured by stories of fine houses with fountains in the middle, memories of the upper class in Old San Juan. Those stories were my weapons against those small town people. *"Hey half-nigger,"* "In Puerto Rico, my people are rich"…*"Hey little spic,"* "They are doctors and lawyers, the whole town are their friends"…*"Little slut,"* "You are all dirt and too stupid to know it, my people matter."

My mind drifted to the time the casket salesman sat in my father's living room. As the illness chewed its way through Mami's body, my father prepared. The salesman spoke gently, efficiently, drew details of various boxes. He had placed catalogues and brochures neatly on the table. "Catafalque," he kept saying, not casket, not coffin, as though the unfamiliar term would ease the pain. With his head buried in his hands, my father began to cry. The tears slipped through openings between his fingers. I wanted to reach out and comfort him. But years of practice made me rise and drift into another room. I heard the casket man comforting him, surprised at the tenderness and sincerity of the smooth salesman.

The last weeks with my mother filled me with emptiness. My emotions surrounded me like still air. I functioned as in a dream. I'd been flying back and forth from Michigan and hadn't seen her in a month. As I rounded the door to her hospital room, the sight of her ninety-pound body made me gasp. I tried to recover, but she'd seen. "Just a bag of bones," she said, shaking her head. For a moment the truth stood thick between us. As she sat up in bed, I noticed the deep red rinse gone from her hair. Soft braids hugged her head. The grey plaits gave an odd look of a little girl grown old too fast. Mami drew her head close to mine, focused through the sheath of drugs. "I'm going to lick this thing," she said in a feverish whisper, "I'm going to lick this thing."

My youngest brother visited the hospital rarely. Sitting silently, his anger and fear cast a sullen veil. He could barely speak to our mother.

I was relieved when his visits stopped. "Don't be angry with the boys," Dad said, "it's hard for them." Kerry, her favorite son, came twice. On my last visit I glimpsed his inability to accept her dying.

"She's just looking for sympathy," Kerry said. His high-pitched voice at thirty-two still held so much of his boyhood. "All we need to do is get her a ten-speed. She can get off her buns and ride." Later, after one of his visits, I'd seen him seated on a couch outside her room, clutching a Bible. He thumbed frantically through its frail pages and begged its testament to keep him strong.

She'd been a busy woman, giving us bits of time between preparing lesson plans, working on another degree, running a travel business. Mami had grown up with cooks and maids. But in her heart she sought more than motherhood. "*¡Caramba muchacha!*" she'd say, impatient with the child I was. Details of home finally gave way to other ambitions. I remember buttons popping off in school when the pins securing them on my dresses would no longer hold. But I wore her achievements like shiny medals, my chest puffed out to children whose mothers mended my clothes when I spent the night. "My mother is working on her doctorate." I knew most of their parents had only finished high school, if that.

I savored the times she spent with me. Once she showed me the first crocus in her garden, deep violet pushed through soil to meet the new warmth of Michigan spring. I'd wanted to bury myself deep in the black earth, have her hands knead me around the roots of the brilliant spring flower. Deep in the soil, deep in my mother's touch.

In the photo I remember her tiny against the sea, but not diminished, standing high and glamorous on the cliff nearby, wearing white slacks and tailored blouse. She was so fashionable then, living in D.C. That pride and arrogance burst from the black and white edges of the photo. Her eyes stared straight out of that flat picture past me. My mother's life had already been as vast with promise as the ocean calling to her back.

The end was difficult. I planned on staying only two weeks. My bags filled the trunk of my father's car. He had taken me to the hospital to say goodbye. I was relieved to be leaving. The well-honed racism of this redneck Florida town scared me. "They only let black people move here two years ago," my father said. Their outright bigotry dwarfed a northern brand of his own. At least at home in Michigan my father belonged. The Swedish immigrants of his father's time had reclaimed their Nordic home in upper Michigan. The snowlands had welcomed them and their children. But here, even his curly black hair stood out like a wild spring couched among beer-bellied southern boys and the frayed bleachy perms of their women.

We left the hospital, headed toward the airport. I was so eager to leave, I felt the heaviness starting to lift with each mile. "Can't he drive faster?" I thought. I wanted to outrun the truth which was pulling at the edge of my senses. "No, I can't stay." I wanted the comfort of my friends, my home. I looked over, my father seemed tight and nervous, maybe scared. I knew I was safe. I knew he wouldn't ask me to stay. I wanted to be free of this hellish ending. "I would never want an open casket," my mother had said years ago at a friend's passing. "I want people to remember me alive, not dead," she said with a hint of anger. The neck of my shirt was wet. I moved in the seat and felt my shirt and legs clinging to the plastic. I remembered her...so thin, frail, only a matter of time. I knew I could not leave. But I didn't want to speak. "Take me back, Dad," I finally said. I felt grief. I felt relief. I saw the tension leave his forehead, felt him breathe a sigh. We both knew that if I left that day, I would not see my mother again. But we could not speak the words.

The next day I moved through the house, cooking, doing laundry. I noticed the plants were dying. They seemed to scream out to me. I was stunned I had not noticed before. The lonely remains, the dry soil, the crunchy leaves echoed a low moan that was building in me. The morning before going back to the hospital, I emptied all the pots in a shed out back. It was as though each plant was seeding the loss deeper within me. I felt my heart open to the sadness. "I'm going to lick this thing," I heard her whisper. She'd always won, wielding her self-assured brilliance, her arrogant privilege like a shield against the mentality of those small Michigan towns. But the dying plants brought the truth gently home. The next day while my father was away, I packed some of my mother's things. I moved slowly, carefully folding all the brilliant-colored clothes that were hardly popular at the time: oranges, purples. I packed methodically, mechanically. The stack of boxes grew taller, the closets emptied. I could not touch the rows and rows of knickknacks. At moments, my hands would stop on a familiar piece of clothing, draw it close to me. Unable to say goodbye, I caressed the smooth material with my hands, imprinting her memory on my fingertips.

The last week at the hospital, my father and I, the only ones to remain, were unable to comfort each other. My grandfather would quietly bring arroz con pollo and platanos stuffed with white cheese to the house. My father and I moved through anger, despair and disbelief as though passing each other on an open stairway, each locked in our own grief, set in our own direction. Each day Mami would crave an old familiar food. Days later a crate from Puerto Rico might arrive packed with smells which stirred a deep memory in me. I was five years old at the market place in Santurce, nose-high to the warm food wrapped in banana leaves. I watched my mother's hand reach for the *tamal*, the *pasteles*. But here in the hospital, three years of chemotherapy and heavy sedatives robbing her of taste and other senses, she would try the *tamarindo*, shake her head, ask for the *leche de avena*, shake her head again. "Slight brain damage," they'd said. By whose measure, I'd wondered.

She floated in and out of consciousness. "I don't believe it," she said over and over again. "I don't believe it. They're chasing me, stop them."

I wanted to comfort her, to reach her, to be the one to ease the pain. To comfort her as she passed. Finally, the tubes were gone from her arms, from her nose, no more Demerol, no more Talwin, no more liquid food. "Take them out," she said. And slowly starving, she drifted home, returned to her motherland, spoke only the language of her heart. "*No lo creo. No lo creo.*" She spoke many things I can't remember, words I didn't understand. The familiar forgotten Spanish filled me with a mourning song as they lifted her from me. And my anger rose.

I don't know at what point I had turned from my native language. "Talk English or don't talk at all," my father had said as my brother and I passed from the warmth of *mi familia*'s arms from the island of my birth to my father's snow-covered home. My mother had left him years earlier, me in her belly, my brother on her arm. "Talk English or don't talk at all," he said when we came to America. I stopped speaking for two years, they said. "We thought you were damaged. We were going to see doctors, then one day you said, 'Bubba gum.'"

Maybe Dad thought he was helping. Maybe he felt threatened that we could leave him with conversation. Years later they both wanted us to learn, to undo the error. "We will speak only Spanish at dinner. *Mantequilla, por favor.*" My father had studied Spanish that summer in Kalamazoo. "Your accent is horrible," my mother would snap. I would think of the dopey man on TV, "*Si, Sen-your.*" Oh, we knew Spanish, my brother and I. We knew "*zapato,*" we knew "*carajo,*" we knew "*mierda.*" Then one day at school, in my third grade class, my father showed up to teach us Spanish. He was a music teacher, but they didn't know. "*Isabel ¿te gustas albondigas?*" and together, 30 seven-year-olds would answer, "*No, no me gusto albondigas.*" But now standing mute at my mother's passing, Mami calling out to us in terror, calling out in her native tongue, I felt awakened in the middle of a rape. Each foreign word another thrust. "*No lo creo. No lo creo.*" Mami, we don't know your language. My rage rising, I understood the lunatic gunning wildly through a crowd.

The end came quickly. I sent my father home early that night. He sat solemnly in the chair across from her hospital bed, staring at the thin frame of the woman he'd shared a bed with for 32 years. His eyes were bloodshot and glassy, and though my mother had asked him not to come drunk, it hardly mattered now. Her eyes were glassed-over, sight gone, her body shrunk a little each day. I abandoned the anger at my mother's last request. I walked across the room. "Dad?" I placed my hand gently on his knee, not wanting to startle him. "Why don't you go home. There is no need for both of us to stay." He resisted at first. I don't recall what made him agree. I eased him home, "I'll call," I said. He needed some sleep, needed a break from this bleak white room, and I was relieved he was gone.

It was nine o'clock at night. Alone in her room, I felt peaceful at first, but the unrest grew quickly. I switched channels on the TV, tried to read, walked to the window, listened to the cicadas' night chatter: they buzzed like bad neon. Soon the walls began to argue for space, closing in on me, opening too wide. I paced, looked at the clock...9:30, listened closely for my mother's breathing. Earlier that evening the nurse had come by. "Why don't you pack some of her things," she'd said. A bit surprised, I accepted the brown bag she had handed me. It had seemed a harsh message. Now I could see she would die soon. I suppose I should have called my father. I packed some things, her toothbrush, her Bible, some earrings. When I was through, the dozen red roses that my grandmother, my father's mother, had sent adorned the top of the brown sack. I remembered my mother's story of Abuelita's death in Puerto Rico. It had been a long painful illness and toward the end the nuns would sit in constant vigil, they prayed through the morning, *"Ruega por nosotros ahora, y en la hora de nuestra muerte, Amen."* They prayed through the long still night. I imagined their heavy habits of devotion, their soft fingers caressing the beads, with the rhythm of their steady chant, *"Dios de salve Maria."* And I longed for them as I longed for my homeland, for its way of life, for its way of death....

The minutes passed so slowly and here in this foreign place, I knew no thought to ease the terror, no inner voice to quiet the restlessness. I could not sit with the slow hand of time, my only companion. My mother had taught me to pray in Spanish. *"En el nombre del padre, del hijo, y del santo cristo...,"* showed me how to make the tiny cross with thumb and forefinger. But my thoughts rested on the Valium on her dresser. I had given up drugs since I'd seen her pain. Measuring it against mine, drugs seemed cowardly and frail. Living daily with my father's alcoholism had reseeded a bitter belief. "I will never be like him. My life is too precious and I have more pride."

The small hospital cot they'd brought for me was next to the wall. I looked again at the clock. Habit stronger than pride, I slipped the pills into my mouth. I crawled into the stiff white sheets of the cot, letting the pills cradle me.

I heard her cough in the night, gasp for air. I wanted to sit up, to go to her. But the pull of the drug held me to the soft bed like an old lover, I rolled back to the comfort. "Get up, go to her, you should help," I heard the voice softly as I heard her cough again, but guilt and compassion only nudged. I did not move.

The nurse shook me gently at first, then a little more firmly. She was so far away. Let me sleep. Was it morning? I searched through the darkness. "Your mother has passed." I watched her lips for the words again. "Your...mother...has...passed." The words stung even through the thick wrap of the drug. When had she left? I had been lying next to her, just Mami and me, our bodies rising and falling like the calm roll of the sea. When had she grown still? When had her breath stopped answering mine?

I arose, walked slowly to where she lay. I touched my mother's cheek, caressing the still warm, peaceful skin. I had wanted to hold her hand as she died. But she was gone. Death cradled her in its arms, quieted the voices, rested the visions.

It was 5:20 in the morning, 1951, Santurce, Puerto Rico. Mami, you brought me in and the sea surrounded me like the waters of your womb. It was 5:14 a.m., 1979, a Florida town, Seventh-day Adventist hospital. I caressed your cheek. You had passed from me.

Mother, he buried you in a thin brown nightie, "Amour" stitched in thick white letters across the bosom. The birthstones of your children hung around your neck. "I thought this would be all right," he'd said, shy at the intimacy, as he showed me the neatly laid-out gown and carefully placed jewelry. I could not tell him I wanted to fold you soft in blankets beneath a blooming magnolia. I wanted to bury you at its base, let its roots cradle you safe, cradle you warm.

Mami, you were the thread reaching through me to the island, my voice on every visit, my memory, my reminder. I thought I could not return without you. But I am just now finding my own way home.

Notes From A Chicana "Coed"

Bernice Zamora

for P.H.

To cry that the *gabacho*
is our oppressor is to shout
in abstraction, *carnal.*
He no more oppresses us
than you do now as you tell me
"It's the gringo who oppresses you, Babe."
You cry "The gringo is our oppressor!"
to the tune of $20,000 to $30,000
a year, brother, and I wake up
alone each morning and ask,
"Can I feed my children today?"

To make the day easier
I write poems about
pájaros, mariposas,
and the fragrance
of perfume I
smell on your collar;
you're quick to point out
that I must write
about social reality,
about "the gringo who
oppresses you, Babe."
And so I write about
how I worked in beet fields
as a child, about how I
worked as a waitress
eight hours at night to
get through high school,
about working as a
seamstress, typist, and field clerk
to get through college, and
about how, in graduate school
I held two jobs, seven days
a week, still alone, still asking,
"Can I feed my children today?"

To give meaning to my life
you make love to me in alleys,
in back seats of borrowed Vegas,
in six-dollar motel rooms
after which you talk about
your five children and your wife
who writes poems at home
about *pájaros, mariposas,*
and the fragrance of perfume
she smells on your collar.
Then you tell me how you
bear the brunt of the
gringo's oppression for me,
and how you would go
to prison for me, because
"The gringo is oppressing you, Babe!"

And when I mention
your G.I. Bill, your
Ford Fellowship, your
working wife, your
three *gabacha guisás*
when you ask me to
write your thesis,
you're quick to shout,
"Don't give me that
Women's Lib trip, *mujer,*
that only divides us,
and we have to work
together for the *movimiento;*
the *gabacho* is oppressing us!"

Oye carnal, you may as well
tell me that moon water
cures constipation, that
penguin soup prevents *crudas,*
or that the Arctic Ocean is *menudo,*
because we both learned in the barrios,
man, that pigeon shit slides easier.

Still, because of the *gabacho,*
I must write poems about
pájaros, mariposas, and the fragrance
of oppressing perfume I smell somewhere.

From *Caracol* 3:9

Corazón de una anciana

Edna Escamill

¡LA CULTURA! ¡LA RAZA!
Sometimes all it means to me is suffering. Tragedy. Poverty. Las caras de los tortured santos y las mujeres en luto, toda la vida en luto. La miseria is not anything I want to remember and everything I cannot forget. Sometimes the bravery in facing and struggling in such life is too little. The courage with which a people siguen luchando against prejudice and injustice is not glory enough. I am not content with that picture—I am only crazy. Even though I am far away from Arizona where I started from, this coming to el estado de California is itself a search for a new life in this cool and distant place by an unknown sea. To someone boiling under a desert sun where only the privileged live surrounded by water and cool air, California was an oasis pictured only in a daydream. It was a place that had to be hospitable, healing and offering the promise of freedom from economic hardship. And so I carry the myth from one place to another. Sometimes I don't want a background, neither brown nor white. I want my identity to start with each moment. I don't want to be from any people. I want to be from nowhere, going to anywhere. If space is a metaphor for the exile and the search, it is also something else. For me it is not a starting place. It is where I end. In all this vastness I can be at home. In the midst of eternal blackness and soundless moving, I thrill to balls of light speeding by. I am at home, I am at peace.

SHE KEPT GOING BACK TO THE PLACE
with a door, not waiting for nightfall or dawn to make the move, walking with certainty, expecting something to happen. Expecting the grasses to move, the mountain to slide apart and the THING, the PLACE she knew was there to appear.

It was a certain kind of place. She had been walking aimlessly, following the curve of the creekbed among oak-studded hills, climbing a small round hill just before sunset when she found it—one of those places where the world can change and another come into being. The place trembled. It trembled in the moments between sunset and nightfall when time runs fluid. She knew it was a place with a door the moment she saw it. The door took shape on the round bodies of the mountain and the watershed between two hills. She watched and she waited, afraid to see, afraid not to keep looking. She sat cross-legged at the top of the small hill watching the sun go down in a great orange ball that set the trees on fire. And at the same time a lucid and delicate moon rose out of the valley cooling the sky, veiling the evening with silver. And she watched the door between the two green hills shimmer, on the verge of opening.

> *I DON'T KNOW WHERE TO BEGIN*
> *to talk about my father. It is simple enough to say he didn't want us*
> *because we looked too white. But too many sins go along with that. And*
> *the fact is, he didn't treat one of my brothers who was dark and looked*
> *Indio any differently from the rest of us when it came down to it. So his*
> *hatred must have started with the blood of his own father and the*
> *European woman who was our mother. She finally succeeded in leaving*
> *him by dying. I would like to be able to say it has been easy to find la*
> *Raza outside myself, but all my life I have struggled toward the race*
> *that rejected me. Brown or white, white or brown, I have been only half*
> *of something without the other. I claim myself. I love your race in me,*
> *my father*, pero no te puedo querer a ti.

SHE SAT CROSS-LEGGED AND STILL on the top of the hill, at first watching and then becoming part of the moonlight, the brilliant sun. Tall yellow grasses stood stiff and dry and were blown down by the first harsh winds of winter. When the rains came, the earth sprouted in green and tender innocence. She listened to the meditative soul of winter and felt the quickening of spring and each of the seasons in turn: she knew that Time was inside of her.

She sat without moving on the top of the hill as night mists gathered around her and the wind began to rise and speak from the hollows of the hills. She waited without waiting, as still and alive as the center of a flame. She waited and burned, making herself one with the desire in her heart: to bring into being the world that was behind the door.

She knew that when the door opened, she would open it with her eyes. With her eyes.

She looked into the space between the hills, feeling the trembling going on in the dark, and when the moment came it did not come toward her, she moved into it—lifted and flying above a long narrow black road. It was the desert unfolding from her eyes, sage bushes on silver sand glowing beneath a deep blue sky. It was both nighttime and not nighttime.

> *WHERE WERE YOU? WHERE WERE YOU,*
> *my father, when we were starving? The child that was hungry was not*
> *white nor brown. The child that was hungry was the white child, was*
> *the brown child. It was not eating corn starch for days at a time that*
> *hurt: the corn starch gave us life. It was the condition of poverty that*
> *hurt, that damaged the soul. The soul of the artist knew you were there,*
> *in Baja, doing the things that made you feel good, like sitting in your*
> *office examining thousand dollar bills. Yes, you earned it yourself, yes,*

it made you feel good to show it to me that time, to see the awe in my eyes. But you were mistaken: it was not awe of you for having it, it was only awe at the fact, the existence of the money itself. It was awe that such a thing should be awesome. It would have been more useful along with the newspapers that I used to line my bed to keep from freezing. I was very good at it: I put layers of papers underneath and then the sheet, then more papers on top, then the cover and more papers on top of that. The papers and the image of your money kept me warm.

THERE WERE ROSE-COLORED SHADOWS beneath the sage bushes, but she did not look back to see what manner of sun was there. She knew that the desert, her birthplace, was unfolding from her eyes to guide her. Her breath was sage, the light behind her eyes the soft light of the moon shining peacefully above giant cactus. Her tears were the raging monsoon storms thundering down sandy washes with the drumming of her heart. And the deepness of her soul brimming with love, the deep dark pools resting at the feet of canyon walls. She created all this out of what she was, just as she herself had been made from this place, this desert.

She reaches the edge of the Pueblo walking without touching the ground beneath her feet, moving down the narrow streets of the Barrio of her childhood. The hour is unknown, but even the dogs are asleep and the wind bounces against the heavy faded doors *de las casas.* And then she hears the voices of the old ones, *de las ancianas* rocking the children to sleep on their wide laps, waiting until the little ones are dreaming to eat their evening bowl of *frijoles con oregano.*

She passes *las tiendas del panadero,* smelling the eloquent, almost religious odor of *pan bidote,* and the sweet, enticing smells of *empanadas* and holiday *viscosuelos. Y alli vive el huesero,* a healer who must always be approached quietly and with respect. Stroking and probing with powerful fingers, he suddenly snaps the bones into place with precise pressures, his face composed and tender in the candlelight.

She comes to the end of the block, jumping down from the steep corner as she did when she was a child. Following the trail to the ancient, spreading *palo verde,* she hears her own resounding whack against the giant piñata as she pulls away the blindfold. None of the children could break the *oya.* Finally, the birthday boy's father broke it himself with the blunt end of an axe. Again, in the wind whipping the branches of the tree over her head, she hears the chanting voices *de las ancianas.* But their prayers dissolve to nothing in the winds of this world. A lonely tumbleweed and the dust of the desert fill the empty passageways as she moves among them. The sepia doors and the adobe walls speak to her heart of the past and the people. She longs to have it again, *la alegría y las voces de las ancianas.* How do we move like adventurers into the next world? she wondered. We who live in the shadows of the broken promises of the past, a past that could not become our future? The children of the people are scattered and will be buried far from the mountain, their Mother. The dreams *de las ancianas* are dusty spirits roaming the twisted streets of the Barrio unable to inhabit the white-washed apartments where young white college students come and go with the opening and closing of the school year.

She stands, an invisible dream at the edge of the Barrio, surrounded by the modern white world *defendiendo con sus mismos suspiros*, her own ancient voice within her breast.

I REMEMBER THINGS BUT I DON'T KNOW if they are real. These things are too outrageous for my life to absorb. My thoughts are bits and pieces of things that really happened but I have made moments of things that may have taken years, or did they?

My father was born in the early 1900s in a Yaqui village in Mexico. I have a photograph of him taken there. He is less than two years old. Everyone else is posing for the picture, but he is naked and crying, running toward the camera. In the background, my Spanish grand- father sits majestically upon his horse, holding it tightly in rein. Then there is a living picture of my father I remember. It is his birthday, an important one, and we are celebrating it at the ranch in Baja. An entire calf has been buried in a pit dug in the ground to cook slowly for hours. The head, also wrapped in gunny sacking, is buried separately, and it is dark out before the beast is ready to be eaten. The women lift out the head first, and the brains are carefully spooned out and passed around in individual servings for the guests to taste. The women's teeth and the silver edge of their spoons gleam in the firelight. From various shadows I watch the laughter and enjoyment of the guests, just as earlier that afternoon I watched the musicians playing and my father picking up and playing one instrument after another. His talent and versatility were the joy of his youth and he is reliving it, though now he is a businessman. I watch from a corner somewhere his unawareness of me. He is a stranger because even though I am related to him, blood of his blood, I have no feelings for him—even when he walks me up and down at night, looking at the stars, and we are the image of a loving father and his daughter. I only pretend to fall asleep in his arms. The truth is, I am wide awake and watching. I am trying to find my father in this person. There is a gulf between us that stretches from the past to the future. In separate events many years apart, he destroyed my mother and a beloved brother.

In separate events many years apart, he condemned all of us to misery. He gave his firstborn son to the boy's grandparents, leaving in him a legacy of cruelty which would later affect all those around him. My mother suffered beatings and starvings, dying soon after I was born. My father beat her to make her abort the children she carried. He denied medical care he could well afford to the younger of my two brothers, and finally, even food and shelter.

My brother lived in alleyways, eating from garbage cans until our grandmother, alerted by a tenant farmer she had befriended, traveled to Mexico and brought him back. The dark, handsome boy I remember with the sparkle in his black eyes and the extraordinary sense of play never recovered from the mental breakdown he suffered at the age of nineteen.

On the day I knew this totality of my father's acts, I walked in circles under the desert sky without feeling, without knowing que habia entrado y que andaba dentro de una cerca de espinas. I was fifteen years old and I would spend much of my adult life pulling the thorns from my heart one by one, with nothing but my fingers and my will. I only went on living, perhaps, out of ignorance, and maybe just a hint of bravery. I never saw my father again, but in these moments of our present, beneath the shining and beautiful stars, we cannot avoid our destiny. My father cannot escape what he has already done, nor what he will do. He is committed to his actions by his passions and by his indifference.

Does the way he is have anything to do with race?

For him it does. He wants children who are like him. He equates being like him with how we look, and we are not dark enough. Even the one who looks the most like him, olive-skinned, with Indio eyes, the image of his Yaqui grandmother, is still not enough like him. He is not hard nor brutal enough to escape the consequences of his father's actions.

Does the way he is have anything to do with race?

For the mother of my mother it does. She hates the Mexican, el Indio first, the man second. For her, the race is the man, down to the last gene of his Indian heritage. Nothing escapes her eyes. She looks past my light skin to my dark eyes and course, straight hair. My independence and my desires, especially to be an artist, are signs of crudity to her. She has examined me minutely, for I am what she has left of the daughter she cherished, and for her, I am not white enough. In me, the French and Spanish blood are tinted by the saliva and heart of the Jaguar. She sees my father looking out of my eyes, and although her heart suffocates with pain, she implicates me in my mother's death. She is the one I must fight the hardest when I choose to recapture all of my heritage. She is the one who could never, in her lifetime, understand why I had to.

But I, too, have been committed to my actions by what I am. The first time I dropped out of graduate school, I went to New York, the most foreign place in this country I could think of. It was to write a story that would explain my father and what he did. Looking back on it, that makes me laugh. But here I am again, talking about him. The only thing that is different after all these years is that I no longer care why he did what he did, why he was the way he was, because I no longer want to excuse him by explanations. A line has to be drawn. Evil must be named and condemned no matter where it appears. And that is that. But it still hurts. And that is okay. These tears are free, unattached. I am not him. The night of his birthday party, I watched his talent and charm the way I've watched it in myself, with distrust and from a distance. Maybe now the things in myself which he also had may flourish. The artist that I am deserves no other end.

AL LLEGAR AL RIO, ALUMBRADO DE LUCES, she contemplates the other side only for a moment, before wading across the waters and walking into a grove of sage. The sage is taller than her head *y cargada de flores amarillas*. Their incense is her very breath. She has returned to a place made sacred by her own blood. Beyond the Barrio, beyond the desert and the mountains that appear in all of her dreams, live the spirit plants and animals that have protected her this long. They come to meet her in the place where the ocotillo grows in a circle and their thorns still run red with her blood. This is the place where she opened her chest, lifted out her heart and tore it to pieces with her own teeth. She stood within the circle, smelling human blood mingled with the odor of sage, waiting. And they came to her. The she coyote, her coat blending with the earth, looked at her with large eyes. *Y el shonte* skipped inside the circle in quick dancing steps. *Y la golondrina encantada*, settling her pure white wings, came with the gentle sounds of peace in her throat. *Y una vibora cascabel* uncoiled at her feet and regarded her with an inscrutable golden eye. *Cada uno tenía en su boca un pedazo de su corazón*, which they touched to the fresh blood and gave to her to swallow. And with the pieces of her heart restored to her, she returned to her body and to her soul, to love and to hope of a future—all the things she had left and forgotten, impaled on the ring of ocotillo.

Sage spirit gave her a crown of yellow flowers, which she held in her hands and looked at long and seriously. Then she gave one flower to each of her friends, each one a bright golden light. Her eyes were brimming with tears as she walked out into the river of the shining lights. The water clung to her until she was covered all over in light. The door that had opened on the high hillside closed behind her.

And now she stands alone above the watershed and looks out upon a day in the world spreading out before her. All the things of the world are like shining jewels to her eyes. Life is waiting for her. She takes a step.

Between Ourselves

Audre Lorde

Once when I walked into a room
my eyes would seek out the one or two black faces
for contact or reassurance or a sign
I was not alone
now walking into rooms full of black faces
that would destroy me for any difference
where shall my eyes look?
Once it was easy to know
who were my people.

If we were stripped to our strength
of all pretense
and our flesh was cut away
the sun would bleach all our bones as white
as the face of my black mother
was bleached white by gold
or Orishala
and how
does that measure me?

I do not believe
our wants have made all our lies
holy.

Under the sun on the shores of Elmina
a black man sold the woman who carried
my grandmother in her belly
he was paid with bright yellow coin
that shone in the evening sun
and in the faces of her sons and daughters.
When I see that brother behind my eyes
his irises are bloodless and without color
his tongue clicks like yellow coins
tossed up on this shore
where we share the same corner
of an alien and corrupted heaven
and whenever I try to eat
the words
of easy blackness as salvation
I taste the color
of my grandmother's first betrayal.

I do not believe
our wants have made all our lies
holy.

But I do not whistle his name at the shrine of Shopona
I do not bring down the rosy juices of death upon him
nor forget Orishala
is called the god of whiteness
who works in the dark wombs of night
forming the shapes we all wear
so that even cripples and dwarfs and albinos
are scared worshipers
when the boiled corn is offered.

Humility lies
in the face of history
I have forgiven myself
for him
for the white meat
we all consumed in secret
before we were born
we shared the same meal.
When you impale me
upon your lances of narrow blackness
before you hear my heart speak
mourn your own borrowed blood
your own borrowed visions.
Do not mistake my flesh for the enemy
do not write my name in the dust
before the shrine of the god of smallpox
for we are all children of Eshu
god of chance and the unpredictable
and we each wear many changes
inside of our skin.

Armed with scars
healed
in many different colors
I look in my own faces
as Eshu's daughter crying
if we do not stop killing
the other
in ourselves

the self that we hate
in others
soon we shall all lie
in the same direction
and Eshidale's priests will be very busy
they who alone can bury
all those who seek their own death
by jumping up from the ground
and landing upon their heads.

From *The Black Unicorn*

En rapport, In Opposition: *Gloria Anzaldúa*
Cobrando cuentas
a las nuestras

Watch For Falling Rocks

The first time I drove from El Paso to San Diego, I saw a sign that read *Watch for Falling Rocks*. And though I watched and waited for rocks to roll down the steep cliff walls and attack my car and me, I never saw any falling rocks. Today, one of the things I'm most afraid of are the rocks we throw at each other. And the resultant guilt we carry like a corpse strapped to our backs for having thrown rocks. We colored women have memories like elephants. The slightest hurt is recorded deep within. We do not forget the injury done to us and we do not forget the injury we have done another. For unfortunately we do not have hides like elephants. Our vulnerability is measured by our capacity for openness, intimacy. And we all know that our own kind is driven through shame or self-hatred to poke at all our open wounds. And we know they know exactly where the hidden wounds are.

> I keep track of all distinctions. Between past and present. Pain and pleasure. Living and surviving. Resistance and capitulation. Will and circumstances. Between life and death. Yes. I am scrupulously accurate. I have become a keeper of accounts.
>
> —IRENA KLEPFISZ[1]

One of the changes that I've seen since *This Bridge Called My Back* was published[2] is that we no longer allow white women to efface us or suppress us. Now we do it to each other. We have taken over the missionary's "let's civilize the savage role," fixating on the "wrongness" and moral or political inferiority of some of our sisters, insisting on a profound difference between oneself and the *Other*. We have been indoctrinated into adopting the old imperialist ways of conquering and dominating, adopting a way of confrontation based on differences while standing on the ground of ethnic superiority.

In the "dominant" phase of colonialism, European colonizers exercise direct control of the colonized, destroy the native legal and cultural systems, and negate non-European civilizations in order to ruthlessly exploit the resources of the subjugated with the excuse of attempting to "civilize" them. Before the end of this phase, the natives internalize Western culture. By the time we reach the "neocolonialist" phase, we've accepted the white colonizers' system of values, attitudes, morality, and modes of production.[3] It is not by chance that in the more rural towns of Texas Chicano neighborhoods are called *colonias* rather than *barrios*.

There have always been those of us who have "cooperated" with the colonizers. It's not that we have been "won" over by the dominant culture, but that it has exploited pre-existing power relations of subordination and subjugation within our native societies.[4] The great White ripoff and they are still cashing in. Like our exploiters who fixate on the inferiority of the natives, we fixate on the fucked-upness of our sisters. Like them we try to impose our version of "the ways things should be"; we try to impose one's self on the *Other* by making her the recipient of one's negative elements, usually the same elements that the Anglo projected on us. Like them, we project our self-hatred on her; we stereotype her; we make her generic.

Just How Ethnic Are You?

One of the reasons for this hostility among us is the forced cultural penetration, the rape of the colored by the white, with the colonizers depositing their perspective, their language, their values in our bodies. External oppression is paralleled with our internalization of that oppression. And our acting out from that oppression. They have us doing to those within our own ranks what they have done and continue to do to us—*Othering* people. That is, isolating them, pushing them out of the herd, ostracizing them. The internalization of negative images of ourselves, our self-hatred, poor self-esteem, makes our own people the *Other*. We shun the white-looking Indian, the "high yellow" Black woman, the Asian with the white lover, the Native woman who brings her white girl friend to the Pow Wow, the Chicana who doesn't speak Spanish, the academic, the uneducated. Her difference makes her a person we can't trust. *Para que sea "legal,"* she must pass the ethnic legitimacy test we have devised. And it is exactly our internalized whiteness that desperately wants boundary lines (this part of me is Mexican, this Indian) marked out and woe to any sister or any part of us that steps out of our assigned places, woe to anyone who doesn't measure up to our standards of ethnicity. *Si no cualifica*, if she fails to pass the test, *le aventamos mierda en la cara, le aventamos piedras, la aventamos.* We throw shit in her face, we throw rocks, we kick her out. *Como gallos de pelea nos atacamos unas a las otras—mexicanas de nacimiento contra* the born-again *mexicanas*. Like fighting cocks, razor blades strapped to our fingers, we slash out at each other. We have turned our anger against ourselves. And our anger is immense. *Es un acido que corroe.*

Internal Affairs *o las que niegan a su gente*

> *Tū traición yo la llevo aquá muy dentro,*
> *la llevo dentro de mi alma*
> *dentro de mi corazón.*
> *Tu traición.*
> —CORNELIO REYNA[5]

I get so tired of constantly struggling with my sisters. The more we have in common, including love, the greater the heartache between us, the more we hurt each other. It's excruciatingly painful, this constant snarling at our own shadows. Anything can set the conflict in motion: the lover getting more recognition by the community, the friend getting a job with higher status, a break-up. As one of my friends said, "We can't fucking get along."

So we find ourselves *entreguerras*,[6] a kind of civil war among intimates, an in-class, in-race, in-house fighting, a war with strategies, tactics that are our coping mechanisms, that once were our survival skills and which we now use upon one another,[7] producing intimate terrorism—a modern form of *las guerras floridas*, the war of flowers that the Aztecs practiced in order to gain captives for the sacrifices. Only now we are each other's victims, we offer the *Other* to our politically correct altar.

El deniego. The hate we once cast at our oppressors we now fling at women of our own race. Reactionary—we have gone to the other extreme—denial of our own. We struggle for power, compete, vie for control. Like kin, we are there for each other, but like kin we come to blows. And the differences between us and this new *Other* are not racial but ideological, not metaphysical but psychological. *Nos negamos a si mismas y el deniego nos causa daño.*

Breaking Out of the Frame

> I'm standing at the sea end of the truncated Berkeley pier. A boat had plowed into the black posts gouging out a few hundred feet of structure, cutting the pier in two. I stare at the sea, surging silver-plated, between me and the loped-off corrugated arm, the wind whipping my hair. I look down, my head and shoulders, a shadow on the sea. Yemaya pours strings of light over my dull jade, flickering body, bubbles pop out of my ears. I feel the tension easing and, for the first time in months, the litany of work yet to do, of deadlines, that sings incessantly in my head, blows away with the wind.
>
> Oh, Yemaya, I shall speak the words
> you lap against the pier.

> But as I turn away I see in the distance a ship's fin fast approaching. I see fish heads lying listless in the sun, smell the stench of pollution in the waters.

From where I stand, *queridas carnalas*—in a feminist position—I see, through a critical lens with variable focus, that we must not drain our energy breaking down the male/white frame (the whole of Western culture) but turn to our own kind and change our terms of reference. As long as we see the world and our experiences through white eyes—in a dominant/subordinate way—we're trapped in the tar and pitch of the old manipulative and strive-for-power ways.

Even those of us who don't want to buy in get sucked into the vortex of the dominant culture's fixed oppositions, the duality of superiority and inferiority, of subject and object. Some of us, to get out of the internalized neocolonial phase, make for the fringes, the Borderlands. And though we have not broken out of the white frame, we at least see it for what it is. Questioning the values of the dominant culture which imposes fundamental difference on those of the "wrong" side of the good/bad dichotomy is the first step. Responding to the *Other* not as irrevocably different is the second step. By highlighting similarities, downplaying divergences, that is, by *rapprochement* between self and *Other* it is possible to build a syncretic relationship. At the basis of such a relationship lies an understanding of the effects of colonization and its resultant pathologies.

We have our work cut out for us. Nothing is more difficult than identifying emotionally with a cultural alterity, with the *Other*. *Alter:* to make different; to castrate. *Altercate:* to dispute angrily. *Alter ego:* another self or another aspect of oneself. *Alter idem:* another of the same kind. Nothing is harder than identifying with an interracial identity, with a mestizo identity. One has to leave the permanent boundaries of a fixed self, literally "leave" oneself and see oneself through the eyes of the *Other*. Cultural identity is "nothing more nor less than the mean between selfhood and otherness...."[8] Nothing scares the Chicana more than a quasi Chicana; nothing disturbs a Mexican more than an acculturated Chicana; nothing agitates a Chicana more than a Latina who lumps her with the *norteamericanas*. It is easier to retreat to the safety of difference behind racial, cultural and class borders. Because our awareness of the *Other* as object often swamps our awareness of ourselves as subject, it is hard to maintain a fine balance between cultural ethnicity and the continuing survival of that culture, between traditional culture and an evolving hybrid culture. How much must remain the same, how much must change.

For most of us our ethnicity is still the issue. Ours continues to be a struggle of identity—not against a white background so much as against a colored background. *Ya no estamos afuera o atras del marco de la pintura*—we not longer stand outside nor behind the frame of the painting. We are both the foreground, the background and the figures predominating. Whites are not the central figure, they are not even in the frame, though the frame of reference is still white, male and heterosexual. But the white is still there, invisible, under our skin—we have subsumed the white.

El desengaño/Disillusionment

And yes I have some criticism, some self-criticism. And no I will not make everything nice. There is shit among us we need to sift through. Who knows, there may be some fertilizer in it. I've seen collaborative efforts between us end in verbal abuse, cruelty and trauma. I've seen collectives fall apart, dumping their ideals by the wayside and treating each other worse than they'd treat a rabid dog. My momma said, "Never tell other people our business, never divulge family secrets." Chicano dirt you do not air out in front of white folks, nor lesbian dirty laundry in front of heterosexuals. The cultural things stay with la Raza. Colored feminists must present a united front in front of whites and other groups. But the fact is we are not united. (I've come to suspect that unity is another Anglo invention like their one sole god and the myth of the monopole.[9]) We are not going to cut through *la mierda* by sweeping the dirt under the rug.

We have a responsibility to each other, certain commitments. The leap into self-affirmation goes hand in hand with being critical of self. Many of us walk around with reactionary, self-righteous attitudes. We preach certain political behaviors and theories and we do fine with writing about them. Though we want others to live their lives by them, we do not live them. When we are called on it, we go into a self-defensive mode and denial just like whites did when we started asking them to be accountable for their race and class biases.

Las opuestas/Those in Opposition

In us, intra- and cross-cultural hostilities surface in not so subtle put-downs. *Las no comprometidas, las que negan a sus gente. Fruncemos las caras y negamos toda responsabilidad.* Where some of us racially mixed people are stuck in now is denial and its damaging effects. Denial of the white aspects that we've been forced to acquire, denial of our sisters who for one reason or another cannot "pass" as 100% ethnic—as if such a thing exists. Racial purity, like language purity, is a fallacy. Denying the reality of who we are destroys the basis needed from which to talk honestly and deeply about the issues between us. We cannot make any real connections because we are not touching each other. So we sit facing each other and before the words escape our mouths the real issues are blanked in our consciousness, erased before they register because it hurts too much to talk about them, because it makes us vulnerable to the hurt the *carnala* may dish out, because we've been wounded too deeply and too often in the past. So we sit, a paper face before another paper face—two people who suddenly cease to be real. *La no compasiva con la complaciente, lo incomunicado atorado en sus gargantas.*

We, the new Inquisitors, swept along with the "swing to the right" of the growing religious and political intolerance, crusade against racial heretics, mow down with the sickle of righteous anger our dissenting sisters. The issue (in all aspects of life) has always been when to resist changes and when to be open to them. Right now, this rigidity will break us.

Recobrando/Recovering

Una luz fria y cenicienta bañada en la plata palida del amanecer entra a mi escritorio and I think about the critical stages we feminists of color are going through, chiefly that of learning to live with each other as *carnalas, parientes, amantes,* as kin, as friends, as lovers. Looking back on the road that we've walked on during the last decade, I see many emotional, psychological, spiritual, political gains—primarily developing an understanding and acceptance of the spirituality of our root ethnic cultures. This has given us the ground from which to see that our spiritual lives are not split from our daily acts. *En recobrando* our affinity with nature and her forces (deities), we have "recovered" our ancient identity, digging it out like dark clay, pressing it to our current identity, molding past and present, inner and outer. Our clay-streaked faces acquiring again images of our ethnic self and self-respect taken from us by the *colonizadores.* And if we've suffered losses, if often in the process we have momentarily "misplaced" our *carnala*hood, our sisterhood, there beside us always are the women, *las mujeres.* And that is enough to keep us going.

By grounding in the earth of our native spiritual identity, we can build up our personal and tribal identity. We can reach out for the clarity we need. Burning sage and sweetgrass by itself won't cut it, but it can be a basis from which we act.

And yes, we are elephants with long memories, but scrutinizing the past with binocular vision and training it on the juncture of past with present, and identifying the options on hand and mapping out future roads will ensure us survival.

So if we won't forget past grievances, let us forgive. Carrying the ghosts of past grievances *no vale la pena.* It is not worth the grief. It keeps us from ourselves and each other; it keeps us from new relationships. We need to cultivate other ways of coping. I'd like to think that the in-fighting that we presently find ourselves doing is only a stage in the continuum of our growth, an offshoot of the conflict that the process of biculturation spawns, a phase of the internal colonization process, one that will soon cease to hold sway over our lives. I'd like to see it as a skin we will shed as we are born into the 21st century.

And now in these times of the turning of the century, of harmonic conversion, of the end of *El Quinto Sol* (as the ancient Aztecs named our present age), it is time we began to get out of the state of opposition and into *rapprochment*, time to get our heads, words, ways out of white territory. It is time that we broke out of the invisible white frame and stood on the ground of our own ethnic being.

From *Sinister Wisdom* 33

Notes

1. Irena Klepfisz, *Keeper of Accounts* (Montpelier, VT: Sinister Wisdom, 1982), 85.

2. According to Chela Sandoval, the publication of *Bridge* marked the end of the second wave of the women's movement in its previous form. *U.S. Third World Feminist Criticism: The Theory and Method of Oppositional Consciousness*, a dissertation in process.

3. Abdul R. JanMohamed, "The Economy of Manichean Allegory: The Function of Racial Difference in Colonialist Literature," *"Race," Writing, and Difference*, ed. Henry Louis Gates, Jr. (Chicago: University of Chicago Press, 1985), 80–81.

4. JanMohamed, 81.

5. A Chicano from Texas who sings and plays *bajo-sexto* in his *música norteña/conjunto*. *"Tu Traición"* is from the album *15 Exitasos*, Reyna Records, 1981.

6. *Entreguerras, entremundos/Inner Wars Among the Worlds* is the title of a forthcoming book of narratives/novel.

7. Sarah Hoagland, "Lesbian Ethics: Intimacy & Self-Understanding," *Bay Area Women's News*, May/June 1987, vol. 1, no. 2, 7.

8. Nadine Gordimer is quoted in JanMohamed's essay, 88.

9. Physicists are searching for a single law of physics under which all other laws will fall.

3 (De) Colonized Selves: Finding Hope Through Horror

I Give You Back

Joy Harjo

I release you, my beautiful and terrible
fear. I release you. You were my beloved
and hated twin, but now, I don't know you
as myself. I release you with all the
pain I would know at the death of
my daughters.

You are not my blood anymore.

I give you back to the white soldiers
who burned down my home, beheaded my children,
raped and sodomized my brothers and sisters.
I give you back to those who stole the
food from our plates when we were starving.

I release you, fear, because you hold
these scenes in front of me and I was born
with eyes that can never close.

I release you, fear, so you can no longer
keep me naked and frozen in the winter,
or smothered under blankets in the summer.

I release you
I release you
I release you
I release you

I am not afraid to be angry.
I am not afraid to rejoice.
I am not afraid to be black.
I am not afraid to be white.
I am not afraid to be hungry.
I am not afraid to be full.
I am not afraid to be hated.
I am not afraid to be loved.

to be loved, to be loved, fear.

Oh, you have choked me, but I gave you the leash.
You have gutted me but I gave you the knife.
You have devoured me, but I laid myself across the fire.
You held my mother down and raped her,
               but I gave you the heated thing.

I take myself back, fear.
You are not my shadow any longer.
I won't hold you in my hands.
You can't live in my eyes, my ears, my voice
my belly, or in my heart my heart
my heart   my heart

But come here, fear
I am alive and you are so afraid
                  of dying.

From *She Had Some Horses*

To Omoni, In Korea

*Anne Mi Ok
Bruining*

Just before falling
asleep you appear before
me, I, slipping

off the foggy edge
into restless oblivion
a vague *nyo* figure hovering
a few inches from my bedroom curtain

then with a brilliant
light
behind the lids of my eyes

oh the glaring
sight of you, the soft
hazy words
of *hangul* sing

to me the sweet notes
of a once familiar song
now harboring only
the mournful *um-ok*
of unremembered memories.

I am your daughter
your child, dear *yo-ja*
I myself a *yo-ja* now
whimpering and crying
to you still
feeling the child
like yearnings
from a previous life when

I feel the comforting
pyong-hwa of your steady
self and am quieted
by the soothing
strokes and caressing
touches and rocking
of your body as I fall
asleep in your arms.

I see your dark, ghostly
sa-mang eyes, moist and lined
from the invisible scars
of an incomplete motherhood
perhaps you still mourn.

Your almost black hair
streaked with white
from
go-saeng of giving me up
and not surviving
the loss after all.

Yet, I see you
no-ryok and resilient
as the warrior
fighting the battle
to survive
in me

when you were alive
before I was left behind
yong-won on the grey, cement
City Hall steps in Seoul
you were living before

my years of sleeping
on a tiny, thin mattress
with dozens of other
children, each clutching
her only possession, a doll
or a broken toy

within the cold, grey walls
of the orphanage
you had a *ttal*

who learned to never
feel *shin-tak*
or wonder aloud about you
after I was adopted
while the questions surfaced
into silence.

I feel neither the regret
nor the anger, and no,
it isn't the pain, nor the cruelty
but a longing *hae-mang* I ache

when we do meet someday
I have abandoned
bitter resentment
I see the *sa-shil* of your tears
touch your face
feel your pain

that what you feel is a small
element of *cha-bu-sim*
and all of our unspoken
questions will be
answered in the reality
of realizing that

the moment I will miss
you the most will be
when I give birth
to my future *ttal.*

Then the circle will be
complete, and a gift
of *ae-jeong* will have entered
into this mortal world
for us, *Omoni.*

---

nyo   female
hangul   our native "Korean" language
um-ok   music
yo-ja   woman
pyong-hwa   peace
sa-mang   death
go-saeng   hardship
no-ryok   strength
yong-won   forever
shin-tak   trust
hae-mang   hope
sa-shil   truth
cha-bu-sim   pride
ttal   daughter
ae-jeong   love
omoni   (birth) mother

A Letter to My Daughter

Siu Wai Anderson

August 1989, Boston

Dear Maya Shao-ming,

You were born at Mt. Auburn Hospital in Cambridge on June 6, 1989, an auspicious date, and for me, the end of a long, long travail. Because you insisted on being breech, with your head always close to my heart, you came into the world by C-section into a chilly O.R. at the opposite end of the labor and delivery suite where, exhausted yet exuberant, I pushed out your brother in a birthing room nearly four years ago.

I couldn't believe my ears when your father exclaimed, "A girl!" All I could do was cry the tears of a long-awaited dream come true. You are so beautiful, with your big dark eyes and silky black hair. Your skin is more creamy than golden, reflecting your particular "happa haole" blend. But your long elegant fingers are those of a Chinese scholar, prized for high intelligence and sensitivity.

You are more than just a second child, more than just a girl to match our boy, to fit the demographical nuclear family with the proverbial 2.5 children. No, ten years ago I wrote a song for an unborn dream: a dark-haired, dark-eyed child who would be my flesh-and-blood link to humanity. I had no other until your brother came. He was my first Unborn Song. But you, little daughter, are the link to our female line, the legacy of another woman's pain and sacrifice thirty-one year ago.

Let me tell your about your Chinese grandmother. Somewhere in Hong Kong, in the late fifties, a young waitress found herself pregnant by a cook, probably a co-worker at her restaurant. She carried the baby to term, suffered to give it birth, and kept the little girl for the first three months of her life. I like to think that my mother—your grandmother—loved me and fought to raise me on her own, but that the daily struggle was too hard. Worn down by the demands of the new baby and perhaps the constant threat of starvation, she made the agonizing decision to give away her girl so that both of us might have a chance for a better life.

More likely, I was dumped at the orphanage steps or forcibly removed from a home of abuse and neglect by a social welfare worker. I will probably never know the truth. Having a baby in her unmarried state would have brought shame on the family in China, so she probably kept my existence a secret. Once I was out of her life, it was as if I had never been born. And so you and your brother and I are the missing leaves on an ancestral tree.

Do they ever wonder if we exist?

I was brought to the U.S. before I was two, and adopted by the Anglo parents who hail you as their latest beautiful grandchild. Raised by a minister's family in postwar American prosperity and nourished on three square meals a day, I grew like a wild weed and soaked up all the opportunities they had to offer—books, music, education, church life and community activities. Amidst a family of blue-eyed blonds, though, I stood out like a sore thumb. Whether from jealousy or fear of someone who looked so different, my older brothers sometimes tormented me with racist name-calling, teased me about my poor eyesight and unsightly skin, or made fun of my clumsy walk. Moody and impatient, gifted and temperamental, burdened by fears and nightmares that none of us realized stemmed from my early years of deprivation, I was not an easy child to love. My adoptive mother and I clashed countless times over the years, but gradually came to see one another as real human beings with faults and talents, and as women of strength in our own right. Now we love each other very much, though the scars and memories of our early battles will never quite fade. Lacking a mirror image in the mother who raised me, I had to seek my identity as a woman on my own. The Asian American community has helped me reclaim my dual identity and enlightened my view of the struggles we face as minorities in a white-dominated culture. They have applauded my music and praised my writings.

But part of me will always be missing: my beginnings, my personal history, all the subtle details that give a person her origin. I don't know how I was born, whether it was vaginally or by Cesarean. I don't know when, or where exactly, how much I weighed, or whose ears heard my first cry of life. Was I put to my mother's breast and tenderly rocked, or was I simply weighed, cleaned, swaddled and carted off to a sterile nursery, noted in the hospital records as "newborn female"?

Someone took the time to give me a lucky name, and write the appropriate characters in neat brush strokes in the Hong Kong city register. "Siu" means "little." My kind of "wai" means "clever" or "wise." Therefore, my baby name was "Clever little one." Who chose those words? Who cared enough to note my arrival in the world?

I lost my Chinese name for eighteen years. It was Americanized for convenience to "Sue." But like an ill-fitting coat, it made me twitch and fret and squirm. I hated the name. But even more, I hated being Chinese. It took many years to become proud of my Asian heritage and work up the courage to take back my birthname. That plus a smattering of classroom Cantonese, are all the Chinese culture I have to offer you, little one. Not white, certainly, but not really Asian, I straddle the two worlds and try to blaze your trails for you. Your name, "Shao-ming," is very much like mine—"Shao" is the Mandarin form of "Siu," meaning "little." And "ming" is "bright," as in a shining sun or moon. Whose lives will you brighten, little Maya? Your past is more complete than mine, and each day I cradle you in your babyhood, lavishing upon you the tender care I lacked for my first two years. When I console you, I comfort the lost baby inside me who still cries out for her mother. No wonder so many adoptees desperately long to have children of their own.

Sweet Maya, it doesn't matter what you "become" later on. You have already fulfilled my wildest dreams.

I love you,

Mommy

Journeys of the Mind

Anne Waters

Seminole/Choctaw/
Chicksaw/Cherokee

You cannot
extricate
my Indianness
my Jewishness
my Lesbianness.
You cannot
reach in and
exorcise that
pain, or joy.

You can take
me to your schools
but you cannot
take my mind
because
Indians and Jews
and Lesbians
don't forget
we don't forget
we remember—always
because we can't
forget.

You can dress me
in your clothes
cut my hair
make up my face
put heeled shoes
on my feet
and force me
to paint
a smile on
my face.
But I won't forget.
I remember.

Because Indians
and Jews and
Lesbians
don't forget.

In the first cycle
I absorb
all that is
about me.
what said
what seen
what heard
what I learn
as a small child
—someone places a
cowboy hat and gun
on my body
I pulling   I tugging
     off
   throwing to the floor
run in silence to
my mother's arms.
We never forget
this first cycle.

In the second cycle
I am taught contradictory
values—schooled in
white ways my father but
not my mother trusted—
forced to assimilate
made forgetful
placed on a path not
of my own choosing
I am dosed with
amnesia for years
and years and years.
I become the light-skinned
terror of my own dreams—
chased by everyone.
I become outside
the frame of the
picture.

The third cycle
begins with
alienated confusion
as the amnesia of
childhood breaks
I dig into my own
I crawl out of lies and
into my mother's life.
I look at her with
new eyes   new sight
and new ears that
demand she re-tell
the stories of old
because *she*
has *not* forgotten.
In the third cycle
I try to sort out
what is
and what is not
mine.

After five months
of not holding down
my food
after reclaiming
re-knowing
re-membering
I pick up the pieces.
and finding myself
I emerge
no longer a victim
of my own self-destruction.
I am a Lesbian of color
who refuses
to be
washed out.

From *Living the Spirit: A Gay American Indian Anthology*

You're Short, Besides!

Sucheng Chan

When asked to write about being a physically handicapped Asian American woman, I considered it an insult. After all, my accomplishments are many, yet I was not asked to write about any of them. Is being handicapped the most salient feature about me? The fact that it might be in the eyes of others made me decide to write the essay as requested. I realized that the way I think about myself may differ considerably from the way others perceive me. And maybe that's what being physically handicapped is all about.

I was stricken simultaneously with pneumonia and polio at the age of four. Uncertain whether I had polio of the lungs, seven of the eight doctors who attended me—all practitioners of Western medicine—told my parents they should not feel optimistic about my survival. A Chinese fortune teller my mother consulted also gave a grim prognosis, but for an entirely different reason: I had been stricken because my name was offensive to the gods. My grandmother had named me "grandchild of wisdom," a name that the fortune teller said was too presumptuous for a girl. So he advised my parents to change my name to "chaste virgin." All these pessimistic predictions notwithstanding, I hung onto life, if only by a thread. For three years, my body was periodically pierced with electric shocks as the muscles of my legs atrophied. Before my illness, I had been an active, rambunctious, precocious, and very curious child. Being confined to bed was thus a mental agony as great as my physical pain. Living in war-torn China, I received little medical attention; physical therapy was unheard of. But I was determined to walk. So one day, when I was six or seven, I instructed my mother to set up two rows of chairs to face each other so that I could use them as I would parallel bars. I attempted to walk by holding my body up and moving it forward with my arms while dragging my legs along behind. Each time I fell, my mother gasped, but I badgered her until she let me try again. After four nonambulatory years, I finally walked once more by pressing my hands against my thighs so my knees wouldn't buckle.

My father had been away from home during most of those years because of the war. When he returned, I had to confront the guilt he felt about my condition. In many East Asian cultures, there is a strong folk belief that a person's physical state in this life is a reflection of how morally or sinfully he or she lived in previous lives. Furthermore, because of the tendency to view the family as a single unit, it is believed that the fate of one member can be caused by the behavior of another. Some of my father's relatives told him that my illness had doubtless been caused by the wild carousing he did in his youth. A well-meaning but somewhat simple man, my father believed them.

Throughout my childhood, he sometimes apologized to me for having to suffer retribution for his former bad behavior. This upset me; it was bad enough that I had to deal with the anguish of not being able to walk, but to have to assuage his guilt as well was a real burden! In other ways, my father was very good to me. He took me out often, carrying me on his shoulders or back, to give me fresh air and sunshine. He did this until I was too large and heavy for him to carry. And ever since I can remember, he has told me that I am pretty.

After getting over her anxieties about my constant falls, my mother decided to send me to school. I had already learned to read some words of Chinese at the age of three by asking my parents to teach me the sounds and meaning of various characters in the daily newspaper. But between the ages of four and eight, I received no education since just staying alive was a full-time job. Much to her chagrin, my mother found no school in Shanghai, where we lived at the time, which would accept me as a student. Finally, as a last resort, she approached the American School, which agreed to enroll me only if my family kept an *amah* (a servant who takes care of children) by my side at all times. The tuition at the school was twenty U.S. dollars per month—a huge sum of money during those years of runaway inflation in China—and payable only in U.S. dollars. My family afforded the high cost of tuition and the expense of employing a full-time *amah* for less than a year.

We left China as the Communist forces swept across the country in victory. We found an apartment in Hong Kong across the street from a school run by Seventh-Day Adventists. By that time I could walk a little, so the principal was persuaded to accept me. An *amah* now had to take care of me only during recess when my classmates might easily knock me over as they ran about the playground.

After a year and a half in Hong Kong, we moved to Malaysia, where my father's family had lived for four generations. There I learned to swim in the lovely warm waters of the tropics and fell in love with the sea. On land I was a cripple; in the ocean I could move with the grace of a fish. I liked the freedom of being in the water so much that many years later, when I was a graduate student in Hawaii, I became greatly enamored with a man just because he called me a "Polynesian water nymph."

As my overall health improved, my mother became less anxious about all aspects of my life. She did everything possible to enable me to lead as normal a life as possible. I remember how once some of her colleagues in the high school where she taught criticized her for letting me wear short skirts. They felt my legs should not be exposed to public view. My mother's response was, "All girls her age wear short skirts, so why shouldn't she?"

The years in Malaysia were the happiest of my childhood, even though I was constantly fending off children who ran after me calling, "*Baikah! Baikah!*" ("Cripple! Cripple!" in the Hokkien dialect commonly spoken in Malaysia). The taunts of children mattered little because I was a star pupil. I won one award after another for general scholarship as well as for art and public speaking. Whenever the school had important visitors my teacher always called on me to recite in front of the class.

A significant event that marked me indelibly occurred when I was twelve. That year my school held a music recital and I was one of the students chosen to play the piano. I managed to get up the steps to the stage without any problem, but as I walked across the stage, I fell. Out of the audience, a voice said loudly and clearly, "Ayah! A *baikah* shouldn't be allowed to perform in public." I got up before anyone could get on stage to help me and, with tears streaming uncontrollably down my face, I rushed to the piano and began to play. Beethoven's "Für Elise" had never been played so fiendishly fast before or since, but I managed to finish the whole piece. That I managed to do so made me feel really strong. I never again feared ridicule.

In later years I was reminded of this experience from time to time. During my fourth year as an assistant professor at the University of California at Berkeley, I won a distinguished teaching award. Some weeks later I ran into a former professor who congratulated me enthusiastically. But I said to him, "You know what? I became a distinguished teacher by *limping* across the stage of Dwinelle 155!" (Dwinelle 155 is a large, cold, classroom that most colleagues of mine hate to teach in.) I was rude not because I lacked graciousness but because this man, who had told me that my dissertation was the finest piece of work he had read in fifteen years, had nevertheless advised me to eschew a teaching career.

"Why?" I asked.

"Your leg..." he responded.

"What about my leg?" I said, puzzled.

"Well, how would you feel standing in front of a large lecture class?"

"If it makes any difference, I want you to know I've won a number of speech contests in my life, and I am not the least bit self-conscious about speaking in front of large audiences.... Look, why don't you write me a letter of recommendation to tell people how brilliant I am, and let *me* worry about my leg!"

This incident is worth recounting only because it illustrates a dilemma that handicapped persons face frequently: those who care about us sometimes get so protective that they unwittingly limit our growth. This former professor of mine had been one of my greatest supporters for two decades. Time after time, he had written glowing letters of recommendation on my behalf. He had spoken as he did because he thought he had my best interests at heart; he thought that if I got a desk job rather than one that required me to be a visible, public person, I would be spared the misery of being stared at.

Americans, for the most part, do not believe as Asians do that physically handicapped persons are morally flawed. But they are equally inept at interacting with those of us who are not able-bodied. Cultural differences in the perception and treatment of handicapped people are most clearly expressed by adults. Children, regardless of where they are, tend to be openly curious about people who do not look "normal." Adults in Asia have no hesitation in asking visibly handicapped people what is wrong with them, often expressing their sympathy with looks of pity, whereas adults in the United States try desperately to be polite by pretending not to notice.

One interesting response I often elicited from people in Asia but have never encountered in America is the attempt to link my physical condition to the state of my soul. Many a time while living and traveling in Asia people would ask me what religion I belonged to. I would tell them that my mother is a devout Buddhist, that my father was baptized a Catholic but has never practiced Catholicism, and that I am an agnostic. Upon hearing this, people would try strenuously to convert me to their religion so that whichever God they believed in could bless me. If I would only attend this church or that temple regularly, they urged, I would surely get cured. Catholics and Buddhists alike have pressed religious medallions into my palm, telling me if I would wear these, the relevant deity or saint would make me well. Once while visiting the tomb of Muhammad Ali Jinnah in Karachi, Pakistan, an old Muslim, after finishing his evening prayers, spotted me, gestured toward my legs, raised his arms heavenward, and began a new round of prayers, apparently on my behalf.

In the United States adults who try to act "civilized" toward handicapped people by pretending they don't notice anything unusual sometimes end up ignoring handicapped people completely. In the first few months I lived in this country, I was struck by the fact that whenever children asked me what was the matter with my leg, their adult companions would hurriedly shush them up, furtively look at me, mumble apologies, and rush their children away. After a few months of such encounters, I decided it was my responsibility to educate these people. So I would say to the flustered adults, "It's okay, let the kid ask." Turning to the child, I would say, "When I was a little girl, no bigger than you are, I became sick with something called polio. The muscles of my leg shrank up and I couldn't walk very well. You're much luckier than I am because now you can get a vaccine to make sure you never get my disease. So don't cry when your mommy takes you to get a polio vaccine, okay?" Some adults and their little companions I talked to this way were glad to be rescued from embarrassment; others thought I was strange.

Americans have another way of covering up their uneasiness: they become jovially patronizing. Sometimes when people spot my crutch, they ask if I've had a skiing accident. When I answer that unfortunately it is something less glamorous than that they say, "I bet you *could* ski if you put your mind to it!" Alternately, at parties where people dance, men who ask me to dance with them get almost belligerent when I decline their invitation. They say, "Of course you can dance if you *want* to!" Some have given me pep talks about how if I would only develop the right mental attitude, I would have more fun in life.

Different cultural attitudes toward handicapped persons came out clearly during my wedding. My father-in-law, as solid a representative of middle America as could be found, had no qualms about objecting to the marriage on racial grounds, but he could bring himself to comment on my handicap only indirectly. He wondered why his son, who had dated numerous high school and college beauty queens, couldn't marry one of them instead of me. My mother-in-law, a devout Christian, did not share her husband's prejudices, but she worried aloud about whether I could have children. Some Chinese friends of my parents, on the other hand, said that I was lucky to have found such a noble man, one who would marry me despite my handicap. I, for my part, appeared in church in a white lace wedding dress I had designed and made myself—a miniskirt!

How Asian Americans treat me with respect to my handicap tells me a great deal about their degree of acculturation. Recent immigrants behave just like Asians in Asia; those who have been here longer or who grew up in the United States behave more like their white counterparts. I have not encountered any distinctly Asian American pattern of response. What makes the experience of Asian American handicapped people unique is the duality of responses we elicit.

Regardless of racial or cultural background, most handicapped people have to learn to find a balance between the desire to attain physical independence and the need to take care of ourselves by not overtaxing our bodies. In my case, I've had to learn to accept the fact that leading an active life has its price. Between the ages of eight and eighteen, I walked without using crutches or braces but the effort caused my right leg to become badly misaligned. Soon after I came to the United States, I had a series of operations to straighten out the bones of my right leg; afterwards though my leg looked straighter and presumably better, I could no longer walk on my own. Initially my doctors fitted me with a brace, but I found wearing one cumbersome and soon gave it up. I could move around much more easily—and more important, faster—by using one crutch. One orthopedist after another warned me that using a single crutch was a bad practice. They were right. Over the years my spine developed a double-S curve and for the last twenty years I have suffered from severe, chronic back pains, which neither conventional physical therapy nor a lighter work load can eliminate.

The only thing that helps my backaches is a good massage, but the soothing effect lasts no more than a day or two. Massages are expensive, especially when one needs them three times a week. So I found a job that pays better, but at which I have to work longer hours, consequently increasing the physical strain on my body—a sort of vicious circle. When I was in my thirties, my doctors told me that if I kept leading the strenuous life I did, I would be in a wheelchair by the time I was forty. They were right on target: I bought myself a wheelchair when I was forty-one. But being the incorrigible character that I am, I use it only when I am *not* in a hurry!

It is a good thing, however, that I am too busy to think much about my handicap or my backaches because pain can physically debilitate as well as cause depression. And there are days when my spirits get rather low. What has helped me is realizing that being handicapped is akin to growing old at an accelerated rate. The contradiction I experience is that often my mind races along as though I'm only twenty while my body feels about sixty. But fifteen or twenty years hence, unlike my peers who will have to cope with aging for the first time, I shall be full of cheer because I will have already fought, and I hope won, that battle long ago.

Beyond learning how to be physically independent and, for some of us, living with chronic pain or other kinds of discomfort, the most difficult thing a handicapped person has to deal with, especially during puberty and early adulthood, is relating to potential sexual partners. Because American culture places so much emphasis on physical attractiveness, a person with a shriveled limb, or a tilt to the head, or the inability to speak clearly, experiences great uncertainty—indeed trauma—when interacting with someone to whom he or she is attracted. My problem was that I was not only physically handicapped, small, and short, but worse, I also wore glasses and was smarter than all the boys I knew! Alas, an insurmountable combination. Yet somehow I have managed to have intimate relationships, all of them with extraordinary men. Not surprisingly, there have also been countless men who broke my heart—men who enjoyed my company "as a friend," but who never found the courage to date or make love with me, although I am sure my experience in this regard is no different from that of many able-bodied persons.

The day came when my backaches got in the way of having an active sex life. Surprisingly that development was liberating because I stopped worrying about being attractive to men. No matter how headstrong I had been, I, like most women of my generation, had had the desire to be alluring to men ingrained into me. And that longing had always worked like a brake on my behavior. When what men think of me ceased to be compelling, I gained greater freedom to be myself.

I've often wondered if I would have been a different person had I not been physically handicapped. I really don't know, though there is no question that being handicapped has marked me. But at the same time I usually do not *feel* handicapped—and consequently, I do not *act* handicapped. People are therefore less likely to treat me as a handicapped person. There is no doubt, however, that the lives of my parents, sister, husband, other family members, and some close friends have been affected by my physical condition. They have had to learn not to hide me away at home, not to feel embarrassed by how I look or react to people who say silly things to me, and not to resent me for the extra demands my condition makes on them. Perhaps the hardest thing for those who live with handicapped people is to know when and how to offer help. There are no guidelines applicable to all situations. My advice is, when in doubt, ask, but ask in a way that does not smack of pity or embarrassment. Most important, please don't talk to us as though we are children.

So, has being physically handicapped been a handicap? It all depends on one's attitude. Some years ago, I told a friend that I had once said to an affirmative action compliance officer (somewhat sardonically since I do not believe in the head count approach to affirmative action) that the institution which employs me is triply lucky because it can count me as non-white, female and handicapped. He responded, "Why don't you tell them to count you four times? ...Remember, you're short, besides!"

From *Making Waves: An Anthology of Writings By and About Asian American Women*

In Magazines (I Found Specimens of the Beautiful)

Ekua Omosupe

Once
I looked for myself
between the covers of
Seventeen
Vogue
Cosmopolitan
among blue eyes, blonde hair, white skin, thin bodies,
this is beauty.
I hated this shroud of
Blackness
that makes me invisible
a negative print
some other one's
nightmare.

In a store front window
against a white back drop
I saw a queenly head of nappy hair
and met this chiseled face
wide wondering eyes,
honey colored, bronzed skin
a mouth with thick lips
bowed   painted red
smiled purple gums and shining pearls
I turned to leave
but this body of
curvacious hips
strong thighs
broad ass
long legs
called me back to look again at likenesses of
African Queens, Dahomey Warriors, statuesque Goddesses.
I stand outside those covers meet
Face to Face
Myself
I am the Beautiful

Notes on Oppression and Violence

Aletícia Tijerina

"Because I am Brown, I am oppressed." When I speak this, I know it is not enough. The knowledge of racism is not enough. Because if I am still bound by my own self-hatred, *I am the oppressor onto myself.*

I ask myself, "How does a Brown sister, a Black sister, free herself?"

Knowing I am oppressed, I must also know that I participate in this oppression. I must realize that I and all my darker sisters take the instruments of oppression and use them on ourselves. Our tools come in many forms.

We take from the oppressor the instrument of hatred and sharpen it on our bodies and souls. The internalization of "spic" and "nigger" begins at birth. Only consciousness must follow—or death.

Migrant Farm Labor Camp No. 109, Ohio, August 17, 1956:
The poor home of a migrant farm worker's family was invaded today by police to rip the children from the groins of the Mexican mother. The Native American father had attempted to kill his three-year-old daughter. The incident was caused by severe economical distress and obvious hunger. The daughter was placed in an orphanage.

The very roots of my radicalism   began in the city streets.

Where was the point of departure from myself   what time was it   what did the feeling look like   how did it taste   why did I swallow it?

Street culture and behavior is a way of surviving in industrial North America. It creates a passionate and violent language.

When I would whisper to a compadre, "I love you," or yell "I hate you" to an enemy, the passion of the language which exploded inside me sprang from the same source. I had learned that both love and hate are potentially violent. When I dared to love someone, he or she shared with me a basic understanding that through our hating we might survive. If we could hate enough and fight back enough we might be jailed less or knifed less or raped less often. As I grew older, I built upon the notion that hatred must seek revenge. I began responding to the harsh reality that I was worthless in society by broadening my violent actions. And in an odd way, I sought justice.

My responses were mixed with a pre-consciousness. A form of resistance.

I was incarcerated when I was sixteen on four felony charges and three misdemeanors. A plea bargain sent me to an experimental maximum security institution in Ohio instead of the Women's prison. When I stole the jail transfer papers on me and others off the prison psychologist's desk, I learned many of us had been sent here because we had high IQs. And, about me, the papers read "She is considered dangerous to society and herself." Dangerous to society...

Dangerous to tell the violence I am. Dangerous to release the anger I am. Dangerous to write the truth of the source of oppression. Dangerous to name it—name the person, the myth and the props. Dangerous to be who I am. Dangerous to the social make-up of this country. Dangerous to write it. Dangerous to myself.

A poem I wrote in 1970 reads:

> i stepped out
>   to meet the Cold
>   only the Cold warmed me
> feeling   winter's naked intent
> the last Cold needle piercing my arm
> feeling   white man's consent
> the lasting supply of bitter Crystals
> thru the dead of Snow.
> i stepped out
>   to meet the Cold
>   only the Cold warmed
> my bleeding   to escape

I was a junkie. Anglos have been consenting to us darkies shootin' hard drugs since the beginning of their colonization. But the white man didn't actually push the spike into my veins. I did. This act is clearly the embodiment of self-hatred. Hatred which goes back a long time. Goes back to the three-year-old girl terrorized by the knife of her father—to the white welfare woman whispering in my ears, "Your momma is a whore, you will grow up to be a no-good whore...." Individual incidents in our lives—in our collective history—we North Americans—colonized and exploiter alike. Yet, it is our collective wills which have created the need for killer drugs. *Violent responses in any form they take are accomplices to the wills which have created the need.* The availability of drugs is not the problem or the dealer down on 122nd Street. They are only players in a far more complex value system of worth which nurtures self-hatred. Self-hatred which is directing and encouraging people to believe suicide is an option—as is alcohol or drug addiction or the reckless homicide on the highways.

We take from the oppressor the instruments of hatred and sharpen them on our bodies and our souls.

For us, because we were misfits—because we were dangerous, the authorities in control of our lives decided to use us as experimental guinea pigs—to monitor our brain waves—test out new drugs—experiment on how to control us, the very dangerous in society—how to mess with our minds.

We were all imprisoned for various crimes against the State: impersonating men; escaping abusive homes; setting fires; taking drugs; robbery 'cause we were hungry; plotting to overthrow the government. Most of our so-called "crimes" against the State were acts of resistance or rebellion against an oppressive family, school, society; for many of us, our cultural identity had been battered and abused since birth.

I was ward of the State from the ages of ten to twenty-one. My adopted mother had given up legal custody of me because of her mental breakdowns.

It was after reading the *Communist Manifesto*,[1] when I was thirteen, that I began to reason that the State had become the parent in my life. And it had been the State which had denied me my real mother, because she was brown and poor and undocumented. I understood too, that the hatred I possessed against the State had been nurtured in this denial. My hatred was more intense than the heat of soldering steel. My reign of revenge followed—robbery—assault on a policeman—possession of narcotics—crossing state lines with narcotics—documents indicating the plot to overthrow the government. The plot to overthrow my parents.

At the maximum security institution all of us darker sisters with curly, kinky, or otherwise offensive hair, had to straighten it to make it more acceptable to our white jailers. In rebellion to this forced cultural exploitation, I purposely jumped another inmate in the straightening room hair shop—breaking her nose and she laying a hot iron across my cheek. I was thrown into solitary confinement for two weeks. Yet, my purpose had been accomplished. Never again did the wardens lead me down the hallway to the hair shop, for fear I would start trouble again.

A radical is born with the will to survive and the strength to make trouble.

Yet, my hatred was consuming me. For all the talk of hatred against the oppressor, true liberation must begin with the liberation of one's self from oneself.

In the basement of the prison was a roller skating rink that a couple of cell groups would use once a week. I liked going there, to watch the other girls round the rink, maybe seeing a good-looking one and making eye contact.

Racial tension in the prison was very high, even more so than on the streets. For there, we could not choose our peers, or escape our enemies.

Descending into the cement basement of the prison, I accidentally bumped into a blue-eyed, brown haired white girl. It took only one half second for me to explode into hatred against her skin. I wanted to strike out at her, but the crowd pushed her forward and out of reach too fast. I hated her like fear loves weakness. Seating myself on the bench, I waited for her to round the floor. Suddenly, everything in the room faded. The music stopped, the sounds of skates weakened then stopped, people disappeared. I was facing a large emptiness alone. I blacked out, yet, while in this void, I heard a voice inside of me say, "See, when you hate so much you are blind to beauty and love can't find you." After hearing these words, the room reappeared, the music began again. I did not move for a long time. I didn't move until I had vowed to myself to cease my hating and let love find me.

I had chosen to cross over, to allow the transcendence of hatred into the opposite, love. A meeting point inside of me let me see clearly there are two roads: one of hatred and one of love. It was still for me to act upon this knowledge to perform human acts which would build upon this vision of love.

When Martin Luther King Jr. said he had a dream—a vision of human love—he knew in the deep well of hatred is love. Love which knows the flesh of every human being is alive with feelings. Still, human love is a vision of love for all of us. Each moment we recall the vision of love *we commit an act of resistance against the oppressor.*

From *Compañeras: Latina Lesbians*

Notes

1. Karl Marx and Friedrich Engels, "The Manifesto of the Communist Party," in *The Marx-Engels Reader*, ed. Robert C. Tucker (New York: W. W. Norton & Company, Inc., 1972), 331–362.

Where Is The Love?   *June Jordan*

I am a feminist, and what that means to me is much the same as the meaning of the fact that I am Black. It means that I must undertake to love myself and respect myself as though my very life depends upon self-love and self-respect. It means that I must seek to cleanse myself of the hatred and contempt that surround and permeate my identity as a woman and as a Black human being in this world. It means that the achievement of self-love and self-respect will require hourly vigilance. It means that I am entering my soul in a struggle that will most certainly transform all the peoples of the earth: the movement into self-love, self-respect and self-determination is the movement now galvanizing the true majority of human beings everywhere.

This movement tests the viability of a moral idea: that the legitimacy of any status quo, any governing force, must be measured according to the experience of those who are, comparatively, powerless. The conduct of the strong vis à vis the strong tells us nothing about a society. The truth is found instead in the behavior of the powerful toward those who are weaker, different, smaller. How do the strong, the powerful, treat children? How do they treat the aged among us? How do the strong and the powerful treat so-called minority members of society? How do the powerful regard women: how do they treat us?

You can see that, according to these criteria, the overwhelming status quo of power and government and tradition is evil, diseased, illegitimate and deserves nothing from us—no loyalty, no accommodation, no patience, no understanding—nothing but clear-minded resolve to utterly change this situation and thereby change our own destiny.

As a Black woman I exist as part of the powerless and as part of the majority peoples of the world. I am powerless compared to any man because women are kept powerless by men. I am powerless compared to anyone white because Black and Third World peoples are kept powerless by whites. And because I am Black and a woman I am the most victimized of the powerless. Yet I am the majority because women constitute the majority gender. I am the majority because Black and Third World peoples constitute the majority of human beings. In short, I am a member of the most powerless majority on the planet.

And it is here—in this extreme coincidence of my status as someone twice stigmatized, my status as someone twice kin to the despised majority—it is here, in this extremity, that I stand in a struggle against demoralization and suicide and toward self-love and self-determination. And it is here, in this extremity, that as a Black feminist I ask myself and anyone who would call me sister, *Where is the love?*

The love growing out of my quest for self-love, self-respect and self-determination must be something one can verify in the ways I present myself to others, the ways I approach people different from myself: How do I reach out to the people I would like to call my sisters, brothers, children, lovers and friends? If I am a Black feminist serious in undertaking self-love, it seems to me that I should gain and gain and gain in strength so that I may without fear be able and willing to love and respect, for example, women who are not feminists, not professionals, not as old or as young as I am, women who have neither job nor income, women who are not Black.

And it seems to me that the strength that should come from Black feminism means that I can, without fear, love and respect all men who are willing and able, without fear, to love and respect me. In short, if acquiring my self-determination is part of a worldwide, inevitable and righteous movement, then I should be willing and able to embrace more and more of the whole world without fear and also without self-sacrifice.

This means that as a Black feminist I cannot be expected to respect what somebody else calls self-love if that concept of self-love requires my self-destruction to any degree. This holds true whether that somebody else is male, female, Black or white. My Black feminism means that you cannot expect me to respect what somebody else identifies as the Good of the People if that so-called Good (often translated as *manhood* or *family* or *nationalism*) requires the deferral or the diminution of my self-fulfillment. We, Blacks and women, are the people. And, as Black women, we are most of the people, any people. Therefore, nothing that is good for the people is actually good unless it is good for me and my people, as I, as we, determine our own lives.

When I speak of Black feminism, I am speaking from an intense consciousness of the truth that we Black women huddle together miserably on the very lowest levels of the economic pyramid. We Black women subsist in the most tenuous economic conditions.

When I speak of Black feminism then, I am not speaking of sexuality; I am not speaking of heterosexuality or homosexuality or bisexuality. Whatever sexuality anyone elects is not my business or the business of the state. Furthermore, I cannot be persuaded that one kind of sexuality will necessarily bring greater happiness to the two people involved. I am not talking about sexuality; I am talking about love, about a deep caring and respect for every other human being, a love that can only derive from secure and positive self-love.

As a Black woman and feminist, I must look about me, with trembling and with shocked anger, at the endless waste, the endless suffocation of my sisters; the bitter sufferings of hundreds of thousands of women who are the sole parents of hundreds of thousands of children, the desolation of women trapped by futile, demeaning, low-paying occupations, the unemployed, the bullied, the beaten, the battered, the ridiculed, the slandered, the trivialized, the raped and the sterilized; the lost millions of beautiful, creative and momentous lives turned to ashes on the pyre of gender identity. I must look about me and, as a Black feminist, I must ask myself: *Where is the love?* How is my own life work serving to end these tyrannies, these corrosions of sacred possibility? How am I earning membership in our worldwide movement for self-determination and self-respect?

As a Black feminist poet and writer I must look behind me with trembling and with shocked anger at the fate of Black women writers. From the terrible graves of the traditional conspiracy against my sisters in art, I must exhume the works of writers and poets such as Georgia Douglas Johnson, Gladys May Caseley-Hayford and Gwendolyn B. Bennett.

Can any of you name two or three other women poets from the Harlem Renaissance? Or, for that matter, how well-known is the work of Margaret Walker, a most signal contemporary of Richard Wright? Why does the work of all women die with no river carrying forward the record of such grace? How is it that whether we have written novels or poetry, whether we have raised our children or cleaned and cooked and washed and ironed, it is all dismissed as "women's work"; it is all, finally, despised as nothing important, and there is no trace, no meaning echo of our days upon the earth?

Here is Georgia Douglas Johnson's poem, "The Heart of A Woman":

> The heart of a woman goes forth with the dawn,
> As a lovebird, softwinging, so restlessly on,
> Afar o'er life's turrets and vales does it roam
> In the wake of those echoes the heart calls home.
>
> The heart of a woman falls back with the night
> And enters some alien cage in its plight,
> And tries to forget it has dreamed of the stars,
> While it breaks, breaks, breaks on the sheltering bars.

It is against such sorrow, such spiritual death, such deliberate strangulation of the lives of women, my sisters, and of powerless peoples—men and women—everywhere, that I work and live, now, as a feminist, trusting that I will learn to love myself well enough to love you (whoever you are), well enough so that you will love me well enough so that we will know, exactly, where is the love: that it is here, between us, and growing stronger and growing stronger.

From *Essence*

This article is an edited version of the opening address delivered by Ms. Jordan on May 4, 1978, as part of the panel on Black Women Writers and Feminism at the National Black Writers' Conference held at Howard University, Washington, D.C.

4

In Silence, Giving Tongue

The Transformation of Silence Into (An)other Alphabet

Periquita

Carmen Morones

Yo me acuerdo I remember
a three year old girl
nicknamed Periquita
by her parents
because she liked to *hacer ruido*

I remember
esa kittenish girl
sitting on her Mama's lap
on the front doorstep
under the moonlight
en México

I remember
her papa and Juan, the neighbor
sitting on rush chairs nearby
taking in the summer breeze
Stars gleaming
Crickets chirping
Fireflies whizzing by...

The men would reminisce
about many things
Good harvests, summer droughts
and the townspeople's misfortunes
Like the time Flaco sold his cow
to Don Hernández

"*¿Por qué?*" Periquita asked

Her papa winked at her
sucked on his cigarette
blew the smoke in circles
Paused...said nothing
Juan elaborated
about Flaco's wife being *muy enferma*
the fever, the difficulty breathing

"*¿Por qué?*" Periquita asked

Juan shrugged
Patted her head
Continued talking about the wife,
taken on a horse to the hospital

Periquita asked
"*¿Hospital? Qué es hospital?*"
Her mama whispered
"*Donde llevan a los enfermos*"

"*¡Oh!*" Periquita exclaimed
Puffed her cheeks like when she had the mumps
"*¡Yo estaba enferma!*" Puffed her cheeks
"*¡Yo estaba enferma!*" Puffed her cheeks
"*¡Yo estaba muy enferma!*"

Her papa nodded
Juan smiled patiently,
then continued
about how Flaco had to sell his cow
to Don Hernández
to pay the hospital bill

Periquita asked her papa,
"*¿Por qué no le das una vaca?*"
the cow with the black and white spots

Juan chuckled
till his laughter fell
like the cigarette from her papa's mouth
crushed beneath his big black boot
Sucked on another one
matchlight in his face
A puff, a jerk of his head
a sideways glance
that told her mama
to-shut-her-up-or-put-her-to-bed

"Shhhhh..."
Her mama said
showed her daughter the palm of her hand
Periquita blinked and closed up
like the sleeping flowers
on the adobe wall

Her kitten eyes
watched the amber glow
of her papa's cigarette
as he sucked on it
Her kitten eyes
watched the flickering of the fireflies
as they passed by
in the night sky.

From *Revista Mujeres* 4:1

Refugee Ship

*Lorna Dee
Cervantes*

Like wet cornstarch, I slide
past my grandmother's eyes. Bible
at her side, she removes her glasses.
The pudding thickens.

Mama raised me without language.
I'm orphaned from my Spanish name.
The words are foreign, stumbling
on my tongue. I see in the mirror
my reflection: bronzed skin, black hair.

I feel I am a captive
aboard the refugee ship.
The ship that will never dock.
El barco que nunca atraca.

From *Revista Chicano-Riqueña* 3:1

Her Rites of Passage   *Lynda Marín*

I

In the stairwell of the apartment building lobby, she had made a tent palace of sheets, bed pillows, and one of Mary's forbidden quilts. Through the palace door flap she marched the buggy, delivering into the great dining hall Corky the rabbit and Brown Doggy. A soft knocking from beyond the palace walls interrupted the feasting. She popped her head under a sheet to see. From the other side of the lobby glass door a large man bent to meet her eyes. He knocked again, pleadingly, as if he were carrying a heavy burden and would be relieved of it only when the big, latched door was opened. Her first impulse—to let him in—was halted instantly by Mary's repeated warning. "Don't ever open that door to anyone who doesn't live here. No matter what!" But now here were his eyes, so sorrowful, and his insistent knocking, so sure, so right. He was a man, after all, and important for that reason. Perhaps just this time.

She was surprised to find that he did not rush right past her but took an interest in her tent palace. He asked if he might have a peek inside. Shyly she lifted the flap, and in he crawled, raising the ceiling with his big head. "What about you?" he asked, cheery. A pause, then she followed. He took up almost all the space. He pointed to his lap and pulled her onto himself jerkily. When she shrank away, his arms tightened around her and his face scratched her cheek. "You be a good girl, and I'll show you something." He fumbled at his pants. His eyes looked cloudy and seemed not to be pointed at her anymore. She thought of screaming but could not. Even now she was not sure he meant to harm her. "Look at this," he commanded. He had taken his pants down to his knees and held a rubbery tube of skin in his hand. "Take a hold of it," he whispered. He grabbed her reluctant hand and rubbed her fisted fingers along the tube. It was warm and smelled like Mary's Chinese herbs only more sour, like stomach flu. She wrenched her nose away, and then, to her surprise, her body sprang free of the sheets and followed after. At the threshold of her own second-story apartment she stopped her legs. If she went in now, heart thumping and wild, Mary might guess, might find him still in her tent palace, his tube hanging from him like a dead bird. And too, she would see the quilt. Better to hide and wait.

The click of the lobby door below released her. She approached the tent warily, but she knew he was gone. In his place, a tidy, piled bowel movement on Mary's quilt. He had used Corky and Brown Doggy to wipe himself. She staggered to the other side of the lobby and wept. Later she was to explain that she'd made the mess herself, for which she received a memorable whipping. That was when she was six years old.

II

Closing the light, she called goodnight to Clayton. Her mother would not be home until eleven o'clock, and by then she was supposed to be asleep. The plumped, sweet-smelling pillows yielded to the weight of her head and she realized that she'd forgotten to remove the ponytail she'd been wearing all day. Shaking out her hair, she heard Clayton at the door, and looked up to see him silhouetted against the bright hallway light. "Goodnight, Daddy," she said, making excuses to herself, god, and her brown-skinned real father for calling the man this way. It was easier though. Her mother insisted, and it gave more a sense of family to the three of them whose bonds felt so fragile, whose relations were so explosive.

He was quiet, just a little half-smile, leaning in at the doorway. And then he was walking around the foot of the bed and sitting beside her, the funny, familiar smile stuck on his face. He reached up and pressed his open hand against the top of her head. She wiggled herself past his weight a few inches farther toward the foot of her bed.

"You shouldn't use so many pillows," he said finally, "not good for your spine." She knew. She said that she knew, said that she always threw all but one off by the time she went to sleep.

"Don't worry!" She laughed a little, wanting to quell the growing discomfort.

"You go right to sleep," he said, leaning his face toward hers. She crinkled her nose at the wine smell, and he squeezed her nostrils shut, kissed her on the forehead.

"Goodnight," she said again, yawning for effect. But he remained seated there, his weight against her hipbone.

"You're becoming a very pretty young lady," he said in a gravelly whisper. His eyes caught glints of the hallway light and she could see them flickering back and forth, as if they were searching for something in hers.

"Thank you," she heard her smallest voice say against the closing of her throat. She shut her mouth tightly, to hold onto the quiet between them before any more words narrowed the possibilities.

"You be a good girl," he said, his face weaving in closer again. And just for a moment, she was not sure. He was the man her mother had married, had fought with, had clung to. He was a professor at the university, and white like her mother. "Always say 'Dr.' in front of his name," her mother had told her. Now it was something he wanted, needed, from her? She only knew she wished to sink deeply into the pillows, through the mattress and into infinite, unbiased space. As his mouth closed in on hers, she felt her body and head collapse. She slumped there, breathless, immobile. His lifted weight rocked the mattress slightly, but she held her stillness until after she heard the click of the door latch. Before going to sleep, she decided to leave Clayton out of the diary she'd just received for her thirteenth birthday.

III

The good thing about Tom Sweeting was that he couldn't pass Spanish without her help, and so she became the freshman girlfriend of the college football quarterback. He wanted to have sex after their second date. She put him off until the end of the semester. But when he finally pressed her one stuporous beer-swilled night in the desert, she was embarrassed by the toughness of her virginity, the resistance of membrane to yield to member. He said she was a hassle. She needed practice.

When Tom left for Christmas vacation with his blonde sorority girl-friend, she was bereft. She found excuses to visit his apartment, to lay claim to his territory, at least, if not his person. His roommate Dave didn't have a girlfriend. He said Tom was a real jerk for leaving her. He offered her beers and TV.

During the second six-pack, she began to cry. Dave lay down beside her on the couch, glancing occasionally at the screen. "Hey," he said, poking at the tears on her nearest cheek. She tried to smile. His pudgy fingers so inept, his beefy linebacker body hanging off the edge. "Hey, that's better!" His eyes were blurry, she noticed, and she blinked hard to clear her own. "You're too pretty to cry over old Sweetass." He was readjusting himself on the cushions, pinning her down with an arm and a leg.

"You're squishing me," she said, pushing a laugh out, pushing against the boulder of weight.

"You're tough," he answered. "You can take it."

She considered, for a moment, the truth of his words and the dubious compliment implied.

"But are you good?"

That was another matter. Good? What did he mean by that? A good girl? True to Tom? A good fuck? His hands were squeezing her body, her behind and her breasts.

"Don't," she said and pushed at him again.

"Don't worry," he smiled, "I'm your buddy."

She knew what he meant. He had been her buddy in a vague way. And he was a varsity athlete, an important person with a public reputation. "Help," a woman was pleading on the screen, but she'd lost the thread of that distant plot. He jabbed fingers under her waistband and dug between her legs. "Really," her voice was still controlled, familiar, "I want you to stop, Dave, really!" With one hand he unfastened his pants. "Dave!" she sounded screechy to herself now.

"Shut up!" he spat.

Her four corners pinned by his whole ponderous weight, she felt his penis slice up through her with a surprising quickness.

Later when Tom asked her if she'd screwed around with Dave, she had simply said no. "Liar, slut," he called her, and she retreated into the company of her old high school boyfriend, hoping her sophomore year would find her more solidly in charge of herself.

IV

The infections began in graduate school. The doctor from Beverly Hills was recommended by the father of one of her roommates. Two sulfa tablets four times a day. Even if the symptoms disappeared soon, she should take the pills for two weeks. But something else happened instead. Wrenching nausea overtook her, laid her out. The doctor said she had the stomach flu. She should keep up the sulfa. But it wouldn't stay down. Nothing would. Not even ice cubes. In the hospital they fed her sulfa intravenously. On the third day, her entire body blossomed purple welts. They added steroids to the I.V. "Could it be the sulfa?" she had asked in little more than a stupor. "No, no," the well-tanned doctor had answered. "We don't have that trouble with sulfa."

When she fell into a coma, another doctor was called in. By whom? she had wondered later. Twenty-four hours off the sulfa, she'd regained consciousness. Twenty-four hours after that, infection reclaimed her kidneys. New drugs, stronger drugs, drugs she would experiment with for years, drugs that would steal her from herself and betray her.

In the middle of her twenty-fifth year she sat before yet another specialist, the head of Urology. His thick red jowls vibrated as he spoke. The exploratory surgery had revealed nothing. Her chronic pain was not physically caused. It was guilt, he explained, because she was having sex out of wedlock with her boyfriend. Oh we all liked to think we were very modern, but there was a reason for the old conventions. Sex out of wedlock brought on symptoms.

Dr. O'Grady leaned heavily back in his chair. She felt him enjoying her dark smallness, her frail response. She knew she should leave quickly, should not let him implant his seeds of fear and doubt, but she found herself fixed in the chair there, unable to dodge the sharp accusations, the jabbing threats. "If you persist in sex outside of marriage," he shrugged his big blue shoulders, "you might always feel guilt, be in pain, be unable to function properly. On the other hand, childbirth might remedy the problem. Who's to say?" He cocked his head and smiled. "Surely all I can do is tell you the truth."

She railed quietly against his diagnosis, but she did, a few months later, divest herself of the boyfriend. And so it was in teeth-clenching privacy that she finished off the rest of her twenties.

V

"Come in!" he said and gestured, a gap-toothed grin flashing. She laid her notebooks on a corner of his desk and seated herself to face him. She had met here with him before, in small groups of division heads or teachers. She was curious as to why he should request to meet with her alone when he had seemed to overlook her in every other instance.

"Well, so, I thought it time we talked a bit, just you and I." He seemed to be staring intently at the book shelves behind her. She fixed her eyes on the vertical furrow sunk into his fleshy forehead. The new chancellor. He had replaced a man found guilty of embezzling the college's funds. "You've been here quite a while for such a young woman."

"Eleven years," she complied.

"You've got a hold of your department. Your colleagues like you. I hear your seminars are jammed."

In the pause, she searched for trail markers, for clues about direction. The furrow seemed to smooth and reform horizontally. His lips stretched across his teeth. He was smiling again, she realized, and her impulse was to smile back, but the muscles just under her cheekbones would not respond.

"Are you always so serious?" A tone she hadn't heard before.

"If you've called me in to compliment me, then, of course, I'm grateful." She searched fast for more words to follow, to stave off a possibility she could only barely imagine. Instead, she became aware of a moldering sweetness hanging in the air. Just to the right of his plump wrist, she located an ashtray where a cigar half, one end wet with gnawing, lay like imitation excrement that kids played jokes with.

"I called you in," cocking his head and voice intimately, "because I'd like to know you better. Would you be more comfortable if we went somewhere for a drink?"

The wrongness of the scene jarred her, pleaded to be reinterpreted. She had sat on the search committee that selected this man. His recommendations (all from white men, she just now considered) had been impeccable. The board had insisted on that. She must be mistaken about the tone of his voice, the tilt of his body. She weighed what she knew against what she felt. All she got were her ribs, expanding and contracting. Intercostals, a word she liked, leapt to the front of her mind and hovered there. But no other words, no sounds even, formed in her throat.

He drew his fleshy hands together under his chin. "I must assume you take better care of school business than you do of your personal life."

Only a slight pause—the space it might take for a mouse to scuttle to the opposite corner. "Which, I might add, many people still talk about."

She considered, for a moment, the possibility that she had been cast, unbeknown to herself, in a bad movie, a low budget venture with amateur actors. Soon the director would appear, would offer assistance, would make up some script for her right on the spot.

"I'm speaking about the Jasper boy. That was his name?"

"Danny Jedson," she complied again. "That's very old history, ten years and well-aired. Students and teachers should not be lovers. Some thought we were. Some knew we weren't."

She watched his eyebrows raise in mock surprise, then feigned compassion. "I'm afraid it's still stewing among some of the board members. I've a mandate to clean up old messes. It's a shame that you're one of them."

Waiting, again, for her own response, she allowed herself to picture Danny, to picture herself telling him about this absurdity. They would all three go out to dinner, she and Danny and Lila, his new lawyer wife. They would laugh at her description of the chancellor's rubbery cheeks and blunt fingers, and especially at his use of the term "boy." But when the picture went blank, the silence bore down.

"What is it you're saying? I'm not really sure." Her voice sounded dim to her, as if it were coming from another room.

"Ah." Back in control, he leaned forward and reached to cover her hand with his own. "Dear girl, just that I can help you—and will—if you'll let me." The stench of old tobacco rode out on his breath, moist and warm, slicing into her head.

All in one motion, she grabbed books, jolted upward. Carried by legs that pre-empted commands, she let herself out of the chancellor's office.

The next day, on her 35th birthday, she received the letter of termination, co-signed by the chancellor and head of the board. And although she spent the next week drafting rejoinders, they all fluttered silently into her wastebasket.

VI

"Sixth floor!" the little girl shouted on her way through the stairwell door and into the large hallway. Her mother, just behind, stood a moment to catch her breath and rehoist grocery bags after the climb, then unlocked the door of their tiny D.C. apartment. At forty-six, she was sorry to admit, she would prefer a building with an elevator but could not afford one close enough to the Capitol where she worked.

Over frying onions she asked, "So who did Mr. Mann yell at today?" Usually she was provided with amusing stories and imitations of her daughter's second grade teacher, but tonight the little girl drew inward and only mumbled, "Nothing." Trying again she asked, "Well, what about

Bullybill?" He had been appointed class president last week by Mr. Mann, much to her daughter's scorn, and had, ever since, used his office to press favors from his classmates. Once, her daughter explained, he had talked her out of her chocolate chip cookies by threatening to break the zipper on her jumpsuit. Bullybill was nearly a nightly topic between them. But instead of an answer to this second question, tonight came only the muffled clicking of the TV channel changer.

Dishing out dinner, she wondered that her child had settled on the Presidential debates. "Wake up!" she said gently, finding her curled on the couch. "Dinner's on."

The small girl rubbed her eyes and then exclaimed at the screen, "Look Mommy, your boss!"

Her mother did not look. She knew well enough what the President looked like. "Mommy, it's like a turkey!" Her small, dark finger, pressed against the bright screen, was following his wiggling underchin as he spoke.

"Yes," she said, matter-of-factly, and went to press the on/off button. But she was stopped in mid-reach by the earnestness of the child's next question.

"He's a good man, isn't he? The President is a good man?"

She marveled at the question, at her six-year-old child's need to have it answered. She tried to remember herself at six, and indeed, by what seemed only a flicker, she could recall needing to believe that men were good—good because they were important. Now her own little girl asked her to verify that truth, to confirm what the child, too, needed to believe.

Caught by the entreating eyes, she searched for words. But the only ones spoken were his, read deftly from the teleprompter, an advantage his advanced age required. He was speaking of women, of comparable worth, of the great work the ladies of this nation would yet perform. The back of her mind grimaced. She thought of her own salary, just over half that of her male colleagues on the same advisory committee. And she thought of the environment she had tokenly been appointed to protect, left barren and exploited for dollars and the pure pleasure of the taking. This chain of thought, she knew, spiraled in on itself; soon followed the picture of the silos, their lids retracting, their contents unsheathed. Aimed at the silent, unsuspecting sky. She reached to enclose the sweet-skinned child in her arms.

"No," she heard herself say, "he's not good."

When they pulled apart, the child said in her smallest voice, "Mr. Mann yelled at me today."

"How come?" her mother asked lightly.

"Because of Bullybill," the girl replied. She waited, then continued. "In the cloak room. He said I had to pull my pants down, or else."

"Or else?" In the background, the President was denouncing terrorists.

"Or else he'd tell Mr. Mann I hit him you know where."

"Did you?" the mother asked.

"No!" the child scrunched up her nose. "I wouldn't want to touch him! You know," she said, lapsing into her most confidential story-telling mode, "he smells like dried-up milk."

"What happened then?"

"I screamed," the girl pronounced.

"You did?" her mother asked, feeling a sudden swelling in her neck and throat. "What did you say?"

"I just screamed, like this, 'aaaaah!'"

"That's not very loud," her mother said soberly. "Is that what made Mr. Mann mad?"

"It was a little louder," the child admitted.

"Like how?" A spark, a glimmer and a spark. "Go ahead, show me how loud." Only a pause (the President was discussing the value of space-based anti-ballistic missiles now), and then, propelled by pure absence of doubt, the full rippling reach of the child's screaming resonated in her own throat. A scream that reduced the President to a Howdy Doody pantomime. A scream that surprised her silence like freshly drawn blood.

The Eskimos

Barbara Ruth

The Eskimos
Make 60 names for snow.
The Balinese
Have words
For fifteen separate
Degrees of trance.
I have spent my life
Searching for the words, the names
To tell you who I am.
I am the eleventh trance
Which comes within
The 27th kind of snow.
I am the note between the ivories
If you play them both together
That is not it.
I am the color between navy blue and black
If you mix them both together
That is not it.
I am the smell you have no words for
You say   You like it
You say   You don't like it
I ask you: Do you know its name?
I believe that every Lesbian Indian Jew
Is exactly like me.
And I believe in dreams of snow
In the nights of Bali.

From *Past, Present & Future Passions*

Palabra de Mujer

Elba Rosario
Sánchez

Todo eso que sabemos,
que por años y descendencia
llevamos clavado en nuestra memoria
del ayer mañana
que incluye el hoy,
todo eso, lo quisieron machacar
como machacábamos
los frijoles de todos los días.

Mudas nos quisieron desde niñas
encarcelándonos en un mundo de:
"No pienses. Así más linda eres."
Nunca nos dieron la palabra
diciéndonos siempre:
"No hay que faltar al respeto."

Nosotras escondimos todo lo prohibido
en los pliegues de nuestro silencio.
Como púas se hundió en nuestra garganta
y de las gotas de sangre brotó la palabra
desafiando lo antes no aclarado.

Elena

Pat Mora

My Spanish isn't enough.
I remember how I'd smile
listening to my little ones,
understanding every word they'd say,
their jokes, their songs, their plots.
    Vamos a pedirle dulces a mamá. Vamos.
But that was in Mexico.
Now my children go to American high schools.
They speak English. At night they sit around
the kitchen table, laugh with one another.
I stand by the stove and feel dumb, alone.
I bought a book to learn English.
My husband frowned, drank more beer.
My oldest said, "*Mamá*, he doesn't want you
to be smarter than he is." I'm forty,
embarrassed at mispronouncing words,
embarrassed at the laughter of my children,
the grocer, the mailman. Sometimes I take
my English book and lock myself in the bathroom,
say the thick words softly,
for if I stop trying, I will be deaf
when my children need my help.

From *Chants*

Unnatural Speech   *Pat Mora*

The game has changed
girl/child, no humming
or singing in these halls,
long, dark, ending at the desk
you want, where you'd sit
adding numbers one by one,
a C.P.A., daisies on your desk.

                    I study hard

you say, your smile true,
like dawn is, fresh, vulnerable,
but my English language scares
you, makes your palms sweat
when you speak before a class

                    I say my speeches
                    to my dolls

you say. Dolls? The game
has changed, girl/child.
I hear you once singing
to those unblinking eyes
lined up on your bed

                    Víbora, víbora de la mar,
your words light in your mouth.

Now at twenty
you stand before
those dolls tense,
feet together,
tongue thick, dry,
pushing heavy English
words out.

                    In class I hide
                    my hands behind
                    my back. They shake.
                    My voice too.

I know the new rules,
girl/child, one by one,
víboras I've lived with
all my life, learned to hold
firmly behind the head.
If I teach you, will your songs
evaporate, like dawn?

From *Borders*

The Three Tongues
Catalina Ríos

Tied to the backs
of some women are
bloody sorrows,
leech-like troubles
that make them weak.

In every strong woman
there are three tongues
all in contradiction,
silenced during the day
by a heavier hand.

At night minutes before bed
the strong woman
must unbraid
the three tongues
and let them speak.
Only then can she sleep.

From *Sinister Wisdom* 34

For Alva Benson, And For Those Who Have Learned To Speak

Joy Harjo

And the ground spoke when she was born.
Her mother heard it. In Navajo she answered
as she squatted down against the earth
to give birth. It was now when it happened,
now giving birth to itself again and again
between the legs of women.

Or maybe it was the Indian Hospital
in Gallup. The ground still spoke beneath
mortar and concrete. She strained against the
metal stirrups, and they tied her hands down
because she still spoke with them when they
muffled her screams. But her body went on
talking and the child was born into their
hands, and the child learned to speak
both voices.

She grew up talking in Navajo, in English
and watched the earth around her shift and change
with the people in the towns and in the cities
learning not to hear the ground as it spun around
beneath them. She learned to speak for the ground,
the voice coming through her like roots that
have long hungered for water. Her own daughter
was born, like she had been, in either place
or all places, so she could leave, leap
into the sound she had always heard,
a voice like water, like the gods weaving
against sundown in a scarlet light.

The child now hears names in her sleep.
They change into other names, and into others.
It is the ground murmuring, and Mt. St. Helens
erupts as the harmonic motion of a child turning
inside her mother's belly waiting to be born
to begin another time.

And we go on, keep giving birth and watch
ourselves die, over and over.
And the ground spinning beneath us
goes on talking.

From *She Had Some Horses*

Prisons of Silence

Janice Mirikitani

1.
The strongest prisons are built
with walls of silence.

2.
Morning light falls between us
like a wall.
We have laid beside each other
as we have for years.
Before the war, when life
would clamor through our windows,
we woke joyfully to the work.

I keep those moments
like a living silent seed.

After day's work, I would
smell the damp soil in his hands,
his hands that felt the outlines
of my body in the velvet
night of summers.

I hold his warm hands to this
cold wall of flesh
as I have for years.

3.
Jap!
Filthy Jap!

Who lives within me?

Abandoned homes, confiscated land,
loyalty oaths, barbed wire prisons
in a strange wasteland.

Go home, Jap!
Where is home?

A country of betrayal.
No one speaks to us.

We would not speak to each other.

We were accused.

Hands in our hair,
hands that spread our legs
and searched our thighs for secret weapons,
hands that knit barbed wire
to cripple our flight.

Giant hot hands flung me,
fluttering, speechless into
barbed wire, thorns in a broken wing.

The stongest prisons are built
with walls of silence.

4.
I watched him depart that day
from the tedious wall of wire,
the humps of barracks,
handsome in his uniform.

I would look each day for letters
from a wall of time,
waiting for approach of my deliverance
from a wall of dust.

I do not remember
reading about his death
only the wall of wind
that encased me, as I turned my head.

5.
U.S. Japs hailed as heroes!

I do not know the face of this country
it is inhabited by strangers
who call me obscene names.

Jap. Go home.
Where is home?

I am alone wandering
in this desert.

Where is home?
Who lives within me?

A stranger with a knife in her tongue
and broken wing,
mad from separations and losses cruel
as hunger.

Walls suffocate her as a tomb,
encasing history.

6.
I have kept myself contained
within these walls shaped to my body
and buried my rage.
I rebuilt my life
like a wall, unquestioning.
Obeyed their laws...their laws.

7.
All persons of Japanese ancestry
    filthy jap.
Both alien and non-alien
    japs are enemy aliens.
To be incarcerated
    for their own good
A military necessity
    The army to handle only the japs
Where is home?
A country of betrayal.

8.
This wall of silence crumbles
from the bigness of their crimes.
This silent wall
crushed by living memory.

He awakens from the tomb
I have made for myself
and unearths my rage.

I must speak.

9.
He faces me in this small
room of myself.
I find the windows
where light escapes.

From this cell of history
this mute grave,
we birth our rage.

We heal our tongues.

We listen to ourselves

    Korematsu, Hirabayashi, Yasui.

We ignite the syllables of our names.

We give testimony.

We hear the bigness of our sounds freed
like many clapping hands,
thundering for reparations.

We give testimony.

Our noise is dangerous.

10.
We beat our hands
like wings healed.

We soar
from these walls of silence.

From *Shedding Silence*

Performed by the Asian American Dance Collective, 1983 Repertory Concert

I Lost It
at the Movies

Jewelle Gomez

My grandmother, Lydia, and my mother, Dolores, were both talking to
me from their bathroom stalls in the Times Square movie theater. I was
washing butter from my hands at the sink and didn't think it at all odd.
The people in my family are always talking; conversation is a life force
in our existence. My great-grandmother, Grace, would narrate her life
story from 7:00 a.m. until we went to bed at night. The only break was
when we were reading or the reverential periods when we sat looking out
of our tenement windows, observing the neighborhood, which we natu-
3rally talked about later.

So it was not odd that Lydia and Dolores talked non-stop from their
stalls, oblivious to everyone except us. I hadn't expected it to happen
there, though. I hadn't really expected an "it" to happen at all. To be a
lesbian was part of who I was, like being left-handed—even when I'd
slept with men. When my great-grandmother asked me in the last days
of her life if I would be marrying my college boyfriend I said yes, knowing
I would not, knowing I was a lesbian.

It seemed a fact that needed no expression. Even my first encounter
with the word "bulldagger" was not charged with emotional conflict. As
a teen in the 1960s my grandmother told a story about a particular
building in our Boston neighborhood that had gone to seed. She described
the building's past through the experience of a party she'd attended there
thirty years before. The best part of the evening had been a woman she'd
met and danced with. Lydia had been a professional dancer and singer
on the black theater circuit; to dance with women was who she was.
They'd danced, then the woman walked her home and asked her out. I
heard the delicacy my grandmother searched for even in her retelling of
how she'd explained to the "bulldagger," as she called her, that she liked
her fine but she was more interested in men. I was struck with how careful
my grandmother had been to make it clear to that woman (and in effect
to me) that there was no offense taken in her attentions, that she just
didn't "go that way," as they used to say. I was so happy at thirteen to
have a word for what I knew myself to be. The word was mysterious and
curious, as if from a new language that used some other alphabet which
left nothing to cling to when touching its curves and crevices. But still a
word existed and my grandmother was not flinching in using it. In fact
she'd smiled at the good heart and good looks of the bulldagger who'd
liked her.

Once I had the knowledge of a word and a sense of its importance to me, I didn't feel the need to explain, confess, or define my identity as a lesbian. The process of reclaiming my ethnic identity in this country was already all-consuming. Later, of course, in moments of glorious self-righteousness, I did make declarations. But they were not usually ones I had to make. Mostly they were a testing of the waters. A preparation for the rest of the world which, unlike my grandmother, might not have a grounding in what true love is about. My first lover, the woman who'd been in my bed once a week most of our high school years, finally married. I told her with my poems that I was a lesbian. She was not afraid to ask if what she'd read was about her, about my love for her. So there, amidst her growing children, errant husband, and bowling trophies I said yes, the poems were about her and my love for her, a love I'd always regret relinquishing to her reflexive obeisance to tradition. She did not flinch either. We still get drunk together when I go home to Boston.

During the 1970s I focused less on career than on how to eat and be creative at the same time. Graduate school and a string of non-traditional jobs (stage manager, mid-town messenger, etc.) left me so busy I had no time to think about my identity. It was a long time before I made the connection between my desire, my isolation, and the difficulty I had with my writing. I thought of myself as a lesbian between girlfriends—except the between had lasted five years. After some anxiety and frustration I deliberately set about meeting women. Actually, I knew many women, including my closest friend at the time, another black woman also in the theatre. She became uncharacteristically obtuse when I tried to open up and explain my frustration at going to the many parties we attended and being too afraid to approach women I was attracted to, certain I would be rejected either because the women were straight and horrified or gay and terrified of being exposed. For my friend theoretical homosexuality was acceptable, even trendy. Any uncomfortable experience was irrelevant to her. She was impatient and unsympathetic. I drifted away from her in pursuit of the women's community, a phrase that was not in my vocabulary yet, but I knew it was something more than just "women." I fell into that community by connecting with other women writers, and that helped me to focus on my writing and on my social life as a lesbian.

Still, none of my experiences demanded that I bare my soul. I remained honest but not explicit. Expediency, diplomacy, discretion, are all words that come to mind now. At that time I knew no political framework through which to filter my experience. I was more preoccupied with the Attica riots than with Stonewall. The media helped to focus our attentions within a proscribed spectrum and obscure the connections between the issues. I worried about who would shelter Angela Davis, but the concept of sexual politics was remote and theoretical.

I'm not certain exactly when and where the theory and reality converged.

Being a black woman and a lesbian unexpectedly blended like that famous scene in Ingmar Bergman's film *Persona*. The different faces came together as one, and my desire became part of my heritage, my skin, my perspective, my politics, and my future. And I felt sure that it had been my past that helped make the future possible. The women in my family had acted as if their lives were meaningful. Their lives were art. To be a lesbian among them was to be an artist. Perhaps the convergence came when I saw the faces of my great-grandmother, grandmother, and mother in those of the community of women I finally connected with. There was the same adventurous glint in their eyes; the same determined step; the penchant for breaking into song and for not waiting for anyone to take care of them.

I need not pretend to be other than who I was with any of these women. But did I need to declare it? During the holidays when I brought home best friends or lovers my family always welcomed us warmly, clasping us to their magnificent bosoms. Yet there was always an element of silence in our neighborhood, and surprisingly enough in our family, that was disturbing to me. Among the regulars in my father, Duke's, bar, was Maurice. He was eccentric, flamboyant, and still ordinary. He was accorded the same respect by neighborhood children as every other adult. His indiscretions took their place comfortably among the cyclical, Saturday night, man/woman scandals of our neighborhood. I regret never having asked my father how Maurice and he had become friends.

Soon I felt the discomforting silence pressing against my life more persistently. During visits home to Boston it no longer sufficed that Lydia and Dolores were loving and kind to the "friend" I brought home. Maybe it was just my getting older. Living in New York City at the age of thirty in 1980, there was little I kept deliberately hidden from anyone. The genteel silence that hovered around me when I entered our home was palpable but I was unsure whether it was already there when I arrived or if I carried it home within myself. It cut me off from what I knew was a kind of fulfillment available only from my family. The lifeline from Grace, to Lydia, to Dolores, to Jewelle was a strong one. We were bound by so many things, not the least of which was looking so much alike. I was not willing to be orphaned by silence.

If the idea of cathedral weddings and station wagons held no appeal for me, the concept of an extended family was certainly important. But my efforts were stunted by our inability to talk about the life I was creating for myself, for all of us. It felt all the more foolish because I thought I knew how my family would react. I was confident they would respond with their customary aplomb just as they had when I'd first had my hair cut as an Afro (which they hated) or when I brought home friends who were vegetarians (which they found curious). While we had disagreed over some issues, like the fight my mother and I had over Vietnam when I was nineteen, always when the deal went down we sided with each other.

Somewhere deep inside I think I believed that neither my grandmother nor my mother would ever censure my choices. Neither had actually raised me; my great-grandmother had done that, and she had been a steely barricade against any encroachment on our personal freedoms and she'd never disapproved out loud of anything I'd done.

But it was not enough to have an unabashed admiration for these women. It is one thing to have pride in how they'd so graciously survived in spite of the odds against them. It was something else to be standing in a Times Square movie theater faced with the chance to say "it" out loud and risk the loss of their brilliant and benevolent smiles.

My mother had started reading the graffitti written on the wall of the bathroom stall. We hooted at each of her dramatic renderings. Then she said (not breaking her rhythm since we all know timing is everything), "Here's one I haven't seen before—'DYKES UNITE'." There was that profound silence again, as if the frames of my life had ground to a halt. We were in a freeze-frame and options played themselves out in my head in rapid succession: Say nothing? Say something? Say what?

I laughed and said, "Yeah, but have you seen the rubber stamp on my desk at home?"

"No," said my mother with a slight bit of puzzlement. "What does it say?"

"I saw it," my grandmother called out from her stall. "It says: 'Lesbian Money!'"

"What?"

"*Lesbian Money*," Lydia repeated.

"I just stamp it on my big bills," I said tentatively, and we all screamed with laughter. The other woman at the sinks tried to pretend we didn't exist.

Since then there has been little discussion. There have been some moments of awkwardness, usually in social situations where they feel uncertain. Although we have not explored the "it," the shift in our relationship is clear. When I go home it is with my lover and she is received as such. I was lucky. My family was as relieved as I to finally know who I was.

From *Testimonies: A Collection of Lesbian Coming Out Stories*

Talking Back

bell hooks

In the world of the southern black community I grew up in, "back talk" and "talking back" meant speaking as an equal to an authority figure. It meant daring to disagree and sometimes it just meant having an opinion. In the "old school," children were meant to be seen and not heard. My great-grandparents, grandparents, and parents were all from the old school. To make yourself heard if you were a child was to invite punishment, the back-hand lick, the slap across the face that would catch you unaware, or the feel of switches stinging your arms and legs.

To speak then when one was not spoken to was a courageous act—an act of risk and daring. And yet it was hard not to speak in warm rooms where heated discussions began at the crack of dawn, women's voices filling the air, giving orders, making threats, fussing. Black men may have excelled in the art of poetic preaching in the male-dominated church, but in the church of the home, where the everyday rules of how to live and how to act were established, it was black women who preached. There, black women spoke in a language so rich, so poetic, that it felt to me like being shut off from life, smothered to death if one were not allowed to participate.

It was in that world of woman talk (the men were often silent, often absent) that was born in me the craving to speak, to have a voice, and not just any voice but one that could be identified as belonging to me. To make my voice, I had to speak, to hear myself talk—and talk I did—darting in and out of grown folks' conversations and dialogues, answering questions that were not directed at me, endlessly asking questions, making speeches. Needless to say, the punishments for these acts of speech seemed endless. They were intended to silence me—the child—and more particularly the girl child. Had I been a boy, they might have encouraged me to speak believing that I might someday be called to preach. There was no "calling" for talking girls, no legitimized rewarded speech. The punishments I received for "talking back" were intended to suppress all possibility that I would create my own speech. That speech was to be suppressed so that the "right speech of womanhood" would emerge.

Within feminist circles, silence is often seen as the sexist "right speech of womanhood"—the sign of woman's submission to patriarchal authority. This emphasis on woman's silence may be an accurate remembering of what has taken place in the households of women from WASP backgrounds in the United States, but in black communities (and diverse ethnic communities), women have not been silent. Their voices can be heard. Certainly for black women, our struggle has not been to emerge from silence into speech but to change the nature and direction of our speech, to make a speech that compels listeners, one that is heard.

Our speech, "the right speech of womanhood," was often the soliloquy, the talking into thin air, the talking to ears that do not hear you—the talk that is simply not listened to. Unlike the black male preacher whose speech was to be heard, who was to be listened to, whose words were to be remembered, the voices of black women—giving orders, making threats, fussing—could be tuned out, could become a kind of background music, audible but not acknowledged as significant speech. Dialogue—the sharing of speech and recognition—took place not between mother and child or mother and male authority figure but among black women. I can remember watching fascinated as our mother talked with her mother, sisters, and women friends. The intimacy and intensity of their speech— the satisfaction they received from talking to one another, the pleasure, the joy. It was in this world of woman speech, loud talk, angry words, women with tongues quick and sharp, tender sweet tongues, touching our world with their words, that I made speech my birthright—and the right to voice, to authorship, a privilege I would not be denied. It was in that world and because of it that I came to dream of writing, to write.

Writing was a way to capture speech, to hold onto it, keep it close. And so I wrote down bits and pieces of conversations, confessing in cheap diaries that soon fell apart from too much handling, expressing the intensity of my sorrow, the anguish of speech—for I was always saying the wrong thing, asking the wrong questions. I could not confine my speech to the necessary corners and concerns of life. I hid these writings under my bed, in pillow stuffings, among faded underwear. When my sisters found and read them, they ridiculed and mocked me—poking fun. I felt violated, ashamed, as if the secret parts of my self had been exposed, brought into the open, and hung like newly clean laundry, out in the air for everyone to see. The fear of exposure, the fear that one's deepest emotions and innermost thoughts will be dismissed as mere nonsense, felt by so many young girls keeping diaries, holding and hiding speech, seems to me now one of the barriers that women have always needed and still need to destroy so that we are no longer pushed into secrecy or silence.

Despite my feelings of violation, of exposure, I continued to speak and write, choosing my hiding places well, learning to destroy work when no safe place could be found. I was never taught absolute silence, I was taught that it was important to speak but to talk a talk that was in itself a silence. Taught to speak and yet beware of the betrayal of too much heard speech, I experienced intense confusion and deep anxiety in my efforts to speak and write. Reciting poems at Sunday afternoon church service might be rewarded. Writing a poem (when one's time could be "better" spent sweeping, ironing, learning to cook) was luxurious activity, indulged in at the expense of others. Questioning authority, raising issues that were not deemed appropriate subjects brought pain, punishments—like telling mama I wanted to die before her because I could not live without her—that was crazy talk, crazy speech, the kind that would lead you to end up in a mental institution. "Little girl," I would be told, "if you don't stop all this crazy talk and crazy acting you are going to end up right out there at Western State."

Madness, not just physical abuse, was the punishment for too much talk if you were female. Yet even as this fear of madness haunted me, hanging over my writing like a monstrous shadow, I could not stop the words, making thought, writing speech. For this terrible madness which I feared, which I was sure was the destiny of daring women born to intense speech (after all, the authorities emphasized this point daily), was not as threatening as imposed silence, as suppressed speech.

Safety and sanity were to be sacrificed if I was to experience defiant speech. Though I risked them both, deep-seated fears and anxieties characterized my childhood days. I would speak but I would not ride a bike, play hardball, or hold the gray kitten. Writing about the ways we are traumatized in our growing-up years, psychoanalyst Alice Miller makes the point in *For Your Own Good* that it is not clear why childhood wounds become for some folk an opportunity to grow, to move forward rather than backward in the process of self-realization. Certainly, when I reflect on the trials of my growing-up years, the many punishments, I can see now that in resistance I learned to be vigilant in the nourishment of my spirit, to be tough, to courageously protect that spirit from forces that would break it.

While punishing me, my parents often spoke about the necessity of breaking my spirit. Now when I ponder the silences, the voices that are not heard, the voices of those wounded and/or oppressed individuals who do not speak or write, I contemplate the acts of persecution, torture—the terrorism that breaks spirits, that makes creativity impossible. I write these words to bear witness to the primacy of resistance struggle in any situation of domination (even within family life); to the strength and power that emerges from sustained resistance and the profound conviction that these forces can be healing, can protect us from dehumanization and despair.

These early trials, wherein I learned to stand my ground, to keep my spirit intact, came vividly to mind after I published *Ain't I A Woman* and the book was sharply and harshly criticized. While I had expected a climate of critical dialogue, I was not expecting a critical avalanche that had the power in its intensity to crush the spirit, to push one into silence. Since that time, I have heard stories about black women, about women of color, who write and publish (even when the work is quite successful) having nervous breakdowns, being made mad because they cannot bear the harsh responses of family, friends, and unknown critics, or becoming silent, unproductive. Surely, the absence of a humane critical response has tremendous impact on the writer from any oppressed, colonized group who endeavors to speak. For us, true speaking is not solely an expression of creative power; it is an act of resistance, a political gesture that challenges politics of domination that would render us nameless and voiceless. As such, it is a courageous act—as such, it represents a threat. To those who wield oppressive power, that which is threatening must necessarily be wiped out, annihilated, silenced.

Recently, efforts by black women writers to call attention to our work serve to highlight both our presence and absence. Whenever I peruse women's bookstores, I am struck not by the rapidly growing body of feminist writing by black women, but by the paucity of available published material. Those of us who write and are published remain few in number. The context of silence is varied and multi-dimensional. Most obvious are the ways racism, sexism, and class exploitation act to suppress and silence. Less obvious are the inner struggles, the efforts made to gain the necessary confidence to write, to re-write, to fully develop craft and skill—and the extent to which such efforts fail.

Although I have wanted writing to be my life-work since childhood, it has been difficult for me to claim "writer" as part of that which identifies and shapes my everyday reality. Even after publishing books, I would often speak of wanting to be a writer as though these works did not exist. And though I would be told, "you are a writer," I was not yet ready to fully affirm this truth. Part of myself was still held captive by domineering forces of history, of familial life that had charted a map of silence, of right speech. I had not completely let go of the fear of saying the wrong thing, of being punished. Somewhere in the deep recesses of my mind, I believed I could avoid both responsibility and punishment if I did not declare myself a writer.

One of the many reasons I chose to write using the pseudonym bell hooks, a family name (mother to Sarah Oldham, grandmother to Rosa Bell Oldham, great-grandmother to me), was to construct a writer-identity that would challenge and subdue all impulses leading me away from speech into silence. I was a young girl buying bubble gum at the corner store when I first really heard the full name bell hooks. I had just "talked back" to a grown person. Even now I can recall the surprised look, the mocking tones that informed me I must be kin to bell hooks—a sharp-tongued woman, a woman who spoke her mind, a woman who was not afraid to talk back. I claimed this legacy of defiance, of will, of courage, affirming my link to female ancestors who were bold and daring in their speech. Unlike my bold and daring mother and grandmother, who were not supportive of talking back, even though they were assertive and powerful in their speech, bell hooks as I discovered, claimed, and invented her was my ally, my support.

That initial act of talking back outside the home was empowering. It was the first of many acts of defiant speech that would make it possible for me to emerge as an independent thinker and writer. In retrospect, "talking back" became for me a rite of initiation, testing my courage, strengthening my commitment, preparing me for the days ahead—the days when writing, rejection notices, periods of silence, publication, ongoing development seem impossible but necessary.

Moving from silence into speech is for the oppressed, the colonized, the exploited, and those who stand and struggle side by side a gesture of defiance that heals, that makes new life and new growth possible. It is that act of speech, of "talking back," that is no mere gesture of empty words, that is the expression of our movement from object to subject—the liberated voice.

From *Talking Back: Thinking Feminist, Thinking Black*

The Girl Who Wouldn't Sing

Kit Yuen Quan

It was really hard deciding how to talk about language because I had to go through my blocks with language. I stumble upon these blocks whenever I have to write, speak in public or voice my opinions in a group of native English speakers with academic backgrounds. All of a sudden as I scramble for words, I freeze and am unable to think clearly. Minutes pass as I struggle to retrieve my thoughts until I finally manage to say something. But it never comes close to expressing what I mean. I think it's because I'm afraid to show who I really am. I cannot bear the thought of the humiliation and ridicule. And I dread having to use a language that has often betrayed my meaning. Saying what I need to say using my own words usually threatens the status quo.

People assume that I don't have a language problem because I can speak English, even when I ask them to take into account that English is my second language. This is the usual reaction I have gotten while working in the feminist movement. It's true that my language problems are different from those of a recent immigrant who cannot work outside of Chinatown because she or he doesn't speak enough English. Unlike my parents, I don't speak with a heavy accent. After twenty years of living in this country, watching American television and going through its school system, I have acquired adequate English skills to function fairly well. I can pass as long as I don't have to write anything or say what I really think around those whom I see as being more educated and articulate than I am. I can spend the rest of my life avoiding jobs that require extensive reading and writing skills. I can join the segment of the population that reads only out of necessity rather than for information, appreciation or enlightenment.

It's difficult for people to accept that I believe I have a literacy problem because they do not understand the nature of my blocks with language. Learning anything new terrifies me, especially if it involves words or writing. I get this overwhelming fear, this heart-stopping panic that I won't understand it. I won't know how to do it. My body tenses up and I forget to breathe if there is a word in a sentence that I don't know or several sentences in a paragraph containing unfamiliar words. My confidence dwindles and I start to feel the ground falling from under me. In my frustration I feel like crying, running out or smashing something, but that would give me away, expose my defect. So I tune out or nod my head as if there is nothing wrong. I've had to cover it up in order to survive, get jobs, pass classes and at times to work and live with people who do not care to understand my reality.

Living with this fear leaves me exhausted. I feel backed against a wall of self-doubt, pushed into a corner, defeated, unable to stretch or take advantage of opportunities. Beyond just being able to read and write well enough to get by, I need to be able to learn, understand, communicate, to articulate my thoughts and feelings, and participate fully without feeling ashamed of who I am and where I come from.

When I first arrived in San Francisco from Hong Kong at age seven and a half, the only English I knew was the alphabet and a few simple words: cat, dog, table, chair. I sat in classrooms for two to three years without understanding what was being said, and cried while the girl next to me filled in my spelling book for me. In music class when other kids volunteered to go up in front of the class to play musical instruments, I'd never raise my hand. I wouldn't sing. The teacher probably wondered why there were always three Chinese girls in one row who wouldn't sing. In art class, I was so traumatized that I couldn't be creative. While other kids moved about freely in school, seeming to flow from one activity to the next, I was disoriented, out of step, feeling hopelessly behind. I went into a "survivor mode" and couldn't participate in activities.

I remember one incident in particular in the fourth grade during a kickball game. I had just missed the ball when Kevin, the class jock, came running across the yard and kicked me in the butt. Had I been able to speak English, I might have screamed my head off or called for the teacher, but I just stood there trying to numb out the pain, feeling everyone's eyes on me. I wasn't sure it wasn't all part of the game.

At home I spoke the sam yup dialect of Cantonese with my parents, who were completely unaware of the severity of my problems at school. In their eyes I was very lucky to be going to school in America. My father had had only a high school education before he had to start working. And we children would not have had any chance to go to college had we stayed in Hong Kong. We had flown over the Pacific Ocean three times between the time I was seven and a half and eight and a half because they were so torn about leaving their home to resettle in a foreign country and culture. At the dinner table after a day of toiling at their jobs and struggling with English, they aired their frustrations about the racism and discrimination they were feeling everywhere: at their jobs, on the bus, at the supermarket. Although they didn't feel very hopeful about their own lives, they were comforted by the fact that my brother and I were getting a good education. Both my parents had made incredible sacrifices for my education. Life would be easier for us, with more opportunities and options, because we would know the language. We would be able to talk back or fight back if need be. All we had to do was study hard and apply ourselves. So every day after school I would load my bag full of textbooks and walk up two hills to where we lived the first few years after we landed here. I remember opening each book and reading out loud a paragraph or two, skipping over words I didn't know until I gave up in frustration.

My parents thought that by mastering the English language, I would be able to attain the Chinese American dream: a college education, a good-paying job, a house in the suburbs, a Chinese husband and children. They felt intimidated and powerless in American society and so clung tightly to me to fulfill their hopes and dreams. When I objected to these expectations using my limited Chinese, I received endless lectures. I felt smothered by their traditional values of how a Chinese girl should behave and this was reason enough not to learn more Chinese. Gradually language came to represent our two or more opposing sets of values. If I asserted my individuality, wanted to go out with my friends, had opinions of my own, or disagreed with their plans for me, I was accused of becoming too smart for my own good now that I had grown wings. "*Cheun neuih*, stupid girl. Don't think you're better than your parents just because you know more English. You don't know anything! We've eaten more salt than you've eaten rice." Everything I heard in Chinese was a dictate. It was always one more thing I wasn't supposed to do or be, one more way I wasn't supposed to think. At school I felt stupid for not knowing the language. At home I was under attack for my rebellious views. The situation became intolerable after I came out to my parents as a lesbian.

When I ran away from home at sixteen, I sought refuge in the women's community working part-time at a feminist bookstore. I felt like I had no family, no home, no identity or culture I could claim. In between hiding from my parents and crashing at various women's houses, I hung out in the Mission playing pool with other young dykes, got high, or took to the streets when I felt like I was going to explode. Sometimes at night I found myself sitting at the counter of some greasy spoon Chinese restaurant longing for a home-cooked meal. I was lonely for someone to talk to who could understand how I felt, but I didn't even have the words to communicate what I felt.

At the bookstore, I was discovering a whole other world: women, dykes, feminists, authors, political activists, artists—people who read and talked about what they were reading. As exciting as it all was, I didn't understand what people were talking about. What was political theory? What was literary criticism? Words flew over my head like planes over a runway. In order to communicate with other feminists, most of whom were white or middle class or both, educated, and at least ten years older than me, I had to learn feminist rhetoric.

Given my uprooted and transplanted state, I have a difficult time explaining to other people how I feel about language. Usually they don't understand or will even dispute what I'm saying. A lot of times I'll think it's because I don't have the right words, I haven't read enough books, or I don't know the language. That's how I felt all the time while working at a feminist bookstore. It wasn't only white, educated people who didn't understand how I felt. Women of color or Third World women who had class privilege and came from literary backgrounds thought the problem was more my age and my lack of political development. I often felt beaten down by these kinds of attitudes while still thinking that my not being understood was the result of my inability to communicate rather than an unreceptive environment.

Even though feminist rhetoric does give me words to describe how I'm being oppressed, it still reflects the same racist, classist standards of the dominant society and of colleges and universities. I get frustrated because I constantly feel I'm being put down for what I'm saying or how I talk. For example, in a collective meeting with other women, I spoke about how I felt as a working class person and why I felt different from them. I told them they felt "middle class" to me because of the way they behaved and because of the values they had, that their "political vision" didn't include people with my experience and concerns. I tried to say all of this using feminist rhetoric, but when I used the term "working class," someone would argue, "You can't use that term...." Because they were educated they thought they owned the language and so could say, "You can't use 'middle class,' you can't use 'working class,' because nowadays everybody is working class and it's just a matter of whether you're poor or comfortable." They did not listen to the point I was trying to make. They didn't care that I was sitting there in the circle stumbling along, struggling to explain how I felt oppressed by them and the structure and policies of the organization. Instead of listening to why I felt that way, they invalidated me for the way I used language and excluded me by defending themselves and their positions and claiming that my issues and feelings were "personal" and that I should just get over them.

Another example of my feeling excluded is when people in a room make all sorts of literary allusions. They make me feel like I should have read those books. They throw around metaphors that leave me feeling lost and confused. I don't get to throw in my metaphors. Instead of acknowledging our different backgrounds and trying to include me in the discussion, they choose to ignore my feelings of isolation. I find that among feminists, white and colored, especially those who pride themselves on being progressive political activists with credentials, there's an assumption that if a person just read more, studied more, she would find the right words, the right way to use them, and even the right thoughts. A lot of times my language and the language of other working class, non-academic people become the target of scrutiny and criticism when others don't want to hear what we have to say. They convince themselves we're using the wrong words: "What definition are you using?" "What do you mean by that?" And then we get into debate about what was meant, we get lost in semantics and then we really don't know what we're saying.

Why should I try to use all of these different words when I'm being manipulated and suppressed by those whose rhetoric is more developed, whether it's feminist, academic, or leftist?

Those of us who feel invisible or misunderstood when we try to name what is oppressing us within supposedly feminist or progressive groups need to realize that our language is legitimate and valid. It comes from our families, our cultures, our class backgrounds, our experiences of different and conflicting realities. And we don't need to read another book to justify it. If I want to say *I'm working class*, I should be able to *say* I'm working class without having to read or quote Marx. But just saying that I'm working class never gives me enough of the understanding that I want. Because our experiences and feelings are far too complex to be capsulized in abstractions like "oppression," "sexism," "racism," etc., there is no right combination of these terms which can express why we feel oppressed.

I knew that I needed to go some place where some of my experiences with language would be mirrored. Through the Refugee Women's Program in the Tenderloin district of San Francisco, I started to tutor two Cambodian refugee girls. The Buth family had been in the U.S. for one and a half years. They lived, twelve people to a room, in an apartment building on Eddy Street half a block from the porno theaters. I went to their home one evening a week and on Sundays took the girls to the children's library. The doorbells in the building were out of order, so visitors had to wait to be let in by someone on their way out. Often I stood on their doorsteps watching the street life. The fragrant smell of jasmine rice wafting from the windows of the apartment building mixed with the smell of booze and piss on the street. Newspapers, candy wrappers and all kinds of garbage swept up by the wind colored the sidewalks. Cars honked and sped past while Asian, Black and white kids played up and down the street. Mothers carrying their babies weaved through loose gatherings of drunk men and prostitutes near the corner store. Around me I heard a medley of languages: Vietnamese, Chinese, Cambodian, English, Black English, Laotian.

Sometimes, I arrived to find Yan and Eng sitting on the steps behind the security gate waiting to let me in. Some days they wore their school clothes, while on other days they were barefooted and wore their traditional sarongs. As we climbed the stairs up to their apartment, we inhaled fish sauce and curry and rice. Six-year-old Eng would chatter and giggle but Yan was quieter and more reserved. Although she was only eight years old, I couldn't help but feel like I was in the company of a serious adult. I immediately identified with her. I noticed how, whenever I gave them something to do, they didn't want to do it on their own. For example, they often got excited when I brought them books, but they wouldn't want to read by themselves. They became quiet and withdrawn when I asked them questions. Their answer was always a timid "I don't know," and they never asked a question or made a request. So I read with them. We did everything together. I didn't want them to feel like they were supposed to automatically know what to do, because I remembered how badly that used to make me feel.

Play time was the best part of our time together. All the little kids joined in and sometimes even their older brothers. Everybody was so excited that they forgot they were learning English. As we played jigsaw sentences and word concentration and chickens and whales, I became a little kid again, except this time I wasn't alone and unhappy. When they made Mother's Day cards, I made a Mother's Day card. When they drew pictures of our field trip to the beach, I sketched pictures of us at the beach. When we made origami frogs and jumped them all over the floor, I went home and made dinosaurs, kangaroos, spiders, crabs and lobsters. Week after week, I added to my repertoire until I could feel that little kid who used to sit like the piece of unmolded clay in front of her in art class turn into a wide-eyed origami enthusiast.

As we studied and played in the middle of the room surrounded by the rest of the family who were sleeping, nursing, doing homework, playing cards, talking, laughing or crying, Yan would frequently interrupt our lesson to answer her mother. Sometimes it was a long conversation, but I didn't mind because English was their second language. They spoke only Cambodian with their family. If they laughed at something on television, it was usually at the picture and not at the dialogue. English was used for schoolwork and to talk to me. They did not try to express their thoughts and feelings in English. When they spoke to each other, they were not alone or isolated. Whether they were living in a refugee camp in the Philippines or in Thailand or in a one-room apartment on Eddy Street, they were connected to each other through their language and their culture. They had survived war, losing family members, their country and their home, but in speaking their language, they were able to love and comfort each other. Sitting there on the bamboo mat next to the little girls, Eng and her younger sister Oeun, listening to their sweet little voices talking and singing, I understood for the first time what it was like to be a child with a voice and it made me remember my first love, the Chinese language.

While searching for an address, I came across a postcard of the San Francisco-Oakland Bay Bridge. I immediately recognized it as the postcard I had sent to my schoolmate in Hong Kong when I first got here. On the back was my eight-and-a-half-year-old handwriting.

In English it says:

Dear Kam Yee, I received your letter. You asked if I've been to school yet. Yes, I've already found a school. My family has decided to stay in America. My living surroundings are very nice. Please don't worry about me. I'm sorry it has taken so long for me to return your letter. Okay lets talk some more next time. Please give my regards to your parents and

your family. I wish you happiness. Signed: Your classmate, Yuen Kit,
August 30th.

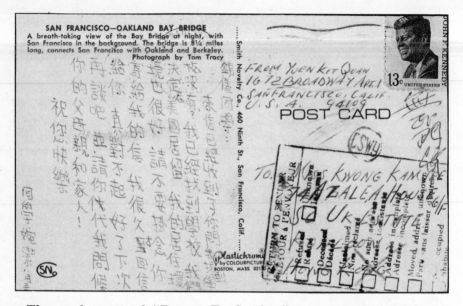

The card, stamped "Return To Sender," is postmarked 1970. Although I have sketchy memories of my early school days in Hong Kong, I still remember the day when Kam Yee and I found each other. The bell rang signaling the end of class. Sitting up straight in our chairs, we had recited "Goodbye, teacher" in a chorus. While the others were rushing out the door to their next class, I rose from my desk and slowly put away my books. Over my left shoulder I saw Kam Yee watching me. We smiled at each other as I walked over to her desk. I had finally made a friend. Soon after that my family left Hong Kong and I wrote my last Chinese letter.

All the time that I was feeling stupid and overwhelmed by language, could I have been having the Chinese blues? By the time I was seven, I was reading the Chinese newspaper. I remember because there were a lot of reports of raped and mutilated women's bodies found in plastic bags on the side of quiet roads. It was a thrill when my father would send me to the newsstand on the corner to get his newspaper. Passing street vendors peddling sweets and fruit, I would run as quickly as I could. From a block away I could smell the stinky odor of *dauh fuh fa*, my favorite snack of slippery, warm, soft tofu in sweet syrup.

Up until a year ago, I could only recognize some of the Chinese characters on store signs, restaurant menus and Chinese newspapers on Stockton and Powell Streets, but I always felt a tingle of excitement whenever I recognized a word or knew its sound, like oil sizzling in a wok just waiting for something to fry.

On Saturdays I sit with my Chinese language teacher on one of the stone benches lining the overpass where the financial district meets Chinatown and links Portsmouth Square to the Holiday Inn Hotel. We have been meeting once a week for me to practice speaking, reading and writing Chinese using whatever material we can find. Sometimes I read a bilingual Chinese American weekly newspaper called the East West Journal, other times Chinese folk tales for young readers from the Chinatown Children's Library, or bilingual brochures describing free services offered by non-profit Chinatown community agencies, and sometimes even Chinese translations of Pacific Bell Telephone inserts. I look forward to these sessions where I reach inward to recover all those lost sounds that once were the roots of my childhood imagination. This exercise in trying to use my eight-year-old vocabulary to verbalize my thoughts as an adult is as scary as it is exhilarating. At one time Chinese was poetry to me. Words, their sounds and their rhythms, conjured up images that pulled me in and gave me a physical sense of their meanings. The Chinese characters that I wrote and practiced were pictographs of water, grass, birds, fire, heart and mouth. With my calligraphy brush made of pig's hair, I made the rain fall and the wind blow.

Now, speaking Chinese with my father is the closest I have felt to coming home. In a thin but sage-like voice, he reflects on a lifetime of hard work and broken dreams and we slowly reconnect as father and daughter. As we sit across the kitchen table from one another, his old and tattered Chinese dictionary by his side, he tells me of the loving relationship he had with his mother, who encouraged him in his interest in writing and the movies. Although our immigrant experiences are generations apart and have been impacted differently by American culture, in his words I see the core of who I am. I cannot express my feelings fully in either Chinese or English or make him understand my choices. Though I am still grappling with accepting the enormous love behind the sacrifices he has made to give me a better life, I realize that with my ability to move in two different worlds I am the fruit of his labor.

For 85 cents, I can have unlimited refills of tea and a *gai mei baau* at The Sweet Fragrance Cafe on Broadway across from the World Theatre. After the first bite, the coconut sugar and butter ooze down my palm. Behind the pastry counter, my favorite clerk is consolidating trays of walnut cupcakes. Pointing to some round fried bread covered with sesame seeds, she urges the customer with "Four for a dollar, very fresh!"

Whole families from grandparents to babies sleeping soundly on mothers' backs come here for porridge, pastries and coffee. Mothers stroll in to get sweets for little ones waiting at home. Old women carrying their own mugs from home come in to chat with their buddies. Workers wearing aprons smeared with pig's blood or fresh fish scales drop in for a bite during their break. Chinese husbands sit for hours complaining and gossiping not unlike the old women in the park.

A waitress brings bowls of beef stew noodles and pork liver porridge. Smokers snub out their cigarettes as they pick up their chopsticks. The man across from me is counting sons and daughters on the fingers of his left hand: one son, another son, my wife, one daughter. He must have family in China waiting to immigrate.

The regulars congregate at the back tables, shouting opinions from one end of the long table to the other. The Chinese are notorious for their loud conversations at close range that can easily be mistaken for arguments and fights until someone breaks into laughter or gives his companion a friendly punch. Here the drama of life is always unfolding in all different dialects. I may not understand a lot of it, but the chuckling, the hand gestures, the raising of voices in protest and in accusation, and the laughter all flow like music, like a Cantonese opera.

Twenty years seems like a long time, but it has taken all twenty years for me to understand my language blocks and to find ways to help myself learn. I have had to create my own literacy program. I had to recognize that the school system failed to meet my needs as an immigrant and that this society and its institutions doesn't reflect or validate my experiences. I have to let myself grieve over the loss of my native language and all the years wasted in classrooms staring into space or dozing off when I was feeling depressed and hopeless. My various activities now help to remind me that my relationship with language is more complex than just speaking enough English to get by. In creative activity and in anything that requires words, I'm still eight years old. Sometimes I open a book and I still feel I can't read. It may take days or weeks for me to work up the nerve to open that book again. But I do open it and it gets a little easier each time that I work through the fear. As long as there are bakeries in Chinatown and as long as I have 85 cents, I know I have a way back to myself.

5 Political Arts, Subversive Acts

Madness Disguises Sanity

Opal Palmer Adisa

Sometimes
I mutter
as I walk
people stare/pass by
on far side

To be
one of those
desolate men
lounging in
stench alleyways
forever talking
to the wind
their words
bullets
people shy from

But I'm woman
conditioned
to nurse screams
like a mute child

I write

From *Morena* February 1988

Not Editable

Chrystos

September 3, 1983

Gloria, dear sister,

I begin to write a little   typed snatches   I ask myself if they
are "Art"   I have lost shreds of myself my confidence and my
judgement   No coherence   my past work came from someone I
can't be anymore   I'm changing don't know where I'm going   no
anchors   no bag to stay inside of   form makes me restless   I
am not editable

This one [woman] thinks I'm a Real Artist   (WHAT is a real
artist? I don't do enough work to be one myself)   I have soul she says
yeah I think   you wanna buy some?

I am so afraid always under my tough exterior   I don't really
believe I have anything unique to say   I've always written from some
compulsion, the necessity to make some damn sense somewhere   a
tool of survival   never been art to me   Colors are different   I
am going to start to cry and I don't know why   even the dahlias hurt
that gave me such joy a few hours ago   I've never been here before
always circumvented it with drug overdoses or hospital   stays
from suicide attempts   anything to distract me from   this unconnected anguish   these letters are masks you know   it is my journal
that is my best self   if there is a best self   I am still trying to find
it   find my way to bone honesty

September 5, 1983

I want a world to be like the dahlias this morning that shock me as
I pass by them with handfuls of dirty clothes   they pulse with life
they sing it   they are coming right out of their skins with it   I
retreat inside myself and wonder what I am supposed to do here   I
keep returning to the same answer   make some dahlia beauty
force it down their throats   wake them up   the sun comes over
the edge of the building and shines down on my wet face   the rainbows
in my eyelashes   the music   hammered dulcimer and celtic harp
the wild roses are so still and the boat hulls gleam with dew   I am
lonely because I am pierced with life and so much is dead   there must
be some place for me   I've been taught so well that functioning is the
appearance of knowing what one is doing   at the dahlia farm I
belonged   I was at home in those tall fat flowers blazing profuse and
generous and full   I want to plant myself in her field and die back in
the fall

I am sure that if I knew others who wrote or painted or SOME-THING   I would feel much differently   but those I know are ordinary folks   I used to seek them out   afraid I would get a big head if I didn't   thought it was so snobbish to only want other creative geniuses for friends   now I feel that anyone else will literally drive me mad   I have decided to open more deeply in letters because I don't have to hold back anything or be correct or any of that shit   and your power is equal to mine, different, very different but you are not afraid of me   that is such a relief

I do want very much to be a good writer   but I am tired of the conventions of poems   I don't know what to do about form   the only "form" that doesn't feel restrictive is letters   I'm afraid I don't make "sense" when I try to move that immediacy to other forms   I'll always write poems of course, but I want to make something else, something new   a joint dialogue or a chorus or something that is very definitely not a "novel"   because they aren't novel anymore

August 21, 1983

I've been calling myself "Captain C" to bring home the fact that *I'm* in charge of my life and if I don't make manifest the beauty I carry in my heart, *use* my gifts—the regret and anger will poison me.

I am beginning to understand the idea of marrying the work. I am wondering why I obsessively save scraps of paper and everyone's letters. I know why. They prove my existence, that I'm cared for a little. That has always seemed necessary to verify through accumulation. Knowing why doesn't stop me.

I ache to belong somewhere, to some place, to some compassionate fellow travelers, to an idea larger than myself. But I make a lousy true believer. Authority is the worst tyranny. Why are we so dependent and rebellious with it?

I vaguely think of churning out art to support myself instead of cleaning toilets but I'll never be interested in success. I want something vastly more difficult—spiritual release, inner and world peace, a body of work I can heal myself through. My materialism is spiritual.

I am a hole rather than a whole. Change screams through me yet I cannot close that gaping wound. It is only when I work that I seem to have a core. I want to be an artist. I fight so many ghost demons just to *say* that. As the wind blows these papers, I wonder if my life has any meaning. I feel so random.

Writing has always been my blanket to pull me through.

Always written to *survive*. A desperation to it. Naming my version of truth to preserve my "sanity" because they are so very busy trying to snatch it away. I'm more sure of my drawings. I go into another state when I draw. Maybe I don't love words as much as I do colors. It's words I'm unsure of. Words are mushy. A line feels so *there*.

I want to spend the next *three* weeks sitting in this chair continuing this letter for you with breaks to eat and piss. *Then* I might begin to find the root...writing is mostly discarding fear *isn't it?* Trusting that one's private voice can give voice for others. Is it necessary to publish though? That's *my* current dilemma.

Yours,
Boca Caliente

A Julia de Burgos

Julia de Burgos

Ya las gentes murmuran que yo soy tu enemiga
porque dicen que en verso doy al mundo tu yo.
Mienten, Julia de Burgos. Mienten, Julia de Burgos.
La que se alza en mis versos no es tu voz: es mi voz;
porque tú eres el ropaje y la esencia soy yo;
y el más profundo abismo se tiende entre las dos.

Tú eres fría muñeca de mentira social,
y yo, viril destello de la humana verdad.

Tú, miel de cortesanas hipocresías; yo no;
que en todos mis poemas desnuda el corazón.

Tú eres como tu mundo, egoísta; yo no;
que todo me lo juego a ser lo que soy yo.

Tú eres sólo la grave señora señorona;
yo no; yo soy la vida, la fuerza, la mujer.

Tú eres de tu marido, de tu amo; yo no;
yo de nadie, o de todos, porque a todos, a todos,
en mi limpio sentir y en mi pensar me doy.

Tú te rizas el pelo y te pintas; yo no;
a mí me riza el viento; a mí me pinta el sol.

Tú eres dama casera, resignada, sumisa,
atada a los prejuicios de los hombres; yo no;
que yo soy Rocinante corriendo desbocado
olfateando horizontes de justicia de Dios.

Tú en ti misma no mandas; a ti todos te mandan;
en ti mandan tu esposo, tus padres, tus parientes,
el cura, la modista, el teatro, el casino,
el auto, las alhajas, el banquete, el champán,
el cielo y el infierno y el qué dirán social.

En mí no, que en mí manda mi solo corazón,
mi solo pensamiento; quien manda en mí soy yo.

Tú flor de aristocracia; y yo la flor del pueblo.
Tú en ti lo tienes todo y a todos se lo debes,
mientras que yo, mi nada a nadie se la debo.

Tú clavada al estático dividendo ancestral,
y yo, un uno en la cifra del divisor social,
somos el duelo a muerte que se acerca fatal.

Cuando las multitudes corran alborotadas
dejando atrás cenizas de injusticias quemadas,
y cuando con la tea de las siete virtudes,
tras los siete pecados, corran las multitudes,
contra ti y contra todo lo injusto y lo inhumano,
yo iré en medio de ellas con la tea en la mano.

From *Obra poética*

To Julia de Burgos

Julia de Burgos

They say I am your enemy
because I give your inmost self to the world in verse.
They lie, Julia de Burgos. They lie, Julia de Burgos.
The voice that sounds in my poems is not your voice; it is my voice;
because you are the trappings and I am the essence;
and between us stretches the deepest divide.

You are the cold doll of social prevarication,
and I the living spark of human truth.

You are the honey of polite hypocrisies; not I,
who lay bare my naked heart in all my poems.

You are like your world, selfish; not I,
who risk everything to be what I am.

You are only the prim ladylike lady;
not I; I am life, strength, woman.

You belong to your husband, to your master; not I;
I belong to no one, or to everyone, because to everyone, everyone,
I give myself in my pure feeling and my thought.

You curl your hair and paint your face; not I;
My hair is curled by the wind, my face is painted by the sun.

You are a housewife, resigned, submissive,
ruled by the prejudices of men; not I;
I am a runaway Rocinante
sniffing at horizons for the justice of God.

You do not command yourself; everyone commands you:
your husband, your parents, your relatives,
the priest, the dressmaker, the theatre, the casino,
the car, the jewels, the banquet, the champagne,
heaven and hell and social gossip.

Not me; to me only my heart gives commands,
only my thought; the one who commands me is myself.

You, flower of the aristocracy, and I, flower of the people.
You have everything and you owe everything to everyone,
while I, my nothingness I owe to no one.

You, nailed to the static ancestral dividend,
and I, a one in the cipher of the social divider,
we are in a duel to the death approaching the inevitable.

While the multitudes race about frantically,
leaving behind ashes from burnt-out injustices,
and while with the torch of the seven virtues
the multitudes pursue the seven sins,
against you, and against everything unjust and inhuman,
I shall go into their midst with the torch in my hand.

Translated by William M. Davis

From *The Defiant Muse: Hispanic Feminist Poems from the Middle Ages to the Present*

Grace

Carmen Morones

There was a rhythmic tapping at the door which Frances recognized as Mrs. Baca's, one of her neighbors in the projects. Frances turned off the stove, swooped the headless Barbie doll from the kitchen floor and went to open the door. "Come on in, Mrs. Baca," she said, holding the screen door open for the large grey-haired woman in the colorful muumuu.

"*¡Buenos dias*, Frances!" Mrs. Baca shuffled across the entrance in cloth slippers, rustling a folded newspaper she used as a fan.

"Sorry it's so hot in here, the cooler's not working," Frances said, more out of concern for Mrs. Baca's comfort than as a complaint. The cooler was constantly breaking down and she had learned to adapt to the humid indoor heat.

"Don' worry about me," Mrs. Baca said, her fanning increasing as she moved farther into the entry way, "I'm jus' gonna be a minute." She inhaled the smell of fried egg and *chorizo* that permeated the house and let out an inadvertent "Umm."

"My mom's in the bathroom combing Rosie's hair."

"I gotta show her this!" Mrs. Baca said, holding up the paper. She smiled as though she were the only person who had seen the paper this morning. "Frances," she said, suddenly grabbing her arm, "you wanna see?" Without waiting for an answer, she unfolded *The Desert Chronicle* and held it in front of her chest. "It's *la Gracie!*"

Frances politely glanced at the large black and white photo that stood out from the other articles. To her surprise, Grace looked stunning. She gave the impression of a queen or movie star in her jeweled tiara, pearl drop earrings and matching necklace. A sleeveless satin dress covered her bosom and her dark, sleek hair dipped perfectly into her bare shoulders. Her face showed no traces of the blemishes Frances noticed at school. Grace smiled a carefree dimpled smile and stared directly at you as though she had never had to be ashamed of anything in her sweet sixteen years. Frances wanted to throw the paper in the trash.

"She's our *primera*, our only one, ever, Frances! It even says it here in the paper. And do you know that she gets all A's and she's even going to reporters' college? No, them other girls that's been in the last few days don't even come close."

Frances wanted to say, "She's not one of us. She's a socie and she may as well be white. She and her kind act as if us Mexicans at school don't even exist. Why should I care if she's running for Homecoming queen?" But she didn't know how to say it, so she kept quiet.

"Oh! I better hurry—I tol' Señora Garcia I'd have *café* with her this morning—Alicia!" Mrs. Baca called out, then suddenly cupped her hand over her mouth. "*Dios mio*, I almos' forgot your papa's sleeping," she whispered.

"It's okay. He's on day shift again at the plant."

"*¡Que bueno!* Those graveyard shif's are awful. They make em so nervous, no? *Gracia a dios*, my Roberto has only two more years before retiremen'." Mrs. Baca fanned herself vigorously with the newspaper. "Alicia!"

Alicia Segura, still in curlers, looked out of the bathroom doorway. "Ah—Señora Baca—*horita voy!* I'm almost done with Rosie's hair."

"Would you like an egg and *chorizo burrito*, Mrs. Baca?" Frances offered.

"No, *gracias*, I ate jus' a little while ago."

"Do you want to sit down in the living room while you wait for my mom?"

"No, *gracias*, I'll jus' wait right here," Mrs. Baca said, fanning herself again.

"Yoohoo!" Frances' friend Della called through the open door, her face pressed against the screen.

Frances grabbed her purse and notebook and dashed out the door.

"Hi, Della," she said, welcoming the dry outdoor heat. Gato, the high school dropout across the street was revving his Chevy. The blast of gasoline smell assaulted Frances' senses. Even though he did this every morning, she had not gotten used to it and was glad when he shot away to his job at the gas station, taking his stink with him. She could now discern the sweet talc fragrance of Della's perfume.

"Girl, you look sharp!" Della said, lifting a long strand of Frances' brown hair which today was wavy. "You perm it?"

"I braided it last night while it was wet," she said, walking away from the house.

"I oughta do that," Della said, lifting a handful of her own hair from her shoulders and twirling it around her finger. The blue-black strands shone in the sun as she contemplated what they would look like wavy.

"You'd look outasight," Frances said, playfully flattening the hump of ratted hair on top of Della's head.

"Then we'd really be twinsies," Della said, raising her foot and thumping her finger on her four-inch-high cork wedgies, identical to Frances'.

"And I'd look taller than you," Frances teased.

"No way," Della softly shoved Frances away. "I'm keeping my hair just like it is," she said, stopping to stare at herself in the window of the old dusty Corvair in the driveway.

Frances dipped into her shoulder bag and came out with a pint-sized bottle of patchouli oil. "My mom and dad can't stand for me to wear this," she said, dabbing the strong resin-like smell behind her ears. Della pinched her nose in a teasing manner.

"You have something against hippies too?!" Frances bared her teeth, mimicking a madwoman and went after Della with her little open bottle of patchouli.

Della backed away, fumbling in her purse for her bottle of perfume. She aimed her Maja at Frances and sprayed freely, without regard for the price of replacing it since she regularly shoplifted it from the pharmacy.

Frances ducked out of the way, missing the talc-smelling spray. She advanced again toward Della, her forefinger shiny with the essential oil. Della kept spraying. Frances covered her face with one arm and braved the mist on her hair in order to dab Della. Even though Della wrestled Frances' arm, she was not able to avoid the oil on her forehead. The girls burst out laughing, waving away the strong, conflicting fragrances.

Della crammed her perfume back in her black purse which was already stuffed to capacity and emerged with a handful of Bazooka bubble gum. "I almost forgot," she said, dropping them in Frances' bag.

"I'll buy tomorrow," Frances promised, ripping the red, white and blue wrapper off a piece which she quickly chewed until the tough little square softened into juicy sweetness. She read the comic and fortune that came underneath the wrapper.

Della, who was doing the same, blew a bubble and then spoke. "Mine says: you will travel to exciting faraway places. How about yours?"

"No one knows what he can do til—" Frances stopped in mid-sentence when she heard her mother, who was escorting Mrs. Baca out the door, yell for them to get going.

"Does my slip show?" asked Della, turning so Frances could see the back hem of her short skirt.

"You're okay, how about mine?"

"Nah."

The friends hurried to get out of McKinley Court, their steps wobbly in their high wedgies. The road that led from the projects toward school was on a hill which they had to descend. From here they could see the gravel rooftops of the houses below, the intersecting of the highway with Main Street where crowded signs advertised gas, fast food and motels. In the distance beyond, railroad tracks crossed the vast desert of Joshua trees to the Calico Mountains where the American Chemical Plant shone like a steel toy in the sun.

"Did you see the coconut in the paper?" Della asked, smacking her gum.

"Mrs. Baca came over and announced it this morning," Frances said, scrunching her face with disapproval.

"Girl, the old man fucking put the paper in my face! 'Why can't you be more like Grace instead of a *pinche loca*' he had the nerve to ask! That little kiss-ass makes me wanna puke!"

"She thinks she's so hot because her parents own that Mexican restaurant," Frances added, blowing a bubble that burst.

"She dresses like a Tricia Nixon clone with those stupid headbands and A-line dresses."

Frances' tone was serious. "Do you think she's as smart as it says in the paper?"

"Cause she's on the honor roll?"

"Yeah, and she's going to college."

"I don't think all them 'socies' get good grades and are going to college because they're smart...it's the moola," Della said, rubbing her thumb against her second and third fingers.

"Yeah...if I had her money I'd go to college too and get the heck out of this hell hole," Frances said with a faraway look in her eyes.

"I'd sure as hell dress better than her," Della said, snapping her gum.

"Ever talked with her?"

Della shook her head. "Who the fuck needs her? *Puta!*"

"Puta?"

"I seen her flirting with all the guys. She ever even look at Gilbert—I'll kick her ass back to Santa Barbara or wherever-the-fuck she came from!"

They burst out laughing.

In their homeroom class, the teacher announced that campus recruiters from Los Angeles would be giving a talk in the auditorium after lunch break and all seniors were required to attend. Frances and Della rolled their eyes: another boring talk. They'd attended more boring talks in the first five weeks of their senior year than all the rest of high school put together. Their plan was to skip the program but they quickly changed their minds when they saw the imposing figure of Mr. Powell, the school dean, searching the hallways for stray students.

Frances and Della reluctantly entered the noisy auditorium. They were annoyed by the Homecoming hysteria that they felt had taken over their town and school, and now took the opportunity to protest by yanking the blue and white crepe streamers that decorated the railing at the bottom of the bleachers. The air-conditioned room was so cold that it made Frances shiver. They chose the bleachers that were the farthest away from the stage and climbed with thumping steps to the highest row. They sat down, chewed another piece of gum and prepared themselves for the ensuing hour: Della filing her fingernails and Frances doodling in her notebook. As soon as the principal appeared beneath the GO SPARTANS GO! banner on the stage, the girls heard nothing beyond their own conversation.

"Girl!" Della said as though she'd just remembered something important. "Guess what Cooksie told me in history class just a little while ago?!"

"What?!"

"Guess!!"

"I don't know—Bobby, the hunk, broke up with his ugly girlfriend?"

"Even better!" Della whispered in Frances' ear: "Candy Schmidt is preggers!"

"Liar!" Frances blurted, playfully shoving Della.

"I swear!" Della stopped filing her nails and looked at Frances with a serious face.

Frances lowered her voice. "That's so hard to believe. How'd Cooksie know?"

"Her sister Arlene filed the lab report at the doctor's office where she works."

"But she's still running for queen as if nothing's happened."

"What do you expect—she'll probably go somewhere and get an abortion."

Frances suddenly felt sorry for Candy, sensing it must be awful to be in that situation. But instead of saying something to Della, she looked towards the stage. A tall, blond man wearing a suit was standing at the microphone. He was saying something about test scores.

"Fuck that shit!" Della whispered.

"You're not kidding," Frances added.

"Hey, how'd you do on that lousy typing test anyway?" Della asked.

"I think I blew it. That bitch, Mrs. Crawford, stood right behind me the whole time and made me nervous. How about you?"

"I think I totally fucked up. I broke my nail and that was it. I don't give a shit about that friggin class anyway." Della said sarcastically, "I'm sure I'm gonna be a secretary!"

A woman in a navy blue suit who reminded Frances of stewardesses in commercials now took over the microphone. She kept repeating, "Get ahead of the competition."

"Which little kiss-ass cheerleader do you think's gonna be queen?" Della asked, shaking her bottle of fingernail polish.

"To be honest, Della," Frances said, concentrating on the large psychedelic bird she was drawing, "I think it's stupid."

"Yeah, you're right. But that's all everybody in this stupid town is talking about."

Frances sketched with quick, furious strokes. "I hate school! I hate football! I hate this boring town!"

"Girl, I hear you." She nudged Frances. "Look, there's the coconut."

"Where?"

"See—with the white headband—over in the front row." Della pointed with her chin to the back of Grace's head.

Frances squinted. She was near-sighted and distant images were fuzzy. She pulled the edges of her eyelids, trying to bring Grace into focus. She was too far and remained a mass of blurred brown hair. "Who's she with? I can't see that far."

Della learned forward and moved her head in various directions trying to see the profile of the guy who sat next to Grace. "I think...it's...that jock...Tim Wilson. Yeah, it's him."

Frances crinkled her nose. "He thinks he's God's gift."

"Hey!" Della said. "There's Billy White!"

"Where?!"

"By the side bleachers, near the exit," she said, pointing with her bottle of nail polish.

Frances pulled her eyelids again. Billy's reddish-blond hair came into focus. His were the longest locks at Rimrock High, for which he braved suspension for not keeping them above his collar. He liked to shake his head as he walked down the hallways as if to remind himself that he was different from the majority, if not superior. Frances was surprised to see him at the assembly, sitting with his friend Doobie, since he had a car and could easily have skipped it. "That jerk!" she said beneath her breath.

"What? Last week he was Mr. Outasight."

"That's before I really thought about what happened."

"What do you mean?" Della, who was opening her bottle of fingernail polish, stopped.

Frances bit on her pencil. "Oh, I don't know. He was late to pick me up...he didn't take me to a movie like I expected."

"That's how all the guys are around here," Della said, applying a coat of bright red polish to a fingernail. "Cheapskates."

"Gilbert doesn't seem that way."

"I mean the white paddies, like the ones I went out with before Gilbert."

"That jerk," Frances repeated, looking in his direction. "He drove me out to Flattop Canyon and we started making out...which was okay. But then he tried to screw me. I had to wrestle the guy even though I said no. He kept saying, 'What's wrong with you? I thought you Mexican chicks were supposed to be real hot lovers.' And he tried to make me feel like I should be grateful he went out with me. He called me a 'prick tease.' And I felt awful when he dropped me home early. 'Later chick.' Those were his last words. 'Later chick.'" Frances' eyes almost filled with tears when she said this.

"How come you never said nothing before?" Della's voice was soft.

"I don't know. I felt kind of weird."

Della put her hand on Frances' shoulder and gently squeezed it. "You're too good for that asshole."

"Thanks Del." Frances felt relief to tell her best friend and yet some questions remained. Why had Billy rejected her? Was it really because she hadn't done it with him? Girls who screwed were the exception, not the rule. Did he think she was ugly? He didn't even give her a chance!

And she still felt very attracted to him. She was angry with him, yet her heart quickened when she rememberd the two of them on the blanket under the moonlight at Flattop Canyon. His sea-blue eyes, his soft, warm lips. It wasn't any use to think about him, she could never have him. She pulled her gaze away from Billy and towards the stage.

The next speaker was a young man in a white shirt and tie who looked Mexican. He introduced himself as Juan Rios and began his speech by saying that anyone could go to college.

"Let's hear this," Frances said with interest, as she had never heard anyone say this before.

"High school sucks—college sucks," Della said, blowing on her finger-nail, wet with bright red polish.

"Shhh."

"Shhh yourself."

Frances heard the recruiter's words loud and clear: "Anyone can go to college. Don't ever let the lack of money stop you. There are scholarships, grants and loans to help the needy student." Could that mean me? she asked herself. Could I go to art school? She imagined herself in a large college studio, light shooting in from skylights and arched windows like she'd seen in books. A nude male model is holding one pose after another, his taut muscles rippling with every change. She is sketching faster and more accurately than she has ever sketched before. She is learning how to stretch her own canvas and getting instruction in oils and acrylics, mediums she has always wanted to try but has not been able to afford. She is sitting in a coffee house with other students, talking passionately about art. Only when she heard the ending applause did she come back to the reality of the auditorium.

Frances was stunned and unusually quiet as she and Della descended the bleachers. Della didn't seem to notice as she was waving to some of her friends. It wasn't until they were filing out of the stuffy auditorium, behind hordes of other students, that Frances finally spoke. "Can you believe that guy just said *anyone* can go to college?!" she asked Della.

"Who the fuck wants to go to college?" Della asked, looking behind her toward the students still exiting from the auditorium.

Frances grabbed Della's arm and pulled her near the hallway wall, away from the chattering, hurrying students. "Listen, Della, if we could go to college in L.A., would you want to?"

"I'm sick of school and I thought you were too." Della looked puzzled.

"But I heard college is better than high school. And what if you could study something you really liked?"

"Like what?" Della asked, looking down at her bright red fingernails.

"I don't know...like...like...like art!"

"You're the artist, girl, not me. Besides, they don't let just anybody in—you gotta take some lousy test—didn't you hear the guy say?" Della started walking again.

Frances walked alongside her. "But the Mexican guy said you could go to community college first...all you need is a diploma. Isn't there a college where your aunt lives in Santa Monica?"

"I think so." Della was frowning. "I thought our plan was to hang out at the beach and do waitressing at night. Now you have us going to school," Della said, a little irritated.

"Maybe we can start out with one or two classes. You know, see if we like it."

"I don't know, Frances. I think college is a lousy idea. Why should we bust our asses? Not only do we have to support ourselves, we gotta work twice as hard as those college-bounds. We got no preparation. Bust our asses—that's all we'll end up doing—and for what?"

"Shit—I don't know. Forget I ever mentioned it," Frances said without any bad feelings. She was used to having ideas that went nowhere.

They stopped in the rest room. The place was stuffy and smelled like someone had been smoking in there recently and tried to hide the odor by spraying cheap cologne. Tinkling sounds alternated with the powerful swoosh of flushing toilets. Ann Taylor, a tall, slender cheerleader wearing her blue and white uniform burst out of a stall and almost bumped into Della as she ran to take a quick peek at herself in the mirror. Della glared at her but she didn't seem to notice.

"*Híjole*, I didn't think I looked this bad," Della said, staring at herself in the mirror. "My blush's rubbed off—my eyeliner's smeared—my lips don't hardly have color. I look pale as a white paddie." She dumped the contents of her purse on the counter above the sink and picked out the make-up she intended to use.

"You look good," Frances said. She was wetting her hair and twirling it with her finger strand by strand. "I'm the one who looks awful. I can't believe this friggin heat has already made my hair go limp." When she realized her hair was not going to curl, she brushed it instead while she waited for Della to finish putting on her make-up.

Della was pressing her bright red lips into a paper towel, to take off the excess color she'd just applied.

"You know, Della, you *could* pass for white, if you wanted to."

"Why'd I wanna do that, they're ugly," Della joked.

Frances laughed.

They gathered their things and went their separate ways: Della to P.E. and Frances to Art.

Frances arrived for class five minutes late and had to rush around setting up her easel and watercolors. She was the only student in her advanced art class who didn't wear painter's smocks and had to depend on the materials the school provided. While most of the other students dabbled in the oils and acrylics they brought to class, Frances had grown very skilled in the use of watercolors. She was good at replicating landscapes from pictures in magazines but preferred experimenting with the spontaneous animals from her imagination whch she painted in bright complementary colors.

Miss Robinson, a tall, thin woman with short, curly blonde hair that always seemed messy, greeted her students. She surveyed her class with blue piercing eyes as she made the announcement that Frances Segura had won first prize in the Downtown Business Association's Homecoming art contest. Her painting of a huge Spartan with a sword leading a trail of lizards and snakes through a purple-hued desert was on display at Brown's Department Store. The $100 award would be used to buy art supplies for the class.

Frances couldn't believe Miss Robinson meant her but it was her painting she had just described. She was afraid to look at her teacher or the other students, afraid that they would somehow see that she wasn't worthy of the prize. She was concentrating on her work, dipping the large wash brush in the grey watercolor cake when Miss Robinson came over and congratulated her. It wasn't a mistake or a figment of her imagination, she had really won. This was the first time she had ever won anything in her life! Her spirit soared, then suddenly plummeted when she thought about the prize money. Why hadn't they given it to her? Especially when she was the student who needed it most. The sketchpads, pencils, pastels, brushes, oils, canvas she could have bought with it! It wasn't fair. But maybe there was a reason for why they did this. She hadn't entered the painting herself, Miss Robinson had, through the school. The supplies she'd used belonged to the school. She was trying to come up with more reasons when a group of students came over and congratulated her. Frances soared again! She had never before gotten so much attention. She felt special and so what if she hadn't gotten any money. She changed her mind about the grey on her brush, cleansed it in the water jar and proceeded to spread a turqoise sky on her paper. On the earth below, a fuchsia lizard with a giant vibrant sunflower growing out of its back crawled across the desert.

After class, Miss Robinson took Frances aside and asked her if she had talked to her counselor about the scholarship she'd announced a few days ago.

"No, I don't think I stand a chance," Frances replied.

"You never know until you try. I'll be happy to write you a letter of recommendation. As I've said before, Frances, you have a lot of potential as an artist."

"But aren't there a lot of students trying for that?"

"Yes, but you could be the one whose work stands out."

"Do you really think I should try?"

"Yes! Promise me you'll see your counselor."

"Okay."

"Don't forget, the deadline is next Friday."

When Frances got home from school that day she told her father the good news.

"I won a prize today," she said, the wind from the cooler blowing in her face.

Her father, in a white t-shirt streaked with oil and grease stains, was crouched by the television set, trying to fix the dial one of the kids had broken the day before.

"Eh?" Her father said without looking up.

"I won a prize today."

"For what, *mi india?*"

"Don't call me that—I hate it!"

Her father looked up at her smirking, his shiny black hair falling across his eyes. "I'm just kiddin'. What'd you win?"

"I won—"

"No, let me guess—Gracie Olmos has the measles and you're her stand-in."

"*Andale*, Frances, I need your help!" her mother yelled from the kitchen.

Frances shook her head in exasperation, "You just don't care," she mumbled repeatedly as she stormed off to the bedroom she shared with her little sister. She went into the closet and closed the door. In the darkness, she felt safe. She stood there, closing her eyes and pushing her feelings deeper and deeper within herself until they were as tiny as a mosquito she could smash with her thumb. "I don't give a shit what he thinks," she said to herself, tearing a tissue she'd had in her pocket to shreds.

She changed into her house clothes and went into the kitchen to help her mother prepare dinner. Baby Petey was walking around the kitchen putting his peanut butter and jelly fingerprints on everything. Her mother, wearing a faded pink gingham smock that did more to reveal her pregnancy than hide it, was standing at the sink washing potatoes.

"Frances, hurry and help me peel these potatoes if we're gonna eat dinner tonight."

"I hear you, mom!"

"Don't get sassy with me, young lady!"

"I'm not...I'm sorry," Frances said, taking the bowl of potatoes to the kitchen table.

"I heard you say something about a prize," her mother said, softening her tone.

"It's no big deal," Frances said, scraping the peel off a potato.

"Frances, don't be like that," her mother said, shaking spices into the hamburger meat.

"I won a prize in art."

"That's great, Frances, be sure you cut those potatoes sliver thin, you know the kids don't like 'em fat—so, what did you win?

"It's more of an award. They gave some money to the class."

"Frances, could you wipe Petey's hands?"

Frances tried to wipe Petey's hands with a paper napkin but he started crying.

"Here, you take over the burgers. I don't want your father coming here and growling at us. Petey, *ven 'aca, mijo.* Let mommy clean your hands and she'll give you a pickle."

"My painting is on display at Brown's Department store."

"That's nice, Frances." Alicia was squatting uncomfortably, cleaning Petey's hands with a wet dish rag.

"My teacher told me I should apply for a scholarship to college."

"College?" Her mother shut the refrigerator door. Momentarily speechless, she stood hugging the jar of pickles. "You never said nothing about college before. *Mija*, we need you at home, especially when the new baby comes."

Frances felt torn between wanting to help her mother who always seemed tired from all the housework she had to do and wanting to go to college. She sensed that she would probably end up like her mother if she didn't do something about it now. "But mom, this could be the chance of a lifetime. My teacher even said she'd write me a letter of recommendation."

"I don't know," she said, handing Petey a pickle, "talk to your dad."

After dinner Frances approached her father, who was sitting in front of the noisy television watching boxing.

"Dad?" she said, standing a few feet away from the frayed plaid lazy-boy where he sat.

"Eh? What you need?" he said, staring ahead at the TV.

"I don't mean to interrupt but...I mean...my teacher thinks I should apply for a scholarship to college."

"Eh?"

"College."

"What you need college for, eh? You're just gonna find yourself a husband and get married anyway."

"I don't want to get married," she said, crossing her arms.

"Yeah, sure. Just don't let yourself get knocked up, eh?" He turned to look at her for the first time during their conversation and shook his finger.

She'd heard this warning before and she felt like yelling her usual reply: "I'm not that stupid!" Instead, she kept her feelings bottled up, as she did not want to ruin her chances of going to college. "I want to go to college."

"Your mama needs you here," he said, staring at the TV again.

"But I don't want to. I mean...I could have a chance at this scholarship."

"What you gonna study?"

The shouting from the television rose. Her father suddenly sat up and yelled at the TV, "*¡Pegale, Ali, Pegale!*"

Frances waited for the excitement to die down. "I want to study A...Art."

"Art? *¡Que locuras!*" He was shaking his head. "Why don't you study something useful like nursing or teaching. An artist? You gonna starve. You crazy or something?"

"My teacher says I have potential."

"You don't think she says that to all the students? That's what they pay her for."

"I want to study art."

"It's too expensive."

"I know. That's why I want this scholarship."

"What scholarship?"

"That's what I've been trying to tell you."

"Okay, Frances, you get that scholarship," he said, chuckling, "and I'll let you go to college. Now let me get back to the fights."

Frances thought that even if he was kidding she'd hold him to it if she got that scholarship.

Before going to sleep, she said a special prayer to her patron saint, Francis of Assisi. The next day, she went to talk with her counselor.

Mr. Lobauer sat behind a big desk; a part-time coach, he had a perennial tan. "The UCLA scholarship? There's terrible competition for that. Terrible competition. I don't think you stand a chance. What'd you say your name was?"

"Frances."

"Well, Frances. Let me put it to you this way. You're competing against the Gordon Smiths, the Matt Bernsteins, the Grace Olmos' of this school."

"But I thought it was an arts scholarship. I mean...I didn't know Gordon or Matt or Grace were art students."

"I meant it as a manner of speaking, dear. There are students such as those here who have great academic and extracurricular backgrounds."

"I thought being a good artist was the most important thing."

"Yes...you must have some ability but you must also prove you're going to succeed. That's the most important thing these schools are looking for."

"What do you mean?"

"Well...the scholarship is intended for someone with proven ability to succeed: high grades, experience in school organizations. I don't recall your name about school."

Frances swallowed hard. "I think my grades are...uh...okay—but I've always gotten A's in art. And I just won the art contest put on by the Downtown Business Association."

"I don't really think you qualify."

"Ms. Robinson told me I should apply."

"To be honest, you'll be wasting your time."

"But I really need that scholarship."

"I know, dear, but so do hundreds of other students."

"Hundreds?! I...I...thanks a lot for your time."

"You're welcome, dear. Glad I could help."

Frances grabbed her books off the floor and was rushing out of Lobauer's office when she accidentally dropped her notebook. Out fell loose papers covered with doodles. Frances felt the blood rushing to her head. She gathered her papers and ran out, letting the door slam behind her.

Frances couldn't go back to class right away. She felt so small. A nobody. A nothing. She felt angry with Mr. Lobauer for treating her like she was stupid. But more than that she was angry at herself for having let herself want something so badly that she knew deep within that she could never have. Just because she won some lousy contest, she let herself get all puffed up. Shit! she was mad at Miss Robinson too. Why didn't she get the award money?! She could have bought a plastic skeleton to study at home, sketch pads, brushes, her very own watercolors! Maybe even a canvas and some oils. She'd always wanted to try oils. But instead she had to rely on the school for her materials and once she graduated, she wouldn't have any.

She shoved the door to the girls' rest room and went into a stall. She put the lid down on the toilet and sat down. She felt like doing something she had never done before. She took a felt pen from her purse and positioned it between "The crabs jump ten feet high" and "La Rosie and Cricket forever" and as darkly as possible wrote: "Fuck everybody!"

She was about to come out of the stall when she heard someone walk into the rest room. Frances hesitated coming out, thinking whoever it was might use her stall, smell the fresh ink and report her. Frances could see between the chink of the stall that someone was standing by the mirror. She smelled lavender. She recognized that smell from gym class. It was Grace's perfume. A strange curiosity came over Frances and she peered through the chink. She could see Grace adjusting her headband, her sleek black hair falling softly to her shoulders. Frances saw something in Grace's reflection that she never noticed before, something so obvious. Grace, the expensive dresser, the straight A student, the cheerleader and soon-to-be journalist; Grace, the girl with the good-looking football player boyfriend; Grace, who could leave them all behind for some fancy college in a big city; Grace, the girl standing only five feet away from her was...darker than she. Frances' eyes dashed from the olive tone of her hand to Grace's *café con leche* color. Back and forth until it had thoroughly sunk in.

Frances sat on the toilet until Grace had left, smiling at her discovery.

That night after all her chores had been done and everyone had gone to bed, Frances tiptoed back to the kitchen, sketch pad under her arm.

She turned on the light and spread her colored pencils and paper on the formica table. She sat down and contemplated the lone orange in the fruit bowl, while the sound of the crickets and the nearby clock's ticking resounded her own solitude. She picked up the orange and played with it, dropping it from one hand to the other, feeling its weight. Her small hands cupped its round shape, turning it so that her fingers ran along the hard dimpled skin. She held it up to her nose, inhaling its sweet citrus smell. She shook it by her ear, and heard its slow, heavy timbre. She set it down on the table, studying its bright color, the interplay of light and shadow upon its surface. Frances imagined herself biting into its juicy center, filling her being with its sweet flavor. She drew a yellow dot upon the blank sheet of paper, then hundreds and thousands more dots that spiraled from the center outward, creating a universe that was in the process of becoming this unique, perfect, little orange.

Commitment from the Mirror-Writing Box

Trinh T. Minh-ha

The Triple Bind

Neither black/red/yellow nor woman but poet or writer. For many of us, the question of priorities remains a crucial issue. Being merely "a writer" without doubt ensures one a status of far greater weight than being "a woman of color who writes" ever does. Imputing race or sex to the creative act has long been a means by which the literary establishment cheapens and discredits the achievements of non-mainstream women writers. She who "happens to be" a (non-white) Third World member, a woman, and a writer is bound to go through the ordeal of exposing her work to the abuse of praises and criticisms that either ignore, dispense with, or overemphasize her racial and sexual attributes. Yet the time has passed when she can confidently identify herself with a profession or artistic vocation without questioning and relating it to her color-woman condition. Today, the growing ethnic-feminist consciousness has made it increasingly difficult for her to turn a blind eye not only to the specification of the writer as historical subject (who writes? and in what context?), but also to writing itself as a practice located at the intersection of subject and history—a literary practice that involves the possible knowledge (linguistical and ideological) of itself as such. On the one hand, no matter what position she decides to take, she will sooner or later find herself driven into situations where she is made to feel she must choose from among three conflicting identities. Writer of color? Woman writer? Or woman of color? Which comes first? Where does she place her loyalties? On the other hand, she often finds herself at odds with language, which partakes in the white-male-is-norm ideology and is used predominantly as a vehicle to circulate established power relations. This is further intensified by her finding herself also at odds with her relation to writing, which when carried out uncritically often proves to be one of domination: as holder of speech, she usually writes from a position of power, creating as an "author," situating herself *above* her work and existing *before* it, rarely simultaneously *with* it. Thus, it has become almost impossible for her to take up her pen without at the same time questioning her relation to the material that defines her and her creative work. As focal point of cultural consciousness and social change, writing weaves into language the complex relations of a subject caught between the problems of race and gender and the practice of literature as the very place where social alienation is thwarted differently according to each specific context.

Silence in Time

Writing, reading, thinking, imagining, speculating. These are luxury activities, so I am reminded, permitted to a privileged few, whose idle hours of the day can be viewed otherwise than as a bowl of rice or a loaf of bread less to share with the family. "If we wish to increase the supply of rare and remarkable women like the Brontës," wrote our reputed foresister Virginia Woolf, "we should give the Joneses and the Smiths rooms of their own and five hundred [pounds] a year. One cannot grow fine flowers in a thin soil."[1] Substantial creative achievement demands not necessarily genius, but acumen, bent, persistence, time. And time, in the framework of industrial development, means a wage that admits of leisure and living conditions that do not require that writing be incessantly interrupted, deferred, denied, at any rate subordinated to family responsibilities. "When the claims of creation cannot be primary," Tillie Olsen observes, "the results are atrophy; unfinished work; minor effort and accomplishment; silences." The message Olsen conveys in *Silences* leaves no doubt as to the circumstances under which most women writers function. It is a constant reminder of those who never come to writing: "the invisible, the as-innately-capable: the born to the wrong circumstances—diminished, excluded, foundered."[2] To say this, however, is not to say that writing should be held in veneration in all milieus or that every woman who fails to write is a disabled being. (What Denise Paulme learned in this regard during her first period of fieldwork in Africa is revealing. Comparing her life one day with those of the women in an area of the French Sudan, she was congratulating herself on not having to do a chore like theirs—pounding millet for the meals day in and day out—when she overheard herself commented upon by one of the women nearby: "That girl makes me tired with her everlasting paper and pencil: what sort of a life is that?" The lesson, Paulme concluded, "was a salutary one, and I have never forgotten it.")[3] To point out that, in general, the situation of women does not favor literary productivity is to imply that it is almost impossible for them (and especially for those bound up with the Third World) to engage in writing as an occupation without their letting themselves be consumed by a deep and pervasive sense of guilt. Guilt over the selfishness implied in such activity, over themselves as housewives and "women," over their families, their friends and all other "less fortunate" women. The circle in which they turn proves to be vicious, and writing in such a context is always practiced at the cost of other women's labor. Doubts, lack of confidence, frustrations, despair: these are sentiments born with the habits of distraction, distortion, discontinuity and silence. After having toiled for a number of years on her book, hattie gossett exclaims to herself:

> Who do you think you are [to be writing a book]? and
> who cares what you think about anything enough to pay

money for it...a major portion of your audience not only
cant read but seems to think readin is a waste of time?
plus books like this arent sold in the ghetto bookshops or
even in airports?[4]

The same doubt is to be heard through Gloria Anzaldúa's voice:

Who gave us permission to perform the act of writing?
Why does writing seem so unnatural for me?...The voice
recurs in me: *Who am I, a poor Chicanita from the sticks,
to think I could write?* How dared I even consider
becoming a writer as I stooped over the tomato fields
bending, bending under the hot sun...

How hard it is for us to *think* we can choose to become
writers, much less *feel* and *believe* that we can.[5]

Rites of Passage

S/he who writes, writes. In uncertainty, in necessity. And does not ask
whether s/he is given the permission to do so or not. Yet, in the context
of today's market-dependent societies, "to be a writer" can no longer
mean purely to perform the act of writing. For a laywo/man to enter the
priesthood—the sacred world of writers—s/he must fulfill a number of
unwritten conditions. S/he must undergo a series of rituals, be baptized
and ordained. S/he must *submit* her writings to the law laid down by the
corporation of literary/literacy victims and be prepared to *accept* their
verdict. Every woman who writes and wishes to become established as a
writer has known the taste of *rejection.* Sylvia Plath's experience is often
cited. Her years of darkness, despair and disillusion, her agony of slow
rebirth, her moments of fearsome excitement at the start of the writing
of *The Bell Jar*, her unsuccessful attempts at re-submitting her first book
of poems under ever-changing titles and the distress with which she
upbraided herself are parts of the realities that affect many women
writers:

Nothing stinks like a pile of unpublished writing, which
remark I guess shows I still don't have a pure motive (O
it's-such-fun-I-just-can't-stop-who-cares-if-it's-publish
ed-or-read) about writing...I still want to see it finally
ritualized in print.[6]

Accumulated unpublished writings do stink. They heap up before your
eyes like despicable confessions that no one cares to hear; they sap your
self-confidence by incessantly reminding you of your failure to incorporate. For publication means the breaking of a first seal, the end of a

"no-admitted" status, the end of a soliloquy confined to the private sphere
and the start of a possible sharing with the unknown other—the reader,
whose collaboration with the writer alone allows the work to come into
full being. Without such a rite of passage, the woman-writer-to-
be/woman-to-be-writer is condemned to wander about, begging for permission to join in and be a member. If it is difficult for any woman to
find acceptance for her writing, it is all the more so for those who do not
match the stereotype of the "real woman"—the colored, the minority,
the physically or mentally handicapped. Emma Santos, who spent her
days running to and fro between two worlds—that of hospitals and that
of the "normal" system—equally rejected by Psychiatry and by Literature, is another writer whose first book has been repeatedly dismissed
(by twenty-two publishing houses). Driven to obsession by a well-known
publisher who promised to send her an agreement but never did, she
followed him, spied on him, called him twenty times a day on the phone,
and ended up feeling like "a pile of shit making after great men of letters."
Writing, she remarks, is "a shameful, venereal disease," and Literature,
nothing more than "a long beseeching." Having no acquaintance, no
friend to introduce her when she sought admission for her work among
the publishers, she describes her experience as follows:

> I receive encouraging letters but I am goitrous. Publish-
> ers, summons, these are worse than psychiatrists, inter-
> rogatories. The publishers perceive a sick and oblivious
> girl. They would have liked the text, the same one, without
> changing a single word, had it been presented by a young
> man from the [Ecole] Normale Superieure, *agrégé* of
> philosophy, worthy of the Goncourt prize.[7]

The Guilt

To capture a publisher's attention, to convince, to negotiate: these
constitute one step forward into the world of writers, one distress, one
guilt. One guilt among the many yet to come, all of which bide their time
to loom up out of their hiding places, for the path is long and there is an
ambush at every turn. Writing: not letting it merely haunt you and die
over and over again in you until you no longer know how to speak. Getting
published: not loathing yourself, not burning it, not giving up. Now I (the
all-knowing subject) feel almost secure with such definite "not-to-do's."
Yet, I/i (the plural, non-unitary subject) cannot set my mind at rest with
them without at the same time recognizing their precariousness. i (the
personal race- and gender-specific subject) have, in fact turned a deaf
ear to a number of primary questions: Why write? For whom? What
necessity? What writing? What impels you and me and hattie gossett to
continue to write when we know for a fact that our books are not going

to be "sold in the ghetto bookshops or even in airports?" And why do we care for their destinations at all? "A writer," proclaims Toni Cade Bambara, "like any other cultural worker, like any other member of the community, ought to try to put her/his skills in the service of the community." It is apparently on account of such a conviction that Bambara "began a career as the neighborhood scribe," helping people write letters to faraway relatives as well as letters of complaint, petitions, contracts and the like.[8] For those of us who call ourselves "writers" in the context of a community whose major portion "not only cant read but seems to think readin is a waste of time" (gossett), being "the neighborhood scribe" is no doubt one of the most gratifying and unpretentious ways of dedicating oneself to one's people. Writing as a social function— as differentiated from the ideal of art for art's sake—is the aim that Third World writers, in defining their roles, highly esteem and claim. *Literacy* and *literature* intertwine so tightly, indeed, that the latter has never ceased to imply both the ability to read and the condition of being well read—and thereby to convey the sense of *polite learning* through the arts of *grammar* and *rhetoric*. The illiterate, the ignorant versus the wo/man of "letters" (of wide reading), the highly educated. With such discrimination and opposition, it is hardly surprising that the writer should be viewed as a social parasite. Whether s/he makes common cause with the upper classes or chooses to disengage her/himself by adopting the myth of the bohemian artist, the writer is a kept wo/man who for her/his living largely relies on the generosity of that portion of society called the literate. A room of one's own and a pension of five hundred pounds per year solely for making ink marks on paper: this, symbolically speaking, is what many people refer to when they say the writer's activity is "gratuitous" and "useless." No matter how devoted to the vocation s/he may be, the writer cannot subsist on words and mere fresh air, nor can s/he really "live by the pen," since her/his work—arbitrarily estimated as it is—has no definite market value. Reading in this context may actually prove to be "a waste of time," and writing, as Woolf puts it, "a reputable and harmless occupation." Reflecting on her profession as a writer (in a 1979 interview), Toni Cade Bambara noted that she probably did not begin "getting really serious about writing until maybe five years ago. Prior to that, in spite of all good sense, I always thought writing was rather frivolous, that it was something you did because you didn't feel like doing any work." The concept of "writing" here seems to be incompatible with the concept of "work." As the years went by and Toni Cade Bambara got more involved in writing, however, she changed her attitude and has "come to appreciate that it is a perfectly legitimate way to participate in struggle."[9]

Commitment as an ideal is particularly dear to Third World writers. It helps to alleviate the Guilt: that of being privileged (Inequality), of "going over the hill" to join the clan of literates (Assimilation), and of indulging in a "useless" activity while most community members "stoop over the tomato fields, bending under the hot sun" (a perpetuation of the same privilege). In a sense, committed writers are the ones who write both to awaken to the consciousness of their guilt and to give their readers a guilty conscience. Bound to one another by an awareness of their guilt, writer and reader may thus assess their positions, engaging themselves wholly in their situations and carrying their weight into the weight of their communities, the weight of the world. Such a definition naturally places the committed writers on the side of Power. For every discourse that breeds fault and guilt is a discourse of authority and arrogance. To say this, however, is not to say that all power discourses produce equal oppression or that those established are necessary. Discussing African literature and the various degrees of propaganda prompted by commitment, Ezekiel Mphahlele observes that although "propaganda is always going to be with us"—for "there will always be the passionate outcry against injustice, war, fascism, poverty"—the manner in which a writer protests reflects to a large extent her/his regard for the reader and "decides the literary worth of a work." "Commitment," Mphahlele adds, "need not give rise to propaganda: the writer can make [her/]his stand known without advocating it...in two-dimensional terms, i.e., in terms of one response to one stimulus."[10] Thus, in the whirlwind of prescriptive general formulas such as: Black art must "respond *positively* to the reality of revolution" or Black art must "expose the enemy, *praise* the people, and *support* the revolution" (Ron Karenga, my italics), one also hears distinct, unyielding voices whose autonomy asserts itself as follows:

> Black pride need not blind us to our own weaknesses: in fact it should help us to perceive our weaknesses...
>   I do not care for black pride that drugs us into a condition of stupor and inertia. I do not care for it if leaders use it to dupe the masses.[11]

> To us, the man who adores the Negro is as sick as the man who abominates him.[12]

Freedom and the masses

The notion of *art engagé* as defined by Jean-Paul Sartre, an influential apologist for socially effective literature, continues to grow and to circulate among contemporary engaged writers. It is easy to find parallels (and it is often directly quoted) in Third World literary discourses. "A free man addressing free men," the Sartrian writer "has only one subject—freedom." He writes to "appeal to the reader's freedom to collaborate in the production of his work" and paints the world "only so that free men may feel their freedom as they face it."[13] The function of literary art, in other words, must be to remind us of that freedom and to defend it. Made to serve a political purpose, literature thus places itself within the context of the proletarian fight, while the writer frees himself from his dependence on elites—or in a wider sense, from any privilege— and creates, so to speak, an art for an unrestricted public known as "art for the masses." From the chain of notions dear to Sartre—choice, responsibility, contingency, situation, motive, reason, being, doing, having—two notions are set forth here as being most relevant to Third World engaged literary theories: freedom and the masses. What is freedom in writing? And what can writing-for-the-masses be? Reflecting on being a writer, "female, black, and free," Margaret Walker, for example, defines freedom as "a philosophical state of mind and exist-ence." She proudly affirms:

> My entire career in writing...is determined by these immutable facts of my human condition...
>
> Writing is my life, but it is an avocation nobody can buy. In this respect I believe I am a free agent, stupid perhaps, but *me* and still free...
>
> The writer is still in the avant-garde for Truth and Justice, for Freedom, Peace, and Human Dignity...Her place, let us be reminded, is anywhere she chooses to be, doing what she has to do, creating, healing, and always being herself.[14]

These lines agree perfectly with Sartre's ideal of liberty. They may be said to echo his concepts of choice and responsibility—according to which each person, being an absolute choice of self, an absolute emergence at an absolute date, must assume her/his situation with the proud conscious-ness of being the author of it. (For one is nothing but this "being-in-situa-tion" that is the total contingency of the world, of one's birth, past and environment, and of the fact of one's fellow wo/man.) By its own rationale, such a sense of responsibility (attributed to the lucid, conscientious, successful man of action) renders the relationship between freedom and commitment particularly problematic. Is it not, indeed, always in the name of freedom that My freedom hastens to stamp out those of others? Is it not also in the name of the masses that My personality bestirs itself to impersonalize those of my fellow wo/men? Do the masses become masses by themselves? Or are they the result of a theoretical and practical operation of "massification"? From where onward can one say of a "free" work of art that it is written for the infinite numbers which constitute the masses and not merely for a definite public stratum of society?

For the people, by the people and from the people

Like all stereotypical notions, the notion of the masses has both an upgrading connotation and a degrading one. One often speaks of the masses as one speaks of the people, magnifying thereby their number, their strength, their mission. One invokes them and pretends to write on their behalf when one wishes to give weight to one's undertaking or to justify it. The Guilt mentioned earlier is always lurking below the surface. Yet to oppose the masses to the elite is already to imply that those forming the masses are regarded as an aggregate of average persons condemned by their lack of personality or by their dim individualities to stay with the herd, to be docile and anonymous. Thus the notion of "art *for* the masses" supposes not only a split between the artist and her/his audience—the spectator-consumer—but also a passivity on the part of the latter. For art here is not attributed to the masses; it is ascribed to the active few, whose role is precisely to produce *for* the great numbers. This means that despite the shift of emphasis the elite-versus-masses opposition remains intact. In fact it must remain so, basically unchallenged, if it is to serve a conservative political and ideological purpose—in other words, if (what is defined as) "art" is to exist at all. One of the functions of this "art for the masses" is, naturally, to contrast with the other, higher "art for the elite," and thereby to enforce its elitist values. The wider the distance between the two, the firmer the stand of conservative art. One can no longer let oneself be deceived by concepts that oppose the artist or the intellectual to the masses and deal with them as with two incompatible entities. Criticisms arising from or dwelling on such a *myth* are, indeed, quite commonly leveled against innovators and more often used as tools of intimidation than as reminders of social interdependency. It is perhaps with this perspective in mind that one may better understand the variants of Third World literary discourse, which claims not exactly an "art for the masses," but an "art for the people, by the people and from the people." In an article on *"Le Poète noir et son peuple"* (The Black Poet and His People), for example, Jacques Rabemananjara virulently criticized Occidental poets for spending their existence indulging in aesthetic refinements and subleties that bear no relation to their peoples' concerns and aspirations, that are merely sterile intellectual delights. The sense of dignity, Rabemananjara said, forbids black Orpheus to go in for the cult of art for art's sake. Inspirer inspired by his people, the poet has to play the difficult role of being simultaneously the torch lighting the way for his fellowmen and their loyal interpreter. "He is more than their spokesman: he is their voice." His noble mission entitles him to be "not only the messenger, but the very message of his people."[15] The concept of a popular and functional art is here poised against that of an intellectual and aesthetic one. A justified regression? A shift of emphasis again? Or an attempt at fusion of the self and the other, of art, ideology and life? Let us listen to other, perhaps less didactic voices; that of Aimé Césaire in *Return to My Native Land:*

> I should come back to this land of mine and say to it: "Embrace me without fear.... If all I can do is speak, at least I shall speak for you."
> And I should say further: "My tongue shall serve those miseries which have no tongue, my voice the liberty of those who founder in the dungeons of despair."
> And I should say to myself: "And most of all beware, even in thought, of assuming the sterile attitude of the spectator, for life is not a spectacle, a sea of griefs is not a proscenium, a man who wails is not a dancing bear."[16]

that of Nikki Giovanni in *Gemini*:

> Poetry is the culture of a people. We are poets even when we don't write poems....We are all preachers because we are One....I don't think we younger poets are doing anything significantly different from what we as a people have always done. The new Black poetry is in fact just a manifestation of our collective historical needs.[17]

and that of Alice Walker in an essay on the importance of models in the artist's life:

> It is, in the end, the saving of lives that we writers are about....We do it because we care....We care because we know this: *The life we save is our own.*[18]

One may say of art for art's sake in general that it is itself a reaction against the bourgeois "functional" attitude of mind which sees in the acquisition of art the highest, purest form of consumption. By making explicit the gratuitousness of their works, artists show contempt for their wealthy customers, whose purchasing power allows them to subvert art in its subversiveness, reducing it to a mere commodity or a service. As a reaction, however, art for art's sake is bound to be "two-dimensional"—"one response to one stimulus" (Mphahlele)—and, therefore, to meet with no success among writers of the Third World. "I cannot imagine," says Wole Soyinka, "that our 'authentic black innocent' would ever have permitted himself to be manipulated into the false position of countering one pernicious Manicheism with another."[19] An art that claims to be at the same time sender and bearer of a message, to serve the people and "to come off the street" (Cade Bambara), should then be altogether "functional, collective, and committing or committed" (Karenga). The reasoning circle closes on the notion of commitment, which again emerges, fraught with questions.

From *Woman Native Other: Writing Postcoloniality and Feminism*

Notes

1. Virginia Woolf, *Women and Writing* (New York: Harcourt Brace Jovanovich, 1979), 54.

2. Tillie Olsen, *Silences* (1978, rpt. New York: Delta/Seymour Lawrence Ed., 1980), 13, 39.

3. Denise Paulme, ed., *Women of Tropical Africa*, tr. H. M. Wright (1963, rpt. Berkeley: University of California Press, 1974), 2.

4. hattie gossett, "Who Told You Anybody Wants To Hear From You? You Ain't Nothing But a Black Woman!" *This Bridge Called My Back: Writings by Radical Women of Color*, ed. Cherrie Morraga & Gloria Anzaldúa (Watertown, MA: Persephone Press, 1981), 175.

5. Gloria Anzaldúa, "Speaking in Tongues: A Letter to 3rd World Women Writers," *This Bridge Called My Back*, 166.

6. Sylvia Plath, *The Bell Jar* (1971, rpt. New York: Bantam Books, 1981), 211. See Biographical Note by Lois Ames.

7. Emma Santos, *L'Itinéraire psychiatrique* (Paris: Des Femmes, 1977), 46–47. For previous quotes see pp. 47, 50, 125 (my translations).

8. Toni Cade Bambara, "What It Is I Think I'm Doing Anyhow," *The Writer on Her Work*, ed. J. Sternburg (New York: W.W. Norton, 1980), 167.

9. "Commitment: Toni Cade Bambara Speaks," interview with Beverly Guy-Sheftall in *Sturdy Black Bridges: Visions of Black Women in Literature*, ed. R. P. Bell, B. J. Parker, & B. Guy-Sheftall (New York: Anchor/Doubleday, 1979), 232.

10. Ezekiel Mphahlele, *Voices in the Whirlwind* (New York: Hill & Wang, 1972), 186–87.

11. Ibid., 196.

12. Franz Fanon, *Black Skin White Masks*, tr. Charles Lam Markmann (New York: Grove Press, 1967), 8.

13. Jean-Paul Sartre, *Situations, II Qu'est-ce que la littérature?* (Paris: Gallimard, 1948), 97, 112.

14. Margaret Walker, "On Being Female, Black, and Free," *The Writer on Her Work*, 95, 102, 106.

15. Jacques Rabemananjara, "Le Poète noir et son peuple," *Présence Africaine* 16 (Oct.–Nov. 1957), 10–13.

16. Aimé Césaire, *Return to My Native Land* (Paris: Présence Africaine, 1971), 60-62.

17. Nikki Giovanni, *Gemini: An Extended Autobiographical Statement on My First Twenty-Five Years of Being a Black Poet* (New York: Viking Press, 1971), 95-96.

18. Alice Walker, "Saving The Life That Is Your Own: The Importance of Models in The Artist's Life," *The Third Woman: Minority Women Writers of The United States*, ed. D. Fisher (Boston: Houghton Mifflin, 1980), 158.

19. Wole Soyinka, *Myth, Literature, and the African World* (New York: Cambridge University Press, 1976), 138.

Judy Baca:
Our People Are The
Internal Exiles

Diane Neumaier

(From an inter-
view with the
Chicana muralist
Judy Baca)

Our people are the internal exiles. To affirm that as a valid experience, when all other things are working against it, is a political act. That's the time we stop being Mexican-Americans and start being Chicanos. When you deny a people's culture you can make them disappear, you can control them.

The people coming over the border from Mexico are the most difficult to organize. Even though they are the most exploited in the Los Angeles sweatshops, even though they are providing a very low-cost labor force, supporting the economy in a very substantial way and using very few social services—they are the people who are being shot at the border, raped at the border, beaten at the border, followed by helicopters with infrared, etc. They don't want to hassle anything; it's too dangerous. They will not resist because they want to have this little bit of money and work. They just want to blend in and be Americans. My point simply is: if you deny the presence of another people and their culture and you deny them their traditions, you are basically committing cultural genocide.

I was born at a time when everybody was working very hard at just being American. In the early fifties, the prevailing idea was that we should all blend in. All separate ethnic groups should disappear and become American. I never did figure out what "American" was. I thought American was hot dogs and Wonderbread. When I went into the school system, I was *forbidden* to speak Spanish. I did not speak English. I remember being in rooms with people speaking this other language. I didn't understand the words they were saying, but I knew clearly that they were saying I was less than they were because I didn't speak their language. In elementary school, most of the Spanish-speaking kids were treated as if they were retarded and held back. I thought to myself, they're not going to be able to do this to me. I'm going to learn what they're saying.

And I learned very quickly. My mother worked on getting me to speak English without an accent. That was real important to her because that accent was an identification. She would have liked me to blend in if I could have, although at this point in her life she's very proud that I didn't. Like a lot of immigrant people, she felt that education was the key if I was to avoid suffering the kind of things that she had suffered.

I was encouraged to be fairly independent—very contrary to the socialization most Latin women are given. However, I also had all those other messages: get married, have children, do all that stuff. But I wanted to be an artist. My family didn't want me to be an artist because it was a crazy thing to be. What impact does your art have on *real life*? I think a lot of the ethic seeped into me: it's not good enough just to be an artist. How will you support yourself? What does it mean to the people you live around? All those questions got to me. So in college I also minored in history and in education. I developed back-up systems, which have proven very valuable in my work.

I went to school in the sixties at the state university in Northridge, California, in the part of the San Fernando Valley which was all white. Looking across that campus I would never see a Mexican or a black person or anybody of color. This was before the EEOP program, during the time when we were beginning to agitate for African-American studies, Chicano studies, American Indian studies. There were groups of people saying, "We're using thousands of Chicano young men in the Vietnamese War." And clearly, in the university system Chicanos had no presence. So the sixties had a very powerful influence on me. I had had all these feelings but no place to hang them. The *Movemiento* gave me a place to focus them and affirm the fact that I wasn't crazy.

I was thrown right in the middle of all that struggle but was very much isolated. The moment I left my community to go to college, I was isolated from my own people because not that many of them went to college, and I was isolated from any sense of my own culture in the university system.

When I got out of school, I brought what I had learned back to my family and listened to their responses. When I showed her my work, my grandmother said to me, "What is this? What's it for?" It was clear to me that somehow I had been encouraged not to be who I was, to use Western European art as my model. I hadn't even learned about *Los Tres Grandes*, the three great muralists. I even had no idea about murals. In fact, I had been doing mural work for a year before I even heard of the Mexican muralists.

My grandmother was no dummy. She knew a lot about healing and had been influenced by the Indians in her understanding of religion. It wasn't straight Catholicism because if you hang an *amuleta* (a little pouch with special herbs and things in it) around somebody's neck to heal them and keep the spirits away, that's not Catholicism in the strictest sense. She, along with my mother, had raised me, and I saw her as an extremely powerful person—spiritually powerful—and I respected her. I thought, these are the people I really know and care about. I love these people, and I really want to make them understand, make them be part of this process I'm going through. If I'm supposed to be interested in communicating, if my work is supposed to elevate the spirit of human beings, have I decided these people are not human beings? It seemed crazy to use Western European models, to be completely inundated by that kind of culture, when in fact we were sitting in southern California—which my grandmother always referred to as Mexico. She used to say things to me like, "English? Why do you want to speak English? English is a language which people spit, spit out words." It is true: in Spanish you can say things in ways you can't in English. It's a much more poetic, musical, lovely kind of language.

My ideas about how I would make art never began with a political analysis. I am moved in the heart. I see an issue, something I can care about, and then I go about finding solutions in the way I can as an artist. If I were a carpenter, I'd go out and rebuild things. If I were an architect, I would redesign the architecture. But I have other skills. I simply use what tools I have at hand to address what I care about.

I got the idea that making art was probably one of the most important human activities that anyone could engage in. Everywhere I looked, all around me I saw people being asked to dehumanize. Crap is pumped into the air so you can't breathe. The streets are overloaded with so many images that you can't see one of them. The sound level is so high that you have to block your sense of hearing. Every aspect of the sensuality and sensibilities of human beings is decreasing. I always had the feeling that art was the celebration of the senses, that it was a place we kept asking people to make a leap, keep it all together, and just let something happen to themselves in a *real* sensual way. A friend of mine, a Mexican muralist, used to tell me, "A painting should be what it is when you stand back from it, just what it is: a painting. But when you get up to it," he said, "when you get up to it, it should be good enough to eat." So I thought to myself, yeah, that's really what it's about. I want to do that. I want to make art that will ask people to use all of their senses. It's an important human endeavor.

I had, of course, the choice of making art and putting it into galleries, seeing if I could shuffle my things around from place to place and get them shown. Artists, especially students, plug into that system as it exists without ever analyzing for whom they make art—the audience they hope to communicate with through their work. In my case, my people and their images had been made to disappear. Images I grew up with in my home had no representation in that world. There was no aesthetic I knew—a certain exuberance for color, for example—that was validated in the art world. I thought to myself, if I get my work into galleries, who will go there? People in my family had never been to a gallery in their entire lives. My neighbors never went to galleries. All the people I knew didn't go to galleries.

But I thought if I took my work to galleries—and if I was lucky—somebody might buy it. Now what does buying something mean? It means limiting people's access to it. That's what ownership is about. Essentially, you buy something, you own it, and you can let people see it or not. And it didn't make sense to me at the time to put art behind some guarded wall.

So for me, then, there wasn't really any choice. How many ethnic artists do you know whose works are being shown, even now? I had no way to apply my work to that structure. You couldn't take an aesthetic that wasn't mainstream into the galleries and have it accepted—especially as a woman, and especially as a Chicana.

From 1969 through roughly 1974, I worked specifically within the Chicano and Mexicano community. That was an interesting process for me, discovering what I could use to address that culture. It was different from my own upbringing, because things change in the streets. The economic and political circumstances change how people can live in those areas. So I had to learn another language—street language. I had to learn what things were impacting that community at that time. I had to deal with gang warfare in a completely different way than when I was a kid, because the barrios that I grew up in didn't have that kind of *organized* gang warfare.

When I got out of college I started teaching at a Catholic high school—in fact, the same school I went to—in a program called Allied Arts, an innovative teaching program which I designed to celebrate the different senses. The kids wrote music, learned basic drama, wrote poetry. We interrelated all the arts. It was a fabulous course for me to teach, because it pulled a lot of things together and helped me understand how to use different techniques to get a desired product. People made presentations using three art forms to express one idea. It took over the whole school and became an incredible event. Kids drove up in a hearse, opened the back door and pulled out coffins to do a presentation on death. There were bands, choral readings, all fabulous stuff that really worked as motivation. We asked these kids to draw up out of themselves something that no one else was requesting of them.

I did my first mural there. I was trying to get team cooperation because there was a problem of division among kids coming from different neighborhoods. So I asked them to draw something together. We took a human figure, divided it up into parts, blew it up ten times its size, reconnected the parts, then dropped it out of a second-story window. Here was a sixty-foot person. It caused an amazing uproar. I saw that you could do an incredible amount of teaching with scale transformation. Changing scale in that way makes people perceive things differently.

Then I got hired in a program for the city with twenty artists. We were supposed to teach at parks all over the city. They looked at us and sent the black people to Watts and the Mexican people to East Los Angeles. So I ended up in East L.A.

I was given two classes, one at ten in the morning and another one at three in the afternoon. It was twenty-six miles from my home, so I would do my morning class and then hang out in the parks. I began to really watch street life. I saw young people, teenagers, adolescents, the throw-away people. Nobody wanted them in the parks; the Recreation and Parks Department had no programs planned for them because they were vandals, because they were involved in gang warfare. So they would play dominoes, drink wine, smoke dope, hang out in various corners. There was always this constant battle. The police would be called to get rid of them, and the kids would come back, like a flock of pigeons that fly up and land again. So I made friends with a lot of them. I met some kids who were involved in tattoo work. Of course, they were also writing all over the walls.

Visual symbols, calligraphy basically, were a focal point in their life on the street. You could read a wall and learn everything you needed to know about that community, about the guys or girls who hung out in the street—who they were, who they hung out with, what generation they were, how many of them had the same nickname—all in what they call *placayasos*.

I became something of an expert reader of street writing. I knew who was who in four or five different neighborhoods because I taught at different places. I realized *I* was moving from one part to the next, but they couldn't. They could not go five blocks without being in danger from other gangs. Some of the feuds were fifty or sixty years old.

That was my constituency. It's certainly not the whole of the Chicano community—I have to say that I get very perturbed when people perceive the Chicano community as being people who write all over the walls—but this is a street phenomenon that has been on the increase. In the sixties, it was more political slogans; now, it's about territory. It has to do with people saying, "Listen, I own nothing here. So I own your wall. Here's who I am." The tattoos are a whole thing, too. Kids with tattooed tears on their cheeks! What does that say about how the kids feel about themselves? What's going on for them is pretty rough, and it's reflected in the highest dropout rate in the entire nation.

I said I wanted to form a mural team. Pretty soon I had a number of people who began to hang with me, who trusted me and would do something I asked them to do. At that point nobody knew what a mural was; it wasn't the phenomenon it is now. I had to explain that we were going to do a big picture on the wall. But I had to figure out how to get the wall back. It was marked. Who do I have to talk to to get permission to use this wall? So I said to the kids, "Listen, I'm going to take off your *placayasos*. Here's what we're going to do. Do you want to work with us?" It was like negotiating treaties.

The most important skill that I've had to develop in this work is to be able to deal with people in City Hall, then jump in my car, drive ten miles to the East Side, change into boots and jeans, and go sit on the curb with the kids. There are people who are bridge people, and my ability to move between those great extremes has made it possible for me to do what I do. Possibly, because I had a university education, because I became Anglicized to a certain degree, I was able to come back to my own community with more information and make things happen.

I formed my first mural team of twenty kids from four different neighborhoods. It was the first time in recent history that they had been able to put aside their differences and work together. That was in 1970. We did three pieces that summer, including *Mi Abuelita*, a giant three-sided bandshell with a grandmother image in it—my grandmother, actually. I had to do it on a volunteer basis, but I got the kids paid.

Vandalism in the city park system is in the millions of dollars. The Recreation and Parks Department paints the walls white and dates them; that way, even if they're marked again, the public will know the department took care of its responsibility. Judging by the way the city spent its dollars, property damage was the concern, not the fact that kids literally die in the parks, overdosing. That's of little significance. What is of significance is that before these kids fall over they write on the walls.

It was distressing to me to see kids die, to see that human beings were not as important as property. I would go to the people in the Recreation and Parks Department thinking that *obviously* if they could see the values their appropriation of money reflected, they would be more responsive to the community. I would say, "Why is it that in East L.A. you have a park built in 1923 with the smallest acreage per capita, when it has one of the largest usages in the city? Why can't you expand this park? Why don't you put in tennis courts?" When they started saying shit to me like, "Mexicans don't like to play tennis," I started getting the picture. I knew that there was racism, but I didn't understand how it was institutionalized.

People were amazed at our work. The *Los Angeles Times* ran sensational articles like "Teenage Youth Gangs Put Down Knives for Brushes." Terrible. The head of Rec and Parks came down to the site—the kids thought he was a narc, and he's lucky he got in and out of there—and said to me, simply, "How can we bottle and package what you do?" I began to understand that I was becoming to the City of Los Angeles a wonderful instrument of graffiti abatement. But I was accomplishing my goals at the same time by doing my own work in the street—which for me was clearly *not* graffiti abatement.

The group of people I was working with was very connected to and influenced by visual symbols—in tattoos, in the kind of writing that went on in the street—but there was no visible reflection of themselves in the larger community. Nothing of the architecture or visual symbols reflected the presence of the people—other than the graffiti. First it was a Jewish community, then Mexican people moved in. What I could see was that any population could move through the place without being reflected in it.

Symbols already had significance in this community, and it made sense to create another set of symbols acknowledging the people's commonality, the fact that they came from the same place and had a common culture. It seemed to me this could break down the divisions among these people, give them information, and change their environment. The murals have been clear forms of expression, reflecting the issues and needs as they see them. I think decorative murals are a waste of time in urban areas. They're urban decoration. Band-Aids on cancer.

In the first years of this work people came by and brought us food and beer, anything we needed. They would volunteer to help us. It was interesting, because there was a real division between the young people from the street and their families; their parents hated them for not being good Mexican kids and thought they had gotten completely out of control. It's that old country-new country stuff. I remember one community meeting when some boys from the White Fence gang were showing their designs. (We always do this to give people a chance to become involved in the process. Then there are no surprises—community people hate surprises.) A woman in the back of the room said, "All you ever do is ruin everything in the community. You write all over everything. You're just worthless. Why should we help you?" I thought, "My, what an outburst of hostility." I thought the kids were doing wonderfully to get up in front of a crowd like that and speak—this from people who were not essentially verbal. I asked, "Who is that?" One of the kids said it was his mother. But when the parents saw their kids doing something positive, connections among the family members began to develop again.

Few girls participated during that time. It was much easier organizing among the young men because girls were not allowed the same mobility. It has been a long process drawing the young girls in, but it's equal. It's taken this many years for that to happen. You see, Latin women are not supposed to be doing things like climbing on scaffolding, being in the public eye.

From 1970 to 1974 there was an incredible outgrowth of murals in East Los Angeles. It wasn't just me—other people were doing it, too. The East Side of Los Angeles was becoming fairly well known for mural imagery. Suddenly there was an upheaval in the barrios; you could drive through them and see giant pieces all over the place. They were powerful and they were strong, and they were political. They talked about who those people were, what they cared about, and what they were mad about. They talked about the issues in their community from police brutality to drug abuse.

By taking a small object and transforming it into a giant image, you teach people to look at it in a different way. Claus Oldenberg knew about that. When your whole body fits into the eye of a monumentally rendered head, you are going to look at it in a way you never looked at the eye before. The same thing is true of the issues included in the mural.

Take a piece of historical information: 350,000 Mexican people were deported from the California region in the thirties, 75,000 from Los Angeles. (It was similar to what's going on now; with the economic recession people are concerned that Mexican people are taking their jobs, and again they're talking about another Bracero program.) But you may not care much about history. That's the attitude you get from a lot of people. "Who cares about that fact?" But then, after four days rendering each person who's getting on the train, and standing next to the oversized face of someone who's feeling the agony of that deportation, there's no way not to identify with that feeling. As the light changes you see them in a different way. You make them real. You make it happen again. Or take a concept: the illusion of prosperity. Make some kind of image that will speak to that. Then have people transform the scale to four times natural size. At the end of that process, they can perceive the concept in a substantially different way.

In 1974 I thought: Well, gee this is really interesting. I think anybody could make a mural. Certainly it's *bleak* in this city. Let's see what we can do about all the grey concrete walls. There were a lot of artists out of work and a lot of people in different communities who could use the opportunity to let the walls speak for them.

I had become fairly friendly with a number of political figures at that point because they had come to the site, seen what I was doing, helped me with the police who were bothering us, and so forth. I wrote a plan to get the city council to help us pay for an East Side brigade. There wasn't one Mexican representative on the whole council, not one in fifteen—even though the population was around forty percent Chicano (not including an uncounted population of probably one or two million undocumented workers). One of the council members told me, "You'll never get this because they don't care about the East Side. They'd like to see it drop off into the ocean." I thought, "He's right. There are fifteen council members, and I have to get it passed by all these votes."

I began to understand a whole lot about the political process. I went before a committee and got slaughtered. I was just devastated. The member from the San Fernando Valley said, "We don't have any gangs in our area. We don't have any youth that need this kind of stuff. Besides, I think we should put them all in jail." A lot of racist stuff came out *that* directly. I couldn't believe it! He said, "What is this, Mexican art?" I had to endure all kinds of abuse.

I went back very discouraged to this black council member who had been friendly with me. He told me, "Judy, you dream too small." I pored over that in my head for days and thought, "He's fuckin' right!" So I wrote a proposal, a very grandiose idea for a citywide mural program. It would incorporate forty murals a year covering a radius of over a hundred miles in every ethnic community of the city. And would cost in the area of $150,000 a year. They gave it to me.

It was a struggle for about six months. I had to appear in front of all types of committees. I would give my spiels over and over again about what it would do for senior citizens, children, professional artists, the black community, the Chicano community, the Asian community, the Korean community, the Thai community, the Chinese community. Then I spent the next three years of my life doing it—a real ordeal. They might give you the money, but they're not going to help you. In fact, they're going to get in your way at every turn. For example, suddenly they would say, "All people hired from now on must have tuberculosis tests." Try getting a thousand people tuberculosis tests who don't have transportation. Or, "All payments will take four to six weeks." The mural would be done in three or four weeks, then you'd get whole gangs of kids coming after you because you haven't paid them. Crazy stuff. That's when I learned administrative skills.

I also learned how to work in a multi-ethnic situation. I no longer was working solely in the Chicano community. I learned that organizing in the Chinese community is *radically* different than organizing in the Chicano community or in the black community. I realized that the Chicano staff was absolutely racist against blacks and saw how the black style of coming in and being able to articulate what's in their mural just turned off my staff, who wanted to veto every black mural that came through.

A lot of the murals done in that program were cultural kinds of pieces; even the tame ones were, in fact, important statements to announce—for example, the presence of Filipinos in a community where no one would acknowledge them. There was a piece on the landing of Filipinos in the Philippine islands, which was very similar to the Mexican legend of the Aztecs arriving in Tenochitilan. This is what gave me the idea about overlapping legends. I thought that was a wonderful thing; people could see how they all connected in some ways.

Some of the pieces were about police brutality and the open warfare that goes on between the police and the people in the communities. Some were about immigration, what the immigration authorities were doing, and the exploitation of illegal workers. Others were about drug abuse, including the government-supported influx of drugs into the communities and the *Las Tres* issue in Los Angeles, where three people were imprisoned for shooting a narcotics agent who was bringing narcotics into the community.

A lot of pieces were on gentrification and urban renewal, on how the developers' interests are taking people's homes away from them. One of the most controversial was a piece that showed, on one side, an idyllic scene in the Venice community done in the style of a Persian miniature; on the other side were bulldozers wiping out the folks, knocking down the small wooden houses on the canals to make room for a plush condo city. In the corner was a little guy spraying, "Stop the pigs. Save Venice." Before the mural was put up, these words had been scrawled on the wall in four-foot red letters. The guy who had done that came to our community meeting and said, "My graffiti is more important than your mural." People thought that he had something there and decided to incorporate it into the mural. So the mural was sort of an illustration of his graffiti. The realtors picked up on it and tried to stop us. In fact, just recently they painted half of it out before the community found out. To keep the mural up, I had to go to about twenty meetings, all the way up to Chief Ed Davis, and explain that in this case "pig" meant greed, not police.

It was truly an *amazing* experience. We were dealing with problems that are manifested in the whole society, going out into these communities and seeing how artists are treated. We did 250 murals (I probably directed around 150) and hired over 1,000 people. It wore me out—to death.

We were putting these pieces up all over the city, which was all fine and good. But at some point, because of the sun and the pollution, and because the murals were in poor communities that were subject to redevelopment, the murals would be torn down. Then the people would get up in arms. For example, somebody would start to paint out a mural when a building owner had changed, and fifty people would be out there with sticks wanting to beat up the guy. We had organized well in the communities, so they protected their murals. But we couldn't get money for maintenance, and it was very difficult to make building owners keep the pieces up.

I also saw artists do just *awful* things in the communities, like coming into an ethnically mixed community and, because the artist was Chicano, painting a Chicano piece with only Chicano kids. Sometimes they would incite people to attack a police officer; everybody would be beaten up and taken to jail—except the artist. Terrible things!

I couldn't handle it anymore. I couldn't control the quality of the pieces. I was tired of supporting other people, breaking my ass and killing myself, and being in this no-man's land position between the community and the city. The community perceived me as being part of the city bureaucracy, while the officials perceived me as being a flaming radical from the community!

It was very hard, and I was very exhausted by the end of it. I decided to start a nonprofit corporation. I had a support group operating for the Citywide Mural Project because I knew at some point the city would withdraw its support. Some of these pieces were *very* political, and I expected that at some point they would want to stop me. In fact, they tried to kill the mural program twice. There were huge battles, letter campaigns, "Citizens to Save the Murals" committees. I didn't want to continue that type of struggle all the time and not get to do my own work—especially since I actually did it better than a lot of people I was supporting to do it. So in 1977 I left the mural project to do *The Great Wall.*

I'd done a number of other big pieces by that time—the Venice murals, the East L.A. murals. I did a 400-foot-long piece and another couple that were about 300-400 feet long. I decided I would pull together all the stuff I had learned into one place and address the issue of having people work together. I had also seen the ghetto-ization of the work, like wonderful pieces done by black artists that were only seen in the black community. They weren't getting the exposure that they deserved. In some ways, murals began to acquire a connotation as "ghetto art." Middle-class and upper-middle-class areas began to resist them in their neighborhoods because they saw them as a ghetto phenomenon. I figured I had to get on that fast. That's why I began SPARC. I formed it with a friend who's an independent filmmaker and another woman who was a printmaker. We began *The Great Wall* as our first project.

I thought that we could generate additional funding to expand the concept of community murals into other art forms. The concept of working in public art or monumental kinds of public pieces with the community could be the basis of the work that we did, the bottom line being to create social change in whatever environment we were working in. I wanted to see other artists be able to address a community with an idea that they had, whatever the form. That's what happened. In 1977, through a lot of political maneuvering, we got the old Venice Jail for free. I wanted to be able to work within an institution. We have to create our own institutions that are sort of deinstitutionalized. It gave me a vehicle through which to have an ongoing connection with the community, not be isolated from other people in my studio.

I originally began the mural thinking that with each artist given the responsibility for a segment of the wall, a wonderful piece would come together in some way. But, in fact, the artists were not as willing to work with each other in the composition of an overall piece as I thought they would be. They created a series of easel paintings. I don't feel that the first thousand feet is a mural. Each hundred-foot segment is different and reflects the personal style of the artist and the people in the artist's crew. Now we're doing it with an overall design.

Probably one of the hardest things for me to do is to recognize my leadership ability because I've always been wanting to give it away whenever possible. I think it's part of my cultural thing that comes up. In the Chicano community, leaders are wiped out. People hate leaders. It's not a good position to be in. Also, it's very hard to acknowledge that I have to say "No," "Yes," "You do what I tell you to do," or "I have leadership on this." Yet I would always take all the responsibility: I would raise all the money; I would do all the preparatory work; I would be the one who would ultimately answer to everyone and see to it that everyone was paid—but I submitted to a collective process all the decision-making power over the planning of the mural. By 1978 I realized I couldn't do that again. I really had to decide whether I wanted the piece to go past what it had been in that first summer. I had a vision for it that I thought was much more encompassing, and I realized if I really wanted to see that happen I had to trust my idea and trust myself to know that it was going to be better for me to make those decisions. And it was.

The thing about muralism, particularly in monumental pieces, is that collaboration is a requirement. It isn't like other art forms you might be able to accomplish by yourself. I've seen a lot of men in Los Angeles do monumental pieces on a two-story or eight-story building, by themselves. But *The Great Wall* is based on a different conception of what art is for. The mural is not just a big picture on a wall. The focus is on cooperation in the process underlying its creation. I could probably go into my studio for a year in advance and design it; but, for one, there's not that kind of funding to support my work for a year, and, two, the process that we use really works in with the overall plan. With what the historians bring in we develop images to put back into public consciousness information that has been lost. It's really incredibly stimulating and exciting. The mural is a conceptual art piece all along, and the finished painting is only one part of it.

To bring talented young people into the design crew fits the goals of the project. It's part of the leadership development aspect of the program, giving kids more and more power to meet and enhance their growth. Also, I think the mural is better because it has a number of minds working on it. The hardest part is making the design work as a unified piece, but the collaboration on ideas really is wonderful.

We sit with the historians and do a "talk-through." We write out a story: "First there was this period in which people thought everything was fine; it was an 'illusion of prosperity.' What was really going on was Prohibition, the whole flapper image, the coming Crash..." It goes like that. You talk it through in a literal way, which develops an attitude that comes from people hashing it out together. In that way, people who are not the best at drawing don't have to be relied on for that. It's orchestrating people's best skills, using their better abilities, putting them together where they match. It's geometric in proportion. It multiplies the power that you have by taking the best of other people and putting it all together in one thing. However, one person must have the overall vision for it to become a whole.

When we get hung up, it's my job to push things forward to set up a situation in which people can be creative. At this point I have the ultimate veto power when I think something is not working. I have to trust my judgement. The people who work with me understand that I have to be able to say, "I just think this is not working." Although the conceptualization takes place in a group, I approve every image idea before it goes to thumbnail.

After we develop the thumbnails, I may do as many as twenty different drawing studies of the woman carrying a child in the Dust Bowl scene. Then I take all the thumbnails and submit them to an overall discipline of a musical division of space—ratio development, musical time 3:5, etc. That's basically how I deal with the overall composition. I also do corrections on everyone's drawings if things are not anatomically correct or whatever. This way there are many minds working on the concepts and one artistic vision pulling it all together.

I think I originally had the idea that leadership meant for me to be the person who created an environment in which other people could be creative. Now I acknowledge the fact that I usually have more experience than anyone else in my group, more mural experience. I've done a tremendous amount of work at this point. I've also watched a whole lot of other people do a tremendous amount of work. And I've made a lot of mistakes. Now, leadership means trusting my intuition, which I think is fairly highly developed, about how to deal with people.

I didn't like any hierarchy. I just thought that we should all be equal. But for now, I really can't say that's possible. I think if I worked in a situation where everybody raised the money, everybody had responsibility, and everybody had the same level of experience, it would be fine. But even then, the world outside would not relate to a collective answering a question. There's got to be one person who ultimately takes it on the chin. Maybe I'm getting tired, but I no longer want to take it for anybody else's mistakes besides my own. Also, when I don't listen to what I think, I screw up.

Of course, if a woman takes this on she's a bitch, a dyke, a macha, a demanding, difficult-to-work-with person—all those kinds of things. Those are stereotypes about what a woman is if she's a leader. I'm conscious all the time of my own body, of what it says to people when I'm talking to them, of the way that I use my words to communicate. I try to use all those parts and pull them together in a way that communicates from a soft place in myself—not the defense/fear place—what I think and what I care about, what I want other people to do and think and care about. They may not care, but at least I'm communicating my attitudes to them. That's how I feel I'm a leader. A lot of times I can plug into the psychology of a group, the overriding feeling, what they're creating for themselves—and pull it out and say, "Let's define it. What is it?" That's part of my role as a leader. So much of it is really being a good teacher. So much of it is drama, being some kind of theater person. But the other part of it is that although I take the consequences for the decisions, I often don't make a decision totally by myself. A lot of times I really am a catalyst, a facilitator. But the other part of it is, I often have to take the responsibility for making decisions myself.

The whole business of learning to be responsible is hard. I have gotten myself in a position a number of times where I've made myself sick. I had acute acrylic poisoning two years ago from mural paint. I was in intensive care with cardiac arrhythmia. I couldn't breathe. It's a little known fact that the metals in acrylic paint are as dangerous as, and in fact are the same as, those in oil paint. Because artists have no power in this country, they don't get any of the safety hazard information that other workers get. I have had a hard time acknowledging that I have to take care of myself. I say all the time in group meetings with my staff at SPARC, "I am one resource. If you use me up we're all in trouble." That means that I have to see myself as a valuable natural resource that has to be preserved in the same way that a river or a tree has to be preserved. I've got to take care of myself. I'm working at it, but I find myself not doing it a lot of the time. It frightens me. That's part of being willful, pushing yourself when your body is telling you something else. We are not taught to be nurturing of ourselves. We're taught to sacrifice, particularly in my culture. The women put on the black mantilla, and they are the mourners and the producers and the nurturers. They make them and they bury them.

People who do this kind of work are in such danger of burnout, or absolutely destroying themselves. We have all those people who have wonderful capabilities out there, people who've been real instrumental in making things happen, and they all get beat up, literally beat up! There's something wrong with how we are perceiving ourselves. That's critical information.

I think the world is becoming interested in what political artists are doing. Political art is now perceived as "avant-garde" or something, and I see people trying to get recognition in this way. I'm not focusing on that, yet some of it happens. For example, a museum is going to be taking *The Great Wall* and blowing it up, doing a whole thing on all the sketches and studies we do to make it happen.

I don't feel that the mainstream art world is something I either want to attack or court. Certainly, it is another kind of audience, and I believe in audience development. But there's a difference between public and personal art, and I'm a public artist.

If I decided now to take the time to do personal work I could pursue putting it in different places, finding a group of my friends who would like it or finding another audience that would respond to it. That's not invalid. But so far I've been trying to have the public at large relate to my work. I think this has also been happening in other areas like artists' books and performance art, which has had the capacity for organizing large groups of people and bringing them to a different state of consciousness very quickly.

I see myself as an urban artist, using the entire environment that I work in, which includes the people in that environment. If I'm talking about transforming an environment—changing, enhancing, making it more beautiful—then I am also talking about changing the people who live in that environment as well. Accepting the whole reality of the space means working with who populates the area and seeing what I can do to better the whole situation. The reason I work with adolescents is not simply because I'm interested in teaching, but because they are the people who populate those public areas. I'm also interested in working with all the power structures—the local authorities, local municipalities, the Army Corps of Engineers, Teamsters' Union—because they are part of the reality of that area. That's how I would define myself as an urban artist. The elements of my designing are not just line, form and color but all the environmental and social factors that are inherent in the space and that cannot be separated from it. That's changing everything and not just the facade.

From *Cultures in Contention*

Object Into Subject: Some Thoughts On the Work Of Black Women Artists

Michelle Cliff

In my room there is a postcard of a sculpture by the Venetian artist Danese Cattaneo, done in the mid-16th century—*Black Venus*. The full-length nude figure is bronze. In one hand she holds a hand-mirror in which she is looking at herself. On her head is a turban, around the edges of which her curls are visible. In her other hand she carries a cloth—or at least what appears to be a cloth. Who was she? A slave? Perhaps in the artist's own household, or maybe that of his patron—one of the many Black women dragged from Africa to enter the service of white Europeans. I have no idea who she actually was: she was an object, then as now.

Around this image are other images of Black women: Bernadette Powell, who killed the man who beat her and is now in Bedford Hills; Fannie Lou Hamer; Billie Holiday; Elizabeth Freeman, who sued for her freedom and won it, in Massachusetts in the nineteenth century; Josephine Baker; Harriet Tubman, portrayed in a linocut by Elizabeth Catlett; women students making basket furniture at the Hampton Institute; Lucy Parsons; Ida B. Wells-Barnett; Audre Lorde; Phillis Wheatley; two women in Botswana seated around a gourd; Sojourner Truth; women in the Black Liberation Movement in England; Betye Saar's Aunt Sally HooDoo; a girlchild balancing a basin on her head in southern Africa.

My moving toward the study of the work—written and visual— of Black women has been a moving toward my own wholeness. My interest in this work is a deeply personal interest, because through these words and images I begin to capture part of who I am.

I should begin with my title—"Object into Subject." What does it mean? We live in a society whose history is drenched in the philosophy and practice of racism, the oppression of Black and other Third World peoples. This is the point at which my definition begins: if you study racism—if you understand the history of the United States—you will find that under racism the person who is oppressed is turned into an object in the mind of the oppressor.

The white anti-racist southern writer Lillian Smith was among the first to offer a metaphysical and psychological explanation of racism as a personal and political American practice[1]—one essential to the maintenance of things as they are in this society. Smith—whose influences included Kierkegaard, Jung, Freud and Sartre—traced the origins of racism, and its more apparent manifestation, segregation, to that place in the human mind she called "mythic": that place where dreams, fantasies and images begin; where they continue and take form as art, literature, politics, religion. The mythic mind is a source of psychic energy—it contributes the motion necessary for sustained thought. But the mythic mind needs a structure in which to function, so that its products will be understood. This structure is provided by reason. Reason, Smith argued, is merely a technic, an enabler; its sole purpose is to create the form which will support the ideas moving out of the mythic mind. Reason is incapable of moral judgement, and therefore will support any idea or image, regardless of its moral basis.

When the mythic idea of whiteness, the obsession with skin color which is the irrational and immoral basis of racism, is given a construct from which the myth takes its form—i.e., the philosophy of white supremacy—the result is cultural or institutionalized racism, contained in the politics, literature, art and religion of the dominant culture. An insane idea now exists within a reasonable reality, not an irrational dream.

Whatever we may feel about Smith's analysis, or her sources for that matter, her treatment of American racism as something embedded in the white mind, regenerating itself within a psychological construct, is extremely important. She recognized early on the character of racism as in a sense "larger than life," something which could not be removed by congressional legislation or Supreme Court decisions, unless these actions were the result of a completely radicalized mindset within the dominant culture. I think that the resurgence of white racism in this country today bears witness to her understanding.

Within the rationale reason lends to racism, Smith argued, is the practice of objectification, an absolute necessity in the racist effort to oppress. (I use the word "effort" because it is and has been so; one which has been carried out on every level of this society, against constant, historic opposition.) Through objectification—the process by which people are dehumanized, made ghostlike, given the status of Other—an image created by the oppressor replaces the actual being. The actual being is then denied speech; denied self-definition, self-realization; and overarching all this, denied selfhood—which is after all the point of objectification. A group of human beings—a people—are denied their history, their language, their music. Their cultural values are ignored. This history, this language, this music, these values exist in the subculture, but in the dominant culture only certain elements are chosen, recast, co-opted and made available to the definition of these people. And these elements presented by the dominant culture tend to serve the purpose of objectification and, therefore, oppression.

The practice of objectification stands between all Black people and full human identity under the white supremacist system: racism requires that

Black people be thought different from white; and this difference is usually translated as less than. This requirement has been stated in various ways throughout the history of America. Did you know, for example, that Thomas Jefferson held the popular view that the Black race was created when Black women mated with orangutans?[2] (I do not know where the original Black women were supposed to have come from.)

Last October on my local PBS station I watched the film *Birth of a Nation*, introduced by a rather hearty film buff as an American classic, the work of a "tragic poet." I had never seen the movie, nor had I read the book *The Clansman*, upon which it is based. I felt I "had to watch it." The first thing I noticed was that all the Black characters were portrayed by white actors in "blackface." Throughout the film the thing most evident to me was that this was a playing-out of a white American's image of Black people, crude and baroque to be sure, but not that far removed from *Gone with the Wind* (another American classic), or even from such white-inspired television programs as "The Jeffersons." If anything, the very coarse brutality of *Birth of a Nation* is closer to the history of the slavocracy than perhaps any other American film. I could see as I watched this film how white people were capable of committing both the acts of the slave period and the lynchings which flourished during Reconstruction and thereafter. D. W. Griffiths's imaginings of Black women and men attempted to justify this history by replacing a people with the fantasies of his tragically racist mind. The very title gives his intention away.

The playwright and activist Lorraine Hansberry, in her essay "The New Paternalists," observed:

> America long ago fell in love with an image. It is a sacred image, fashioned over centuries of time: this image of the unharried, unconcerned, glandulatory, simple, rhythmic, amoral, dark creature who was, above all else, a *miracle of sensuality*. It was created, and it persists, to provide a personified pressure valve for fanciful longings in [white] American dreams, literature, and life....I think, for example, of that reviewer writing in a Connecticut newspaper about *A Raisin in the Sun*...and marvelling, in the rush of a quite genuine enthusiasm, that the play proved again that there was a quaint loveliness in how our "dusky brethren" can come up with a song and hum their troubles away. It did not seem to disturb him one whit that there is no single allusion to that particular mythical gift in the entire play. He did not need it there; it was in his head.[3]

Just as this white reviewer could hear Black people humming as he watched Hansberry's play, others could declare it a play about insurance money, one which proved that all Black people really wanted was to live alongside whites. Many white people perceived the ending of *Raisin* as "happy," unaware perhaps of what it meant for a Black family to move into a white neighborhood in Chicago in the post-World War II years. Did any of these white people know of Hansberry's own childhood experience when her family moved into a white Chicago neighborhood? The response to this move was white violence: the eight-year-old Hansberry had a brick thrown through her bedroom window by the white mob. Her father, supported by the NAACP, took the case all the way to the Supreme Court and established a precedent for nondiscriminatory housing—but nothing in Chicago actually changed.

If anything, the ending of *Raisin* is hopeful, not happy. And the hopefulness one feels derives not from any expectation of a white change-of-heart, but from the fact that Hansberry has tested her characters throughout the play and they have emerged as people of integrity, capable of facing reality and white racism. She was, I think, attempting to create Black characters who would disrupt white imagery of Black people. But many in her audience could only see these characters through their own screen of objectification.

It is objectification that gives the impression of sanity to the process of oppression. The centuries-old image of which Hansberry speaks, actually a collection of images, is necessary to maintain racism. To hate with no justification for hatred, to oppress with no reason for oppression, would be recognizably insane. Once an object is provided—an object endowed by the oppressor with characteristics that allow hatred, that allow oppression—then hatred and oppression of the object can be defended as logical. An insane idea has been made rational. Lillian Smith portrayed this basic insanity of segregation in the South she knew:

> As I sit here writing, I can almost touch that little town, so close is the memory of it. There it lies, its main street lined with great oaks, heavy with matted moss that swings softly even now as I remember. A little white town rimmed with Negroes, making a deep shadow on the whiteness. There it lies, broken in two by one strange idea. Minds broken in two. Hearts broken. Conscience torn from acts. A culture split into a thousand pieces. That is segregation. I am remembering: a woman in a mental hospital walking four steps out, four steps in, unable to go any further because she has drawn an invisible line around her small world and is terrified to take one step beyond it....A man

in a Disturbed Ward assigning "places" to the other patients and violently insisting that each stay in his place.[4]

"Segregation," for Smith, described a phenomenon deeper than legal statute or town custom. She saw segregation as a form of dichotomizing within the white Western male tradition. She observed, for example, that white women are segregated from Black women and also objectified within the dominant culture:

> Another split took place....Somehow much in the white woman that [man] could not come to terms with, the schizophrenic split he had made in her nature—the sacred madonna and the bitch he had created of her— could now be projected, in part, onto another female: under slavery, he could keep his pure white "madonna" and have his dark tempestuous "prostitute." ...Back of southern people's fear of giving up segregation is this fear of giving up the "dark woman" who has become a symbol which the men no longer wish to attach to their own women.[5]

Smith's observation is important: white and Black women were/are both objectified and split from one another. I feel that Smith oversimplified the split, however. For example, the sacred madonna, in order to maintain her status (and most often she was intent on maintaining her status), had to objectify the Black woman according to the white male imagination. The white woman on the slave plantation knew that white men used rape against Black women. She knew that Black women were for the most part fieldhands, working alongside men—when they were pregnant, when they were nursing. The Black woman was made into a sex object, yes, but Smith's use of the word "prostitute," even in quotes, suggests more choice than any slave woman ever had. It also denies or glosses over the use of rapism by white men against Black women as an instrument of terror, of oppression.

Black women have been doubly objectified—as Black, as women; under white supremacy, under patriarchy. It has been the task of Black women artists to transform this objectification: to become the subject commenting on the meaning of the object, or to become the subject rejecting the object and revealing the real experience of being. In her essay "In Search of Our Mothers' Gardens," Alice Walker ponders the degree of difficulty faced by a Black woman in the United States with artistic ambition: "What did it mean for a black woman to be an artist in our grandmothers' time? In our great-grandmothers' day? It is a question with an answer cruel enough to stop the blood."[6]

In her novel *Sula*, Toni Morrison makes the following observation about the seemingly destructive nature of her main character:

> In a way, her strangeness, her naiveté, her craving for the other half of her equation was the consequence of an idle imagination. Had she paints, or clay, or knew the discipline of the dance, or strings; had she anything to engage her tremendous curiosity and her gift for metaphor, she might have exchanged the restlessness and preoccupation with whim for an activity that provided her with all she yearned for. And like any artist with no art form, she became dangerous.[7]

Sula's tragedy, and the tragedy she represents, is "cruel enough to stop the blood." Because of her race, perhaps also because of her sex, she has been shut out from art and denied access to art forms. She is an intelligent, thinking woman, who ultimately has nowhere to go.

The objectification of Black women has taken many forms: The Mammy, Mama—wetnurse, midwife, cook—usually large, usually dark, combining humility and capability. The temptress, sex-object, whore—sometimes mulatto (from the Latin for mule, i.e., a creature unable to reproduce herself)—misbegotten and tragic, the power of the master coursing through her powerless veins. These are but two examples which recur in white Western literature and art. And these have been repeated by white women as well as white men. There is, of course, "Mammy" in *Gone with the Wind*; and there is Julie, the woebegone quadroon in Edna Ferber's *Showboat*. Another novel, *Imitation of Life* by Fanny Hurst, attempts to "deal with" both Mammy and mulatto.

By many accounts, Fanny Hurst was a well-intentioned liberal. Much has been made, for example, of the fact that she employed Zora Neale Hurston as her secretary in 1925. But some of that history suggests Hurst's insensitivity to Hurston's identity as a Black woman, not to mention a brilliant novelist and writer, among whose subjects was the self-definition of Black women. On one occasion Hurst, intent on integrating a restaurant in Vermont, prevailed upon Hurston to accompany her—passing Hurston off as an "African princess." Hurston remarked, "Who would have thought that a good meal could be so bitter."[8] In this incident Hurst, the would-be liberator, reveals herself as objectifier. This phenomenon occurred over and again during the Civil Rights Movement. It was most commonly expressed in the notion that unless Black people behaved in certain ways, allowing whites to oversee and control their access to liberation, that liberation would not be achieved. What is present is the need for whites to maintain power, and limit the access of Black people to that power, which, finally, is the power of self-definition.

Imitation of Life, published in 1933, concerns the relationship between two dyads: a white woman and her daughter and a Black woman and her daughter. Both pairs are essentially alone in the world. The Black woman, Delilah, is hired to run the house by the white woman, Miss B., who has been recently widowed. Delilah carries with her various recipes, and these prove to be the "salvation" of Miss B. and family. In a relatively short time, Miss B. is the proprietor of a chain of restaurants in which Delilah's food is the main attraction, and which are recognized by a likeness of Delilah on the sign. When Miss B. hits on the idea of photographing Delilah as the advertising gimmick for the enterprise, she dresses Delilah as a chef. Delilah, faithful servant throughout the book, in this one instance asks her employer not to humiliate her but to allow her to wear her best clothes.

Miss B., however, prevails. Hurst describes the final result: "Breaking through a white background, as through a paper-covered hoop, there burst the chocolate-and-cream effulgence that was Delilah."[9] Here is Aunt Jemima; the female server of Sanka; even Mrs. Butterworth, whose color literally pours forth. Here is an instance of the brainchild of a Black woman, her recipe, her art form, passed through generations of Black women; co-opted and sold, with a caricature of the artist used to ensure its success.

In and around the main theme of the novel—the "success" of Miss B. as an "independent businesswoman"—is the subplot concerning Delilah's light-skinned daughter, Peola—unable to be white, unwilling to be Black, in the course of her dilemma denying her mother. Peola moves west, works as a librarian, passes for white, and marries a white man. She has herself "sterilized," eliminating any chance of "throwback." Her husband is also mutilated, having lost part of a hand. Perhaps he is all she is entitled to. Delilah has the final say: "Black women who pass, pass into damnation."

Taken together, Delilah and Peola represent what George Frederickson has characterized as "soft" and "hard" stereotypes.* Bell Hooks also juxtaposes two stereotypes of Black women: Mammy and Sapphire.

> It is not too difficult to imagine how whites came to create the black mammy figure....She was first and foremost asexual and consequently had to be fat (preferably obese); she also had to give the impression of not being clean so she was the wearer of a greasy dirty headrag; her too tight shoes from which emerged her large feet were

---

*Although Frederickson's *The Black Image in the White Mind* deals primarily with stereotypes of Black men, with some alterations his categories apply to stereotypes of Black women.

further confirmation of her bestial cowlike quality. Her greatest virtue was of course her love for white folk which she willingly and passively served....In a sense whites created in the mammy figure a black woman who embodied solely those characteristics they as colonizers wished to exploit.[10]

As Sapphires, black women were depicted as evil, treacherous, bitchy, stubborn, and hateful, in short all that the mammy was not. White men could justify their de-humanization and sexual exploitation of black women by arguing that they possessed inherent evil demonic qualities....And white women could use the image of the evil sinful black woman to emphasize their own innocence and purity.[11]

To talk about the history of Black women in America, and of the various images I have mentioned, we must begin with the woman who was a slave. Who was she? How did she survive? How many of her did survive? What did she teach her children? What was her relationship to her husband? What were her options?

She could be lynched, beaten, tortured, mutilated, raped. She could have her children sold away from her. She was forbidden education. She was considered a beast of burden. She was subject to the white man's power and the white woman's powerlessness masking as whim. Her womb was a commodity of the slavemaster, and her childlessness, a liability of the slavemaster. She was not expected to love—but she did. She was not expected to run away—but she did. She was known to commit infanticide and induce abortion rather than have her child be a slave. She was known to commit acts of violence and rebellion—with magic, poison, force, even with spit. And she sometimes learned to read and write and sustain the art forms she had carried with her.

In 1960 Lorraine Hansberry was commissioned to write a play about slavery for national television. She wrote *The Drinking Gourd*, about a Black family and a white family under slavery. In it, as in *Raisin*, Hansberry attempted to contradict the myths about Black people and to recapture and recast history. Her play was never performed; it was judged "too controversial" by the network. Hansberry had described Lena Younger, her mother-figure in *Raisin*, as an "affirmation," as

the black matriarch incarnate, the bulwark of the Negro family since slavery, the embodiment of the Negro will to transcendence. It is she, who in the mind of the black poet scrubs the floors of a nation in order to create black diplomats and university professors. It is she, while

seeming to cling to traditional restraints, who drives the
young on into the fire hoses. And one day simply refuses
to move to the back of the bus in Montgomery. Or goes
out and buys a house in an all-white neighborhood where
her children may possibly be killed by bricks thrown
through the windows by a shrieking racist mob.[12]

With her mother-figure in *The Drinking Gourd*, Hansberry went further.
Rissa, the slavemother, does what the Black mother-figure in white
American mythology has never done: she, in effect, kills a white man (the
"good" white man), and gives his guns to her children, after her son has
been blinded for learning to read. The play ends as Rissa and her band
of revolutionaries escape into the woods.

We know that Black women—mothers and nonmothers—have been
intrinsic to the activism of Black history. There is the following story, for
example, quoted by Angela Davis:

> She didn't work in the field. She worked at a loom. She
> worked so long and so often that once she went to sleep
> at the loom. Her master's boy saw her and told his
> mother. His mother told him to take a whip and wear her
> out. He took a stick and went out to beat her awake. He
> beat my mother till she woke up. When she woke up, she
> took a pole out of the loom and beat him nearly to death
> with it. He hollered, "Don't beat me no more, and I won't
> let 'em whip you."
>
> She said. "I'm going to kill you. These black titties
> sucked you, and then you come out here to beat me." And
> when she left him, he wasn't able to walk.
>
> And that was the last I seen of her until after freedom.
> She went out and got an old cow that she used to
> milk—Dolly, she called it. She rode away from the
> plantation because she knew they would kill her if she
> stayed.[13]

This story tells of a Black woman in the act of freeing herself. A selfish
need for freedom, and a recognition that freedom is their right, is
something usually denied to Black women historically, even when they
are recognized as liberators of their race. But Fannie Lou Hamer, Ida
B. Wells, Mary McLeod Bethune, Sojourner Truth—and the many
women whose names we do not know—all felt a personal desire for
freedom, which came from a feeling of self-esteem, self-worth, and they
translated this into a political commitment that their people also be free.
Harriet Tubman said:

> I looked at my hands to see if I was de same person now
> I was free. Dere was such a glory ober eberything, de sun
> came like gold trou de trees, and ober de fields, and I felt
> like I was in heaven.
>
> I had crossed de line of which I had so long been
> dreaming. I was free; but dere was no one to welcome me
> to de land of freedom. I was a stranger in a strange land,
> and my home after all was down in de ole cabin quarter,
> wid de ole folks, and my brudders and sisters. But to dis
> solemn resolution I came; I was free, and dey should be
> free also; I would make a home for dem in de North, and
> de Lord helping me, I would bring dem all dere.[14]

The artist, like the liberator, must begin with herself.

Edmonia Lewis (1843-1900?) is the first woman of color we know
whose work as a visual artist was recognized by the dominant culture.
During her life as a sculptor she was confronted with the objectification
of herself as Black and female. While her work was not ignored, it was
given a secondary place of importance by most critics. Lewis was seen as
a "wonder," a work of art in herself—a curiosity. The following excerpt
from an abolitionist newspaper describes the artist and her marble group
Forever Free (1867):

> No one...could look upon this piece of sculpture without
> profound emotion. The noble figure of the man, his very
> muscles seeming to swell with gratitude; the expression of
> the right now to protect, with which he throws his arms
> around his kneeling wife; the "Praise de Lord" hovering
> on their lips; the broken chain—all so instinct with life,
> telling in the very poetry of stone the story of the last ten
> years. And when it is remembered who created this group,
> an added interest is given to it....Will anyone believe it
> was the small hand of a girl that wrought the marble and
> kindled the light within it?—a girl of dusky hue, mixed
> Indian and African, who not more than eight years ago
> sat down on the steps of City Hall to eat the dry crackers
> with which alone her empty purse allowed her to satisfy
> her hunger; but as she sat and thought...of her homeless
> state, something caught her eye, the hunger of the
> stomach ceased, but the hunger of the soul began. That
> quiet statue of the good old Franklin...kindled the latent
> genius which was enshrined within her, as her own group
> was in marble, till her chisel brought it out. For weeks
> she haunted that spot and the State House, where she

could see Washington and Webster. She asked questions, and found that such things were first made in clay. She got a lump of hard mud, shaped her some sticks, and, her heart divided between art and the terrible need for freedom...she wrought out...an admirable bust of [Col. Robert Gould Shaw, white Bostonian commander of the company of Black troops organized due to pressure from Frederick Douglass].[15]

When this article was written Lewis was a well-known sculptor living in Rome, with a degree in liberal arts from Oberlin College. She had studied sculpture with Edward Brackett, a prominent neoclassical artist. She was not particularly interested in creating likenesses of Franklin, Washington, or Webster—her interest in these pieces would have been purely technical, not inspirational. The only "leader" of white America she ever depicted was Abraham Lincoln. All her other subjects were drawn from her history as the daughter of a Black man and a Chippewa woman, and her consciousness of racism.

Just as the author patronizes the artist, so does he minimize the political statement of her work. For instance, he uses the word "gratitude" rather than "pride," or "triumph," in his comments on the male figure; he focuses on the arm which embraces the woman, rather than on the hand which is raised, the broken chain dangling from the wrist. He cites the struggle of the last "ten" years with typical white solipsism. In addition, his "Praise de Lord" does not allow us knowledge of the politics of Black Americans, to which religion has been historically intrinsic. Rather, it can be read in such a way that the triumph is taken from the hands of those who have won it and placed somewhere "out there."

It is commonly believed that the slaves were freed by white Northerners. But as W.E.B. Du Bois observed: "In proportion to population, more Negroes than whites fought in the Civil War. These people, withdrawn from the support of the Confederacy, with the threat of the withdrawal of millions more, made the opposition of the slaveholder useless, unless they themselves freed and armed their own slaves."[16] The journey out of slavery was one in which Black people played a dominant role. It is this that Lewis is commemorating in her work. She had earlier commemorated the slave-woman in her piece *Freedwoman on First Hearing of Her Liberty* (which has been lost to us).

In an interview with the *Lorain County News*, Lewis spoke of her childhood:

> My mother was a wild Indian and was born in Albany, of copper color and with straight black hair. There she made and sold moccasins. My father, who was a Negro, and a gentleman's servant, saw her and married her....Mother

often left home and wandered with her people, whose
habits she could not forget, and thus we were brought up
in the same wild manner. Until I was twelve years old, I
led this wandering life, fishing and swimming...and
making moccasins.[17]

Alice Walker speaks about looking "high—and low" for the artistic
antecedents of Black women; she speaks specifically of her own mother's
garden—how this was the place of her mother's creative expression, the
background against which Walker's own work proceeded: "Guided by
my heritage of a love of beauty and a respect for strength—in search of
my mother's garden I found my own."[18] This statement makes me think
of Lewis's mother, her independence and her craft. The fact that she
trained her daughter in her art form. That she taught her strength.

Lewis's sculpture, because she chose primarily to depict subjects
directly related to her own and her people's experience, has a certain
power. Where her pieces lose power is in the style she adopted and the
material she used: the neo-classical style, with its emphatic focus on Greek
idealization, and the pristine whiteness of the marble, which supports the
narrowness of the style—so that a black face must appear white and be
carved according to principles of beauty which are white, "fine" features
as perfection. The nineteenth century was the century of jubilee, of a
women's movement, and of a revolutionary movement in Europe. But
these moral reactions need to be understood against the immorality which
dominated that century: the "white man's burden," the political/relig-
ious/economic affirmation of the supremacy of the white race. The
neo-classical style arose quite naturally from all this, based as it was on
the imitation of fifth-century Athens, a slave-owning, gynephobic society,
but one popularly regarded as high-minded and democratic. In Lewis's
Forever Free the limitations placed on a Black and Indian artist working
in this style and with this material are evident: the curly hair of the male
figure and the broken chain are the only signs that these are people of
color.

Of her sculpture *Hagar* (1875), Lewis said: "I have a strong sympathy
for all women who have struggled and suffered."[19] Again, we have to look
beyond the actual figure to the story Lewis is illustrating to find the
political/historical statement in her work. Hagar was an Egyptian, a
woman of color, the slave of Abraham's wife, Sarah. Hagar was "given"
to Abraham by Sarah so that he might have an heir; and she was the
mother of his first-born son, Ishmael. Then Isaac was born to Abraham
and Sarah. The book of Genesis continues the story:

Sarah saw the son of Hagar the Egyptian, whom she had
borne to Abraham, playing with her son Isaac. So she said
to Abraham, "Cast out this slave woman with her son; for

the son of this slave woman shall not be heir with my son
Isaac." And the thing was very displeasing to Abraham
on account of his son. But God said to Abraham, "Be not
displeasing because of the lad and because of your slave
woman; whatever Sarah says to you, do as she tells you,
for through Isaac shall your descendents be named.... So
Abraham rose early in the morning...and sent [Hagar]
away. And she departed, and wandered in the wilderness
of Beer-sheba.[20]

It is quite impossible to read this story and not think of the Black woman
under slavery, raped by the white master, serving the white master's wife,
bearing a child by the white master and bearing the responsibility for
that child—with no power over her own fate, or that of her child. Lewis's
choice of Hagar as a symbol for Black slave-women also fits into the Black
tradition in America, one immersed in the stories of the Bible (often the
Bible was the only access slaves had to the written word), and characterized by the translation of these stories according to Black history.

In reading this account from Genesis, I am also thrown back to Lillian
Smith's description of the split between Black and white women. It is
Sarah who is made responsible for the banishment of Hagar. Her husband
and his god remain blameless, even noble.

After approximately ten years of recognition, Edmonia Lewis "disappeared." This sort of falling out of fame is usually seen as tragic, but I
wonder what happened to her? Was her disappearance by choice? Or did
she disappear because she was a Black woman artist who was no longer
in vogue, because she was no longer seen as "exotic"?

In contrast to Lewis's white marble sculptures, Elizabeth Catlett's
figures are done in brown wood or terra cotta, or another material which
suggests the color of her subjects, or at least that her subjects are people
of color. No white Western features replace the characteristics of Black
and other Third World people. But Catlett is a contemporary artist, one
who relatively early in her career left this country and moved to a country
of colored people—Mexico.

Yet her piece *Homage to My Young Black Sisters* (1969), when we
make allowances over time and across space, is not that far removed in
political intent from Lewis's *Hagar*. In form the differences are enormous: Hagar's hands are clasped in front of her, in resignation, in
supplication—in the wilderness she has to turn to Abraham's god to save
the life of her son. The female figure of *Homage* has one arm raised in a
powerful and defiant fist. The similarity between the two pieces is that
both, I think, represent part of the history of Black women, particularly
Black motherhood, in America. The midsection of the *Homage* figure is
an open space, which I take as Catlett's statement of the historical white
denial of Black women's right to motherhood in any self-defining way,

and of the theft of the children of Black women and of what these children represent—whether through the laws of the slavocracy or those of postindustrial America.

Catlett uses the theme of Black women and children often in her work, depicting over and again the heroism required of Black women simply to survive. In her lithographs, engravings and linocuts, Catlett seeks to tell the history of Black women, breaking away from the objectification of the dominant culture. We might, for example, look at her wood engraving of Harriet Tubman (1975), in contrast to Judy Chicago's Sojourner Truth plate in the *Dinner Party*.[21] Catlett's Harriet dominates the foreground; one powerful arm points forward, the other holds a rifle. She is tall and she is strong and she is Black. In the background are the men and women she leads. What is interesting to me is the expression on Tubman's face—she is fiercely determined. This expression is repeated in the group she leads. There is no passivity here, no resignation, no impotent tears, no "humming." Rather, this is a portrait of the activity of a people in conflict with their oppression.

Catlett has stated that art should be obviously political, available to the people who are its subject. We have no such clear statement from Lewis, but we must wonder for whom her work was done, finally; and whether she stopped working as she did because of a distance between her art and her subjects.

Harriet Powers (1837-1911) was a quilt-maker (only two of her quilts are known to survive). She worked in applique, a method of needlework devisd by the Fon of Dahomey, brought to this country on slave ships.[22] Betye Saar is a collector; an artist who constructs images with various objects, mementos, photographs, bits and pieces picked up here and there and saved; things used in another context, by other hands. Bot Powers and Saar endow their work with a belief in the spiritual nature of the ordinary. Power's quilts, constructed from the scraps saved by a poor Black woman, convey a real portrait of one Black woman's religion and politics. Marie Jeane Adams states: "The more one examines the style and content of Harriet Power's work, the more one sees that it projects a grand spiritual vision that breaks out of the confines of folk art."[23]

The employment of once-used objects by these artists is one aspect of their work which needs further thought. In the history of white Western art there is an obsession with the purity of materials. And also with their value. For one example: in the art of fifteenth-century Italy, and even earlier, the color ultramarine was often used to depict the most important figure or feature in a painting or fresco. This choice was made with the knowledge that the color was created by crushing lapis lazuli, the most expensive source of pigment after gold.[24] And this choice extended to the very meaning of the work produced. In the art of Powers and Saar, the sources of the artist's materials are also important, but the choice is more deeply personal. We might ask: how much does the power of a work of art consist in the material which makes up that work? What is the difference between a work of art made with things specifically employed in that work and never before, and one which uses only things used before? Is one more useful than the other? More magical than the other?

We know of Harriet Powers's work partly because of a white woman—Jennie Smith, herself an artist—who left an eighteen-page monograph on the artist. She recorded the following in 1891, when Powers finally agreed to sell her a quilt:

> I found the owner, a negro woman, who lived in the country on a little farm whereon she and her husband made a respectable living.... Last year I sent word that I would buy it if she still wanted to dispose of it. She arrived one afternoon in front of my door...with the precious burden...encased in a clean crocus sack.
>
> She offered it for ten dollars, but I told her I only had five to give. After going out consulting with her husband she returned and said, "Owin' to de hardness of de times, my old man 'lows I'd better teck hit." Not being a new woman she obeyed.
>
> After giving me a full description of each scene with great earnestness, she departed but has been back several times to visit the darling offspring of her brain.[25]

Power's second quilt—now in the Boston Museum of Fine Arts—was commissioned in 1898 by the wives of professors at Atlanta University. This quilt, known as the second Bible quilt, consists of five columns, each divided into three frames. All the frames deal with the theme of God's vengeance and redemption, illustrated through Biblical images and representations of cataclysmic events in eighteenth- and nineteenth-century America.

> This...much-exhibited quilt portrays fifteen scenes. Ten are drawn from familiar Bible stories which concern the threat of God's judgment inextricably fused with His mercy and man's redemption, among which are the Fall, Moses in the wilderness, Job's trials, Jonah and the whale, the Baptism of Christ and the Crucifixion....Four others depict astronomical or meteorological events, only one of which, an extremely cold spell in 1895 in the eastern United States, occurred in Mrs. Powers' adult life. Given Mrs. Powers' intensely religious outlook, she interpreted these events in the celestial atmosphere as messages from God to mankind about punishment, apocalypse, and salvation.[26]

The one frame which does not fit into this categorization is the one which, as Marie Jeane Adams observes, is the key to the quilt. Powers left a description in her own words of all the scenes in the quilt; of this particular frame, she said:

> Rich people who were taught nothing of God. Bob Johnson and Kate Bell of Virginia. They told their parents to stop the clock at one and tomorrow it would strike one and so it did. This was the signal that they had entered everlasting punishment. The independent hog which ran 500 miles from Ga. to Va. Her name was Betts.[27]

The frame has a clock in the center, stars and a moon scattered around, two human figures. At the bottom is the independent hog named Betts, the largest figure of the quilt. Metallic thread outlines the clockface and creates a tiara around the head of the white woman, Kate Bell. Betts is made from gray cloth, but she is placed over a swatch of orange so that her figure unmistakably stands out.

This quilt represents a great spiritual vision, but it also represents a great political vision: as well as hope, it represents rage. It is a safe guess that Bob Johnson and Kate Bell of Virginia were a son and daughter of the slavocracy. They stand surrounded by scenes representing the punishment meted out to those who are arrogant and self-serving, and the redemption promised those who are righteous. In this particular frame it is their sin of pride which has damned them; and Powers is clear in her belief that their damnation is well-earned. In contrast is the dominating figure of Betts, who in an act of self-liberation goes free. Her 500-mile flight from Georgia to Virginia is, as Adams points out, a reference to one route traveled by runaway slaves. And Betts is undeniably female—her teats hang down from her gray-cloth body. I think of Dolly—the cow in the anecdote cited above—being ridden away by a Black woman. And I think of the white idea of Black women as beasts of burden, "mules," farm animals; of the image of Harriet Tubman being forced to draw a wagon for the entertainment of white folks. I take Betts to be a metaphor for this experience. Angela Davis has quoted Frederick Law Olmstead's description of a slave crew in Mississippi returning from the fields:

> [I saw] forty of the largest and strongest women I ever saw together; they were all in a simple uniform dress of a bluish check stuff; their legs and feet were bare; they carried themselves loftily, each having a hoe over the shoulder, and walking with a free, powerful swing like chausseurs on the march.[28]

It would be very simple to romanticize this group of women. But, as Davis says, it is not slavery and the slave system that have made them strong; it is the experience of their labor and their knowledge of themselves as producers and creators. She quotes Marx: "labor is the living, shaping fire; it represents the impermanence of things, their temporality." Davis makes a brilliant connection here:

> ...perhaps these women had learned to extract from the oppressive circumstances of their lives the strength they needed to resist the daily dehumanization of slavery. Their awareness of their endless capacity for hard work may have imparted to them a confidence in their ability to struggle for themselves, their families and their people.[29]

Black women were not dehumanized under slavery; they were dehumanized in white minds. I return again and again in my own mind to the adjective "independent," which Powers uses to describe Betts, a "chasseur on the march."

It is not that far a distance from Lewis's *Hagar*, to Catlett's *Homage*, to Powers's Betts, to Betye Saar's *Aunt Jemima*. Saar's construction, entitled *The Liberation of Aunt Jemima*, is perhaps the most obvious illustration of what I mean by the title of this essay: "Object into Subject." Here is the most popularized image of the Mammy—in the center of the piece she is a cookie jar, the source of nourishment for others: behind her are faces cut from the pancake mix. In front of the central figure is another image of Mammy, holding a white baby. And there is a broom alongside the central figure. But she also holds a pistol and a rifle; and the skirt of Mammy with the white baby forms an unmistakable Black fist. Saar's message is clear: Aunt Jemima will free herself.

In an interview in *Black Art*, Saar described the components she uses in her work:

> They are all found objects or discarded objects, so they have to be remnants. They are connected with another sensitivity so it has to be a memory of belonging to another object, or at least having another function.[30]

Aunt Jemima has been created by another sensitivity than that of the artist who has made this portrait. Aunt Jemima has a memory of belonging to someone else, of being at the service of someone else. She exists against an image, which exists in another mind. The cookie jar is a remnant of another life: most likely she "lived" on the kitchen counter of a white family, maybe Saar found her discarded on a white elephant table, or at a garage sale. She has appeared to me in my travels, usually turning up in rural antique stores or church basements, labeled "collectible." The picture of Mammy with the white baby reminds me first of old magazine advertisements, usually, as I recall, for soap or cereal or other necessities of the servant role. And I additionally recall the many films of the forties and fifties about white middle-class America, in which a large Black woman who worked in the kitchen was always present but only occasionally given a line to speak. She was played by Louise Beavers, Hattie McDaniel or Ethel Waters—and she was usually characterized by her loyalty to the white family for whom she worked. She also appeared on television: "Beulah" was a program in which she was featured. She was kind, honest, a good cook, always with a song to hum her troubles away; and as usual, devoted to those white folks.

All but three of the elements in Saar's construction are traditional to Aunt Jemima; the two guns and the fist are not. Saar, by including these unfamiliar aspects has changed the function of the figure she is representing. She has combined the myth with the reality of Black women's historic opposition to their oppression.

This representation of Aunt Jemima is startling. All of us who have grown up with the mythical figure of Aunt Jemima and her equally mythical attributes—whether or not we recognized they were mythic— have been affected. We may not have known her, but aren't we somehow convinced that somewhere she exists, or at least has existed? The last thing we would expect would be that she would carry a gun, or raise a hand. As a child in Jamaica I was taught that the women who worked for us were to be respected and obeyed, and yet I remember my twelve-year-old light-skinned self exercising what I felt was my authority over these women, and being quite taken aback when one of the women threatened to beat me—and my mother backed her up. Just as I was shocked to find that another houseworker had tied up my cousins and shut them on the verandah because they were interfering with her work.

So while we may know the image is an image, the expectations of Black women behaving according to this image persist. As far as I can tell, Harriet Tubman carried both a carbine and a pistol. And she threatened to shoot any slave who decided to turn back on the journey north. Just as Lorraine Hansberry's slavemother armed her children and set out with them—after leaving a white man to die.

From *Heresies* 15

Notes

1. For Lillian Smith's definition of racism, see "The Mob and the Ghost" and "Words That Chain Us and Words That Set Us Free," in *The Winner Names the Age*, ed. Michelle Cliff (New York: Norton, 1978).

2. Erlene Stetson, "Studying Slavery," in *All The Women Are White, All The Blacks Are Men, But Some of Us Are Brave*, ed. Gloria T. Hull, Patricia Bell Scott & Barbara Smith (Old Westbury, N.Y.: Feminist Press, 1981).

3. Lorraine Hansberry, quoted in *Les Blancs: The Collected Last Plays of Lorraine Hansberry*, ed. Robert Nemiroff (New York: Vintage, 1973), 206.

4. Lillian Smith, *Killers of the Dream* (New York: Norton, 1949), 31.

5. Smith, *Winner*, 204.

6. Alice Walker, "In Search of Our Mothers' Gardens," in *Working It Out*, ed. Sara Ruddick & Pamela Daniels (New York: Pantheon, 1977), 94.

7. Toni Morrison, *Sula* (New York: Bantam, 1975), 105.

8. Quoted by Robert Hemenway, *Zora Neale Hurston* (Urbana: University of Illinois Press, 1977), 24.

9. Fannie Hurst, *Imitation of Life* (New York: Harper & Bros., 1933), 105.

10. Bell Hooks, *Ain't I A Woman* (Boston: South End, 1981), 84.

11. Ibid., 85.

12. Hansberry, *Winner*, 210.

13. Angela Davis, "The Black Woman's Role in the Community of Slaves," *Black Scholar* (1971), 13.

14. Quoted by Sarah Bradford, *Harriet Tubman: Moses of Her People* (Secaucus, NJ: Citadel, 1974, rpt.), 30–32.

15. Quoted by Phebe A. Hanaford, *Daughters of America* (Augusta, ME: True, n.d.), pp. 296–7.

16. Quoted by Sara Bennett & Joan Gibbs, "Racism and Classism in the Lesbian Commuity," in *Top Ranking*, ed. Bennett & Gibbs (Brooklyn: February 3rd Press, 1980), 14–15.

17. Quoted by Eleanor Tufts, *Our Hidden Heritage* (New York: Paddington, 1974), 159.

18. Walker, "Gardens," 101.

19. Tufts, *Heritage*, 163.

20. Genesis. 21:9–14.

21. For a brilliant analysis of the Sojourner Truth plate in Chicago's *Dinner Party*, see Alice Walker, "One Child of One's Own," in *But Some of Us Are Brave*.

22. This detail, and most of the information about Powers and her quilt, comes from Marie Jeane Adams, "The Harriet Powers Pictorial Quilts," *Black Art*, vol. 3, no. 4, 12–28.

23. Ibid., 16.

24. Michael Baxandall, *Painting and Experience in Fifteenth-Century Italy* (London: Oxford University Press, 1972), 9 ff.

25. Quoted by Mirra Bank, *Anonymous Was a Woman* (New York: St. Martin's, 1979), 118.

26. Adams, "Powers," 14.

27. Mrs. Powers's description of the quilt appears in both Adams and Bank.

28. Davis, "Black Woman's Role," 11.

29. Ibid.

30. Betye Saar, "Interview with Houston Conwill," *Black Art*, vol. 3, no. 1, 9.

"Nopalitos": The Making of Fiction

Helena María Viramontes

Testimonio

Fiction is my jugular. For me it is a great consolation to know that whatever miserable things happen in my lifetime, goodness will inevitably result because I will write about it. There is strength in this when none is left in the soul.

I was born and raised in the U.S., East L.A., Califas, to be more exact, on First Street not too far from Whittier Blvd., close enough to enable me to see the smoke from the Chicano Moratorium riots. I come from a family of eleven, six sisters and three brothers, but the family always extended its couch or floor to whomever stopped at our house with nowhere else to go. As a result, a variety of people came to live with us. Former boyfriends of my sisters who were thrown or pushed out of their own homes, friends who stayed the night but never left, relatives who crossed the border and stayed until enough was saved. Through all this I remember two things well: first, the late night kitchen meetings where everyone talked and laughed in low voices, played cards, talked of loneliness, plans for the future, of loves lost or won. I heard men cry, drunken stories, women laughing. It was fascinating to listen in the dark, peek into the moments of their lives. For me, it seemed like a dream to wake up at midnight and hear the voices and listen to the soft music, see the light under the door. This was adulthood and I yearned to one day be the one on the other side of that door.

Little did I realize that this is the stuff good fiction is made of: the stories, the fascination of the subject matter, capturing the moments and fleeing with them like a thief or lover. I began my apprenticeship without even knowing it.

The other thing I remember is my mother. Her relentless energy. She must have been tired a good part of her life and yet she had to keep going and going and going. I also remember her total kindness, the way a sad story made her cry, the way she always found room somehow in an already-crowded household for those with the sad stories. The nights she would stay up, a small black and white TV blaring, waiting for the girls to come home. The mornings she would get up, KWKW Spanish radio low, making the big stack of tortillas for the morning breakfast.

These two things, love of stories and love of my mother, or all that seemed female in our household, influenced me to such an extent that it became an unconscious part of me, so unconscious that I didn't realize it until just moments ago. In fact, the first story that I wrote, titled "Requiem for the Poor," opened with my mother awaking to make breakfast. To think: she was the first image in my mind, my heart, my hand. Naturally.

If my mother was the fiber that held a family together, it was my father who kept snapping it with his oppressive cruelty. With virtually no education, stressed with the responsibility of supporting such a large family, he worked as a hod carrier—a carrier of cement in construction. He drank, and was mean. Impatient, screaming a lot of the time, temper tantrums, we were often trembling in his presence. If my mother showed all that is good in being female, my father showed all that is bad in being male. I'm only now understanding the depth of this conclusion, and am making a serious effort to erase this black and white. See the good and bad in both sexes. That's the power of imagination, peeking beyond the fence of your personal reality and seeing the possibilities thereafter.

A basic problem for any writer is time. I lament the lack of time. As I pass my shelves of books, I think, these are books I will never read; or as my notebooks pile up, spilling over with plots, characters, great and moving sentences, I think, these are the words that will never find a story. Ideally, it would be bliss to manipulate the economic conditions of our lives and thus free our minds, our hands, to write. But there is no denying that this is a privilege limited to a certain sex, race and class. The only bad thing about privilege, Virginia Woolf wrote (I'm paraphrasing from Tillie Olsen), was that not everyone could have it.

How does one solve the problem of time? Fortunately, we *mujeres* are an inventive people. My mother, for example, faced the challenge of feeding eleven people every evening. Time and time again, I saw her cut four pork chops, add this and that and this, pour water, and miraculously feed all of us with a tasty *guiso*. Or the *nopales* she grew, cleaned, diced, scrambled with eggs, or meat, or chile, or really mixed with anything her budget could afford, and we had such a variety of tasty dishes!

I have never been able to match her *nopales*, but I have inherited her capacity for invention. I myself invent time by first conjuring up the voices and spirits of the women living under brutal repressive regimes. In the light of their reality, my struggles for a few hours of silence seem like such a petty problem. I am humbled, and no sooner do I think of their courage that I find my space on the kitchen table, my time long after midnight and before the start of the children's hectic morning. Because I want to do justice to their voices. To tell these women, in my own gentle way, that I will fight for them, that they provide me with my own source of humanity. That I love them, their children. Once seen in this perspective, the lack of sleep is more of an inconvenience than a sacrifice.

What little time we do invent we guard like our children. Interruption is a fact in our lives and is as common as pennies. Solely because we are women. A man who aspires to write is sanctioned by society. It is an acceptable and noble endeavor. As for us, writing is seen as a hobby we do after all our responsibilities are fulfilled. Nay, to write while the baby is crying is a crime punishable by guilt. Guilt is our Achilles' heel. Thus the work of the *mujer* suffers immensely, for the leisure of returning to her material, to rework it, polish it, is almost impossible. Because phones will ring, children will cry, or mothers will ask for favors. My mother, it seemed for a time, believed me to be half-baked for wanting desperately to write. It was inconceivable to her that I spent mornings scratching a sharpened pencil against paper. She would stand and look over my shoulder, try to read a paragraph or two, and seeing that I was simply wasting my time staring into space, she'd ask me to go get some *tortillas*, or could you vacuum the living room, maybe water the plants outside? After turning her away with a harsh no, guilt would engulf me like a blob, and although I hated myself for doing it, there I was, once again, holding a garden hose, watering her roses.

We must come to understand that stifling a woman's imagination is too costly a price to pay for servitude. The world would be void of any depth or true comprehension if we were not allowed to exercise our imaginations. We must challenge those beliefs which oppress us within our family, our culture, in addition to those in the dominant culture.

Family ties are fierce. Especially for *mujeres*. We are raised to care for. We are raised to stick together, for the family unit is our only source of safety. Outside our home there lies a dominant culture that is foreign to us, isolates us, and labels us illegal alien. But what may be seen as a nurturing, close unit, may also become suffocating, manipulative, and sadly victimizing. As we slowly examine our own existence in and out of these cultures, we are breaking stereotypes, reinventing traditions for our own daughters and sons.

What a courageous task! In the past, we have been labeled as the weaker sex, and it is logical to assume that we are of weaker minds as well. As women, we have learned to listen, rather than speak, causing us, historically, to join with others who maintain we have nothing to say. Only now we are discovering that we do. And those who do not seem interested in knowing our voices are just plain foolish. To limit their knowledge of people, places, cultures, and sexes is to live in a narrow, colorless world. It is not only a tragedy, but just plain silly, for only foolish people would not be interested in embracing such knowledge.

We cannot, nor will we divorce ourselves from our families. But we need a change in their attitudes. If I am to succeed as a writer, I need my family to respect my time, my words, myself. This goes for my parents, brothers, sisters, my children, my husband. Respectability is a long and sometimes nasty struggle. But you'd be surprised at the progress one can make. Eventually, my mother proved to be very flexible. When I signed my first honorarium over to her, she discreetly placed it in her pocket. Later, as I spread my notebooks over the dining room table, she carried in a steaming cup of coffee, sweetened just the way I like it.

Now for some *nopalitos*.

From *Breaking Boundaries: Latina Writing and Critical Readings*

6 If You Would Would Be My Ally

For the white person who wants to know how to be my friend

Pat Parker

The first thing you do is to forget that i'm Black.
Second, you must never forget that i'm Black.

You should be able to dig Aretha,
but don't play her every time i come over.
And if you decide to play Beethoven—don't tell me
his life story. They made us take music appreciation too.

Eat soul food if you like it, but don't expect me
to locate your restaurants
or cook it for you.

And if some Black person insults you,
mugs you, rapes your sister, rapes you,
rips your house or is just being an ass—
please, do not apologize to me
for wanting to do them bodily harm.
It makes me wonder if you're foolish.

And even if you really believe Blacks are better lovers than
whites—don't tell me. I start thinking of charging stud fees.

In other words—if you really want to be my friend—*don't*
make a labor of it. I'm lazy. Remember.

From *Movement In Black*

Some Like Indians Endure

Paula Gunn Allen

Laguna Pueblo/Sioux

i have it in my mind that
dykes are indians

they're a lot like indians
they used to live as tribes
they owned tribal land
it was called the earth

they were massacred
lots of times
they always came back
like the grass
like the clouds
they got massacred again

they thought caringsharing
about the earth and each other
was a good thing
they rode horses
and sang to the moon

but i don't know
about what was so longago
and it's now that dykes
make me think i'm with indians
when i'm with dykes

because they bear
witness bitterly
because they reach
and hold
because they live every day
with despair laughing
in cities and country places
because earth hides them
because they know
the moon

because they gather together
enclosing
and spit in the eye of death

indian is an idea
some people have
of themselves
dyke is an idea some women
have of themselves
the place where we live now
is idea
because whiteman took
all the rest
because father
took all the rest
but the idea which
once you have it
you can't be taken
for somebody else
and have nowhere to go
like indians you can be
stubborn

the idea might move you on,
ponydrag behind
taking all your loves and
children maybe downstream

maybe beyond the cliffs
but it hangs in there
an idea
like indians
endures

it might even take your
whole village with it
stone by stone
or leave the stones
and find more
to build another village
someplace else

like indians
dykes have fewer and fewer
someplace elses to go
so it gets important
to know
about ideas and
to remember or uncover
the past
and how the people
traveled
all the while remembering
the idea they had
about who they were
indians, like dykes
do it all the time

dykes know all about dying
and that everything belongs
to the wind
like indians
they do terrible things
to each other
out of sheer cussedness
out of forgetting
out of despair
so dykes
are like indians
because everybody is related
to everybody
in pain
in terror
in guilt
in blood
in shame
in disappearance
that never quite manages
to be disappeared
we never go away
even if we're always
leaving

because the only home
is each other
they've occupied all
the rest
colonized it; an
idea about ourselves is all
we own

and dykes remind me of indians
like indians   dykes
are supposed to die out
or forget
or drink all the time
or shatter
go away
to nowhere
to remember what will happen
if they don't

they don't anyway—even
though the worst happens

they remember and they
stay
because the moon remembers
because so does the sun
because the stars
remember
and the persistent stubborn grass
of the earth

From *Living the Spirit: A Gay American Indian Anthology*

Girlfriends

*Andrea R.
Canaan*

You know, the kind of woman friend you
can be a girl with.
You know what I mean a woman you giggle
with one minute and can be dead serious
the next.
The kind of friend that you can be a bitch
with and she thinks that you were being
a bitch just then, and tells you so.
The kind of friend that you usually
tell all to and when you forget to tell
her some secret that you have been holding
and casually mention it to her, you are
surprised that you hadn't told her.
You know, the kind of friend that you can
go out with and it's not always dutch.
The kind of woman friend that you
play with and sleep with and go to
the movies with and gossip half the day
or night with and argue politics with and
never agree yet always agree with...you know?
The kind of friend that you keep secrets
for and with and can be P.I. with, in fact
you both insist upon it.
I mean the kind of friend that you laugh
and cry with over some woman breaking your
heart even though this is the fourth time
this year it's happened, and she will hold
you and let you wail
just like it was the very first time your
heart was ever broken.
The kind of woman that will leave
no stone unturned to find out why she hurt
your feelings even if she didn't mean to and
especially if she did.
The kind of friend that you will accept
an apology from graciously even when you feel
now that you might have been being hyper-
sensitive that day and revel in the knowing

that someone cares so much how you feel and
you don't have to worry about monogamy or
polygamy or which side of the bed is yours
or nothing.
The kind of woman friend that you can tell
how your lover done you so wrong and she
doesn't get mad when you don't do all those
things you swore you would.
The kind of friend that you can get
mad with or strongly disagree with or lose
it with and she will not give up on you
or stop loving you.
The kind of friend that will give
you space to fall in love even though your
new affair is taking the spontaneity out
of her being able to pop over or to
call you late about some small bit of
info to hear your voice and be assured
about some fear that you can not
yet name.
The kind of friend that doesn't get mad
until she has not seen or heard from you
for two solid weeks and then she comes
over or calls and cusses your ass out for days
and then you go out for an ice cream cone.
I mean the kind of friend that stays mad
with the people that fuck over you long
after you have forgiven them.
The kind of friend that
allows you to wallow in self pity for
just so long and then gives you a swift
kick.
The kind of friend that close or far apart
she will be there for you, the distance wiped
away instantly to meet some outside enemy or
trouble.
I mean the kind of woman who always honors
what is private and vulnerable for you.

You know, I mean girlfriends.

From *Feminary* 13

Developing Unity Among Women of Color: Crossing the Barriers of Internalized Racism and Cross-Racial Hostility

Virginia R. Harris and Trinity A. Ordoña

The struggle against racism and sexism should be a unifying force among women of color. The additional struggle against heterosexism and homophobia should make a strong base for unity among lesbians of color. But unity has generally eluded heterosexual women of color and lesbians of color. Clearly, shared oppression by itself does not override the forces that keep us apart.

We are African American and Filipino lesbians. As individuals, we have worked with women of color for the past ten years. In the last few years, our efforts have focused on lesbians of color. In 1987, we created a consultation service focused on developing unity among women of color. The purpose of this paper is to present some of our observations of the racially based conflicts among women of color, to discuss underlying causes and to begin a long-needed dialogue on these issues among ourselves.

Women of color coming together in our common struggle against racism and sexism is seen as the epitome of unity. Indeed, the struggle against these twin oppressions is a powerful unifying foundation. Yet, unity within the women of color community is often short-lived. Few coalitions survive past the project or issue which brought us together. When the "honeymoon" ends, we find ourselves tormented by in-fighting and unaddressed conflicts. Internalized racism, cross-racial hostility, internalized sexism, homophobia and heterosexism are the particular dynamics which keep us from resolving these antagonisms and forming lasting coalitions and relationships. These conflicts are part of interactions between women of the same racial group, between women of different racial groups and between heterosexual women of color and lesbians of color.

I

Racism is all around us. We eat, sleep, speak and breathe it. We see it everywhere. We feel it inside us. We are discouraged by it more often than not—discouraged because fewer and fewer perpetrators of racism are even conscious of their racist behavior—or perhaps they don't care. Their behaviors, which insure that racism remains a part of our lives, are efforts to instill in our minds—deeply and permanently—ideas, attitudes and motivations regarding [racial] purity and pollution.[1]

A small corporation. Of approximately 700 employees there are ten to fifteen mostly white, mostly late twenties and early thirties, out lesbians. That they declare themselves lesbians in a hostile corporate environment is commendable. This is especially true since there is a higher number of closeted lesbians in the company.

One of the out, white lesbians was told she would be promoted from her clerical job to a technical one. She had been doing technical work in addition to her clerical job, so, clearly, she was qualified. The manager who told her this was, simultaneously, giving two heterosexual women of color a difficult time—trying to get one fired and sexually harassing the other. He had previously been instrumental in terminating a lesbian of color. His sexism, racism and homophobia were discussed by the three women constantly. When the white lesbian was told of her proposed promotion, her behavior toward the women of color changed. She became the manager's ally and withheld information from the women of color which laid out his plans against them.

After five weeks of doing the new job, papers still had not been processed for her promotion. When asked why, the manager told her she had not been promoted, but had been given a lateral transfer, made a trainee and would not get a raise. She went to the women of color for understanding, for sympathy and support.

Racism seeps into our systems like poison, kills off pieces of our selves as we build a tolerance for it. We have learned to survive with our insides, our essential selves, rotting away. We build protective walls to ward off the poison and the "protection" becomes a prison. The prison limits our choices to be and we live only as others have determined. The poison of oppression becomes our food, food that nourishes the prison but not the self. Just like our bodies build up a tolerance for additives and chemicals and may seem to thrive on them, our psyches build a tolerance for the pain inflicted by oppression.

A Sunday afternoon in May, 1989. I have the television set on. "Who Dunnit?" the voice says, louder than the voices had been on the program. An "Old Spice" commercial. "What boxer held the heavyweight title of the world for the longest period of time?" (Cut to the usual "Old Spice" man so the viewer has time to think.) Clips of Joe Louis' fights flash by. In each clip Joe Louis, Heavyweight

Champion of the World for twelve consecutive years, was being beaten up by a white contender. Joe Louis was Black.

The racism in the commercial stayed with me. By the end of that day, I wondered if I had really seen what I saw.

My anger and bewilderment turned into self-doubt: the feeling that I had somehow misinterpreted what I saw. Self-doubt is the soul of internalized racism; self-hatred is its substance. The self-doubt and self-hatred that result from internalized racism determine how we react to just about every situation we encounter. "As children we absorbed that hatred [for our color, for our sex, for our effrontery in daring to presume we had any right to live], passed it through ourselves, and for the most part, we still live our lives outside of the recognition of what that hatred really is and how it functions."[2]

What does it mean to internalize, to ingest, the poison of oppression? It means deep down we believe the basis of the oppression: dark is inferior and evil; woman is inferior, evil and must be controlled sexually. It means we must prove we do not fit the stereotypes born out of these beliefs: Asian women are quiet and inscrutable; Black women are angry and aggressive; Latin women are emotional and sexy; Native women are strong and earthy. In our desire to prove we do not to fit a stereotype, we often mirror the behavior of the dominant society. "How the English colonists would have been pleased that they had fathered such mimics of themselves!"[3]

We try to live up to standards set by white, dominant society, standards and definitions which often compete with the values of our individual cultures. America, the "melting pot," steals from everyone's culture and denigrates those parts it cannot duplicate. For example, until whites called it rock and roll, the original rhythm and blues was relegated to black radio stations late at night and was considered unfit for listening. Yet Elvis Presley became famous singing Big Mama Thorton's "Hound Dog." And Pat Boone made more money singing Fats Domino's music than Fats ever did. To this day, there are separate categories for rock and roll and rhythm and blues in the Top Forty. Is it a surprise that the 1989 American Music Award for rhythm and blues went to a white, English performer?

Our legitimate cultures can offer us a great source of strength, but we often find ourselves fighting against that very source. It is a real struggle to see our cultures without the white overlay. It is a struggle to own the characteristics from our cultures which the dominant culture has turned into vilifying caricatures. We try to deny and avoid those stereotypes by assimilation. We adopt the basic tenet that we must be "better than" to have real worth. "Nothing is more difficult than identifying emotionally with a cultural alterity,* with the Other."[5] Striving to be "better than" another; one language is "better than" another; one color is "better than" another; one size is "better than" another; one type of hair is "better than" another, ad nauseam. We find ways to legitimize the "privileges" this hierarchy provides us while being victims of it.

Racism treats women of different racial backgrounds differently, but racism is still a common oppression of women of color. Our experiences may be different, but we all internalize racism ("struggle to become something we're not while denying who we are"[6]) and feel the powerlessness which results from that internalization. The racial hierarchy is calculated and has definite purpose. One purpose is to produce the antagonisms we experience in groups of supposedly similar women. We are unable to talk to each other. We are unable to accept differences. We are unable to see and admit the stereotypes and predispositions we have about ourselves and other women. We are unable to get situations resolved.

In order to feel powerful and to hold on to our "privilege," we have developed sophisticated coping mechanisms. Tense and charged situations generally put us on the defensive. Being on the defensive makes us feel under attack. Being under attack makes us feel our survival is threatened. Coping mechanisms which may have protected us when our survival was threatened are now patterns of behavior which get in the way of our working together. If in tense or charged situations each of us resorts to behavior designed to make us feel "powerful," or in "control," or designed for us to "win," it is no wonder our interactions are crammed with animosity and frustration.

The dominant culture has taught us well that any behavior or value not ascribed to getting ahead, achieving or acquiring is not worth having. Cooperation is for those who cannot cut it on their own, or to be used in certain circumstances when others are needed for our individual glorification, acquisition and achievement. If we cannot convince those with whom we are interacting to come over to our point of view, our frustration increases. If they are as fortified for battle as we are, the feelings of powerlessness and loss of privilege, which we are trying not to feel, intensify. The battle escalates as each tries to "win." Feelings of frustration and powerlessness breed hostility. Something must be done, because whatever the consequences, it is better than the gnawing emptiness of impotence.

The two of us shared with each other what coping mechanisms we most often use to get through situations which evoke feelings of powerlessness. One image was an armed tank charging across the battlefield. The other

---

*al-ter'i-ty, n. the state or quality of being different; oppositeness.[4]

image was tunneling—to go around, to go under, to avoid. Attack and avoidance—two very different coping mechanisms which come directly out of our legitimate cultures and out of our internalized racism. These different coping mechanisms can scuttle any attempt at working together if we are not conscious of our retreat into fighting for "survival," fighting to "win." One or both of us will do something to feel less frustrated—more powerful. What we do will probably be destructive.

> *An organization formed to provide women of color support around their jobs.* After a year, almost all the women of one ethnic group had left in disagreement on the organization's direction. A meeting was scheduled to deal with this issue. Group A came to the meeting with a plan and presented it in a direct, straightforward way. Group B disagreed, but did not openly state their disagreement. One or two women of Group B took up most of the meeting time and focused on past antagonisms with members of the "opposing" group. After much argument, both groups agreed on Group A's plan. Later, women from Group B met secretly to discuss how all the problems were the de facto leader of Group A. "If she were gone, then…"
>
> The antagonism was racialized but everyone called it "a personality conflict." Groups A and B were predominantly different races. Frustration at their inability to agree drove deeper wedges between them. The predispositions each had about the "other" group were "proven" correct—once again. All the women went their separate ways, angry, disillusioned and believing the "other" at fault.

How many times have you left organizations of women supposedly like you or like other women of color, disappointed, angry and frustrated? How many times have you gotten so angry with another woman of color that you refuse to work with her again—refuse to *speak* to her again? How many times have you wondered why women of color are harder to deal with than white women? How many times have you felt that women of color are the enemy? Too many times for comfort.

II

We know racism from whites. When someone like us or another woman of color exhibits the same racist behavior we experience from whites, it feels the same, tastes the same, but because it is coming from another person of color the impact is orders of magnitude greater. We do not have a tolerance for this dose of poison. Our "protection" no longer works. We react with a different emotion and hostility than we do to racism from a white person. The rage and hostility implodes.

> *Third day of the new semester, new school, new city, new people.* I happened across a group of Asian students, and a Filipina, like myself, was among them. We all greeted each other and exchanged a few introductory remarks. "Are you here on EOP (Economic Opportunity Program)?" the Filipina asked me. "No," I responded. "Then you're a preppy," she declared. I was angry and confounded at the same time. Hot air spun circles in my head. If a white person tried to put me down, I immediately shot back a counter. Instead, I was silent. I asked myself, "Is something wrong with me?" The Filipina and I never became friends. I avoided her. Whenever I saw her during our time together in school or since, our original confrontation was the first thing that came to mind. I have never spoken of this incident until now.

To call another woman of color "racist" or to say she's "trying to act white" may describe the behavior but it does not clarify the whys of the behavior. The phenomenon is not racism even though the actions and reactions are the same as those we experience from racism.

To many, it looks like women of color hate and oppress each other as much as whites hate and oppress people of color. Is it a different "kind" of racism? Horizontal racism? This term does not take into account the racial hierarchy set up by racism. In the U.S. different women of color have similar but very different experiences of racism. We use the term cross-racial hostility to differentiate what goes on between and among women of color from racism. Racism is prejudice *plus* power—control of others' lives, power over. Cross-racial hostility is prejudice *plus* trying to *feel* powerful. Very different!

"We colored women have memories like elephants. The slightest hurt is recorded deep within."[7] Women of color have the power to hurt each other. Some of us may individually have the power to affect another woman's economic stability. It is important to understand, though, that we do not have the power to determine quality of life, backed by law and institution, over groups of people or even over a single woman.

Cross-racial hostility is complex. Case in point:

> *A woman of color writing group.* Trinity read a piece in our writing group about her mother coming to the United States after World War II with the survivors of the death march from a place spelled B-a-t-a-a-n. Trinity said

Ba-ta-an. I "corrected" her, giving the American pro-
nunciation, Ba-tan. I was appalled at, but immediately
defended, my behavior. When I stopped, listened to what
had happened, I saw I had trivialized Trinity. I had not
intended to. I had no conscious intent, it all happened
too fast. When the movie *Bataan*, starring Robert
Taylor, was made after the war, I identified totally with
the American, alone in his foxhole, waiting for death,
firing his machine gun at the charging "yellow hoards."

*A large, important fund-raising event for a multiracial
organization.* The steering committee was made up of two
black women, a white woman and the coordinator, also a
woman of color. Well before the event was to take place,
the black women and the white woman call the
coordinator's attention to projects not getting done. The
coordinator (not black) went to white women outside
the steering committee with stories about the black women.
The black women were a problem, impossible to work
with. After the event (which appeared successful but
did not raise any money), the committee disbanded, with
the women of color not speaking to each other.

Internalized patterns of behavior are acted out unconsciously and make
cross-racial hostility both pervasive and difficult to confront. But no
matter how much women of color hate, harm and exploit one another,
white power and privilege remain intact.

The American nation was founded on racism. Compare the rapid
emergence and eventual world dominance of the U.S. with the centuries-
long process of national formation in Europe. This dominance was *not*
the result of "Yankee ingenuity" and would not have been accomplished
without the resources and wealth first created by stolen Native American
land and enslaved black labor.

America created a simple system of privilege for whites based on the
exploitation and oppression of people of color. This social division along
the color line crossed class, nationality, language and religious barriers.
The simple fact of "whiteness"[8] meant the overall life, fortune and destiny
of white people and their white children were qualitatively better than
those of people of color. White people were exempt from slavery, land
grab and genocide—the first forms of white privilege. Whites enjoyed a
wide latitude of opportunities, personal freedom and democratic rights
protected by the State. Even though poor American-born and immigrant
whites were viciously exploited by rich white people, they were not on
the bottom. The bottom was reserved for Indians, blacks and other people
of color.

All people of color face the oppression of racism. The commonality could serve as a powerful unifying bond of solidarity between us. But instead of unifying, we fight one another to stay "one step up" from the bottom of the racial hierarchy. However, we do not *choose* our place in the racial pecking order. We are *placed* in it.

Cross-racial hostility is the stepchild of racism. The dynamics of cross-racial hostility are created by the imbalances in treatment between racially oppressed people based on exaggerated differences among us. Each group has its own unique history of discrimination, racial violence and institutionalized prejudice. Historically, each group "served" a particular role in meeting the socio-economic needs of white America. For example, during western expansion in the 1800s, while the debate over free versus slave state raged, thousands of Chinese men were brought in to work the mines and railroads. The Chinese were not slaves but they were not free. The Chinese were also subject to lynching and other forms of violence from whites because of their race. They did not have the legal legacy of slavery and its subsequent Jim Crow laws to overcome. However, they faced severe legal and social restrictions—racist violence, anti-alien hysteria, as well as anti-miscegenation, school segregation and employment exclusion laws. After working the mines and railroads, Chinese were barred from the trades and all but domestic employment. For the most part, they were left to support their own through family-owned stores, laundries and restaurants in Chinatown ghettoes. The same, yet not the same. Different, yet not different.

Where differences among white people tend to be evened out by white privilege, differences among people of color are blown out of proportion with personal jealousies and betrayal, encouraged by whites. The difference between the house nigger and the field nigger is a classic example of how differential/preferential treatment split and divided us. Both were slaves for life, but one was treated conspicuously better than the other. For example, "the light-skinned blacks, usually the offspring of white men and black women, were typically given the preferred [*sic*] work inside the master's home, while darker-skinned blacks were relegated to [grueling] field work."[9] There was no guarantee this exemption would continue from one day to the next. The house nigger's situation was always precarious. Their "privileges" and "status" could be taken away for any or no reason. In the daily, ruthless life and death struggle, the desire for preferential treatment often overshadowed feelings of hatred for the master and replaced it with jealous hatred for each other.

Slaves were also used to hunt down and punish runaway slaves. Worse yet, some slaves were promised freedom if they betrayed their runaway brothers and sisters. Freedom was an individual privilege whose benefits defy comparison, even though the black person could be sold back into slavery with no legal recourse. If the "benefits" of betrayal did not persuade them, defiant slaves were beaten until the information was forced from them. They were tortured, maimed and/or killed as examples to all others who might resist.

These practices created deep emotional, spiritual and ideological chasms among black people. The chasms grew wider and became a way of life for many. The legacy? Colorism. In 1790 free mulattoes in Charleston, South Carolina formed the Brown Fellowship Society, which restricted membership to the light-skinned. In retaliation, free dark-skinned blacks formed the Free Dark Men of Color, permitting only the darkest to belong. These two groups maintained segregated burial plots for their members in an already segregated cemetery.[10] The legacy continues—color is the basis of a discrimination lawsuit filed by a lighter-skinned black woman against her darker-skinned supervisor, also a black woman. The *New York Times* ran the story on the front page.[11]

This lawsuit comes from hundreds of years of intra-racial conflict and internal strife. We were/are consciously and constantly used against each other. American history offers countless examples. Indian scouts helped the U.S. Cavalry in campaigns against rival Indian tribes. Black soldiers have been part of the ground troops in all the U.S. racist conquests—the Indian wars, the Spanish-American War of 1898, the Vietnam War, the 1985 invasion of Grenada. Legal versus illegal immigrant status continually divides the Latino community. The ongoing struggle at Big Mountain pits Indian against Indian in a bitter dispute over land, resources and sovereignty.

Recent changes in U.S. immigration laws have altered social and economic progress for peoples of color and put us solidly on a collison course. In the 1960s, the government and big business realized a need to invest in the scientific and technical training of a work force to meet the growing demands of a high-tech society.* This education could have affected large numbers of people of color in America who were unskilled, *i.e.*, low-paid garment workers, domestics and farm workers. Instead, government and big business looked overseas for cheap *skilled* labor.

In 1965, new legislation gave preference to professional and technically skilled immigrants from countries in Asia, Africa and Latin America. (Ironically, this law was signed two years after the historic March on Washington.) Asian and Latin American immigrants have filled the quotas, most coming from countries tied to U.S. foreign debt and

---

*The neglect of U.S. science education is now under sharp criticism. The National Assessment of Educational Progress states: "Alarming numbers of young Americans...emerge from the nation's elementary and secondary schools with an inadequate grounding in mathematics, science and technology. ...At age 17, students' science achievement remains well below that of 1969. ...[While] the average proficiency of 13 to 17 year old black and Hispanic students remains at least 4 years behind that of their white peers."[12]

U.S.-dominated multinational corporations. U.S.-born unskilled workers are unable to compete with the more highly skilled and educated immigrants. Within the Asian community, third and fourth generation Asian Americans, often the first in their families to receive a college education, find themselves competing with immigrants from their home countries for the same few positions. In the meantime, the recent arrivals experience discrimination from Americans based on language, culture, foreign education and citizenship status. They work for cheap wages, unable to get jobs in their chosen professions or at salaries commensurate to their education, experience or training.

The classrooms are being filled with Asian children due to the large influx of Asians in California. (Between 1980 and 1995, the Asian population in California will increase from 1.6 million to 3.8 million, or *140 %* in 15 years.[13]) At prestigious U.C. Berkeley, the large population of Asian students triggered a reactionary backlash among white students fearful of losing dominance in science, engineering and computer technology. The administration threatens to close affirmative action opportunities to all Asians while proclaiming Asians the "model minority," pitting Asians against other people of color.[14]

Prejudice toward immigrants is not the exclusive property of whites. People of color have joined the chorus of growing American national chauvinism. In 1986, Proposition 63—to uphold "English as the official language" and thus eliminate the legal basis for bilingual education and ballots—was supported in California by a margin of three to one. The measure surprisingly won support in cities where people of color were in the majority. In Oakland, where the population is 63% "minority,"[15] the measure was passed by 51%.[16] Most notably, the nationally publicized campaign was led by S. I. Hayakawa,[17] a Japanese Canadian (and naturalized U.S. citizen) who first gained notoriety in 1968 for his fight *against* Ethnic Studies at San Francisco State University.

In day-to-day terms, Asians compete against blacks and others for jobs, while their accomplishments are used to threaten affirmative action opportunities for Asian Americans. Racial antagonism, competition and hostility characterize the social interactions between these groups in the workplace, neighborhood and schools. Yet, none are aware of the greater socio-economic and political forces orchestrating this conflict.

III

[Racism] has consistently dehumanized peoples of color, especially those who questioned or refused normative socialization. It has fostered privileges to the privileged; it has solidified a normative white culture, and it continues to make unjust social institutions and oppressive relations seem legitimate. ...Racism is only one of the several bases of social differentiation; nevertheless, it is probably the strongest, and it is fueled by class and gender-related "isms." Racial differentiation continues to interact with class and gender distinctions which keep the majority of Black folks on the "outside" while the society extends color, class, and gender privileges to the socially acceptable "insiders," even for "Negro" insiders as long as they use the "master's" tools.[18]

Over a long, insidious and brutal process of being conquered, peoples of color have been instilled with the same racist, chauvinist and supremacist values and attitudes which have oppressed us. Is it then a mystery that we find unity so elusive? While people, and especially women, of color are, in broad, general terms, commonly oppressed by racism, we are exploited differently by racism. Depending on one's class, racial group, gender, nationality, cultural background, education, English fluency, citizenship status, sexual preference, physical appearance and ability, and history in or with this country, we are "given" our place in the racial hierarchy. It is arbitrary and subject to the socio-political needs of the U.S. economy and for the benefit and maintenance of white privilege.

Unity is not automatically bequeathed to people of color. Racism translates the differences among us into *relatively* preferential treatment for some at the expense of others, promoting internalized racism and cross-racial hostility. Disunity among people of color due to the exploitation of differences is an inherent part of the system of racism. The *potential* for unity is there and the *power* is tremendous—witness the recent Civil Rights Movement. For unity to develop and continue to exist, the distrust and discord ever-present among us must be replaced. How?

In the groups we conduct with women of color, we begin by acknowledging and sharing our own internalized racism. The face of racism inside each of us is an ugly one, but we find that confronting the stereotypes and predispositions we have about ourselves leads to understanding others. In group process, it becomes clear that our definitions of unity mean sameness—same feelings, thoughts, ideas and behaviors. This mentality commonly develops a tenuous agreement to co-exist as long as differences—not just political and organizational, but personal differences as well—are denied and disregarded. Our *sameness* brings us together, our *differences* drive us apart. We stay together as long as we do *not* confront the issues. Witness how the struggle against sexism in the Civil Rights Movement was put on hold because racism was the "unifying" issue and sexism "divided" us.

We live in a time when the assault on women of color is increasing. Laws that were marginally enforced are now being rolled back—legalized abortion for one. Recruitment in the Ku Klux Klan is the highest it has ever been. Colored children are being drugged to death—if they survive their first year. So why spend time on internalized racism and cross-racial hostility when racism is still so rampant? We have spent years fighting racism and other oppressions through legislation. No legislation, however, can give a person self-esteem. Slogans like "Black Is Beautiful" did not eliminate salf-hatred. Internalized racism cannot be legalized or constitutionalized or sloganized away.

Women of color must challenge our racist attitudes and internalized racism with the same vigor we challenge racism. We must honestly admit and confront the stereotypes and predispositions we have about ourselves and others. We must think and act equitably in a society that honors the hierarchical. We must learn and know our existence cannot be at the expense of another person.

Individually, we cannot eliminate the institution of racism. But we *can change* how we individually interact with each other and internalize racism—internalize oppression. The conflict and hostility between and among women of color can only be resolved by women of color. This is a long, painful process. Internalized racism and cross-racial hostility have been around as long as institutionalized racism. This is *our* work and we have to do it if we want *real* freedom.

"Now that we've begun to break the silence and begun to break through the diabolically erected barriers and can hear each other and see each other, we can sit down with trust and break bread together."[19]

Notes

1. William Ryan, *Equality* (New York: Pantheon Books, 1981), 140.

2. Audre Lorde, "Eye to Eye: Black Women, Hatred and Anger," *Sister Outsider* (Trumansburg, NY: The Crossing Press, 1984), 146.

3. Elizabeth Nunez-Harrell, *When Rocks Dance* (New York: Ballantine Books, 1986), 75.

4. Webster's New Twentieth Century Dictionary Unabridged, 2nd edition, 1983.

5. Gloria Anzaldúa, *"En Rapport,* In Opposition: *Cobrando Cuentas A Las Nuestras,"* *Sinister Wisdom* 33 (1987): 14.

6. Elana Featherson, in conversation, 1989.

7. Anzaldúa, *Sinister Wisdom* 33, 11.

8. See *The Subjective Side of Politics* by Margo Adair and Sharon Howell for further analysis of what "whiteness" means in the U.S. Available from Tools of Change, P.O. Box 14141, San Francisco, CA 94114, (415) 861–6838.

9. *New York Times*, 23 May 1989, National Edition, A11.

10. Walter B. Weare, *Black Business in the South: A Social History of North Carolina Mutual Life Insurance Company* (Urbana: University of Illinois Press, 1973), 9–10.

11. *New York Times*, 23 May 1989, 1.

12. Ina V. S. Mullis and Lynn B. Jenkins, *The Science Report Card* (Princeton: Educational Testing Service, 1988), 6–7.

13. *California Population Characteristics* (1988), 46.

14. Chinese for Affirmative Action, *1988–89 Annual Report* (San Francisco), 24–31.

15. 1980 Census Data for Oakland: 46.9% black, 14.8% other, 38.2% white. 1988 Census Data for Oakland: 50.4% black, 15.2% other, 34.5% white.

16. "Supplement to the Statement of Vote," *Statement of Vote* (General Elections, Oakland, 4 November 1986), 198.

17. S. I. Hayakawa, Editorial, "For: A United People," *San Francisco Chronicle*, 1 November 1986, 34.

18. Joyce Elaine King and Thomasyne Lightfoote Wilson, *On Being African American: Beyond Cultural Democracy and Racist Education* (1988, unpublished), 3.

19. Toni Cade Bambara, Foreword, *This Bridge Called My Back: Writings by Radical Women of Color* (Latham, NY: Kitchen Table: Women of Color Press, 1981), vi.

Nods That Silence

Lynet Uttal

I have participated regularly in Anglo feminist groups and Women of Color feminist groups for almost a decade now, and I am still wondering why each engages me so differently. In the Anglo feminist groups, I feel distanced and disconnected from the ways things get done. My relationships with the other women are always smooth and politely managed. I always feel that my presence is welcomed, but I usually don't agree wholeheartedly with the ideas, the analyses and the organizational tactics. Yet I continue to participate because I am concerned with many of the issues these groups address.

In contrast, my experiences in groups with women from many different racial/ethnic groups have been more connected while at the same time more conflictual. I feel much more understanding from these women, and membership in the ideas we pursue together, even though I more frequently find myself frustrated and heated up.

The major disagreement I have with the practices of Anglo feminist groups is the strong message they send out that our discussions need to be smooth, orderly, efficient and supportive. The idea is that we are not going to do to one another what men have always done to us—we are not going to silence one another nor be competitive. Instead, we are going to provide a space which is supportive and respectful of different opinions. We are not going to trash each other. So we tell ourselves to make space for everyone to talk. Nod supportively. We each have the right to speak after being silenced for so long.

But are we being supportive and respectful when we hear but fail to listen to one another? As I sit and listen in Anglo feminist groups, I often wonder if we are silencing ourselves in yet another way. When someone speaks and says something I don't fully understand or agree with, I search the faces of others in the group to see if they understand and are really in agreement with the speaker, or if they are silently acquiescing to the person speaking only to be supportive? I see some heads nodding, yet I see many others still, frozen, holding their thoughts inside because they don't feel it's okay to speak up and ask for clarification or disagree. Every time I try to verbalize my thoughts, I think over and over again in my head how to state my thoughts diplomatically. Yet even with this careful attention to words, after I speak I always end up feeling that I have breached a code of conduct. I always regret ever having spoken. When my over-rehearsed thoughts come bursting out, the sea of heads nods politely, acknowledging my right to speak, but it appears that their souls have failed to listen to what I have said.

These groups seem to gain their strength from a collectivity of women who are generally in agreement with one another. Those are the ones who come back again and again. Others come for awhile, remain quiet and then silently disappear without ever having been missed because they were never noticed. A few attempt to speak up. But they too fade away, silenced and subtly excluded by blank looks of "supportive" listening.

Yet without more interactive discussions in Anglo feminist groups, these "safe" spaces have set limits on how much we can learn from participating in these groups. Little can be carried over to other parts of our lives in an effective way. So if this is all that feminist sisterhood is about—protecting ourselves from any differences, maintaining at all costs an image of solidarity—it's a fruitless practice that leaves us at a standstill.

I worry constantly about this issue of hearing without listening. I have become even more concerned recently because Anglo middle class feminist groups are actively recruiting women of color. Can a sisterhood that has historically provided safe and supportive spaces based on the commonalities between women also provide room for dialogue between women's differences? Thinking about the consciousness-raising groups of the sixties, I wonder how many women came to these groups and didn't stay. I hear that the groups were powerful because women were given a voice and learned strength from finding others who had their same struggles. Or was this an illusion which resulted when those who differed didn't stick around? Did practices of aligning around common experiences silence some women then, too?

I felt tremendous relief when I read Bonnie Thornton Dill's discussion on the problems of "sisterhood" in the women's movement.[1] She wrote that the political practice of sisterhood is based on bonding around common experiences. This concept assumes that all women in all societies experience patriarchal subordination in the same way. The experiences of Anglo middle class women have defined what these commalities are in the contemporary women's movement and have ignored how race and class dynamics create different experience for other women. She verbalized what I had sensed all along.

We are limited when we organize women's groups around assumed and certain sets of shared experiences. Instead of simply reproducing our past shared experiences, I think that we need to create new shared understandings by working with one another in women's groups. We need to learn more about each other. We need to ask each other, "How are you making sense of this situation?" "What's going on with you?" and "What do you think should be done?" and then negotiate a path we can all walk together. But in order for this to happen we must stop politely and passively hearing one another. We need to begin to actively listen and discuss our differences as well as our similarities so that we may accomplish what this sisterhood stuff is really supposed to be all about.

When I speak, I am tired of getting polite nods which hear me, but don't tell me if anyone is really listening. I am tired of the polite silences and the lack of responses or requests for clarification. I am tired of feeling that my words were given space, but they might as well have not been said because they didn't get built upon or incorporated into the conversation. I can feel the polite bridge built from the speaker before me, over my words, to the next speaker—a useless bridge because the ideas under it are already dried up by the silence from the banks.

The sisterhood I envision would mean *creating* a sense of unity that comes from all of us working together, building on our diverse experiences. But how is this going to happen? How do we learn to listen as well as hear one another? How can we learn to validate one another while at the same time provide room for questioning and expressing disagreement and misunderstanding? How can we do all this without seeming unsupportive and too competitive?

I believe it means that we have to be allowed to "get messy." A polite nod does not incorporate ideas into an ongoing discussion. Nods of validation simply further silence women by not giving serious consideration to what has just been said. No one is listening when they have no responses. Nor does it help any of us to question our own beliefs. On the other hand, a question or response lets me know that someone is listening to me and working with me to understand. Instead of a patronizing nod, I prefer the query which makes my comments a building block in the discussion. Laughter and disagreements are also responses which help us think further.

In each of the Women of Color groups I have been in, there is always a great deal of confusion caused by disagreements. Our ideas are threads that don't always weave together and colors that clash. Our ideas of how to structure time come into conflict. Some of us are very goal-directed and want to be efficient with our time together. Others of us are more willing to sacrifice efficiency in order to figure things out carefully. The distinction between Anglo feminist groups and Women of Color feminist groups is that differences are more explicitly acknowledged in discussions in Women of Color groups. By discussing them, these differences become less threatening and conflictual.

Our shared efforts to figure out the differences make us feel closer to women whom we each initially perceived as "others." There is a genuine commitment to work through the confusion no matter how much time it takes. It comes in the form of questions, hurt feelings, taking sides, feeling frustrated, and "aha, so that's what you mean. Okay." expressions. It doesn't always work out. Sometimes we stop with hurt feelings. But just as frequently we plow through the confusion as a group, putting ideas in order and creating a shared picture which we all can see. And all of this is possible because disagreements and confusion are not received as invalidation of our individual ideas.

As women's groups (especially Anglo women's groups) become more established and more institutionalized, I think we need to be careful of how we are going to incorporate diversity. Especially if becoming more established means becomeing more bureaucratized and hierarchical in our way of making decisions. Incorporating diversity, if it is going to be successful, will require a great deal more of active listening, instead of passive hearing. It is going to require more active discussion instead of turn-taking, space-given talking. It's going to mean expressing disagreements, asking for clarifications and incorporating our differences in creating a shared vision together. A "sisterhood" that I want to belong to allows me to be different and still be able to work together. To this sisterhood, I will bring my individual history, listen to others' stories and know that we are building a foundation together.

Notes

1. Bonnie Thornton Dill, "Race, Class and Gender: Prospects for an All-Inclusive Sisterhood," *Feminist Studies* 9, no. 1 (1983): 131–150.

I Am Your Sister: Black Women Organizing Across Sexualities

Audre Lorde

Whenever I come to Medgar Evers College I always feel a thrill of anticipation and delight because it feels like coming home, like talking to family, having a chance to speak about things that are very important to me with people who matter the most. And this is particularly true whenever I talk at the Women's Center. But, as with all families, we sometimes find it difficult to deal constructively with the genuine differences between us and to recognize that unity does not require that we be identical to each other. Black women are not one great vat of homogenized chocolate milk. We have many different faces, and we do not have to become each other in order to work together.

It is not easy for me to speak here with you as a Black Lesbian feminist, recognizing that some of the ways in which I identify myself make it difficult for you to hear me. But meeting across difference always requires mutual stretching, and until you *can* hear me as a Black Lesbian feminist, our strengths will not be truly available to each other as Black women.

Because I feel it is urgent that we not waste each other's resources, that we recognize each sister on her own terms so that we may better work together toward our mutual survival, I speak here about heterosexism and homophobia, two grave barriers to organizing among Black women. And so that we have a common language between us, I would like to define some of the terms I use: *Heterosexism*—a belief in the inherent superiority of one form of loving over all others and thereby the right to dominance; *Homophobia*—a terror surrounding feelings of love for members of the same sex and thereby a hatred of those feelings in others.

In the 1960s, when liberal white people decided that they didn't want to appear racist, they wore dashikis, and danced Black, and ate Black, and even married Black, but they did not want to feel Black or think Black, so they never even questioned the textures of their daily living (why should flesh-colored bandaids always be pink?) and then they wondered, "Why are those Black folks always taking offense so easily at the least little thing? Some of our best friends are Black...."

Well, it is not necessary for some of your best friends to be Lesbian, although some of them probably are, no doubt. But it is necessary for you to stop oppressing me through false judgement. I do not want you to ignore my identity, nor do I want you to make it an insurmountable barrier between our sharing of strengths.

When I say I am a Black feminist, I mean I recognize that my power as well as my primary oppressions come as a result of my Blackness as well as my womanness, and therefore my struggles on both these fronts are inseparable.

When I say I am a Black Lesbian, I mean I am a woman whose primary focus of loving, physical as well as emotional, is directed to women. It does not mean I hate men. Far from it. The harshest attacks I have ever heard against Black men come from those women who are intimately bound to them and cannot free themselves from a subservient and silent position. I would never presume to speak about Black men the way I have heard some of my straight sisters talk about the men they are attached to. And of course that concerns me, because it reflects a situation of noncommunication in the heterosexual Black community that is far more truly threatening than the existence of Black Lesbians.

What does this have to do with Black women organizing?

I have heard it said—usually behind my back—that Black Lesbians are not normal. But what is normal in this deranged society by which we are all trapped? I remember, and so do many of you, when being Black was considered *not normal*, when they talked about us in whispers, tried to paint us, lynch us, bleach us, ignore us, pretend we did not exist. We called that racism.

I have heard it said that Black Lesbians are a threat to the Black family. But when 50 percent of children born to Black women are born out of wedlock, and 30 percent of all Black families are headed by women without husbands, we need to broaden and redefine what we mean by *family*.

I have heard it said that Black Lesbians will mean the death of the race. Yet Black Lesbians bear children in exactly the same way other women bear children, and a Lesbian household is simply another kind of family. Ask my son and daughter.

The terror of Black Lesbians is buried in that deep inner place where we have been taught to fear all difference—to kill it or ignore it. Be assured: loving women is not a communicable disease. You don't catch it like the common cold. Yet the one accusation that seems to render even the most vocal straight Black woman totally silent and ineffective is the suggestion that she might be a Black Lesbian.

If someone says you're Russian and you know you're not, you don't collapse into stunned silence. Even if someone calls you a bigamist, or a childbeater, and you know you're not, you don't crumple into bits. You say it's not true and keep on printing the posters. But let anyone, particularly a Black man, accuse a straight Black woman of being a Black *Lesbian*, and right away that sister becomes immobilized, as if that is the most horrible thing she could be, and must at all costs be proven false. That is homophobia. It is a waste of woman energy, and it puts a terrible weapon into the hands of your enemies to be used against you to silence you, to keep you docile and in line. It also serves to keep us isolated and apart.

I have heard it said that Black Lesbians are not political, that we have not been and are not involved in the struggles of Black people. But when I taught Black and Puerto Rican students writing at City College in the SEEK program in the sixties I was a Black Lesbian. I was a Black Lesbian when I helped organize and fight for the Black Studies Department of John Jay College. And because I was fifteen years younger then and less sure of myself, at one crucial moment I yielded to pressures that said I should step back for a Black man even though I knew him to be a serious error of choice, and I did, and he was. But I was a Black Lesbian then.

When my girlfriends and I went out in the car one July 4th night after fireworks with cans of white spray paint and our kids asleep in the back seat, one of us staying behind to keep the motor running and watch the kids while the other two worked our way down the suburban New Jersey street, spraying white paint over the black jockey statues, and their little red jackets, too, we were Black Lesbians.

When I drove through the Mississippi Delta to Jackson in 1968 with a group of Black students from Tougaloo, another car full of redneck kids trying to bump us off the road all the way back into town, I was a Black Lesbian.

When I weaned my daughter in 1963 to go to Washington in August to work in the coffee tents along with Lena Horne, making coffee for the marshals because that was what most Black women did in the 1963 March on Washington, I was a Black Lesbian.

When I taught a poetry workshop at Tougaloo, a small Black college in Mississippi, where white rowdies shot up the edge of the campus every night, and I felt the joy of seeing young Black poets find their voices and power through words in our mutual growth, I was a Black Lesbian. And there are strong Black poets today who date their growth and awareness from those workshops.

When Yoli and I cooked curried chicken and beans and rice and took our extra blankets and pillows up the hill to the striking students occupying buildings at City College in 1969, demanding open admissions and the right to an education, I was a Black Lesbian. When I walked through the midnight hallways of Lehman College that same year, carrying Midol and Kotex pads for the young Black radical women taking part in the action, and we tried to persuade them that their place in the revolution was not ten paces behind Black men, that spreading their legs to the guys on the tables in the cafeteria was not a revolutionary act no matter what the brothers said, I was a Black Lesbian. When I picketed for Welfare Mothers' Rights, and against the enforced sterilization of young Black girls, when I fought institutionalized racism in the New York City schools, I was a Black Lesbian.

But you did not know it because we did not identify ourselves, so now you can say that Black Lesbians and Gay men have nothing to do with the struggles of the Black Nation.

And I am not alone.

When you read the words of Langston Hughes you are reading the words of a Black Gay man. When you read the words of Alice Dunbar-Nelson and Angelina Weld Grimké, poets of the Harlem Renaissance, you are reading the words of Black Lesbians. When you listen to the life-affirming voices of Bessie Smith and Ma Rainey, you are hearing Black Lesbian women. When you see the plays and read the words of Lorraine Hansberry, you are reading the words of a woman who loved women deeply.

Today, Lesbians and Gay men are some of the most active and engaged members of Art Against Apartheid, a group which is making visible and immediate our cultural responsibilities against the tragedy of South Africa. We have organizations such as the National Coalition of Black Lesbians and Gays, Dykes Against Racism Everywhere, and Men of All Colors together, all of which are committed to and engaged in antiracist activity.

Homophobia and heterosexism mean you allow yourselves to be robbed of the sisterhood and strength of Black Lesbian women because you are afraid of being called a Lesbian yourself. Yet we share so many concerns as Black women, so much work to be done. The urgency of the destruction of our Black children and the theft of young Black minds are joint urgencies. Black children shot down or doped up on the streets of our cities are priorities for all of us. The fact of Black women's blood flowing with grim regularity in the streets and living rooms of Black communities is not a Black Lesbian rumor. It is a sad statistical truth. The fact that there is widening and dangerous lack of communication around our differences between Black women and men is not a Black Lesbian plot. It is a reality that is starkly clarified as we see our young people becoming more and more uncaring of each other. Young Black boys believing that they can define their manhood between a sixth-grade girl's legs, growing up believing that Black women and girls are the fitting target for their justifiable furies rather than the racist structures grinding us all into dust, these are not Black Lesbian myths. These are sad realities of Black communities today and of immediate concern to us all. We cannot afford to waste each other's energies in our common battles.

What does homophobia mean? It means that high-powered Black women are told it is not safe to attend a Conference on the Status of Women in Nairobi simply because we are Lesbians. It means that in a political action, you rob yourselves of the vital insight and energies of political women such as Betty Powell and Barbara Smith and Gwendolyn Rogers and Raymina Mays and Robin Christian and Yvonne Flowers. It means another instance of the divide-and-conquer routine.

How do we organize around our differences, neither denying them nor blowing them up out of proportion?

The first step is an effort of will on your part. Try to remember to keep certain facts in mind. Black Lesbians are not apolitical. We have been a part of every freedom struggle within this country. Black Lesbians are not a threat to the Black family. Many of us have families of our own. We are not white, and we are not a disease. We are women who love women. This does not mean we are going to assault your daughters in an alley on Nostrand Avenue. It does not mean we are about to attack you if we pay you a compliment on your dress. It does not mean we only think about sex, any more than you only think about sex.

Even if you *do* believe any of these stereotypes about Black Lesbians, begin to practice acting like you don't believe them. Just as racist stereotypes are the problem of the white people who believe them, so also are homophobic stereotypes the problem of the heterosexuals who believe them. In other words, those stereotypes are yours to solve, not mine, and they are a terrible and wasteful barrier to our working together. I am not your enemy. We do not have to become each other's unique experiences and insights in order to share what we have learned through our particular battles for survival as Black women.

There was a poster in the 1960s that was very popular: HE'S NOT BLACK, HE'S MY BROTHER! It used to infuriate me because it implied that the two were mutually exclusive—*he* couldn't be both brother and Black. Well, I do not want to be tolerated, nor misnamed. I want to be recognized.

I am a Black Lesbian, and I *am* your sister.

From *A Burst of Light*

Recognizing, Accepting and Celebrating Our Differences*

Papusa Molina

Querida Gloria:

You called me and your call takes me through an eight years journey. *Me pides que te escriba* a piece of work about alliances, about my work with the Women Against Racism Committee. About this family of women housed in my *gringo* home, Iowa City. And Gloria, the fear kicks in. *Ese miedo* that comes late at night when I am there lying in bed withough being able to sleep because I am *sola*; because everything that is familiar has stayed behind in Merida, on the beach of Isla Mujeres, in the pyramids of Uxmal. *Ese miedo* that enters me when I am afraid of not being able to express my deepest feelings because *el Ingles no da*—it's too short, too practical, not romantic enough, not soft enough for me when I want to call my lover *caracolito*. Gloria, *este es el miedo* of always being an outsider; no matter who I am with, the sense of belonging is always temporary; the fear of living in the Borderlands paralyzes and silences me. You have written about it, I know you understand. I know you know what needs to be overcome to build alliances, to trust. So I cleanse myself. I do the things that mamma Teish has taught me. I start thinking about Cindy and Joan and Mary and Rusty and *el miedo* starts disappearing. It is like magic. I just need to sit in front of the computer now. I just need to let my memory run, and my fingers will speak for my mind and soul. I will speak clear and loud so my silence does not become an accomplice of my fear. Some truths need to be said, and they will. Some experiences need to be accounted for, and they will. I will start the journey.

October of 1981. I'd been in Iowa City only three months when Rusty—a Chicana who has taught me more than anyone else about being Mexican—called to invite me to a meeting where a group of women of color expressed their rage at our invisibility in the Women's Center's programs and staff. The people working and organizing out of the Center

---

*This is the Women Against Racism Committee workshops title. It is also the title of our 1986 conference. I decided to start my piece with this title as a way to acknowledge that my voice is not an individual one. My voice is the product of a collective effort. It is my personal experiece as a member of a family of women who struggle each day to get clearer and clearer about who we are and about the task in front of us.

responded and a multicultural committee was formed. We decided that one way to address the issues raised would be learning about the experience of people of color in the U.S. The Women Against Racism Committee organized its first anti-racism conference on May 2, 1982. By this date you and Cherríe Moraga had edited and published *This Bridge Called My Back*.[1] We invited Cherríe to be our keynote speaker, and she accepted. We put together a packet of readings, sent out invitations and established that our conference would be free and open to the public. It was empowering for the women of color—all 80 of us who came from the eastern part of the state. It was the first time so many of us were together in the same room, reaffirming each other with *ajas*, with hugs, with clenched fists and with tears when memories of isolation brought back the pain. For the white women, it was time only for guilt. There was no understanding of our rage, no clear sense of what we were talking about. The closing session was chaotic, to say the least. We ended up calling each other every single name in the book. A lot of tears and screaming and silencing and interrupting. The group disbanded after this conference. At the time, it seemed almost impossible that white women and women of color in Iowa City could ever be in the same room together, working for the same cause. However, some of us hung together. In September of 1983 we called former members to reconstitute the committee. Some women could not come back. Maybe *el miedo* came in, maybe the anger, the guilt or pure pain kept them away. The ones who returned once again began the process of questioning, of learning, of talking honestly and of exercising listening skills. We started reading everything that we could get our hands on: *The Combahee River Collective Statement*,[2] speeches by Audre Lorde; *This Bridge* became our bible. We organized another local conference in April of 1984. Once again, we needed to admit that we hadn't learned how to work together, hadn't learned how to work across our differences. The fact that almost all of us were lesbians and/or feminists, with an intellectual understanding of racism, classism and homophobia didn't mean a damn thing. We were stuck. We knew that something was missing but we didn't know what. *Pero Gloria*, we were hardheaded. We kept meeting each Monday, we kept reading, we kept arguing. It seems that at some intuitive level we knew that our survival on this planet depended on our ability to go beyond coalitions and form alliances.

Some time during the 1984–1985 academic year, a couple of women from Iowa City attended the first national conference of the National Black Women's Health Project and they met Lillie Allen. They came back to the Committee and proposed that we invite her to our next conference. We had already contacted Barbara Smith to be our keynote speaker, but we realized that we didn't have anything to lose by adding Lillie and maybe we could learn something. So an invitation went out to Lillie, and she accepted. She brought with her Ann Mackie, and for the first time since we started our work, there was something that looked a little different. A white woman and a black woman, both southern, were working together. They were loving and respecting each other, and above all they were presenting us with a model where the individual consequences of racism were addressed and a healing process was started. They conducted workshops for the conference participants and then, after the conference, the committee got together for a session with Lillie. We weren't really prepared for what happened. From the very beginning, the purpose of having an ongoing group was to educate ourselves and others about racism. We were to serve as a laboratory. Before sharing with others we were going to explore among ourselves. It was rough. Again, Gloria, *el canijo miedo* of exploring, of exposing ourselves, of daring to be vulnerable and risk looking at each other in our totality without masks and false postures, rose up. The struggle between the intellectual and the touchy-feely approach erupted from the first moment when Lillie hugged one of us or—worst of all—encouraged our tears. This conference forever changed the life of the committee.

Years passed and we kept organizing conferences. The majority of the women—by this time we were about 25—continued struggling in the committee. Those who left did so mainly because they moved away from Iowa City. We kept mixing the more intellectual approach—a process by which we corrected misinformation and provided new information—with what we called "personal work." Gloria Joseph, Merle Woo, Rachel Sierra, Toni Cade Bambara, Nellie Wong, Winona La Duke and you, among others, were our keynote speakers. All of you challenged our prejudices, corrected our thoughts and were vital for bringing into our small community a world existing outside the limits of our small town. Meanwhile, Barbara Love, Vivian Carlo, Lillian Roybal-Rose, Pat Roselle and Ricki Sherover-Marcuse were taking us on an experiential journey of our personal encounters with racism. At the same time, we started to discover, as we dealt with racism, that we needed to deal with other oppressions which separated us from each other.

At the end of our 1987 conference, we realized that we had something on our hands and maybe the time had arrived to share it with other people who were doing anti-racism work in particular and liberation work in general. So, during the committee's Retreat of June 20, 1987, we decided that the Conference *Parallels and Intersections: Racism and Other Forms of Oppression* would take place in April of 1989 in Iowa City. The other part of our resolution that day was the commitment to train ourselves more and more as facilitators in order to conduct anti-oppression workshops around the county. We accomplished both. On April 9, 1989, we held the closing session of a conference attended by 1,500 people. Many of the participants came because they had attended our workshops in their own communities or knew somebody who had done so. We had over 60 workshops, 20 speakers divided in panels and special interest sessions, concerts, dances, plays and singers. At the end of four days, 150 volunteers and the 30 committee members were exhausted but confident that a new vision had been created: that in order to dismantle the socio-political and economic structures of oppression, we needed to form alliances with very specific characteristics; we needed to make into reality the old adage that the "political is personal and the personal is political": and we needed to dismantle—as Angela Davis reminded us—white people's organizations and recreate them with diversity at their core and people of color as their leaders.[3] We needed to work at the personal level, unlearning attitudes and behaviors of oppression; and at the institutional level, we needed to actively dismantle the structures which privileged some by excluding and silencing others.

At this moment in the reading you may be asking yourself: "All this sounds fine, but how did they do it?" I don't know exactly how, Gloria. I don't think that exact recipes exist. I can only share what we found after eight years of searching. It is almost a matter of faith. You may smile or almost laugh, but *no te rias*. Like the words of the old Lennon song, "You may say I'm a dreamer, but I'm not the only one."[4] If I didn't believe that it is possible, I could not wake up every morning and face living in a country which practices oppression at every level, a country where internal and external colonizations follow the same patterns but *al fin y al cabo*, a country where multicultural society is an unavoidable reality. So let me share with you what I have learned.

I have learned that coalitions and alliances are different. Coalitions are intellectual/political exercises where individual needs are sacrificed for the cause. I think all of us, in one way or another, have had that experience. We all have experienced burn-out. We have acquired ulcers, alcoholism, broken hearts, insomnia, sore throats, and we have stopped smoking and have started again at least 1,000 times. We know the rewards of coalitions: a successful march, strike, rally, land preservation. But people get hurt, sick, angry, demoralized and, once in a while, might even produce a right wing fundamentalist. When we build coalitions we forget to take care of ourselves. We dismiss our own importance because winning the battle is the goal. But don't misunderstand me: coalitions are necessary as long as we keep in mind that they are temporary, formed with specific goals in mind, and they need to be disbanded as soon as the objective is achieved. Alliances, on the other hand, are about individuals, they are about love, they are about commitment and they are about responsibility. They are about concrete manifestations of our rebellious spirits and our sense of justice. They are about shared visions of a better society for all of us.

Now I think I know what you may be saying at this moment: "*Ay Papusa, cuando vas a aprender m'hijita*, here you go again with your idealism." Well, Gloria, let me tell you how I think this is possible.

I believe there are some ways of thinking and being that we need to implement in order to be allies. Audre Lorde, in a paper delivered at the Copeland Colloquium at Amherst College in April of 1980, told us:

"...[I]t is not those differences between us that are separating us. It is rather our refusal to recognize those differences."[5] In the Women Against Racism Committee we say: "It is our refusal to recognize, accept and celebrate those differences that keeps us apart." I think, Gloria, that in the feminist movement especially, we have been very good about recognizing the differences; we have named them; we have analyzed their construction, and we have even deconstructed them. However, we have a hard time accepting and celebrating differences. Why? I think it is because we are immersed in a society where "sameness" is venerated as the most desirable quality. It is so internalized that even when we construct alternative organizations, we establish norms and regulations that create just another category of sameness—the politically correct person. We chastise each other if we do not speak the same language, look at society with the same eyes, or even dress and eat the same food. It takes an act of love, then, to recognize, accept and celebrate our differences.

Another qualitative change consists in looking at every human being—including ourselves—as victims and perpetrators of oppression. Because we live in a society that emphasizes a dichotomous world view, we live our lives making either-or choices, labeling each other by opposition and dividing the planet into good and bad, black and white, yes and no. Everything around us tells us that in order to affirm who we are, we need to negate the other or define it as the opposite. I think that especially as people of color, we have a hard time seeing ourselves as oppressors. Because we look at ourselves in just one dimension—race—we aren't aware of the many times we also participate and, with our daily actions, maintain a system that distributes rewards based on gender, age, class, sexual orientation, religious/cultural background, physical and mental ability, etc, etc, etc. It is only recently that some feminists have at least started asking for an analysis based on gender, sexuality, class and race. However, we are very quick to blame the white, upper class, Christian, heterosexual, able-bodied man as the Oppressor with capital *O*. I think it is important that we start assuming some responsibility for our contribution to this patriarchal, imperialist system which ends up oppressing most of us.

Maybe the most idealistic of our proposals is the belief that because behaviors and attitudes of oppression are learned, they can be unlearned.* Mary Arnold, one of the members of the Committee, always talks about the smog in which we all live. We all breathe the same prejudices, the same assumptions and, with small differences, the same

---

*I would like to acknowledge the contributions of Ricki Sherover-Marcuse to the liberation movement. The incorporation of this concept in our framework derives from our work with her.

values. The process of clearing the air then has to be a conscious one. We have to dare to question the myths and misinformations transmitted to us by the main actors in charge of the superstructures of society. We need to challenge the teachings of our parents, religious leaders, educators, politicians and to increase our ability to respond with an ever clearer sense of who we are, how our prejudices get reinforced and how we create institutions to enact our collective prejudices. Understanding personal and institutional power becomes, then, the main task in the process of liberation and in this revolution where allies are struggling for life and not for death.

El miedo comes back, Gloria. I feel like I have poured my mind and my soul as I write. Maybe this will make sense to you and you would like to include it in the anthology, maybe it rambles too much and you will decide to leave it out. However, it has been good for me. I have confronted the fear of saying it as I see it. I have survived. And I serve as a testimony that change is not reached without struggle. Our journey has just begun.

En la lucha,

Papusa
Iowa City, Fall of 1989

Notes

1. *This Bridge* was first published by Persephone Press in 1981. When Persephone closed, Kitchen Table: Women of Color Press picked it up and it can be obtained from them. Their address is P.O. Box 908, Latham, NY 12110.

2. You can find it in: Barbara Smith, ed., *Home Girls: A Black Feminist Anthology* (New York: Kitchen Table: Women of Color Press, 1983), 272.

3. Closing session of *Parallels and Intersections*.

4. *Imagine* by John Lennon.

5. Lorde, Audre, *Sister Outsider* (New York: The Crossing Press, 1984).

7 "Doing" Theory in Other Modes of Consciousness

The Race for Theory

Barbara Christian

I have seized this occasion to break the silence among those of us, critics, as we are now called, who have been intimidated, devalued by what I call the race for theory. I have become convinced that there has been a takeover in the literary world by Western philosophers from the old literary élite, the neutral humanists. Philosophers have been able to effect such a takeover because so much of the literature of the West has become pallid, laden with despair, self-indulgent and disconnected. The New Philosophers, eager to understand a world that is today fast escaping their political control, have redefined literature so that the distinctions implied by that term, that is, the distinctions between everything written and those things written to evoke feeling as well as to express thought, have been blurred. They have changed literary critical language to suit their own purposes as philosophers, and they have reinvented the meaning of theory.

My first response to this realization was to ignore it. Perhaps, in spite of the egocentrism of this trend, some good might come of it. I had, I felt, more pressing and interesting things to do, such as reading and studying the history and literature of black women, a history that had been totally ignored, a contemporary literature bursting with originality, passion, insight and beauty. But unfortunately it is difficult to ignore this new takeover, since theory has become a commodity which helps determine whether we are hired or promoted in academic institutions—worse, whether we are heard at all. Due to this new orientation, works (a word which evokes labor) have become texts. Critics are no longer concerned with literature, but with other critics' texts, for the critic yearning for attention has displaced the writer and has conceived of himself as the center. Interestingly in the first part of this century, at least in England and America, the critic was usually also a writer of poetry, plays or novels. But today, as a new generation of professionals develops, he or she is increasingly an academic. Activities such as teaching or writing one's response to specifc works of literature have, among this group, become subordinated to one primary thrust, that moment when one creates a theory, thus fixing a constellation of ideas for a time at least, a fixing which no doubt will be replaced in another month or so by somebody else's competing theory as the race accelerates. Perhaps because those who have effected the takeover have the power (although they deny it) first of all to be published, and thereby to determine the ideas which are deemed valuable, some of our most daring and potentially radical critics (and by *our* I mean black, women, third world) have been influenced, even co-opted, into speaking a language and defining their discussion in terms alien to and opposed to our needs and orientation. At least so far, the creative writers I study have resisted this language.

For people of color have always theorized—but in forms quite different from the Western form of abstract logic. And I am inclined to say that our theorizing (and I intentionally use the verb rather than the noun) is often in narrative forms, in the stories we create, in riddles and proverbs, in the play with language, since dynamic rather than fixed ideas seem more to our liking. How else have we managed to survive with such spiritedness the assault on our bodies, social institutions, countries, our very humanity? And women, at least the women I grew up around, continuously speculated about the nature of life through pithy language that unmasked the power relations of their world. It is this language, and the grace and pleasure with which they played with it, that I find celebrated, refined, critiqued in the works of writers like Morrison and Walker. My folk, in other words, have always been a race for theory— though more in the form of the hieroglyph, a written figure which is both sensual and abstract, both beautiful and communicative. In my own work I try to illuminate and explain these hieroglyphys, which is, I think, an activity quite different from the creating of the hieroglyphs themselves. As the Buddhists would say, the finger pointing at the moon is not the moon.

In this discussion, however, I am more concerned with the issue raised by my first use of the term, *the race for theory*, in relation to its academic hegemony, and possibly of its inappropriateness to the energetic emerging literatures in the world today. The pervasiveness of this academic hegemony is an issue continually spoken about—but usually in hidden groups, lest we, who are disturbed by it, appear ignorant to the reigning academic élite. Among the folk who speak in muted tones are people of color, feminists, radical critics, creative writers, who have struggled for much longer than a decade to make their voices, their various voices, heard, and for whom literature is not an occasion for discourse among critics but is necessary nourishment for their people and one way by which they come to understand their lives better. Clichéd though this may be, it bears, I think, repeating here.

The race for theory, with its linguistic jargon, its emphasis on quoting its prophets, its tendency towards "Biblical" exegesis, its refusal even to mention specific works of creative writers, far less contemporary ones, its preoccupations with mechanical analyses of language, graphs, algebraic equations, its gross generalizations about culture, has silenced many of us to the extent that some of us feel we can no longer discuss our own literature, while others have developed intense writing blocks and are puzzled by the incomprehensibility of the language set adrift in literary circles. There have been, in the last year, any number of occasions on which I had to convince literary critics who have pioneered entire new areas of critical inquiry that they did have something to say. Some of us are continually harassed to invent wholesale theories regardless of the complexity of the literature we study. I, for one, am tired of being asked to produce a black feminist literary theory as if I were a mechanical man. For I believe such theory is prescriptive—it ought to have some relationship to practice. Since I can count on one hand the number of people attempting to be black feminist literary critics in the world today, I consider it presumptuous of me to invent a theory of how we *ought* to read. Instead, I think we need to read the works of our writers in our various ways and remain open to the intricacies of the intersection of language, class, race and gender in the literature. And it would help if we share our process, that is, our practice, as much as possible since, finally, our work *is* a collective endeavor.

The insidious quality of this race for theory is symbolized for me by the very name of this special issue—Minority Discourse—a label which is borrowed from the reigning theory of the day and is untrue to the literatures being produced by our writers, for many of our literatures (certainly Afro-American literature) are central, not minor, and by the titles of many of the articles, which illuminate language as an assault on the other, rather than as possible communication, and play with, or even affirmation of another. I have used the passive voice in my last sentence construction, contrary to the rules of Black English, which like all languages has a particular value system, since I have not placed responsibility on any particular person or group. But that is precisely because this new ideology has become so prevalent among us that it behaves like so many of the other ideologies with which we have had to contend. It appears to have neither head nor center. At the least, though, we can say that the terms "minority" and "discourse" are located firmly in a Western dualistic or "binary" frame which sees the rest of the world as minor, and tries to convince the rest of the world that it *is* major, usually through force and then through language, even as it claims many of the ideas that we, its "historical" other, have known and spoken about for so long. For many of us have never conceived of ourselves only as somebody's *other*.

Let me not give the impression that by objecting to the race for theory I ally myself with or agree with the neutral humanists who see literature as pure expression and will not admit to the obvious control of its production, value and distribution by those who have power, who deny, in other words, that literature is, of necessity, political. I am studying an entire body of literature that has been denigrated for centuries by such terms as *political*. For an entire century Afro-American writers, from Charles Chestnutt in the nineteenth century through Richard Wright in the 1930s, Imamu Baraka in the 1960s, Alice Walker in the 1970s, have protested the literary hierarchy of dominance which declares when literature is literature, when literature is great, depending on what it thinks is to its advantage. The Black Arts Movement of the 1960s, out of which Black Studies, the Feminist Literary Movement of the 1970s and Womens' Studies grew, articulated precisely those issues, which came *not* from the declarations of the New Western Philosophers but from these groups' reflections on their own lives. That Western scholars have long believed their ideas to be universal has been strongly opposed by many such groups. Some of my colleagues do not see black critical writers of previous decades as eloquent enough. Clearly they have not read Wright's "Blueprint for Negro Writing," Ellison's *Shadow and Act*, Chestnutt's resignation from being a writer, or Alice Walker's "Search for Zora Neale Hurston." There are two reasons for this general ignorance of what our writer-critics have said. One is that black writing has been generally ignored in this country. Since we, as Toni Morrison has put it, are seen as a discredited people, it is no surprise, then, that our creations are also discredited, but this is also due to the fact that until recently dominant critics in the Western World have also been creative writers who have had access to the upper middle-class institutions of education and until recently our writers have decidedly been excluded from these institutions and in fact have often been opposed to them. Because of the academic world's general ignorance about the literature of black people and of women, whose work too has been discredited, it is not surprising that so many of our critics think that the position arguing that literature is political begins with these New Philosophers. Unfortunately, many of our young critics do not investigate the reasons *why* that statement—literature is political—is now acceptable when before it was not; nor do we look to our own antecedents for the sophisticated arguments upon which we can build in order to change the tendency of any established Western idea to become hegemonic.

For I feel that the new emphasis on literary critical theory is as hegemonic as the world which it attacks. I see the language it creates as one which mystifies rather than clarifies our condition, making it possible for a few people who know that particular language to control the critical scene—that language surfaced, interestingly enough, just when the literature of peoples of color, of black women, of Latin Americans, of Africans began to move to "the center." Such words as *center* and *periphery* are themselves instructive. *Discourse, canon, texts*, words as latinate as the tradition from which they come, are quite familiar to me. Because I went to a Catholic Mission school in the West Indies I must confess that I cannot hear the word "canon" without smelling incense, that the word "text" immediately brings back agonizing memories of Biblical exegesis, the "discourse" reeks for me of metaphysics forced down my throat in those courses that traced *world* philosophy from Aristotle through Thomas Aquinas to Heidegger. "Periphery" too is a word I heard throughout my childhood, for if anything was seen as being at the periphery, it was those small Caribbean islands which had neither land mass nor military power. Still I noted how intensely important this periphery was, for U.S. troops were continually invading one island or another if any change in political control even seemed to be occurring. As I lived among folk for whom language was an absolutely necessary way of validating our existence, I was told that the minds of the world lived only in the small continent of Europe. The metaphysical language of the New Philosophy, then, I must admit, is repulsive to me and is one reason why I raced from philosophy to literature, since the latter seemed to me to have the possibilites of rendering the world as large and as complicated as I experienced it, as sensual as I knew it was. In literature I sensed the possibility of the integration of feeling/knowledge, rather than the split between the abstract and the emotional in which Western philsophy inevitably indulged.

Now I am being told that philosophers are the ones who write literature, that authors are dead, irrelevant, mere vessels through which their narratives ooze, that they do not work nor have they the faintest idea what they are doing; rather they produce texts as disembodied as the angels. I am frankly astonished that scholars who call themselves Marxists or post-Marxists could seriously use such metaphysical language even as they attempt to deconstruct the philosophical tradition from which their language comes. And as a student of literature, I am appalled by the sheer ugliness of the language, its lack of clarity, its unnecessarily complicated sentence constructions, its lack of pleasurableness, its alienating quality. It is the kind of writing for which composition teachers would give a freshman a resounding F.

Because I am a curious person, however, I postponed readings of black women writers I was working on and read some of the prophets of this new literary orientation. These writers did announce their dissatisfaction with some of the cornerstone ideas of their own tradition, a dissatisfaction with which I was born. But in their attempt to change the orientation of Western scholarship, they, as usual, concentrated on themselves and were not in the slightest interested in the worlds they had ignored or controlled. Again I was supposed to know *them*, while they were not at all interested in knowing *me*. Instead they sought to "deconstruct" the tradition to which they belonged even as they used the same forms, style, language of that tradition, forms which necessarily embody its values. And increasingly as I read them and saw their substitution of their philosophical writings for literary ones, I began to have the uneasy feeling that their folk were not producing any literature worth mentioning. For they always harkened back to the masterpieces of the past, again reifying the very texts they said they were deconstructing. Increasingly, as *their* way, *their* terms, *their* approaches remained central and became the means by which one defined literary critics, many of my own peers who had previously been concentrating on dealing with the other side of the equation, the reclamation and discussion of past and *present* third world literatures, were diverted into continually discussing the new literary theory.

From my point of view as a critic of contemporary Afro-American women's writing, this orientation is extremely problematic. In attempting to find the deep structures in the literary tradition, a major preoccupation of the new New Criticism, many of us have become obsessed with the nature of reading itself to the extent that we have stopped writing about literature being written today. Since I am slightly paranoid, it has begun to appear to me that the literature being produced *is* precisely one of the reasons why this new philosophical-literary-critical theory of relativity is so prominent. In other words, the literature of blacks, women of South America and Africa, etc., as overtly "political" literature was being pre-empted by a new Western concept which proclaimed that reality does not exist, that everything is relative and that every text is silent about something—which indeed it must necessarily be.

There is, of course, much to be learned from exploring how we know what we know, how we read what we read, an exploration which, of necessity, can have no end. But there also has to be a "what," and that "what," when it is even mentioned by the New Philosophers, are texts of the past, primarily Western male texts, whose norms are again being transferred onto third world, female texts as theories of reading proliferate. Inevitable a hierarchy has now developed between what is called theoretical criticism and practical criticism, as mind is deemed superior to matter. I have no quarrel with those who wish to philosophize about how we know what we know. But I do resent the fact that this particular orientation is so privileged and has diverted so many of us from doing the first readings of the literature being written today as well as of past works about which nothing has been written. I note, for example, that there is little work done on Gloria Naylor, that most of Alice Walker's works have not been commented on—despite the rage around *The Color Purple*—that there has yet to be an in-depth study of Frances Harper, the nineteenth-century abolitionist poet and novelist. If our emphasis on theoretical criticism continues, critics of the future may have to reclaim the writers we are now ignoring, that is, if they are even aware these artists exist.

I am particularly perturbed by the movement to exalt theory, as well, because of my own adult history, I was an active member of the Black Arts Movement of the sixties and know how dangerous theory can become. Many today may not be aware of this, but the Black Arts Movement tried to create Black Literary Theory and in doing so became prescriptive. My fear is that when Theory is not rooted in practice, it becomes prescriptive, exclusive, élitist.

An example of this prescriptiveness is the approach the Black Arts Movement took towards language. For it, blackness resided in the use of black talk which they defined as hip urban language. So that when Nikki

Giovanni reviewed Paule Marshall's *Chosen Place, Timeless People*, she criticized the novel on the grounds that it was not black, for the language was too elegant, too white. Blacks, she said, did not speak that way. Having come from the West indies where we do, some of the time, speak that way, I was amazed by the narrowness of her vision. The emphasis on *one way* to be black resulted in the works of southern writers being seen as non-black since the black talk of Georgia does not sound like the black talk of Philadelphia. Because the ideologues, like Baraka, come from the urban centers they tended to privilege their way of speaking, thinking, writing, and to condemn other kinds of writing as not being black enough. Whole areas of the canon were assessed according to the dictum of the Black Arts Nationalist point of view, as in Addison Gayle's *The Way of the New World*, while other works were ignored because they did not fit the scheme of cultural nationalism. Older writers like Ellison and Baldwin were condemned because they saw that the intersection of Western and African influences resulted in a new Afro-American culture, a position with which many of the Black Nationalist ideologues disagreed. Writers were told that writing love poems was not being black. Further examples abound.

It is true that the Black Arts Movements resulted in a necessary and important critique both of previous Afro-American literature and of the white-established literary world. But in attempting to take over power, it, as Ishmael Reed satirizes so well in *Mumbo Jumbo*, became much like its opponent, monolithic and downright repressive.

It is this tendency towards the monolithic, monotheistic, etc., which worries me about the race for theory. Constructs like the *center* and the *periphery* reveal that tendency to want to make the world less complex by organizing it according to one principle, to fix it through an idea which is really an ideal. Many of us are particularly sensitive to monolithism since one major element of ideologies of dominance, such as sexism and racism, is to dehumanize people by stereotyping them, by denying them their variousness and complexity. Inevitably, monolithism becomes a metasystem, in which there is a controlling ideal, especially in relation to pleasure. Language as one form of pleasure is immediately restricted, and becomes heavy, abstract, prescriptive, monotonous.

Variety, multiplicity, eroticism are difficult to control. And it may very well be that these are the reasons why writers are often seen as *persona non grata* by political states, whatever form they take, since writers/artists have a tendency to refuse to give up their way of seeing the world and of playing with possibilities; in fact, their very expression relies on that insistence. Perhaps that is why creative literature, even when written by politically reactionary people, can be so freeing, for in having to embody ideas and recreate the world, writers cannot merely produce "one way."

The characteristics of the Black Arts Movement are, I am afraid, being repeated again today, certainly in the other area to which I am especially tuned. In the race for theory, feminists, eager to enter the halls of power, have attempted their own prescriptions. So often have I read books on feminist literary theory that restrict the definition of what *feminist* means and overgeneralize about so much of the world that most women as well as men are excluded. Nor seldom do feminist theorists take into account the complexity of life—that women are of many races and ethnic backgrounds with different histories and cultures and that as a rule women belong to different classes that have different concerns. Seldom do they note these distinctions, because if they did they could not articulate a theory. Often as a way of clearing themselves, they do acknowledge that women of color, for example, do exist, then go on to do what they were going to do anyway, which is to invent a theory that has little relevance for us.

That tendency towards monolithism is precisely how I see the French feminist theorists. They concentrate on the female body as the means to creating a female language, since language, they say, is male and necessarily conceives of woman as other. Clearly many of them have been irritated by the theories of Lacan for whom language is phallic. But suppose there are peoples in the world whose language was invented primarily in relation to women, who after all are the ones who relate to children and teach language. Some Native American languages, for example, use female pronouns when speaking about non-gender specific activity. Who knows who, according to gender, created languages. Further, by positing the body as the source of everything, French feminists return to the old myth that biology determines everything and ignore the fact that gender is a social rather than a biological construct.

I could go on critiquing the positions of French feminists who are themselves more various in their points of view than the label which is used to describe them, but that is not my point. What I am concerned about is the authority this school now has in feminist scholarship—the way it has become *authoritative discourse*, monologic, which occurs precisely because it does have access to the means of promulgating its ideas. The Black Arts Movement was able to do this for a time because of the political movements of the 1960s—so too with the French feminists who could not be inventing "theory" if a space had not been created by the Women's Movement. In both cases, both groups posited a theory that excluded many of the people who made that space possible. Hence one of the reasons for the surge of Afro-American women's writing during the 1970s and its emphasis on sexism in the black community is precisely that when the ideologues of the 1960s said *black*, they meant *black male*.

I and many of my sisters do not see the world as being so simple. And perhaps that is why we have not rushed to created abstract theories. For we know there are countless women of color, both in America and in the rest of the world to whom our singular ideas would be applied. There is, therefore, a caution we feel about pronouncing black feminist theory that might be seen as a decisive statement about third world women. This is not to say we are not theorizing. Certainly our literature is an indication of the ways in which our theorizing, of necessity, is based on our multiplicity of experiences.

There is at least one other lesson I learned from the Black Arts Movement. One reason for its monolithic approach had to do with its desire to destroy the power which controlled black people, but it was a power which many of its ideologues wished to achieve. The nature of our context today is such that an approach which desires power single-mindedly must of necessity become like that which it wished to destroy. Rather than wanting to change the whole model, many of us want to be at the center. It is this point of view that writers like June Jordan and Audre Lorde continually critique even as they call for empowerment, as they emphasize the fear of difference among us and our need for leaders rather than a reliance on ourselves.

For one must distinguish the desire for power from the need to become empowered—that is, seeing oneself as capable of and having the right to determine one's life. Such empowerment is partially derived from a knowledge of history. The Black Arts Movement did result in the creation of Afro-American Studies as a concept, thus giving it a place in the university where one might engage in the reclamation of Afro-American history and culture and pass it on to others. I am particularly concerned that institutions such as Black Studies and Women's Studies, fought for with such vigor and at some sacrifice, are not often seen as important by many of our black or women scholars precisely because the old hierarchy of traditional departments is seen as superior to these "marginal" groups. Yet, it is in this context that many others of us are discovering the extent of our complexity, the interrelationships of different areas of knowledge in relation to a distinctly Afro-American or female experience. Rather than having to view our world as subordinate to others, or rather than having to work as if we were hybrids, we can pursue ourselves as subjects.

My major objection to the race for theory, as some readers have probably guessed by now, really hinges on the question, "for whom are we doing what we are doing when we do literary criticism?" It is, I think, the central question today especially for the few of us who have infiltrated the academy enough to be wooed by it. The answer to that question determines what orientation we take in our work, the language we use, the purposes for which it is intended.

I can only speak for myself. But what I write and how I write is done in order to save my own life. And I mean that literally. For me literature is a way of knowing that I am not hallucinating, that whatever I feel/know *is*. It is an affirmation that sensuality is intelligence, that sensual language is language that makes sense. My response, then, is directed to those who write what I read and to those who read what I read—put concretely—to Toni Morrison and to people who read Toni Morrison (among whom I would count few academics). That number is increasing, as is the readership of Walker and Marshall. But in no way is the literature that Morrison, Marshall or Walker create supported by the academic world. Nor given the political context of our society, do I expect that to change soon. For there is no reason, given who controls these intitutions, for them to be anything other than threatened by these writers.

My readings do presuppose a need, a desire among folk who like me also want to save their own lives. My concern, then, is a passionate one, for the literature of people who are not in power has always been in danger of extinction of co-optation, not because we do not theorize, but because what we can even imagine, far less who we can reach, is constantly limited by societal structures. For me, literary criticism is promotion as well as understanding, a response to the writer to whom there is often no response, to folk who need the writing as much as they need anything. I know, from literary history, that writing disappears unless there is a response to it. Because I write about writers who are now writing, I hope to help ensure that their tradition has continuity and survives.

So my "method," to use a new "lit. crit." word, is not fixed but relates to what I read and to the historical context of the writers I read *and* to the many critical activities in which I am engaged, which may or may not involve writing. It is a learning from the language of creative writers, which is one of surprise, so that I might discover what language I might use. For my language is very much based on what I read and how it affects me, that is, on the surprise that comes from reading something that compels you to read differently, as I believe literature does. I, therefore, have no set method, another prerequisite of the new theory, since for me every work suggests a new approach. As risky as that might seem, it is, I believe, what intelligence means—a tuned sensitivity to that which is alive and therefore cannot be known until it is known. Audre Lorde puts it in a far more succinct and sensual way in her essay "Poetry is not a Luxury":

> As they become known to and accepted by us, our feelings and the honest exploration of them become sanctuaries and spawning grounds for the most radical and daring of ideas. They become a safe-house for that difference so necessary to change and the conceptualization of any meaningful action. Right now, I could name at least ten ideas I would have found intolerable or incomprehensible and frightening, except as they came after dreams and poems. This is not idle fantasy, but a disciplined attention to the true meaning of "it feels right to me." We can train ourselves to respect our feelings and to transpose them into a language so they can be shared. And where that

language does not yet exist, it is our poetry which helps
to fashion it. Poetry is not only dream and vision; it is the
skeleton architecture of our lives. It lays the foundations
for a future of change, a bridge across our fears of what
has never been before.[1]

From *Cultural Critique* 6

Notes

1. Audre Lorde, *Sister Outsider* (Trumansburg, N.Y.: The Crossing Press, 1984), 37.

The Politics of Poetics: Or, What Am I, A Critic, Doing in This Text Anyhow?

Tey Diana Rebolledo

In an essay "Retrieving our Past, Determining our Future" poet Pat Mora chose to begin with a pre-Colombian poem:

> Also they grow cotton
> of many colors:
> red, yellow, pink,
> purple, green, bluish-green,
> blue, light green,
> orange, brown, and dark gold.
> These were the colors of the cotton itself.
> It grew that way from the earth,
> no one colored it.
> And also they raised these
> fowl of rare plumage:
> small birds the color of turquoise,
> some with green feathers,
> with yellow, with flame-colored breasts.
> Every kind of fowl
> that sang beautifully,
> like those that warble in the mountains.[1]

Mora chose this poem because she liked the images of music, color and nature. But then she is a poet. I would like to underscore Mora's choice and begin with some definitions. *"Politics:* intrigue or maneuvering within a group; one's position or attitude on political subjects. *Poetics:* literary criticism dealing with the nature, form and laws of poetry; a study of or treatise on poetry or aesthetics. *Criticism:* the art, skill or profession of making discriminating judgements, especially of literary or artistic works, detailed investigation of the origin and history of literary documents. *Discourse:* to run about, to speak at length, the process or power of reasoning."[2]

My understanding several months ago was that this symposium "Chicana Creativity and Criticism: Charting New Frontiers in American Literature," would undertake a dialogue between Chicana creative writers and Chicana literary critics with regard to several topics: are Chicana critics friends or foes to the writers? What function do or can we Chicana critics play in relationship to our literature? And, what the heck are we doing in and to these texts anyway? As Chicanas we are all in this *revoltura* and explosion of literature and poetics together. It is time, perhaps, to take a step back and analyze where we are and where we might be going.

I do not mean the remarks I am about to make to be anti-intellectual, anti-theoretical or anti-aesthetic. Nor do I mean to assume the position of any critic other than myself. Nor am I criticizing the work of any particular literary critic. Nevertheless, I am commenting on what I see as a general phenomenon: one that we need to take stock of and one which affects Chicano male critics as well as the females. Juan Bruce-Novoa, in his recent article "Canonical and Noncanonical Texts," thinks there is now a "body of work" which constitutes Chicano literature and which is recognized as such. He recognizes that previously "any mention of canon was clearly understood as a reference to mainstream literature" and, he adds, "to state we were excluded from the canon was to state the obvious. Moreover, there was an ironic sense of worth associated with being outside the canon, almost a sense of purity, because, beyond the exclusionary ethnocentrism implied by the canon, Chicanos infused the term with a criticism of the very existence of a privileged body of texts."[3]

It seems to me that in spite of the explosion of creative and critical activity on the part of both critics and writers, Chicana writers and critics are still within a framework of marginality among Chicano writing as well as in mainstream writing. Some of this may be attributed to time; that is, time for the maturing of our literature as well as of our criticism. In addition to the creation of new insights and perspectives, we are also at a moment of rupture in which we are just beginning to look back to uncover our traditions, whether they be written or oral, and to talk back—to unsay what had been said and frozen in time and place. We are at the moment of questioning everything, even ourselves. Only when it is accomplished can we, with clear conscience, proceed towards some understanding of critical difference.

At the recent Chicano Studies Conference in Salt Lake City (1987), it became clear that for the past several years social scientists and literary critics alike have been engaged in a desperate search for a theoretical/critical discourse in which to situate what is happening to us. There have been discourses and counter-discourses. We talk about historical/materialist perspectives, transformative perspectives, pluralism (which some called a pre-prostituted dominant discourse) and the word hegemony was used in one session alone thirty-two times. Some of the talks began with a few of the questions to be asked, then discussed the methods used to answer those questions, mostly the methods used. I would say a typical talk could be summarized in the following way: the speaker begins, "This paper will focus on the ideology of cultural practice and its modes of signifying." S/he then spends twenty minutes discussing how the works of whatever theoretical greats s/he selects will define, inform and privilege the work s/he is doing. Such names as Jameson, Said, Williams, Hall, Burke and other contemporary *meros, meros* (mostly male) will be invoked over and over. The speaker is then sent a note by the chair of the panel that there is no time left. And whatever the Chicano/a writing or phenomenon that was to be discussed is quickly summarized in two minutes. The talk is over. We have talked so much about theory we never get to our conclusion nor focus on the texts. By appropriating mainstream theoreticians and critics we have become so involved in intellectualizing that we lose our sense of our literature and therefore our vitality. This priority of placing our literature in a theoretical framework to "legitimize" it, if the theory overshadows it, in effect undermines our literature or even places it, once again, in a state of oblivion. Privileging the theoretical discourse de-privileges ourselves.

In puzzling over this scenario, which in fact occurred many times in Salt Lake, one could be left with various insights about what is happening to us:

1. We have internalized the dominant ideology so that only by talking theory (construed as a superior form of logic) can our literature and our cultural practices be intellectually viable, that is, accepted within the traditional academic canon as "legitimate."

2. We are trying to impress ourselves and others with our ability to manipulate theoretical discourse, to use buzz words such as hegemony, signifying and even the word discourse. Someone once said to me "you are so articulate. You are able to talk in *their* language." I am not sure what this means. On the one hand they may be telling me I am totally assimilated or they may, in reality, be saying that no Chicana can truly be articulate. (I myself often feel that it is only our baroque *conceptismo* that has been transferred into English.)

3. We have entered into the "Age of Criticism" which could be defined as a preoccupation with theoretical structures often not internalized: we feel that theory is power.

4. We have a genuine desire to look beyond the elements (the texts) to the conditions that structured them. We are truly in search of a theoretical framework which yet eludes us or at least some of us (and I count myself among those eludees).

I would like to outline some of the problems that I think we Chicana critics face or that at least I, as a critic in training, think about from time to time. They often as not deal with the question, what am I doing in this text anyhow?

1. First of all I am a reader. But I am not just a reader. My job, as a university professor, is to bring the attention of my students to the text itself. How can I do this if the text is not included in the general course curriculum, in the anthologies or in any way accessible to the student or to the population at large? Perhaps my primary responsibility, therefore, is the promulgation of the works of these writers, to make the writers known. We all know that the material production of Chicana writers is often limited to chapbooks, journals and the few texts that are accepted by Arte Publico Press and Bilingual Press. It is limited even to the Chicano audience and from one region to the next, from one big city to the next, we may not know what is happening. The work being done by Juan Rodríguez, *Third Woman* and the Centro de Escritores de Aztlán, for example, helps but as these texts go out of print, this production becomes more difficult to find. At Salt Lake City a copy of the first printing of Quinto Sol's *El Grito* was proudly held up as the rarity it has become. Of the chapbooks that were and are produced in the 1960s, 1970s and 1980s, many will end up in a rare book room in a library if we are fortunate. Fortunate because they will be preserved as artifacts—the same phenomenon which will make the book even more inaccessible.

If this product is inaccessible to those who are its target, in terms of interest, it is virtually unavailable to a larger audience. The role of the Chicana critic then becomes one of facilitator: reproducing and making known the texts of our authors. In itself this may not be an insignificant task since, for example, in a recent struggle with some of my co-authors (not the editors) of a book to be published by Yale University Press, I was told that my method of writing, that is, including entire poems written by Chicanas instead of dissecting them by including between slashes "pertinent" quotes from the text, made my article "hard to read" and "jumpy." While this may be true of my *own* writing, it certainly was not true of those texts of the authors I had included. I was very troubled by the inadequacies of a vision which presumed to have me speak for all Chicanas when they were perfectly able to speak for themselves. My arguments for entire text inclusion were the following: a) These texts were unknown and therefore needed to be reproduced in their entirety; b) These writers were more passionate, forceful and graphic than I; c) I did not want to do to these writers what others have been doing to all of us for centuries, that is, to appropriate their discourse through my discourse. I commented that I had no problem with my strategy and if they were not happy with publishing my chapter as it was, I did not wish it to be included in the volume. Fortunately the article will be published in its jumpy entirety in *The Desert Is No Lady*, title poem by Pat Mora.[4]

2. The second function of a critic may be to analyze the content of the literary production—stepping back from the product in order to see what

may be the dominant concerns and themes. I myself have indulged in this type of descriptive thematic analysis (adding, I hope, some analysis in depth as to cultural context and history). One example is a paper I wrote on *abuelitas*, noting the scope and complexity of this recurring figure and offering an explanation as to why this figure was approaching what I considered to be mythic proportions.[5] This article has brought mixed reviews. My secretary, who was typing it, asked to take it home to read to her children, and many others have used it in their classrooms for teaching. Recently, a contemporary writer remarked to me about critics writing descriptively about things that "everyone already knew about," such as *abuelitas*. Yet descriptive thematic analysis serves its purpose too, particularly as it grows in sophistication, and as historical and cultural analysis are linked to it. I hope that since my *abuelitas* article was published and as I have grown as a scholar that my analysis has too.

3. Another important current function for us as critics is to remember our literary history. While contemporary writers may feel that they are seeing the world anew, those of us who are searching out our literary roots are finding women writers who were raising many of the same concerns women voice today—written in a different tone and style and conforming to a different mode; nevertheless, contemporary writers have not arisen from a complete void. If the written word did not survive in enough texts to be known today, nonetheless the oral forms of women's concerns, of women's images have lived in the tradition from one generation, from one century to another. Thus the critic as literary historian is able to fill in the lacunae and to connect the past and the present.

4. Chicana literary discourse, like most feminist discouse, is a troubled one. It is always searching, questioning and fraught with tensions and contradictions, just as is the creative writing arising from the same creative context. A truly Chicana literary theory would result from the attempt to resolve these things, to mend the rift between doers and thinkers. I think we would all agree that Chicana criticism and theory are still in a state of flux looking for a theoretical, critical framework that is our own, whatever the perspective. I personally find it difficult to have theory (male-oriented, French feminist, post-structural or whatever is the current fad) be what dictates what we find in our literature. I prefer to have the literature speak for itself and as a critic try to organize and understand it. Perhaps from a more open perspective our own theoretical critical analysis will arise, rather than finding the theory first and imposing it upon the literature.

Recently several Chicana critics have taken up the issue of a theoretical approach to our literature. Norma Cantú in "The Chicana Poet and Her Audience: Notes Towards a Chicana Feminist Aesthetic" acknowledges the lack of a methodological approach in our work but feels that it is a sense of place and world as embedded in particular language use that the Chicana poet communicates to her Chicana audience. For Cantú it is the special relationship between writer and listener, the shared cultural referents that make the poems work.[6] Norma Alarcón, in her perceptive study on the image of La Malinche, reevaluates and reconstructs the symbolic and figurative meaning this figure holds for us as Chicana writers and critics, dealing with the significance of language use and silence within our literature.[7] She also sees significant evolution of the Chicana as "speaking subject," one who brings within herself her race, class and gender, expressing this from a self-conscious point of view. Both of these critics, it seems to me, in addition to being theoretically well-grounded, look at literature from within, in an integrative sense.

5. It is very difficult to work on living authors: authors who read what you write and agree or don't agree. But it is just as difficult to work on authors no longer living. In the practice of literary criticism one (or perhaps I speak for myself only) must practice sound and honorable as well as rigorous criticism. That is, facts must be checked, scholarship must be sound. There is always the danger that the critic, immersed in pursuing some essential point, will become over enthusiastic and confuse the authorial voice with that of the narrative or poetic voice. If structuralism has taught us anything at all, it is that the lyric/narrative speaker is just that. As critics we must be careful not to confuse author with speaker.

When dealing with a vigorously living author we must also not be too timid to analyze symbolically what we, as critics, may see in the text—that which the author may not consciously have intended. We know that there are many levels of symbolic discourse that we may not be aware of at any given moment. When the text is published, when the author gives it up to the public domain, it is released and opened up to interpretation by the reader. It exists on its own, separate from the author. The textual interpretation, therefore, is one of integration between the authorial intent, and the text itself, *and* the third (and separate) interpretation or grasping of those two aspects by the reader.

6. We must, as critics, also be careful in our criticism to be honest. I think Chicana critics are often too benign. Our close network between writers and critics makes it difficult to have caustic criticism (which might ruin friendships) but at the same time we may hesitate to be as critical as we should be. One way I know I cope with this, and I imagine others have the same problem is simply to ignore those texts I don't like of writers that I do like or to ignore those writers who say nothing to me. This seems to me to be a function of human nature. What is important, however, is that the critic be conscious of her biases. And while we women

may be benign to each other, there are still many Chicano critics who refuse to recognize their own biases and misogyny. Raymond Paredes, in a recent review article, is only able to see Chicana literature through a particularly phallocentric focus. If we were to accept his views we would see "if there is one quality that runs consistently through *their* (italics mine) stories, plays and novels, it is the conviction that men know and care very little about women and that everyone is the worse for it."[8] His review continues with the assumption that men are the focus of Chicana literature, as he assails Beverly Silva, Cherrie Moraga and Ana Castillo as faulted writers, their work, he says, is more interesting "ideologically" than aesthetically. Back to the old notion of "Are They Any Good?" Those writers whose perspectives Paredes does not agree with he considers superficial, and Denise Chávez, with whom he is more in agreement, is merely "flawed."[9]

7. Perhaps more dangerous than ignoring texts we dislike is excluding the works of authors whose perspective we do not share or whose perspective we might feel uncomfortable with. Here I mean specifically the perspective of sexual preference. There are some fine Lesbian writers such as Cherríe Moraga, Gloria Anzaldúa, and Veronica Cunningham whose works are often excluded (although less so recently) from our critical thinking. Certainly if critics are serious about historical, cultural and gender context, then all writers need to be included within the general cultural framework. Then too some critics feel more comfortable with socially conscious literature and exclude that coming from the middle class. As the complexities and shades of our literature grows, we must be careful not to canonize a certain few to the exclusion of other equally fine writers.

8. While some scholars see the need for some resolution of dichotomies, for example of Chicana and feminist, Chicana and poet—as if they were mutually exclusive—others examine the relationship between dominant and ethnic communities. The dominant discourse, if we internalize it, would have us believe that we function under such labels, and to some extent we do. I believe, however, as Bernice Zamora so succinctly expressed it, that our complexities are infinite: that we have grown up and survived along the edges, along the borders of so many languages, worlds, cultures and social systems that we constantly fix and focus on the spaces in between, Nepantla as Sor Juana would have seen it. Categories that try to define and limit this incredibly complex process at once become diminished for their inability to capture and contain. Those of us who try to categorize these complexities inevitably fail.

Margarita Cota-Cárdenas in her novel *Puppet* examines the way in which this ideology is imposed. She sees this in part as arising from a single vision of what being Chicana should be.

> Are you Malinche a malinche? Who are you (who am I
> Mal inche)? Seller or buyer? Sold or bought and at what
> price? What is it to be what so many should say sold-out
> malinchi who is who are/are we what? At what price
> without having been there naming putting label tags what
> who have bought sold malinchismo what other-ismos
> invented shouted with hate reacting, striking like vipers
> like snakes THEIR EYES like snakes what who what[10]

Her Malinche breaks the silence of centuries and she does not do so
quietly:

> yes yes I went yelling loud too why why and they said tie
> her up she's too forward too flighty she thinks she's a
> princess thinks she's her father's daughter thinks she's
> hot stuff that's it doesn't know her place a real threat to
> the tribe take her away haul her off she's a menace to our
> cause that's it only learned to say crazy things accuse with
> HER EYES and they didn't want then troublemakers in
> their country.[11]

These labels, specific here to La Malinche but clearly extended to all
Chicanas, are of course the very labels culture uses to restrict and limit
women's activity, socially as well as intellectually. Women are so silenced
that they are only left to speak with "their eyes." In a country defined
as "their" country, one that does not belong to her, Cota-Cárdenas makes
the connection between Mexico and the United States:

> This country, well I suppose Mexico, Aztlán...? Well, it
> could have been a little more to the north or a little more
> to the south, it makes no difference now, what I was telling
> you was my version, that's it, my version...as a woman,
> that's right, and they can establish the famous dialectic
> with the other versions that you already know very well.[12]

Cota-Cárdenas thus introduces the complexities, the ambiguities in our
lives and, while she does not deny the legitimacy of the other versions
(acknowledging them for what they are), overlays another perspective
that is hers alone.

These remarks I have made may seem to be arising from some simplistic
assumptions. I myself was trained as a structuralist, semiotic critic. But
increasingly I have become suspicious and yes, even bored, by a criticism
which seems alien to the text about which it purports to talk; by a

theoretical basis of patriarchal norms or a theory which does not take the particular concerns of minority writers and culture into account. I am suspicious of criticism which ignores the texts of our writers and which turns the vitality and the passion of those texts of our writers into an empty and meaningless set of letters. This sort of criticism, it seems to me, might as well be analyzing a menu or a telephone directory, and would perhaps be better directed in doing so. As Sor Juana criticized Aristotle—he would have been a better philosopher had he studied cooking—I believe that our critical discourse should come from within, within our cultural and historical perspective. This is not to say that I am advocating limited, regional, small-minded descriptive literary analysis. But I think we should internalize and revolutionize theoretical discourse that comes from outside ourselves, accepting that which is useful and discarding that which is merely meant to impress. In the search for our own aesthetic, for our own analytical direction, we need to look to each other, to recognize that our literature and our cultural production does not need legitimization from the academy, that it already is legitimate in itself. Above all, we must not forget that the most important aspect of our analysis are the texts themselves. As we ask ouselves where are we, what are we doing, we must never appropriate into our own discouse the discourse of the writer herself. If we are to diffuse, support, promote, analyze and understand the work of our writers, we must let them speak for themselves. As a critic I desire the same as poet Pat Mora, I want to see the cotton of many colors, the small birds the color of turquoise and hear the birds that warble in the mountains.

From *Chicana Creativity and Criticism: Charting New Frontiers in American Literature*

Notes

1. Miguel León-Portilla, *Pre-Columbian Literature of Mexico* (Norman: University of Oklahoma Press, 1969), 41, cited in Mora, "Tradition and Mythology: Signatures of Landscape in Chicana Literature"; forthcoming in Tey Diana Rebolledo, ed., *Writing From the Margins.*

2. *Webster's II New Riverside Dictionary* (Boston: Houghton Mifflin Co., 1984).

3. *The Americas Review* 14:3–4 (Fall–Winter, 1986), 119.

4. *The Desert Is No Lady: Southwestern Landscapes in Women's Writing and Art*, Vera Norwood and Janice Monk, eds. (New Haven: Yale University Press, 1987), 96–124.

5. "Abuelitas: Mythology and Integration in Chicana Literature," *Woman of Her Word: Hispanic Women Write*, Evangelina Vigil,ed. Revista Chicano-Riqueña 11:3–4 (1983), 148–58.

6. Rebolledo, ed., *Writing From the Margins*.

7. Norma Alarcón, "Traddutora, Traditora: A Paradigmatic Figure of Chicana Feminism," in Rebolledo, *Writing From the Margins*.

8. Raymond Paredes, "Review Essay: Recent Chicano Writing," *Rocky Mountain Review* 41:1–2 (1987), 126.

9. Paredes, 128.

10. Margarita Cota-Cárdenas, *Puppet* (Austin, TX: Relámpago Books Press, 1985), 85.

11. Cota-Cárdenas, 86.

12. Cota-Cárdenas, 86.

The Theoretical Subject(s) of This Bridge Called My Back and Anglo-American Feminism

Norma Alarcón

This Bridge Called My Back: Writings by Radical Women of Color, edited by Chicana writers Cherríe Moraga and Gloria Anzaldúa,* was intended as a collection of essays, poems, tales and testimonials that would give voice to the contradictory experiences of "women of color." In fact, the editors state:

> We are the colored in a white feminist movement.
> We are the feminists among the people of our culture.
> We are often the lesbians among the straight.[1]

By giving voice to such experiences, each according to her style, the editors and contributors believed they were developing a theory of subjectivity and culture that would demonstrate the considerable differences between them and Anglo-American women, as well as between them and Anglo-European men and men of their own culture. As speaking subjects of a new discursive formation, many of *Bridge*'s writers were aware of the displacement of their subjectivity across a multiplicity of discourses: feminist/lesbian, nationalist, racial, socioeconomic, historical, etc. The peculiarity of their displacement implies a multiplicity of positions from which they are driven to grasp or understand themselves and their relations with the real, in the Althusserian sense of the word.[2] *Bridge* writers, in part, were aware that these positions are often incompatible or contradictory, and others did not have access to the maze of discourses competing for their body and voice. The self-conscious effort to reflect on their "flesh and blood experiences to concretize a vision that can begin to heal our 'wounded knee'"[3] led many *Bridge* speakers to take a position in conflict with multiple intercultural and intracultural discursive interpretations in an effort to come to grips with "the many-headed demon of oppression."[4]

Since its publication in 1981, *Bridge* has had a diverse impact on Anglo-American feminist writings in the United States. Teresa de Laure-

---

*Hereafter cited as *Bridge*, the book has two editions. I use the second edition published by Kitchen Table Press, 1983. The first edition was published by Persephone Press, 1981.

tis, for example, claims that *Bridge* has contributed to a "shift in feminist consciousness,"[5] yet her explanation fails to clarify what the shift consists of and for whom. There is little doubt, however, that *Bridge*, along with the 1980s writings by many women of color in the United States, has problematized many a version of Anglo-American feminism, and has helped open the way for alternate feminist discourses and theories. Presently, however, the impact among most Anglo-American theorists appears to be more cosmetic than not because, as Jane Flax has recently noted, "The modal 'person' in feminist theory still appears to be a self-sufficient individual adult."[6] This particular "modal person" corresponds to the female subject most admired in literature which Gayatri Chakravorty Spivak had characterized as one who "articulates herself in shifting relationship to...the constitution and 'interpellation' of the subject not only as individual but as 'individualist'."[7] Consequently, the "native female" or "woman of color" can be excluded from the discourse of feminist theory. The "native female"—object of colonialism and racism—is excluded because, in Flax's terms, white feminists have not "explored how our understanding of gender relations, self, and theory are partially constituted in and through experiences of living in a culture in which asymmetric race relations are a central organizing principle of society."[8] Thus, the most popular subject of Anglo-American feminism is an autonomous, self-making, self-determining subject who first proceeds according to the *logic of identification* with regard to the subject of consciousness, a notion usually viewed as the purview of man, but now claimed for women.[9] Believing that in this respect she is the same as man, she now claims the right to pursue her own identity, to name herself, to pursue self-knowledge, and, in the words of Adrienne Rich, to effect "a change in the concept of sexual identity."[10]

Though feminism has problematized gender relations, indeed, as Flax observes, gender is "the single most important advance in feminist theory,"[11] it has not problematized the subject of knowledge and her complicity with the notion of consciousness as "synthetic unificatory power, the centre and active point of organization of representations determining their concatenation."[12] The subject (and object) of knowledge is now a woman, but the inherited view of consciousness has not been questioned at all. As a result, some Anglo-American feminist subjects of consciousness have tended to become a parody of the masculine subject of consciousness, thus revealing their ethnocentric liberal underpinnings. In 1982, Jean Bethke Elshtain had noted the "masculine cast" of radical feminist language, for example, noting the terms of "raw power, brute force, martial discipline, law and order with a feminist face—and voice."[13] Also in critiquing liberal feminism and its language, she notes that "no vision of the political community that might serve as the groundwork of a life in common is possible within a political life dominated by a self-interested, predatory individualism."[14] Althusser argues that this tradition "has privileged the category of the 'subject' as Origin, Essence and Cause, responsible in its internality for all determinations of the external object. In other words, this tradition has promoted Man, in his ideas and experience, as the source of knowledge, morals and history."[15] By identifying in this way with this tradition, standpoint epistemologists have substituted, ironically, woman for man. This 'logic of identification' as a first step in constructing the theoretical subject of feminism is often veiled from standpoint epistemologists because greater attention is given to naming female identity, and describing women's ways of knowing as being considerably different than men's.[16] By emphasizing 'sexual difference,' the second step takes place, often called oppositional thinking (counteridentifying). However, this gendered standpoint epistemology leads to feminism's bizarre position with regard to other liberation movements, working inherently against the interests of non-white women and no one else. For example, Sandra Harding argues that oppositional thinking (counteridentification) with white men should be retained even though "[t]here are suggestions in the literature of Native Americans, Africans, and Asians that what feminists call feminine versus masculine personalities, ontologies, ethics, epistemologies, and world views may be what these other liberation movements call Non-Western versus Western personalities and world views.... I set aside the crucial and fatal complication for this way of thinking—the fact that one half of these people are women and that most women are not Western."[17] She further suggests that feminists respond by relinquishing the totalizing "master theory" character of our theory-making: "This response to the issue [will manage] to retain the categories of feminist theory...and simply set them alongside the categories of the theory making of other subjugated groups.... Of course, it leaves bifurcated (and perhaps even more finely divided) the identities of all except ruling-class white Western women...."[18] The apperception of this situation is precisely what led to the choice of title for the book *All The Women Are White, All The Blacks Are Men, But Some of Us Are Brave*, edited by Gloria T. Hull, Patricia Bell Scott and Barbara Smith.[19]

Notwithstanding the power of *Bridge* to affect the personal lives of its readers, *Bridge*'s challenge to the Anglo-American subject of feminism has yet to effect a newer discourse. Women of color often recognize themselves in the pages of *Bridge*, and write to say, "The women writers seemed to be speaking to me, and they actually understood what I was going through. Many of you put into words feelings I have had that I had no way of expressing.... The writings justified some of my thoughts telling me I had a right to feel as I did."[20] On the other hand, Anglo feminist readers of *Bridge* tend to appropriate it, cite it as an instance of difference between women, and proceed to negate that difference by subsuming women of color into the unitary category of woman/women. The latter is often viewed as the "common denominator" in an oppositional (counteridentifying) discourse with some white men, that leaves us unable to explore relationships among women.

Bridge's writers did not see the so-called "common denominator" as the solution for the construction of the theoretical feminist subject. In the call for submissions the editors clearly stated: "We want to express to all women—especially to white middle class women—the experiences which divide us as feminists; we want to explore the causes, and sources of, and solutions to these divisions. We want to create a definition that expands what 'feminist' means to us."[21] Thus, the female subject of *Bridge* is highly complex. She is and has been constructed in a crisis of meaning situation which includes racial and cultural divisions and conflicts. The psychic and material violence that gives shape to that subjectivity cannot be underestimated nor passed over lightly. The fact that not all of this violence comes from men in general but also from women renders the notion of "common denominator" problematic.

It is clear, however, that even as *Bridge* becomes a resource for the Anglo-American feminist theory classroom and syllabus, there's a tendency to deny differences if those differences pose a threat to the "common denominator" category. That is, unity would be purchased with silence, putting aside the conflictive history of groups' interrelations and interdependence. In the words of Paula Treichler, "[h]ow do we address the issues and concerns raised by women of color, who may themselves be even more excluded from theoretical feminist discourse than from the women's studies curriculum?... Can we explore our 'common differences' without overemphasizing the division that currently seems to characterize the feminism of the United States and the world?"[22] Clearly, this exploration appears impossible without a reconfiguration of the subject of feminist theory, and her relational position to a multiplicity of others, not just white men.

Some recent critics of the "exclusionary practices in Women's Studies" have noted that its gender standpoint epistemology leads to a 'tacking on' of "material about minority women" without any note of its "significance for feminist knowledge."[23] The common approaches noted were the tendency to 1) treat race and class as secondary features in social organization (as well as representation) with primacy given to female subordination; 2) acknowledge that inequalities of race, class and gender generate different experiences and then set race and class inequalities aside on the grounds that information was lacking to allow incorporation into an analysis; 3) focus on descriptive aspects of the ways of life, values, customs and problems of women in subordinate race and class categories with little attempt to explain their source or their broader meaning. In fact, it may be impossible for gender standpoint epistemology to ever do more than a "pretheoretical presentation of concrete problems."[24] Since the subject of feminist theory and its single theme—gender—go largely unquestioned, its point of view tends to suppress and repress voices that question its authority, and as Jane Flax remarks, "The suppression of these voices seems to be a necessary condition for the (apparent) authority, coherence, and universality of our own."[25] This may account for the inability to include the voices of "women of color" into feminist discourse, though they are not necessarily under-represented in the reading list.

For the standpoint epistemologists, the desire to construct a feminist theory based solely on gender, on the one hand, and the knowledge or implicit recognition that such an account might distort the representation of many women and/or correspond to that of some men, on the other, gives rise to anxiety and ambivalence with respect to the future of that feminism, especially in Anglo-America. At the core of that attitude is the often unstated recognition that if the pervasiveness of women's oppression is virtually 'universal' on some level, it is also highly diverse from group to group and that women themselves may become complicitous with that oppression. "Complicity arises," says Macdonell, "where through lack of a positive starting point either a practice is driven to make use of prevailing values or a critique becomes the basis for a new theory."[26] Standpoint epistemologists have made use of the now gendered and feminist notion of consciousness, without too much question. (This notion, of course, represents the highest value of European culture since the Enlightenment.) The inclusion of other analytical categories such as race and class becomes impossible for a subject whose consciousness refuses to acknowledge that "one becomes a woman" in ways that are much more complex than in a simple opposition to men. In cultures in which "asymmetric race and class relations are a central organizing principle of society," one may also "become a woman" in opposition to other women. In other words, the whole category of woman may also need to be problematized, a point that I shall take up later. In any case, one should not step into that category nor that of man that easily or simply.

Simone de Beauvoir and her key work *The Second Sex* have been most influential in the development of feminist standpoint epistemology. She may even be responsible for the creation of Anglo-American feminist theory's "episteme": a highly self-conscious ruling class white Western female subject locked in a struggle to the death with "Man." De Beauvoir has shaken the world of women, most especially with the ramification of her phrase, "One is not born, but rather becomes, a woman."[27] For over 400 pages of text after that statement, de Beauvoir demonstrates how a female is constituted as a "woman" by society as her freedom is curtailed from childhood. The curtailment of freedom incapacitates her from affirming "herself as a subject."[28] Very few women, indeed, can escape the cycle of indoctrination except perhaps the writer/intellectual because "[s]he knows that she is a conscious being, a subject."[29] This particular kind of woman can perhaps make of her gender a project and transform her sexual identity.[30] But what of those women who are not so privileged, who neither have the political freedom nor the education? Do they now, then, occupy the place of the Other (the 'Brave') while some women become subjects? Or do we have to make a subject of the whole world?

Regardless of our point of view in this matter, the way to becoming a female subject has been effected through consciousness-raising. In 1982, in a major theoretical essay, "Feminism, Method and the State: An Agenda for Theory," Catharine A. MacKinnon cited *Bridge* as a book that explored the relationship between sex and race and argued that "consciousness-raising" was *the* feminist method.[31] The reference to *Bridge* was brief. It served as an example, along with other texts, of the challenge that race and nationalism have posed for Marxism. According to her, Marxism has been unable to account for the appearance of these emancipatory discourses nor has it been able to assimilate them. Nevertheless, MacKinnon's major point was to demonstrate the epistemological challenge that feminism and its primary method, "consciousness-raising," posed for Marxism. Within Marxism, class as method of analysis has failed to reckon with the historical force of sexism. Through "consciousness-raising" (from women's point of view), women are led to know the world in a different way. Women's experience of politics, of life as sex objects, gives rise to its own method of appropriating that reality: feminist method. It challenges the objectivity of the "empirical gaze" and "rejects the distinction between knowing subject and known object."[32] By having women be the subject of knowledge, the so-called "objectivity" of men is brought into question. Often, this leads to privileging women's way of knowing in opposition to men's way of knowing, thus sustaining the very binary opposition that feminism would like to change or transform. Admittedly, this is only one of the many paradoxical procedures in feminist thinking, as Nancy Cott confirms: "It acknowledges diversity among women while positing that women recognize their unity. It requires gender consciousness for its basis, yet calls for the elimination of prescribed gender roles."[33]

However, I suspect that these contradictions or paradoxes have more profound implications than is readily apparent. Part of the problem may be that as feminist practice and theory recuperate their sexual differential, through "consciousness-raising," women reinscribe such a differential as feminist epistemology or theory. With gender as the central concept in feminist thinking, epistemology is flattened out in such a way that we lose sight of the complex and multiple ways in which the subject and object of possible experience are constituted. The flattening effect is multiplied when one considers that gender is often solely related to white men. There's no inquiry into the knowing subject beyond the fact of being a "woman." But what is a "woman," or a "man" for that matter? If we refuse to define either term according to some "essence," then we are left with having to specify their conventional significance in time and space, which is liable to change as knowledge increases or interests change. The fact that Anglo-American feminism has appropriated the generic term for itself leaves many a woman in this country having to call herself otherwise, i.e., "woman of color," which is equally "meaningless" without further specification. It also gives rise to the tautology "Chicana women." Needless to say, the requirement of gender consciousness only in relationship to man leaves us in the dark about a good many things, including interracial and intercultural relations. It may be that the only purpose this type of differential has is as a political strategy. It does not help us envision a world beyond binary restrictions, nor does it help us to reconfigure feminist theory to include the "native female." It does, however, help us grasp the paradox that within this cultural context one cannot be a feminist without becoming a gendered subject of knowledge, which makes it very difficult to transcend gender at all and to imagine relations between women.

In *Feminist Politics and Human Nature*, Alison M. Jaggar, speaking as a socialist feminist, refers repeatedly to *Bridge* and other works by women of color. In that work, Jaggar states that subordinated women are unrepresented in feminist theory. Jaggar claims that socialist feminism is inspired by Marxist and radical feminist politics though the latter has failed to be scientific about its insights. *Bridge* is cited various times to counter the racist and classist position of radical feminists.[34] Jaggar charges that "[r]adical feminism has encouraged women to name their own experience but it has not recognized explicitly that this experience must be analyzed, explained and theoretically transcended."[35] In a sense, Jaggar's charge amounts to the notion that radical feminists were flattening out their knowledge by an inadequate methodology, i.e. gender consciousness-raising. Many of Jaggar's observations are a restatement of *Bridge*'s challenge to Anglo-American feminists of all persuasions, be it Liberal, Radical, Marxist, and Socialist, the types sketched out by Jaggar. For example, "[a] representation of reality from the standpoint of women must draw on the variety of all women's experience"[36] may be compared to Barbara Smith's view in *Bridge* that "Feminism is the political theory and practice to free *all* women: women of color, working-class women, poor women, physically challenged women, lesbians, old women, as well as white economically privileged heterosexual women."[37] Jaggar continues, "Since historically diverse groups of women, such as working-class women, women of color, and others have been excluded from intellectual work, they somehow must be enabled to participate as subjects as well as objects of feminist theorizing."[38] Writers in *Bridge* did appear to think that "consciousness-raising" and the naming of one's experience would deliver some theory and yield a notion of "what 'feminist' means to us."[39] Except for Smith's statement, there is no overarching view that would guide us as to "what 'feminist' means to us." Though there is a tacit political identity—gender/class/race-encapsulated in the phrase "women of color" that connects the pieces—they tend to split apart into "vertical relations" between the culture of resistance and the culture resisted or from which excluded. Thus, the binary restrictions become as prevalent between race/ethnicity of oppressed versus oppressor as between the sexes. The problems inherent in Anglo-American feminism and race relations are so locked into the "Self/Other" theme that it is no surprise that *Bridge*'s co-editor Moraga would remark, "In the last three years I have learned that Third World feminism does not provide the kind of easy political framework that women of color are running to in droves. The *idea* of Third World feminism has proved to be much easier between the covers of a book than between real live women."[40] She refers to the United States, of course, because feminism is alive and well throughout the Third World largely within the purview of women's rights, or as a class struggle.[41]

The appropriation of *Bridge*'s observations in Jaggar's work differs slightly from the others in its view of linguistic use, implying to a limited extent that language is also reflective of material existence. The crucial question is how, indeed, can women of color be subjects as well as objects of feminist theorizing? Jaggar cites María Lugones' doubts: "We cannot talk to you in our language because you do not understand it…. The power of white Anglo women vis-à-vis Hispanas and Black women is in inverse proportion to their working knowledge of each other…. Because of their ignorance, white Anglo women who try to do theory with women of color inevitably disrupt the dialogue. Before they can contribute to collective dialogue, they need to 'know the text,' to have become familiar with an alternative way of viewing the world…. You need to learn to become unintrusive, unimportant, patient to the point of tears, while at the same time open to learning any possible lessons. You will have to come to terms with the sense of alienation, of not belonging, of having your world thoroughly disrupted, having it criticized and scrutinized from the point of view of those who have been harmed by it, having important concepts central to it dismissed, being viewed with mistrust…."[42] One of *Bridge*'s breaks with prevailing conventions is linguistic. Lugones' advice to Anglo women to listen was post-*Bridge*. If prevailing conventions of speaking/writing had been observed, many a contributor would have been censored or silenced. So would have many a major document or writing of minorities. *Bridge* leads us to understand that the silence and silencing of people begins with the dominating enforcement of linguistic conventions, the resistance to relational dialogues, as well as the disenablement of peoples by outlawing their forms of speech. Anglo-American feminist theory assumes a speaking subject who is an autonomous, self-conscious individual woman. Such theory does not discuss the linguistic status of the person. It takes for granted the linguistic status which founds subjectivity. In this way it appropriates woman/women for itself, and turns its work into a theoretical project within which the rest of us are compelled to 'fit.' By 'forgetting' or refusing to take into account that we are culturally constituted in and through language in complex ways and not just engendered in a homogeneous situation, the Anglo-American subject of consciousness cannot come to terms with her (his) own class-biased ethnocentrism. She is blinded to her own construction not just as a woman but as an Anglo-American one. Such a subject creates a theoretical subject that could not possibly include all women just because we are women. It is against this feminist backdrop that many "women of color" have struggled to give voice to their subjectivity and which effected the publication of the writings collected in *Bridge*. However, the freedom of women of color to posit themselves as multiple-voiced subjects is constantly in peril of repression precisely at that point where our constituted contradictions put us at odds with women different from ourselves.

The pursuit of a "politics of unity" solely based on gender forecloses the "pursuit of solidarity" through different political formations and the exploration of alternative theories of the subject of consciousness. There is a tendency in more sophisticated and elaborate gender standpoint epistemologists to affirm "an identity made up of heterogeneous and heteronomous representations of gender, race, and class, and often indeed across languages and cultures"[43] with one breath, and with the next to refuse to explore how that identity may be theorized or analyzed, by reconfirming a unified subjectivity or "shared consciousness" through gender. The difference is handed over with one hand and taken away with the other. If it be true, as Teresa de Lauretis has observed, that "[s]elf and identity...are always grasped and understood within particular discursive configurations...,"[44] it does not necessarily follow that one can easily and self-consciously decide "to reclaim [an identity] from a history of multiple assimilations,"[45] and still retain a "shared consciousness." Such a practice goes counter to the homogenizing tendency of the subject of consciousness in the United States. To be oppressed means to be disenabled not only from grasping an "identity," but also from reclaiming it. In this culture, to grasp or reclaim an identity means always already to have become a subject of consciousness. The theory of the subject of consciousness as a unitary and synthesizing agent of knowledge is always already a posture of domination. One only has to think of Gloria Anzaldúa's essay in *Bridge*, "Speaking in Tongues: A Letter to Third World Women Writers."[46] Though de Lauretis concedes that a racial "shared consciousness" may have prior claims than gender, she still insists on unity through gender: "the female subject is always constructed and defined in gender, starting from gender."[47] One is interested in having more than an account of gender, there are other relations to be accounted for. De Lauretis insists, in most of her work, that "the differences among women may be better understood as differences within women."[48] This position returns us all to our solitary, though different, consciousness, without noting that some differences are (have been) a result of relations of domination of women by women; that differences may be purposefully constituted for the purpose of domination or exclusion, especially in oppositional thinking. Difference, whether it be sexual, racial, social, has to be conceptualized within a political and ideological domain.[49] In *Bridge*, for example, Mirtha Quintanales points out that "in this country, in this world, racism is used *both* to create false differences among us *and* to mask very significant ones—cultural, economic, political."[50]

One of the most remarkable tendencies in the work reviewed is the implicit or explicit acknowledgement that women of color are excluded from feminist theory, on the one hand, and on the other the reminder that though excluded from theory, their books are read in the classroom and/or duly footnoted. It is clear that some of the writers in *Bridge* thought at some point in the seventies that feminism could be the ideal answer to their hope for liberation. Chrystos, for example, states her disillusionment as follows: "I no longer believe that feminism is a tool which can eliminate racism or even promote better understanding between different races and kinds of women."[51] The disillusionment is eloquently reformulated in the theme poem by Donna Kate Ruchin, "The Bridge Poem."[52] The dream of helping the people who surround her to reach an interconnectedness that would change society is given up in favor of self-translation into a "true self." In my view, the speaker's refusal to play "bridge," an enablement to others as well as self, is the acceptance of defeat at the hands of political groups whose self-definition follows the view of self as unitary, capable of being defined by a single "theme." The speaker's perception that the "self" is multiple ("I'm sick of mediating with your worst self/on behalf of your better selves,"[53] and its reduction harmful, gives emphasis to the relationality between one's selves and those of others as an ongoing process of struggle, effort and tension. Indeed, in this poem the better "bridging self" of the speaker is defeated by the overriding notion of the unitary subject of knowledge and consciousness so prevalent in Anglo-American culture. Consciousness as a site of multiple voicings is the theoretical subject, par excellence, of *Bridge*. Concomitantly, these voicings (or thematic threads) are not viewed as necessarily originating with the subject, but as discourses that transverse consciousness and which the subject must struggle with constantly. Rosario Morales, for example, says "I want to be whole. I want to claim myself to be puertorican, and U.S. American, working class and middle class, housewife and intellectual, feminist, marxist and anti-imperialist."[54] Gloria Anzaldúa observes, "What am I? *A third world lesbian feminist with Marxist and mystic leanings*. They would chop me up into little fragments and tag each piece with a label."[55] The need to assign multiple registers of existence is an effect of the belief that knowledge of one's subjectivity cannot be arrived at through a single discursive "theme." Indeed, the multiple-voiced subjectivity is lived in resistance to competing notions for one's allegiance or self-identification. It is a process of disidentification[56] with prevalent formulations of the most forcefully theoretical subject of feminism. The choice of one or many themes is both theoretical and a political decision. Like gender epistemologists and other emancipatory movements, the theoretical subject of *Bridge* gives credit to the subject of consciousness as the site of knowledge but problematizes it by representing it as a weave. In Anzaldúa's terms, the woman of color has a "plural personality." Speaking of the new mestiza in *Borderlands/La Frontera*, she says, "[s]he learns to juggle cultures. ...[the] juncture where the mestiza stands is where phenomena tend to collide."[57] As an object of multiple indoctrinations that heretofore have collided upon her, their new recognition as products of the oppositional thinking of others can help her come to terms with the politics of varied discourses and their antagonistic relations.

Thus, current political practices in the United States make it almost impossible to go beyond an oppositional theory of the subject, which is the prevailing feminist strategy and that of others; however, it is not the theory that will help us grasp the subjectivity of women of color. Socially and historically, women of color have been now central, now outside antagonistic relations between races, classes, and gender(s); this struggle of multiple antagonisms, almost always in relation to culturally different groups and not just genders, gives configuration to the theoretical subject of *Bridge*. It must be noted, however, that each woman of color cited here, even in her positing of a "plurality of self," is already privileged enough to reach the moment of cognition of a situation for herself. This should suggest that to privilege the subject, even if multiple-voiced, is not enough.

Notes

1. Moraga and Anzaldúa, 23.

2. Louis Althusser, *Lenin and Philosophy and Other Essays*, Ben Brewster, tr. (London: New Left Books, 1971).

3. Moraga and Anzaldúa, 23.

4. Moraga and Anzaldúa, 195.

5. Teresa de Lauretis, *Technologies of Gender* (Bloomington: Indiana University Press, 1987), 10.

6. Jane Flax, "Postmodernism and Gender Relations in Feminist Theory," *Signs* 12:4 (Summer 1987), 640.

7. Gayatri Chakravorty Spivak, "Three Women's Texts and a Critique of Imperialism," *Critical Inquiry* 12:1 (Autumn 1985), 243–44.

8. Flax, 640.

9. Julia Kristeva, "Women's Time," *Signs* 7:1 (Autumn 1981), 19.

10. Adrienne Rich, *On Lies, Secrets and Silence* (New York: W.W. Norton, 1979), 35.

11. Flax, 627.

12. Michel Pecheux, *Language, Semantics and Ideology* (New York: St. Martin's Press, 1982), 122.

13. Jean Bethke Elshtain, "Feminist Discourse and Its Discontents: Language, Power, and Meaning," *Signs* 7:3 (Spring 1981), 611.

14. Elshtain, 617.

15. Diane Macdonell, *Theories of Discourse: An Introduction* (New York: Basil Blackwell, 1986), 76.

16. For an intriguing demonstration of these operations, see Seyla Benhabib, "The Generalized and the Concrete Other: The Kohlberg-Gilligan Controversy and Feminst Theory" in Seyla Benhabib and Drucilla Cornell, *Feminism as Critique* (Minneapolis: University of Minnesota Press, 1987), 77–95.

17. Sandra Harding, "The Instability of the Analytical Categories of Feminist Theory," *Signs* 11:4 (Summer 1986), 659.

18. Harding, 660.

19. Gloria T. Hull, Patricia B. Scott and Barbara Smith, eds., *All The Women Are White, All The Blacks Are Men, But Some of Us Are Brave* (Westbury, N.Y.: Feminist Press, 1982).

20. Moraga and Anzaldúa, Foreword to the Second Edition, n.p.

21. Moraga and Anzaldúa, Introduction to the First Edition, xxiii.

22. Paula Treichler, "Teaching Feminist Theory," *Theory in the Classroom*, Cary Nelsen, ed. (Urbana: University of Illinois Press, 1986), 79.

23. Maxine Baca Zinn, Lynn Weber Cannon, Elizabeth Higginbotham and Bonnie Thornton Dill, "The Cost of Exclusionary Practices in Women's Studies," *Signs* 11:4 (Summer 1986), 296.

24. Baca Zinn *et al.*, 296–97.

25. Flax, 633.

26. Macdonell, 62.

27. Simone de Beauvoir, *The Second Sex* (New York: Vintage Books, 1974), 301.

28. de Beauvoir, 316.

29. de Beauvoir, 761.

30. For a detailed discussion of this theme, see Judith Butler, "Variations on Sex and Gender: Beauvoir, Wittig, and Foucault" in Benhabib and Cornell, 128–42.

31. Catharine MacKinnon, "Feminism, Marxism, Method and the State: An Agenda for Theory," *Signs* 7:3 (Spring 1982), 536–38.

32. MacKinnon, 536.

33. Nancy F. Cott, "Feminist Theory and Feminist Movements: The Past Before Us," *What is Feminism: A Re-Examination*, Juliet Mitchell and Ann Oakley, eds. (New York: Pantheon Books, 1986), 49.

34. Alison M. Jaggar, *Feminist Politics and Human Nature* (Totowa, N.J.: Rowman & Allanheld, 1983), 249–50; 295–96.

35. Jaggar, 381.

36. Jaggar, 386.

37. Moraga and Anzaldúa, 61.

38. Jaggar, 386.

39. Moraga and Anzaldúa, Introduction, xxiii.

40. Moraga and Anzaldúa, Foreword to the Second Edition, n.p.

41. Miranda Davies, *Third World: Second Sex* (London: Zed Books, 1987).

42. Jaggar, 386.

43. Teresa de Lauretis, "Feminist Studies/Critical Studies: Issues, Terms, and Contexts," *Feminist Studies/Critical Studies* Teresa de Lauretis, ed. (Bloomington: Indiana University Press 1986), 9.

44. de Lauretis, *Feminist Studies*, 8.

45. de Lauretis, *Feminist Studies*, 9.

46. Moraga and Anzaldúa, 165–74.

47. de Lauretis, *Feminist Studies*, 14.

48. de Lauretis, *Feminist Studies*, 14.

49. Monique Wittig, cited in Elizabeth Meese, *Crossing the Double-Cross: The Practice of Feminist Criticism* (Chapel Hill: University of North Carolina Press, 1986), 74.

50. Moraga and Anzaldúa, 153.

51. Moraga and Anzaldúa, 69.

52. Moraga and Anzaldúa, xxi–xxii.

53. Moraga and Anzaldúa, xxii.

54. Moraga and Anzaldúa, 91.

55. Moraga and Anzaldúa, 205.

56. Pecheux, 158–59.

57. Gloria Anzaldúa, *Borderlands/La Frontera: The New Mestiza* (San Francisco: Spinsters/Aunt Lute, 1987), 79.

Definition of Womanist

Alice Walker

Womanist   1. From *womanish.* (Opp. of "girlish," i.e., frivolous, irresponsible, not serious.) A black feminist or feminist of color. From the black folk expression of mothers to female children, "You acting womanish," i.e., like a woman. Usually referring to outrageous, audacious, courageous or *willful* behavior. Wanting to know more and in greater depth than is considered "good" for one. Interested in grown-up doings. Acting grown up. Being grown up. Interchangeable with another black folk expression: "You trying to be grown." Responsible. In charge. *Serious.*

2. *Also:* A woman who loves other women, sexually and/or nonsexually. Appreciates and prefers women's culture, women's emotional flexibility (values tears as a natural counterbalance of laughter), and women's strength. Sometimes loves individual men, sexually and/or nonsexually. Committed to survival and wholeness of entire people, male *and* female. Not a separatist, except periodically, for health. Traditionally universalist, as in: "Mama, why are we brown, pink, and yellow, and our cousins are white, beige, and black?" Ans.: "Well, you know the colored race is just like a flower garden, with every color flower represented." Traditionally capable, as in: "Mama, I'm walking to Canada and I'm taking you and a bunch of other slaves with me." Reply: "It wouldn't be the first time."

3. Loves music. Loves dance. Loves the moon. *Loves* the Spirit. Loves love and food and roundness. Loves struggle. *Loves* the Folk. Loves herself. *Regardless.*

4. Womanist is to feminist as purple is to lavender.

From *In Search of Our Mothers' Gardens*

Not You/Like You: Post-Colonial Women and the Interlocking Questions of Identity and Difference

Trinh T. Minh-ha

To raise the question of identity is to reopen again the discussion on the self/other relationship in its enactment of power relations. Identity as understood in the context of a certain ideology of dominance has long been a notion that relies on the concept of an essential, authentic core that remains hidden to one's consciousness and that requires the elimination of all that is considered foreign or not true to the self, that is to say, not-I, other. In such a concept the other is almost unavoidably either opposed to the self or submitted to the self's dominance. It is always condemned to remain its shadow while attempting at being its equal. Identity, thus understood, supposes that a clear dividing line can be made between I and not-I, he and she; between depth and surface, or vertical and horizontal identity; between us here and them over there. The further one moves from the core the less likely one is thought to be capable of fulfilling one's role as the real self, the real Black, Indian or Asian, the real woman. The search for an identity is, therefore, usually a search for that lost, pure, true, real, genuine, original, authentic self, often situated within a process of elimination of all that is considered other, superfluous, fake, corrupted or Westernized.

If identity refers to the whole pattern of sameness within a being, the style of a continuing me that permeated all the changes undergone, then difference remains within the boundary of that which distinguishes one identity from another. This means that at heart X must be X, Y must be Y and X cannot be Y. Those running around yelling X is not X and X can be Y usually land in a hospital, a rehabilitation center, a concentration camp or a reservation. All deviations from the dominant stream of thought, that is to say, the belief in a permanent essence of woman and in an invariant but fragile identity whose loss is considered to be a specifically human danger, can easily fit into the categories of the mentally ill or the mentally underdeveloped.

It is probably difficult for a normal, probing mind to recognize that to seek is to lose, for seeking presupposes a separation between the seeker and the sought, the continuing me and the changes it undergoes. Can identity, indeed, be viewed other than as a by-product of a manhandling of life, one that, in fact, refers no more to a consistent pattern of sameness than to an inconsequential process of otherness. How am I to lose, maintain or gain a female identity when it is impossible for me to take up a position outside this identity from which I presumably reach in and feel for it? Difference in such a context is that which undermines the very idea of identity, differing to infinity the layers of totality that forms I.

Hegemony works at leveling out differences and at standardizing contexts and expectations in the smallest details of our daily lives. Uncovering this leveling of differences is, therefore, resisting that very notion of difference which defined in the master's terms often resorts to the simplicity of essences. Divide and conquer has for centuries been his creed, his formula of success. But a different terrain of consciousness has been explored for some time now, a terrain in which clear cut divisions and dualistic oppositions such as science versus subjectivity, masculine versus feminine, may serve as departure points for analytical purpose but are no longer satisfactory if not entirely untenable to the critical mind.

I have often been asked about what some viewers call the lack of conflicts in my films. Psychological conflict is often equated with substance and depth. Conflicts in Western contexts often serve to define identities. My suggestion to the "lack" is: let difference replace conflict. Difference as understood in many feminist and non-Western contexts, difference as foreground in my film work is not opposed to sameness, nor synonymous with separateness. Difference, in other words, does not necessarily give rise to separatism. There are differences as well as similarities within the concept of difference. One can further say that difference is not what makes conflicts. It is beyond and alongside conflict. This is where confusion often arises and where the challenge can be issued. Many of us still hold on to the concept of difference not as a tool of creativity to question multiple forms of repression and dominance, but as a tool of segregation, to exert power on the basis of racial and sexual essences. The apartheid type of difference.

Let me point to a few examples of practices of such a notion of difference. There are quite a few, but I'll just select three and perhaps we can discuss those. First of all, I would take the example of the veil as reality and metaphor. If the act of unveiling has a liberating potential, so does the act of veiling. It all depends on the context in which such an act is carried out, or more precisely, on how and where women see dominance. Difference should neither be defined by the dominant sex nor by the dominant culture. So that when women decide to lift the veil one can say that they do so in defiance of their men's oppressive right to their bodies. But when they decide to keep or put on the veil they once took off they might do so to reappropriate their space or to claim a new difference in defiance of genderless, hegemonic, centered standardization.

Second, the use of silence. Within the context of women's speech silence has many faces. Like the veiling of women just mentioned, silence can only be subversive when it frees itself from the male-defined context of absence, lack and fear as feminine territories. On the one hand, we face the danger of inscribing femininity as absence, as lack and as blank in rejecting the importance of the act of enunciation. On the other hand, we understand the necessity to place women on the side of negativity and to work in undertones, for example, in our attempts at undermining patriarchal systems of values. Silence is so commonly set in opposition with speech. Silence as a will not to say or a will to unsay and as a language of its own has barely been explored.

Third, the question of subjectivity. The domain of subjectivity understood as sentimental, personal and individual horizon as opposed to objective, universal, societal, limitless horizon is often attributed to both women, the other of man, and natives, the Other of the West. It is often assumed, for example, that women's enemy is the intellect, that their apprehension of life can only wind and unwind around a cooking pot, a baby's diaper or matters of the heart. Similarly, for centuries and centuries we have been told that primitive mentality belongs to the order of the emotional and the affective, and that it is incapable of elaborating concepts. Primitive man feels and participates. He does not really think or reason. He has no knowledge, "no clear idea or even no idea at all of matter and soul," as Lévi-Bruhl puts it. Today this persistent rationale has taken on multiple faces, and its residues still linger on, easily recognizable despite the refined rhetoric of those who perpetuate it.

Worth mentioning again here is the question of outsider and insider in ethnographic practices. An insider's view. The magic word that bears within itself a seal of approval. What can be more authentically other than an otherness by the other, herself? Yet, every piece of the cake given by the master comes with a double-edged blade. The Afrikanners are prompt in saying, "you can take a Black man from the bush, but you can't take the bush from the Black man." The place of the native is always well-delimitated. "Correct" cultural filmmaking, for example, usually implies that Africans show Africa; Asians, Asia; and Euro-Americans, the world. Otherness has its laws and interdictions. Since you can't take the bush from the Black man, it is the bush that is consistently given back to him, and as things often turn out it is also this very bush that the Black man shall make his exclusive territory. And he may do so with the full awareness that barren land is hardly a gift. For in the unfolding of power inequalities, changes frequently require that the rules be reappropriated so that the master be beaten at his own game. The conceited giver likes to give with the understanding that he is in a position to take back whenever he feels like it and whenever the accepter dares or happens to trespass on his preserves. The latter, however, sees no gift. Can you imagine such a thing as a gift that takes? So the latter only sees debts that, once given back, should remain his property—although land owning is a concept that has long been foreign to him and that he refused to assimilate.

Through audiences' responses and expectations of their works, non-white filmmakers are often informed and reminded of the territorial boundaries in which they are to remain. An insider can speak with authority about her own culture, and she's referred to as the source of authority in this matter—not as a filmmaker necessarily, but as an insider, merely. This automatic and arbitrary endowment of an insider with legitimized knowledge about her cultural heritage and environment only exerts its power when it's a question of validating power. It is a paradoxical twist of the colonial mind. What the outsider expects from the insider is, in fact, a projection of an all-knowing subject that this outsider usually attributes to himself and to his own kind. In this unacknowledged self/other relation, however, the other would always remain the shadow of the self. Hence not really, not quite all-knowing. That a white person makes a film on the Goba of the Zambezi, for example, or on the Tasaday of the Philippine rainforest, seems hardly surprising to anyone, but that a Third World member makes a film on other Third World peoples never fails to appear questionable to many. The question concerning the choice of subject matter immediately arises, sometimes out of curiosity, most often out of hostility. The marriage is not consumable, for the pair is no longer outside/inside, that is to say, objective versus subjective, but something between inside/inside—objective in what is already claimed as objective. So, no real conflict.

Interdependency cannot be reduced to a mere question of mutual enslavement. It also consists in creating a ground that belongs to no one, not even to the creator. Otherness becomes empowerment, critical difference when it is not given but recreated. Furthermore, where should the dividing line between outsider and insider stop? How should it be defined? By skin color, by language, by geography, by nation or by political affinity? What about those, for example, with hyphenated identities and hybrid realities? And here it is worth noting, for example, a journalist's report in a recent *Time* issue which is entitled, "The Crazy Game of Musical Chairs." In this brief report attention is drawn to the fact that people in South Africa who are classified by race and placed into one of the nine racial categories that determine where they can live and work, can have their classification changed if they can prove they were put in a wrong group. Thus, in an announcement of racial reclassifications by the Home Affairs Ministers one learns that 9 whites became colored, 506 coloreds became white, 2 whites became Malay, 14 Malay became white, 40 coloreds became Black, 666 Blacks became colored and the list goes on. However, says the minister, no Blacks apply to become whites. And no whites became Black.

The moment the insider steps out from the inside she's no longer a mere insider. She necessarily looks in from the outside while also looking out from the inside. Not quite the same, not quite the other, she stands in that undetermined threshold place where she constantly drifts in and out. Undercutting the inside/outside opposition, her intervention is necessarily that of both not quite an insider and not quite an outsider. She is, in other words, this inappropriate other or same who moves about with always at least two gestures: that of affirming 'I am like you' while persisting in her difference and that of reminding 'I am different' while unsettling every definition of otherness arrived at.

This is not to say that the historical I can be obscured and ignored and that differentiation cannot be made, but that I is not unitary, culture has never been monolithic and is always more or less in relation to a judging subject. Differences do not only exist between outsider and insider—two entities. They are also at work within the outsider herself, or the insider herself—a single entity. She who knows she cannot speak of them without speaking of herself, of history without involving her story, also knows that she cannot make a gesture without activating the to and fro movement of life.

The subjectivity at work in the context of this inappropriate other can hardly be submitted to the old subjectivity/objectivity paradigm. Acute political subject awareness cannot be reduced to a question of self-criticism toward self-improvement, nor of self-praise toward greater self-confidence. Such differentiation is useful, for a grasp of subjectivity as, let's say, the science of the subject or merely as related to the subject, makes the fear of self-absorption look absurd. Awareness of the limits in which one works need not lead to any form of indulgence in personal partiality, nor to the narrow conclusion that it is impossible to understand anything about other peoples, since the difference is one of essence. By refusing to naturalize the I, subjectivity uncovers the myth of essential core, of spontaneity and depth as inner vision. Subjectivity, therefore, does not merely consist of talking about oneself, be this talking indulgent or critical. In short, what is at stake is a practice of subjectivity that is still unaware of its own constituted nature, hence, the difficulty to exceed the simplistic pair of subjectivity and objectivity; a practice of subjectivity that is unaware of its continuous role in the production of meaning, as if things can make sense by themselves, so that the interpreter's function consists of only choosing among the many existing readings, unaware of representation as representation, that is to say, the cultural, sexual, political inter-reality of the filmmaker as subject, the reality of the subject film and the reality of the cinematic apparatus. And finally unaware of the inappropriate other within every I.

From *Inscriptions* 3/4

Lecture given at the Feminism and the Critique of Colonial Discourse Conference, U.C. Santa Cruz, April 25, 1987.

Legal Alien

Pat Mora

Bi-lingual, Bi-cultural,
able to slip from "How's life?"
to *"Me'stan volviendo loca,"*
able to sit in a paneled office
drafting memos in smooth English,
able to order in fluent Spanish
at a Mexican restaurant,
American but hyphenated,
viewed by Anglos as perhaps exotic,
perhaps inferior, definitely different,
viewed by Mexicans as alien,
(their eyes say, "You may speak
Spanish but you're not like me")
an American to Mexicans
a Mexican to Americans
a handy token
sliding back and forth
between the fringes of both worlds
by smiling
by masking the discomfort
of being pre-judged
Bi-laterally.

From *Chants*

La conciencia de la mestiza: Towards a New Consciousness

Gloria Anzaldúa

> *Por la mujer de mi raza*
> *hablará el espíritu.*[1]

Jose Vasconcelos, Mexican philosopher, envisaged *una raza mestiza, una mezcla de razas afines, una raza de color—la primera raza síntesis del globo.* He called it a cosmic race, *la raza cósmica*, a fifth race embracing the four major races of the world.[2] Opposite to the theory of the pure Aryan, and to the policy of racial purtiy that white America practices, his theory is one of inclusivity. At the confluence of two or more genetic streams, with chromosomes constantly "crossing over," this mixture of races, rather than resulting in an inferior being, provides hybrid progeny, a mutable, more malleable species with a rich gene pool. From this racial, ideological, cultural and biological cross-pollinization, an "alien" consciousness is presently in the making—a new *mestiza* consciousness, *una conciencia de mujer.* It is a consciousness of the Borderlands.

Una lucha de fronteras/A Struggle of Borders

> Because I, a *mestiza*,
> continually walk out of one culture
> and into another,
> because I am in all cultures at the same time,
> *alma entre dos mundos, tres, cuatro,*
> *me zumba la cabeza con lo contradictorio.*
> *Estoy norteada por todas las voces que me hablan*
> *simultáneamente.*

The ambivalence from the clash of voices results in mental and emotional states of perplexity. Internal strife results in insecurity and indecisiveness. The *mestiza*'s dual or multiple personality is plagued by psychic restlessness.

In a constant state of mental nepantilism, an Aztec word meaning torn between ways, *la mestiza* is a product of the transfer of the cultural and spiritual values of one group to another. Being tricultural, monolingual, bilingual or multilingual, speaking a patois, and in a state of perpetual transition, the *mestiza* faces the dilemma of the mixed breed: which collectivity does the daughter of a darkskinned mother listen to?

El choque de un alma atrapado entre el mundo del espíritu y el mundo de la técnica a veces la deja entullada. Cradled in one culture, sandwiched between two cultures, straddling all three cultures and their value systems, *la mestiza* undergoes a struggle of flesh, a struggle of borders, an inner war. Like all people, we perceive the version of reality that our culture communicates. Like others having or living in more than one culture, we get multiple, often opposing messages. The coming together of two self-consistent but habitually incompatible frames of reference[3] causes *un choque*, a cultural collision.

Within us and within *la cultura chicana*, commonly held beliefs of the white culture attack commonly held beliefs of the Mexican culture, and both attack commonly held beliefs of the indigenous culture. Subconsciously, we see an attack on ourselves and our beliefs as a threat and we attempt to block with a counterstance.

But it is not enough to stand on the opposite river bank, shouting questions, challenging patriarchical, white conventions. A counterstance locks one into a duel of oppressor and oppressed; locked in mortal combat, like the cop and the criminal, both are reduced to a common denominator of violence. The counterstance refutes the dominant culture's views and beliefs, and, for this, it is proudly defiant. All reaction is limited by, and dependent on, what it is reacting against. Because the counterstance stems from a problem with authority—outer as well as inner—it's a step towards liberation from cultural domination. But it is not a way of life. At some point, on our way to a new consciousness, we will have to leave the opposite bank, the split between the two mortal combatants somehow healed so that we are on both shores at once and, at once, see through serpent and eagle eyes. Or perhaps we will decide to disengage from the dominant culture, write it off altogether as a lost cause, and cross the border into a wholly new and separate territory. Or we might go another route. The possibilities are numerous once we decide to act and not react.

A Tolerance For Ambiguity

These numerous possibilities leave *la mestiza* floundering in uncharted seas. In perceiving conflicting information and points of view, she is subjected to a swamping of her psychological borders. She has discovered that she can't hold concepts or ideas in rigid boundaries. The borders and walls that are supposed to keep the undesirable ideas out are entrenched habits and patterns of behavior; these habits and patterns are the enemy within. Rigidity means death. Only by remaining flexible is she able to stretch the psyche horizontally and vertically. *La mestiza* constantly has to shift out of habitual formations; from convergent thinking, analytical reasoning that tends to use rationality to move toward a single goal (a Western mode), to divergent thinking,[4] characterized by movement away from set patterns and goals and toward a more whole perspective, one that includes rather than excludes.

The new *mestiza* copes by developing a tolerance for contradictions, a tolerance for ambiguity. She learns to be an Indian in Mexican culture, to be Mexican from an Anglo point of view. She learns to juggle cultures. She has a plural personality, she operates in a pluralistic mode—nothing is thrust out, the good, the bad and the ugly, nothing rejected, nothing abandoned. Not only does she sustain contradictions, she turns the ambivalence into something else.

She can be jarred out of ambivalence by an intense, and often painful, emotional event which inverts or resolves the ambivalence. I'm not sure exactly how. The work takes place underground—subconsciously. It is work that the soul performs. That focal point or fulcrum, that juncture where the *mestiza* stands, is where phenomena tend to collide. It is where the possibility of uniting all that is separate occurs. This assembly is not one where severed or separated pieces merely come together. Nor is it a balancing of opposing powers. In attempting to work out a synthesis, the self has added a third element which is greater than the sum of its severed parts. That third element is a new consciousness—a *mestiza* consciousness—and though it is a source of intense pain, its energy comes from a continual creative motion that keeps breaking down the unitary aspect of each new paradigm.

En unas pocas centurias, the future will belong to the *mestiza*. Because the future depends on the breaking down of paradigms, it depends on the straddling of two or more cultures. By creating a new mythos—that is, a change in the way we perceive reality, the way we see ourselves and the ways we behave—*la mestiza* creates a new consciousness.

The work of *mestiza* consciousness is to break down the subject-object duality that keeps her a prisoner and to show in the flesh and through the images in her work how duality is transcended. The answer to the problem between the white race and the colored, between males and females, lies in healing the split that originates in the very foundation of our lives, our culture, our languages, our thoughts. A massive uprooting of dualistic thinking in the individual and collective consciousness is the beginning of a long struggle, but one that could, in our best hopes, bring us to the end of rape, of violence, of war.

La encrucijada/The Crossroads

> A chicken is being sacrificed
>   at a crossroads, a simple mound of earth
> a mud shrine for *Eshu*,
>   *Yoruba* god of indeterminacy,
> who blesses her choice of path.
>   She begins her journey.

Su cuerpo es una bocacalle. La mestiza has gone from being the sacrificial goat to becoming the officiating priestess at the crossroads.

As a *mestiza* I have no country, my homeland cast me out; yet all countries are mine because I am every woman's sister or potential lover. (As a lesbian I have no race, my own people disclaim me; but I am all races because there is the queer of me in all races.) I am cultureless because, as a feminist, I challenge the collective cultural/religious male-derived beliefs of Indo-Hispanics and Anglos; yet I am cultured because I am participating in the creation of yet another culture, a new story to explain the world and our participation in it, a new value system with images and symbols that connect us to each other and to the planet. *Soy un amasamiento*, I am an act of kneading, of uniting and joining that not only has produced both a creature of darkness and a creature of light, but also a creature that questions the definitions of light and dark and gives them new meanings.

We are the people who leap in the dark, we are the people on the knees of the gods. In our flesh, (r)evolution works out the clash of cultures. It makes us crazy constantly, but if the center holds, we've made some kind of evolutionary step forward. *Nuestra alma el trabajo*, the opus, the great alchemical work; spiritual *mestizaje*, a "morphogenesis,"* an inevitable unfolding. We have become the quickening serpent movement.

Indigenous like corn, like corn, the *mestiza* is a product of crossbreeding, designed for preservation under a variety of conditions. Like an ear of corn—a female seed-bearing organ—the *mestiza* is tenacious, tightly wrapped in the husks of her culture. Like kernels she clings to the cob; with thick stalks and strong brace roots, she holds tight to the earth—she will survive the crossroads.

Lavando y remojando el maíz en agua de cal, despojando el pellejo. Moliendo, mixteando, amasando, haciendo tortillas de masa.** She steeps the corn in lime, it swells, softens. With stone roller on *metate*, she grinds the corn, then grinds again. She kneads and moulds the dough, pats the round balls into *tortillas*.

---

*To borrow chemist Ilya Prigogine's theory of "dissipative structures." Prigogine discovered that substances interact not in predictable ways as it was taught in science, but in different and fluctuating ways to produce new and more complex structures, a kind of birth he called "morphogenesis," which created unpredictable innovations.[5]

***Tortillas de masa harina*: corn tortillas are of two types, the smooth uniform ones made in a tortilla press and usually bought at a tortilla factory or supermarket, and *gorditas*, made by mixing *masa* with lard or shortening or butter (my mother sometimes puts in bits of bacon or *chicharrones*).

We are the porous rock in the stone *metate*
squatting on the ground.
We are the rolling pin, *el maíz y agua,*
la masa harina. Somos el amasijo.
Somos lo molido en el metate.
We are the *comal* sizzling hot,
the hot *tortilla,* the hungry mouth.
We are the coarse rock.
We are the grinding motion,
the mixed potion, *somos el molcajete.*
We are the pestle, the *comino, ajo, pimienta,*
We are the *chile colorado,*
the green shoot that cracks the rock.
We will abide.

El camino de la mestiza/The *Mestiza* Way

Caught between the sudden contraction, the breath sucked in and the endless space, the brown woman stands still,
looks at the sky. She decides to go down, digging her way
along the roots of trees. Sifting through the bones, she
shakes them to see if there is any marrow in them. Then,
touching the dirt to her forehead, to her tongue, she takes
a few bones, leaves the rest in their burial place.

She goes through her backpack, keeps her journal and
address book, throws away the muni-bart metromaps.
The coins are heavy and they go next, then the greenbacks
flutter through the air. She keeps her knife, can opener
and eyebrow pencil. She puts bones, pieces of bark,
hierbas, eagle feather, snakeskin, tape recorder, the
rattle and drum in her pack and she sets out to become
the complete *tolteca.*

Her first step is to take inventory. *Despojando, desgranando, quitando
paja.* Just what did she inherit from her ancestors? This weight on her
back—which is the baggage from the Indian mother, which the baggage
from the Spanish father, which the baggage from the Anglo?

Pero es difícil differentiating between *lo heredado, lo adquirido, lo
impuesto.* She puts history through a sieve, winnows out the lies, looks
at the forces that we as a race, as women, have been a part of. *Luego
bota lo que no vale, los desmientos, los desencuentros, el embrutecimiento.
Aguarda el juicio, hondo y enraízado, de la gente antigua.* This step is
a conscious rupture with all oppressive traditions of all cultures and
religions. She communicates that rupture, documents the struggle. She
reinterprets history and, using new symbols, she shapes new myths. She

adopts new perspectives toward the darkskinned, women and queers. She strengthens her tolerance (and intolerance) for ambiguity. She is willing to share, to make herself vulnerable to foreign ways of seeing and thinking. She surrenders all notions of safety, of the familiar. Deconstruct, construct. She becomes a *nahual*, able to transform herself into a tree, a coyote, into another person. She learns to transform the small "I" into the total Self. *Se hace moldeadora de su alma. Según la concepción que tiene de sí misma, así será.*

Que no se nos olvide los hombres

> "Tú no sirves pa' nada—
> you're good for nothing.
> *Eres pura vieja.*"

"You're nothing but a woman" means you are defective. Its opposite is to be *un macho*. The modern meaning of the word "machismo," as well as the concept, is actually an Anglo invention. For men like my father, being "macho" meant being strong enough to protect and support my mother and us, yet being able to show love. Today's macho has doubts about his ability to feed and protect his family. His "machismo" is an adaptation to oppression and poverty and low self-esteem. It is the result of hierarchical male dominance. The Anglo, feeling inadequate and inferior and powerless, displaces or transfers these feeling to the Chicano by shaming him. In the Gringo world, the Chicano suffers from excessive humility and self-effacement, shame of self and self-deprecation. Around Latinos he suffers from a sense of language inadequacy and its accompanying discomfort; with Native Americans he suffers from a racial amnesia which ignores our common blood, and from guilt because the Spanish part of him took their land and oppressed them. He has an excessive compensatory hubris when around Mexicans from the other side. It overlays a deep sense of racial shame.

The loss of a sense of dignity and respect in the macho breeds a false machismo which leads him to put down women and even to brutalize them. Coexisting with his sexist behavior is a love for the mother which takes precedence over that of all others. Devoted son, macho pig. To wash down the shame of his acts, of his very being, and to handle the brute in the mirror, he takes to the bottle, the snort, the needle and the fist.

Though we "understand" the root causes of male hatred and fear, and the subsequent wounding of women, we do not excuse, we do not condone and we will not longer put up with it. From the men of our race, we demand the admission/acknowledgement/disclosure/testimony that they wound us, violate us, are afraid of us and of our power. We need them to say they will begin to eliminate their hurtful put-down ways. But more than the words, we demand acts. We say to them: we will develop equal power with you and those who have shamed us.

It is imperative that *mestizas* support each other in changing the sexist elements in the Mexican-Indian culture. As long as woman is put down, the Indian and the Black in all of us is put down. The struggle of the *mestiza* is above all a feminist one. As long as *los hombres* think they have to *chingar mujeres* and each other to be men, as long as men are taught that they are superior and therefore culturally favored over *la mujer*, as long as to be a *vieja* is a thing of derision, there can be no real healing of our psyches. We're halfway there—we have such love of the Mother, the good mother. The first step is to unlearn the *puta/virgen* dichotomy and to see *Coatlapopeuh—Coatlicue* in the Mother, *Guadalupe*.

Tenderness, a sign of vulnerability, is so feared that it is showered on women with verbal abuse and blows. Men, even more than women, are fettered to gender roles. Women at least have had the guts to break out of bondage. Only gay men have had the courage to expose themselves to the woman inside them and to challenge the current masculinity. I've encountered a few scattered and isolated gentle straight men, the beginnings of a new breed, but they are confused, and entangled with sexist behaviors that they have not been able to eradicate. We need a new masculinity and the new man needs a movement.

Lumping the males who deviate from the general norm with man, the oppressor, is a gross injustice. *Asombra pensar que nos hemos quedado en ese pozo oscuro donde el mundo encierra a las lesbianas. Asombra pensar que hemos, como femenistas y lesbianas, cerrado nuestros corazónes a los hombres, a nuestros hermanos los jotos, desheredados y marginales como nosotros.* Being the supreme crossers of cultures, homosexuals have strong bonds with the queer white, Black, Asian, Native American, Latino and with the queer in Italy, Australia and the rest of the planet. We come from all colors, all classes, all races, all time periods. Our role is to link people with each other—the Blacks with Jews with Indians with Asians with whites with extraterrestrials. It is to transfer ideas and information from one culture to another. Colored homosexuals have more knowledge of other cultures; have always been at the forefront (although sometimes in the closet) of all liberation struggles in this country; have suffered more injustices and have survived them despite all odds. Chicanos need to acknowledge the political and artistic contributions of their queer. People, listen to what your *jotería* is saying.

The *mestizo* and the queer exist at this time and point on the evolutionary continuum for a purpose. We are a blending that proves that all blood is intricately woven together, and that we are spawned out of similar souls.

Somos una genta

> *Hay tantísimas fronteras*
> que dividen a la gente,
> pero por cada frontera
> existe también un puente.
> —GINA VALDÉS[6]

Divided Loyalties. Many women and men of color do not want to have any dealings with white people. It takes too much time and energy to explain to the downwardly mobile, white middle-class women that it's okay for us to want to own "possesions," never having had any nice furniture on our dirt floors or "luxuries" like washing machines. Many feel that whites should help their own people rid themselves of race hatred and fear first. I, for one, choose to use some of my energy to serve as mediator. I think we need to allow whites to be our allies. Through our literature, art, *corridos* and folktales we must share our history with them so when they set up committees to help Big Mountain Navajos or the Chicano farmworkers or *los Nicaragüenses* they won't turn people away because of their racial fears and ignorances. They will come to see that they are not helping us but following our lead.

Individually, but also as a racial entity, we need to voice our needs. We need to say to white society: we need you to accept the fact that Chicanos are different, to acknowledge your rejection and negation of us. We need you to own the fact that you looked upon us as less than human, that you stole our lands, our personhood, our self-respect. We need you to make public restitution: to say that, to compensate for your own sense of defectiveness, you strive for power over us, you erase our history and our experience because it makes you feel guilty—you'd rather forget your brutish acts. To say you've split yourself from minority groups, that you disown us, that your dual consciousness splits off parts of yourself, transferring the "negative" parts onto us. (Where there is persecution of minorities, there is shadow projection. Where there is violence and war, there is repression of shadow.) To say that you are afraid of us, that to put distance between us, you wear the mask of contempt. Admit that Mexico is your double, that she exists in the shadow of this country, that we are irrevocably tied to her. Gringo, accept the doppelganger in your psyche. By taking back your collective shadow the intracultural split will heal. And finally, tell us what you need from us.

By Your True Faces We Will Know You

I am visible—see this Indian face—yet I am invisible. I both blind them with my beak nose and am their blind spot. But I exist, we exist. They'd like to think I have melted in the pot. But I haven't, we haven't.

The dominant white culture is killing us slowly with its ignorance. By taking away our self-determination, it has made us weak and empty. As a people we have resisted and we have taken expedient positions, but we have never been allowed to develop unencumbered—we have never been allowed to be fully ourselves. The whites in power want us people of color to barricade ourselves behind our separate tribal walls so they can pick us off one at a time with their hidden weapons; so they can whitewash and distort history. Ignorance splits people, creates prejudices. A misinformed people is a subjugated people.

Before the Chicano and the undocumented worker and the Mexican from the other side can come together, before the Chicano can have unity with Native Americans and other groups, we need to know the history of their struggle and they need to know ours. Our mothers, our sisters and brothers, the guys who hang out on street corners, the children in the playgrounds, each of us must know our Indian lineage, our afro-*mestisaje*, our history of resistance.

To the immigrant *mexicano* and the recent arrivals we must teach our history. The 80 million *mexicanos* and the Latinos from Central and South America must know of our struggles. Each one of us must know basic facts about Nicaragua, Chile and the rest of Latin America. The Latinoist movement (Chicanos, Puerto Ricans, Cubans and other Spanish-speaking people working together to combat racial discrimination in the market place) is good but it is not enough. Other than a common culture we will have nothing to hold us together. We need to meet on a broader communal ground.

The struggle is inner: Chicano, *indio*, American Indian, *mojado*, *mexicano*, immigrant Latino, Anglo in power, working class Anglo, Black, Asian—our psyches resemble the bordertowns and are populated by the same people. The struggle has always been inner, and is played out in the outer terrains. Awareness of our situation must come before inner changes, which in turn come before changes in society. Nothing happens in the "real" world unless it first happens in the images in our heads.

El día de la Chicana

> I will not be shamed again
> Nor will I shame myself.

I am possessed by a vision: that we Chicanas and Chicanos have taken back or uncovered our true faces, our dignity and self-respect. It's a validation vision.

Seeing the Chicana anew in light of her history. I seek an exoneration, a seeing through the fictions of white supremacy, a seeing of ourselves in our true guises and not as the false racial personality that has been given to us and that we have given to ourselves. I seek our woman's face, our true features, the positive and the negative seen clearly, free of the tainted biases of male dominance. I seek new images of identity, new beliefs about ourselves, our humanity and worth no longer in question.

Estamos viviendo en la noche de la Raza, un tiempo cuando el trabajo se hace a lo quieto, en el oscuro. El día cuando aceptamos tal y como somos y para en donde vamos y porque—ese día será el día de la Raza. Yo tengo el conpromiso de expresar mi visión, mi sensibilidad, mi percepción de la revalidación de la gente mexicana, su mérito, estimación, honra, aprecio y validez.

On December 2nd when my sun goes into my first house, I celebrate *el día de la Chicana y el Chicano*. On that day I clean my altars, light my *Coatlalopeuh* candle, burn sage and copal, take *el baño para espantar basura*, sweep my house. On that day I bare my soul, make myself vulnerable to friends and family by expressing my feelings. On that day I affirm who we are.

On that day I look inside our conflicts and our basic introverted racial temperament. I identify our needs, voice them. I acknowledge that the self and the race have been wounded. I recognize the need to take care of our personhood, of our racial self. On that day I gather the splintered and disowned parts of *la gente mexicana* and hold them in my arms. *Todas las partes de nosotros valen.*

On that day I say, "Yes, all you people wound us when you reject us. Rejection strips us of self-worth; our vulnerability exposes us to shame. It is our innate identity you find wanting. We are ashamed that we need your good opinion, that we need your acceptance. We can no longer camouflage our needs, can no longer let defenses and fences sprout around us. We can no longer withdraw. To rage and look upon you with contempt is to rage and be contemptuous of ourselves. We can no longer blame you, nor disown the white parts, the male parts, the pathological parts, the queer parts, the vulnerable parts. Here we are weaponless with open arms, with only our magic. Let's try it our way, the *mestiza* way, the Chicana way, the woman way.

On that day, I search for our essential dignity as a people, a people with a sense of purpose—to belong and contribute to something greater than our *pueblo*. On that day I seek to recover and reshape my spiritual identity. *¡Anímate! Raza, a celebrar el día de la Chicana.*

El retorno

> All movements are accomplished in six stages,
> and the seventh brings return.
>   —I CHING[7]

> *Tanto tiempo sin verte casa mía,*
> mi cuna, mi hondo nido de la huerta.
> —"SOLEDAD"[8]

I stand at the river, watch the curving, twisting serpent, a serpent nailed to the fence where the mouth of the Rio Grande empties into the Gulf.

I have come back. *Tanto dolor me costó el alejamiento.* I shade my eyes and look up. The bone beak of a hawk slowly circling over me, checking me out as potential carrion. In its wake a little bird flickering its wings, swimming sporadically like a fish. In the distance the expressway and the slough of traffic like an irritated sow. The sudden pull in my gut, *la tierra, los aguaceros.* My land, *el viento soplando la arena, el lagartijo debajo de un nopalito. Me acuerdo como era antes. Una región desértica de vasta llanuras, costeras de baja altura, de escasa lluvia, de chaparrales formados por mesquites y huizaches.* If I look real hard I can almost see the Spanish fathers who were called "the cavalry of Christ" enter this valley riding their burros, see the clash of cultures commence.

Tierra natal. This is home, the small towns in the Valley, *los pueblitos* with chicken pens and goats picketed to mesquite shrubs. *En las colonias* on the other side of the tracks, junk cars line the front yards of hot pink and lavender-trimmed houses—Chicano architecture we call it, self-consciously. I have missed the TV shows where hosts speak in half and half, and where awards are given in the category of Tex-Mex music. I have missed the Mexican cemeteries blooming with artificial flowers, the fields of aloe vera and red pepper, rows of sugar cane, of corn hanging on the stalks, the cloud of *polvareda* in the dirt roads behind a speeding truck, *el sabor de tamales de rez y venado.* I have missed *la yequa colorada* gnawing the wooden gate of her stall, the smell of horse flesh from Carito's corrals. *He hecho menos las noches calientes sin aire, noches de linternas y lechuzas* making holes in the night.

I still feel the old despair when I look at the unpainted, dilapidated, scrap lumber houses consisting mostly of corrugated aluminum. Some of the poorest people in the U.S. live in the Lower Rio Grande Valley, an arid and semi-arid land of irrigated farming, intense sunlight and heat, citrus groves next to chaparral and cactus. I walk through the elementary school I attended so long ago, that remained segregated until recently. I remember how the white teachers used to punish us for being Mexican.

How I love this tragic valley of South Texas, as Ricardo Sánchez calls it; this borderland between the Nueces and the Rio Grande. This land has survived possession and ill-use by five countries: Spain, Mexico, the

Republic of Texas, the Confederacy, and the U.S. again. It has survived Anglo-Mexican blood feuds, lynchings, burnings, rapes, pillage.

Today I see the Valley still struggling to survive. Whether it does or not, it will never be as I remember it. The borderlands depression that was set off by the 1982 peso devaluation in Mexico resulted in the closure of hundreds of Valley businesses. Many people lost their homes, cars, land. Prior to 1982, U.S. store owners thrived on retail sales to Mexicans who came across the borders for groceries and clothes and appliances. While goods on the U.S. side have become 10, 100, 1000 times more expensive for Mexican buyers, goods on the Mexican side have become 10, 100, 1000 times cheaper for Americans. Because the Valley is heavily dependent on agriculture and Mexican retail trade, it has the highest unemployment rates along the entire border region; it is the Valley that has been hardest hit.*

"It's been a bad year for corn," my brother, Nune, says. As he talks, I remember my father scanning the sky for a rain that would end the drought, looking up into the sky, day after day, while the corn withered on its stalk. My father has been dead for 29 years, having worked himself to death. The life span of a Mexican farm laborer is 56—he lived to be 38. It shocks me that I am older than he. I, too, search the sky for rain. Like the ancients, I worship the rain god and the maize goddess, but unlike my father I have recovered their names. Now for rain (irrigation) one offers not a sacrifice of blood, but of money.

"Farming is in a bad way," my brother says. "Two to three thousand small and big farmers went bankrupt in this country last year. Six years ago the price of corn was $8.00 per hundred pounds," he goes on. "This year it is $3.90 per hundred pounds." And, I think to myself, after taking inflation into account, not planting anything puts you ahead.

I walk out to the back yard, stare at *los rosales de mamá*. She wants me to help her prune the rose bushes, dig out the carpet grass that is choking them. *Mamagrande Ramona también tenía rosales*. Here every Mexican grows flowers. If they don't have a piece of dirt, they use car tires, jars, cans, shoe boxes. Roses are the Mexican's favorite flower. I think, how symbolic—thorns and all.

Yes, the Chicano and Chicana have always taken care of growing things and the land. Again I see the four of us kids getting off the school bus,

---

*Out of the twenty-two border counties in the four border states, Hidalgo County (named for Father Hidalgo who was shot in 1810 after instigating Mexico's revolt against Spanish rule under the banner of *la Virgen de Guadalupe*) is the most poverty-stricken county in the nation as well as the largest home base (along with Imperial in California) for migrant farmworkers. It was here that I was born and raised, I am amazed that both it and I have survived.

changing into our work clothes, walking into the field with Papí and Mamí, all six of us bending to the ground. Below our feet, under the earth lie the watermelon seeds. We cover them with paper plates, putting *terremotes* on top of the plates to keep them from being blown away by the wind. The paper plates keep the freeze away. Next day or the next, we remove the plates, bare the tiny green shoots to the elements. They survive and grow, give fruit hundreds of times the size of the seed. We water them and hoe them. We harvest them. The vines dry, rot, are plowed under. Growth, death, decay, birth. The soil prepared again and again, impregnated, worked on. A constant changing of forms, *renacimientos de la tierra madre*.

> This land was Mexican once
> was Indian always
> and is.
>   And will be again.

From *Borderlands/La Frontera: The New Mestiza*

Notes

1. This is my own "take-off" on Jose Vasconcelos' idea. Jose Vasconcelos, *La Raza Cósmica: Missión de la Raza Ibero-Americana* (México: Aguilar S.A. de Ediciones, 1961).

2. Vasconcelos.

3. Arthur Koestler termed this "bisociation." Albert Rothenberg, *The Creative Process in Art, Science, and Other Fields* (Chicago, IL: University of Chicago Press, 1979), 12.

4. In part, I derive my definitions for "convergent" and "divergent" thinking from Rothenberg, 12–13.

5. Harold Gilliam, "Searching for a New World View," *This World* (January, 1981), 23.

6. Gina Valdés, *Puentes y Fronteras: Coplas Chicanas* (Los Angeles, CA: Castle Lithograph, 1982), 2.

7. Richard Wilhelm, *The I Ching or Book of Changes*, trans. Cary F. Baynes (Princeton, NJ: Princeton University Press, 1950), 98.

8. *"Soledad"* is sung by the group Haciendo Punto en Otro Son.

Playfulness, "World"-Travelling, and Loving Perception

María Lugones

A paper about cross-cultural and cross-racial loving that emphasizes the need to understand and affirm the plurality in and among women as central to feminist ontology and epistemology. Love is seen not as fusion and erasure of difference but as incompatible with them. Love reveals plurality. Unity—not to be confused with solidarity—is understood as conceptually tied to domination.

This paper weaves two aspects of life together. My coming to consciousness as a daughter and my coming to consciousness as a woman of color have made this weaving possible. The weaving reveals the possibility and complexity of a pluralistic feminism, a feminism that affirms the plurality in each of us and among us as richness and as central to feminist ontology and epistemology.

The paper describes the experience of "outsiders" to the mainstream White/Anglo organization of life in the U.S, and stresses a particular feature of the outsider's existence: the acquired flexibility in shifting from the mainstream construction of life to other constructions of life where she is more or less "at home." This flexibility is necessary for the outsider but it can also be willfully exercised by those who are at ease in the mainstream. I recommend this willful exercise which I call "world"-travelling and I also recommend that the willful exercise be animated by a playful attitude.

As outsiders to the U.S. mainstream, women of color practice "world"-travelling, mostly out of necessity. I affirm this practice as a skillful, creative, rich, enriching and, given certain circumstances, as a loving way of being and living. I recognize that we do much of our travelling, in some sense against our wills, to hostile White/Anglo "worlds." The hostility of these "worlds" and the compulsory nature of the "travelling" have obscured for us the enormous value of this aspect of our living and its connection to loving. Racism has a vested interest in obscuring and devaluing the complex skills involved in this. I recommend that we affirm this travelling across "worlds" as partly constitutive of cross-cultural and cross-racial loving. Thus I recommend to women of color in the U.S. to learn to love each other by travelling to each other's "worlds."

On the other hand, the paper makes a connection between what Marilyn Frye has named "arrogant perception" and the failure to identify with persons that one views arrogantly or has come to see as the products of

arrogant perception. A further connection is made between this failure
of identification and a failure to love. Love is not used in the sense Frye
has identified as consistent with arrogant perception and as promoting
unconditional servitude. "We can be taken in by this equation of servitude
with love," Frye says, "because we make two mistakes at once: we think,
of both servitude and love that they are selfless or unselfish."[1] Rather,
the identification of which I speak is constituted by what I come to
characterize as playful "world"-travelling. To the extent that we learn to
perceive others arrogantly or come to see them only as products of
arrogant perception and continue to perceive them that way, we fail to
identify with them—fail to love them—in this particularly deep way.

Identification and Love

As a child, I was taught to perceive arrogantly. I have also been the object
of arrogant perception. Though I am not a White/Anglo woman, it is clear
to me that I had early training in arrogant perception. I was brought up
in Argentina watching men and women of moderate and of considerable
means graft the substance[2] of their servants to themselves. I also learned
to graft my mother's substance to my own. It was clear to me that both
men and women were the victims of arrogant perception and that
arrogant perception was systematically organized to break the spirit of
all women and of most men. I valued my rural 'gaucho' ancestry because
its ethos has always been one of independence in poverty through
enormous loneliness, courage and self-reliance. I found inspiration in this
ethos and made a commitment not to be broken by arrogant perception.
I can say this only because I have learned from Frye's "In and Out of
Harm's Way: Arrogance and Love." She has given me a way of understanding and articulating something important in my own life.

Frye is not particularly concerned with women as arrogant perceivers
but as the objects of arrogant perception. Her focus is, in part, on
enhancing our understanding of women "untouched by phallocratic
machinations."[3] She proposes an understanding of what it is to love
women inspired by a vision of women unharmed by arrogant perception.
To love women is, at least in part, to perceive them with loving eyes. "The
loving eye is a contrary of the arrogant eye."[4]

I am concerned with women as arrogant perceivers because I want to
explore further what it is to love women. I want to explore two failures
of love: my failure to love my mother and White/Anglo women's failure
to love women across racial and cultural boundaries in the U.S. As a
consequence of exploring these failures I will offer a loving solution to
them. My solution modifies Frye's account of loving perception by adding
what I call playful "world"-travel.

It is clear to me that at least in the U.S. and Argentina women are
taught to perceive many other women arrogantly. Being taught to

perceive arrogantly is part of being taught to be a woman of a certain class in both countries. It is part of being taught to be a White/Anglo woman in the U.S. and it is part of being taught to be a woman in both places: to be both the agent and the object of arrogant perception. My love for my mother seemed to me thoroughly imperfect as I was growing up because I was unwilling to become what I had been taught to see my mother as being. I thought that to love her was consistent with my abusing her (using, taking for granted, and demanding her services in a far-reaching way that, since four other people engaged in the same grafting of her substance onto themselves, left her little of herself for herself) and was to be in part constituted by my identifying with her, my seeing myself in her: to love her was supposed to be of a piece with both my abusing her and with my being open to being abused. It is clear to me that I was not supposed to love servants: I could abuse them without identifying with them, without seeing myself in them. When I came to the U.S. I learned that part of racism is the internalization of the propriety of abuse without identification: I learned that I could be seen as a being to be used by White/Anglo men and women without the possibility of identification, i.e. without their act of attempting to graft my substance onto theirs, rubbing off on them at all. They could remain untouched, without any sense of loss.

So, women who are perceived arrogantly can perceive other women arrogantly in their turn. To what extent those women are responsible for their arrogant perceptions of other women is certainly open to question, but I do not have any doubt that many women have been taught to abuse women in this particular way. I am not interested in assigning responsibility. I am interested in understanding the phenomenon so as to find a loving way out of it.

There is something obviously wrong with the way I was taught to love and something right with my failure to love my mother in this way. There is something wrong with my being taught to practice enslavement of my mother and to learn to become a slave through this practice. There is something wrong with my having been taught that love is consistent with abuse, consistent with arrogant perception. But I do not think that what is wrong is my profound desire to identify with her, to see myself in her.

The love I was taught is the love that Frye speaks of when she says "We can be taken in by this equation of servitude with love."[5] Even though I could both abuse and love my mother, I was not supposed to love servants. This is because in the case of servants one is and is supposed to be clear about their servitude and the "equation of servitude with love" is never to be thought clearly in those terms. But I could love my mother because deception is part of this "loving." Servitude is called abnegation and abnegation is not analyzed any further. Abnegation is not instilled in us through an analysis of its nature but rather through a heralding of it as beautiful and noble. We are coaxed, seduced into abnegation not through analysis but through emotive persuasion. When I say that there is something obviously wrong with the loving that I was taught, I do not mean to say that the connection between loving and abuse is obvious. Rather this connection has to be unveiled. Once it is unveiled, what is obvious is that there is something wrong with the loving.

I did not learn my lessons about loving well. This failure necessitated a separation from my mother: I saw us as beings of quite a different sort. I abandoned my mother while I longed to love her, though, given what I was taught, "love" could not be the right word for what I longed for.

I was disturbed by my not wanting to be what she was. I had a sense of not being quite integrated, my self was missing because I could not identify with her, I could not see myself in her, I could not welcome her world. I saw myself as separate from her, a different sort of being, not quite of the same species. This separation, this lack of love, I saw as a lack in myself, not a fault, but a lack. *Love has to be rethought, made anew.*

There is something similar between my relation to my mother as someone I was not able to love and the relation between women of color in the U.S. and White/Anglo women: there is a failure of love. I want to note here that Frye has helped me understand one of the aspects of this failure, the directly abusive aspect. I think part of the failure of love includes the failure to identify with another woman, the failure to see oneself in other women who are quite different from oneself.

Frye's emphasis on independence in her analysis of loving perception is not particularly helpful in explaining this failure of love. She says that in loving perception, "the object of the seeing is another being whose existence and character are logically independent of the seer and who may be practically or empirically independent in any particular respect at any particular time."[6] But this is not helpful, for example, in allowing me to understand how my failure of love toward my mother (when I ceased to be her parasite) left me not quite whole. It is not helpful since I saw her as logically independent from me. Neither does Frye's emphasis on independence help me understand why the racist or ethnocentric failure of love of White/Anglo women should leave me not quite real among them.

I am not particularly interested in cases of White/Anglo women's parasitism onto women of color but more pointedly in cases where the failure of identification is the central feature of the "relation." I am particularly interested in those cases in which White/Anglo women behave in one or more of the following ways towards women of color: they ignore, ostracize, stereotype, classify us as crazy and render us invisible. This behavior is exhibited *while we are in their midst.* Frye's emphasis on independence as key to loving is unhelpful because the more independent I am, the more independent I am left to be, the more alone I am left to be. Their world and their integrity have no use for me. Yet they rob me of my solidity through indifference, an indifference they can afford and which often seems studied. This points toward separatism in communities where our substance is seen and celebrated; where we become substantive, solid, real through this celebration. But many of us have to work among White/Anglos and our best shot at recognition has seemed to be among White/Anglo women because many of them have expressed a *general* sense of being pained at their failure of love.

Many times White/Anglo women seem to want women of color out of their field of vision. Their lack of concern is a harmful failure of love that leaves me independent from them in the same way that my mother became independent from me once I ceased to be her parasite. But of course, because my mother and I wanted to love each other well, we were not whole in this independence. White/Anglo women are independent from me, I am independent from them, I am independent from my mother, she is independent from me, and we cannot love each other in this independence.

I am incomplete and unreal without other women. I am profoundly dependent on others without having to be their subordinate, their slave, their servant.

Since I am emphasizing here that the failure of love lies in part in the failure to identify, and since I agree with Frye that in perceiving others lovingly one "must consult something other than one's own will and interests and fears and imagination,"[7] I will proceed to explain what I think needs to be consulted. Loving my mother was not possible for me so long as I retained a sense that it was fine to see her through arrogant eyes. Loving my mother also required that I see with her eyes, that I go into my mother's world, that I see both of us as we are constructed in her world, that I witness her own sense of herself from within her world. Only through this travelling to her "world" could I identify with her because only then could I cease to ignore her and to be excluded and separate from her. Only then could I see her as a subject even if one subjected and only then could I see how meaning could arise fully between us. We are fully dependent on each other for the possibility of being understood without which we are not intelligible, we do not make sense, we are not solid, visible, integrated; we are lacking. Travelling to each other's "worlds" enables us to *be* through *loving* each other.

I will lead you to see what I mean by a "world" in the way I proposed the concept to myself: through the kind of ontological confusion that we, women of color, refer to half-jokingly as "schizophrenia" and through my effort to make sense of this ontological confusion.

"Worlds" and "world"-travelling

Some time ago I was in a state of profound confusion as I experienced myself as both having and not having a character trait: the trait is playfulness. I experienced myself both as a playful person and as a person who is not playful, a person who would be acting out of character if she were to express playfulness. At first I thought that the "multiple personality" problem could be explained away by lack of ease. Maybe my playfulness is very difficult to express or enact in certain worlds. So, it may be that in those worlds I lack the trait. But, of course, I need to explain what "world" means if that explanation is to be serviceable to me in my confusion as to who I am characterwise.

I can explain some of what I mean by a "world." I do not want the fixity of a definition because I think the term is suggestive and I do not want to lose this. A "world" has to be presently inhabited by flesh and blood people. That is why it cannot be a utopia. It may also be inhabited by some imaginary people. It may be inhabited by people who are dead or people that the inhabitants of this "world" met in some other "world" and now have in this "world" in imagination.

A "world" need not be a construction of a whole society. It may be a construction of a tiny portion of a particular society. It may be inhabited by just a few people. Some "worlds" are bigger than others.

A "world" may be incomplete in that things in it may not be altogether constructed or some things may be constructed negatively (they are not what 'they' are in some other "world"). Or the "world" may be incomplete because it may have references to things that do not quite exist in it, references to things like Brazil. Given lesbian feminism, the construction of 'lesbian' in 'lesbian community' (a "world" in my sense) is purposefully and healthily still up in the air, in the process of becoming. To be Hispanic in this country is, in a dominant Anglo construction purposefully incomplete. Thus one cannot really answer questions like "What is a Hispanic?" "Who counts as a Hispanic?" "Are Latinos, Chicanos, Hispanos, black dominicans, white cubans, korean-colombians, italian-argentinians Hispanic?" What it means to be a 'Hispanic' in the varied so-called Hispanic communities in the U.S. is also up in the air. We have not yet decided whether there are any 'Hispanics' in our varied "worlds."

So a "world" may be an incomplete visionary non-utopian construction of life or it may be a traditional construction of life. A traditional Hispano construction of Northern New Mexican life is a "world." Such a traditional construction, in the face of a racist, ethnocentric, money-centered anglo construction of Northern New Mexican life, is highly unstable because Anglos have the means for imperialist destruction of traditional Hispano "worlds."

Some of the inhabitants of a "world" may not understand or accept the way in which they are constructed in it. So, for example, a recent Latin-American immigrant may not understand how she is constructed in White/Anglo "worlds." So, there may be "worlds" that construct me in ways that I do not even understand or I may not accept the construction as an account of myself, a construction of myself. And yet, I may be *animating* such a construction, even though I may not intend my moves, gestures, acts in that way.

One can "travel" between these "worlds" and one can inhabit more than one of these "worlds" at the very same time. I think that most of us who are outside the mainstream U.S. construction or organization of life are "world-travellers" as a matter of necessity and of survival. It seems to me that inhabiting more than one "world" at the same time and "travelling" between "worlds" is part and parcel of our experience and our situation. One can be at the same time in a "world" that constructs one as stereotypically latin, for example, and in a "world" that constructs one as latin. Being sterotypically latin and being simply latin are different simultaneous constructions of persons that are part of different "worlds." One animates one or the other or both at the same time without necessarily confusing them, though simultaneous enactment can be confusing to oneself.

In describing a "world" I mean to be offering a description of experience, something that is true to experience even if if is ontologically problematic. Though I would think that any account of identity that could not be true to this experience of outsiders to the mainstream would be faulty even if ontologically unproblematic. Its ease would constrain, erase, or deem aberrant experience that has within it significant insights into non-imperialistic understanding between people.

Those of us who are "world"-travellers have the distinct experience of being different in different "worlds" and ourselves in them. We can say "That's me there, and I am happy in that 'world'." The experience is one of having memory of oneself as different without any underlying "I." So, I can say "That's me in there and I am so playful in that 'world'." I say "That's *me* in that 'world'" *not* because I recognize myself in that person. Rather that person may be very different from myself in this "world" and yet I can say *without inference* "That's me." I may well recognize that that person has abilities that I do not have and yet the having or not having of the abilities is always an "I have..." and "I do not have...," i.e., it is always experienced in the first person.

The shift from being one person to being a different person is what I call "travel." This shift may not be willful or even conscious, and one may be completely unaware of being different than one is in a different "world." Even though the shift can be done willfully, it is not a matter of acting. One does not pose as someone else, one does not pretend to be, for example, someone of a different personality or character or someone who uses space or language differently than the other person. Rather one *is* someone who has that personality or character or uses space and language in that particular way.

Being at ease in a "world"

In investigating what I mean by "being at ease in a 'world,'" I will describe different ways of being at ease. One may be at ease in one or in all of these ways. A maximal way of being at ease, being at ease in all of these ways, is somewhat dangerous because people who are at ease in this way tend not to have any inclination to travel across "worlds" or tend not to have any experience of "world" travelling.

The first way of being at ease in a particular "world" is by being a fluent speaker in that "world." I know all the norms that there are to be followed, I know all the words that there are to be spoken. I know all the moves. I am confident.

Another way of being at ease is by being normatively happy. I agree with all the norms, I could not like any norms better. I am asked to do just what I want to do or what I think I should do. At ease.

Another way of being at ease in a "world" is by being humanly bonded. I am with those I love and they love me too. It should be noticed that I may be with those I love and be at ease because of them in a "world" that is otherwise as hostile to me as "worlds" can get.

Finally one may be at ease because one has a shared history that one sees exemplified by the response to the question "Do you remember poodle skirts?" There you are, with people you do not know at all. The question is posed and then they all begin talking about their poodle skirt stories. I have been in such situations without knowing what poodle skirts, for example, were and I felt so ill at ease because it was not *my* history. The other people did not particularly know each other. It is not that they were humanly bonded. Probably they did not have much politically in common either. But poodle skirts were in their shared history.

Given the clarification of what I mean by a "world," "world"-travel, and being at ease in a "world," we are in a position to return to my problematic attribute, playfulness. It may be that in this "world" in which I am so unplayful I am a different person than in the "world" in which I am playful. Or it may be that the "world" in which I am unplayful is constructed in such a way that I could be playful in it. I could practice, even though that "world" is constructed in such a way that my being playful in it is hard.

My description of what I mean by a "world" favors the first possibility as the one that is truest to the experience of "outsiders" to the mainstream. But that description also makes this possibility problematic because the "I" is identified in some sense as one and in some sense as plural (I am one and many at the same time). I identify myself as myself through memory and retain myself as different in memory. I can be in a particular "world" and have a double image of myself as, for example, playful and unplayful. This is a very familiar and recognizable phenomenon to the outsider to the mainstream in some *central* cases:

when in one "world" I animate, for example, that "world's" caricature or stereotype of the person I am in the other "world." I can have both images of myself, and to the extent that I can materialize or animate both images at the same time, I become an ambiguous being. This is very much a part of trickery and foolery. It is worth remembering that the trickster and the fool are significant characters in many non-dominant or outsiders' cultures.

As one sees any particular "world" with these double edges and sees absurdity in them, one animates the person one is in that world differently. Given that latins are constructed in Anglo "worlds" as sterotypically intense and given that many latins, myself included, are genuinely intense, I can say to myself "I am intense" and take a hold of the double meaning. Furthermore, I can be stereotypically intense or be the real thing and, if you are Anglo, you do not know when I am which *because* I am Latin-American. As Latin-American I am an ambiguous being, a two-imaged self: I can see that gringos see me as stereotypically intense because I am, as a Latin-American, constructed that way in their "world." I may or may not *intentionally* animate the stereotype or the real thing knowing that you may not see it in anything other than in the stereotypical construction. This ambiguity is not just funny, it is survival-rich. We can also make a funny picture of those who dominate us precisely because we can see the double edges, we can see *them* doubly constructed, we can see the plurality in us and in them. So we know truths that only the fool can speak and only the trickster can play out without harm. We inhabit "worlds" and travel across them and keep all the memories.

Sometimes the "world"-traveller has a double image of herself and each self includes as important ingredients of itself one or more attributes of the other self: for example being playful and being unplayful. To the extent that an attribute is personality or character central, the "world" in which she has that attribute would have to be changed if she is to cease to have it. For example, the "world" in which I am unplayful would have to be changed for me to be playful in it. It is not as if, if I were to be at ease in that "world," I would be my own playful self. Because the attribute is personality central and there is such a good fit between the "world" in which I am unplayful and my being constructed unplayful in it, I cannot become playful, *I am unplayful* in that "world." To become playful would be for me to become a contradictory being. So, lack of ease cannot be a solution for my problematic case. My problem is not one of lack of ease.

I am suggesting that I can understand my confusion about whether I am or am not playful by saying that I am both and that I am different persons in different "worlds" and can remember myself in both as I am in the other. I am a plurality of selves. This is to understand my confusion because *it is to come to see it as of a piece* with much of the rest of my experience as an outsider in some of the "worlds" that I inhabit and of a piece with significant aspects of the experience of non-dominant people in the "worlds" of their dominators.

So, though I may not be at ease in the "worlds" in which I am not constructed playful, it is not that I am not playful *because* I am not at ease. The two are compatible. But lack of playfulness is not caused by lack of ease but lack of health. I am not a healthy being in the "worlds" that construct me as unplayful.

Playfulness

I had a very personal stake in investigating this topic. Playfulness is not only the attribute that was the source of my confusion and the attitude that I recommend as the loving attitude in travelling across "worlds" but also what I am scared to do without—ending up a serious human being, someone with no multi-dimensionality, with no fun in life, someone who has had the fun constructed out of her. I am seriously scared of getting stuck in a "world" that constructs me that way. A "world" that I have no escape from and in which I cannot be playful.

I thought about what it is to be playful and what it is to play and I did this thinking in a "world" in which I only remember myself as playful and in which all of those who know me as playful are imaginary beings. A "world" in which I am scared of losing my memories of myself as playful or have them erased from me. Because I live in such a "world," after I formulated my own sense of what it is to be playful and to play I decided that I needed to see what other people had said about play and playfulness. I read two classics on the subject: Johan Huizinga's *Homo Ludens*[8] and Hans-Georg Gadamer's chapter on the concept of play in his *Truth and Method*.[9] I discovered, to my amazement, that what I thought about play and playfulness was in contradiction with their accounts. Though I will not provide the arguments for this interpretation of Gadamer and Huizinga here, I understood that both of them have an agonistic sense of 'play.' Play and playfulness have, ultimately, to do with contest, with winning, losing, battling. The sense of playfulness that I have in mind has nothing to do with those things. So, I tried to elucidate both senses of play and playfulness by contrasting them to each other. The contrast helped me see the attitude that I have in mind as the loving attitude in travelling across "worlds" more clearly.

An agonistic sense of playfulness is one in which *competence* is supreme. You'd better know the rules of the game. In agonistic play, contest, competition, there is risk, there is *uncertainty*, but the uncertainty is about who is going to win and who is going to lose. There are rules that inspire hostility. The attitude of *playfulness is conceived as secondary to or derivative from play*. Since play is agon, contest, then the only conceivable playful attitude is an agonistic, combative, competitive one. One of the paradigmatic ways of playing for both Gadamer and Huizinga is role-playing. In role-playing, the person who is participating in the game has a *fixed conception of him or herself*. I also think that the players are imbued with *self-importance* in agonistic play since they are so keen on winning given their own merits, their very own competence.

When considering the value of "world"-travelling and whether playfulness is the loving attitude to have while travelling, I recognized the agonistic attitude as inimical to travelling across "worlds." The agonistic traveller is a conqueror, an imperialist. Given the agonistic attitude one *cannot* travel across "worlds," though can kill other "worlds" with it. So for people who are interested in crossing racial and ethnic boundaries, an arrogant western man's construction of playfulness is deadly. One needs to give such an attitude up if one wants to travel. Huizinga in his classic book on play, interprets Western civilization as play. That is an interesting thing for Third World people to think about. Western civilization has been interpreted by a white western man as play in the agonistic sense of play: he reviews western law, art, and many other aspects of western culture and sees agon, contest, in all of them.

So then, what is the loving playfulness that I have in mind? Let me begin with one example: We are by the river bank. The river is very, very low. Almost dry. Bits of water here and there. Little pools with a few trout hiding under the rocks. But mostly wet stones, grey on the outside. We walk on the stones for awhile, You pick up a stone and crash it onto the others. As it breaks, it is quite wet inside and it is very colorful, very pretty. I pick up a stone and break it and run toward the pieces to see the colors. They are beautiful. I laugh and bring the pieces back to you and you are doing the same with your pieces. We keep on crashing stones for hours, anxious to see the beautiful new colors. We are playing. The playfulness of our activity does not presuppose that there is something like "crashing stones" that is a particular form of play with its own rules. Rather *the attitude that carries us through the activity, a playful attitude, turns the activity into play*. Our activity has no rules, though it is certainly intentional activity and we both understand what we are doing. The playfulness that gives meaning to our activity includes uncertainty, but in this case the uncertainty is an *openness to surprise*. This is a particular metaphysical attitude that does not expect the world to be neatly packaged, ruly. Rules may fail to explain what we are doing. We are not self-important, we are not fixed in particular constructions of ourselves, which is part of saying that we are *open to self-construction*. We may not have rules, and when we do have rules, *there are no rules that are to us sacred*. We are not worried about competence. We are not wedded to a particular way of doing things. While playful we have not abandoned ourselves to, nor are we stuck in, any particular "world," We are *there creatively*. We are not passive.

Playfulness is, in part, an openness to being a fool, which is a combination of not worrying about competence, not being self-important, not taking norms as sacred and finding ambiguity and double edges a source of wisdom and delight.

So, positively, the playful attitude involves openness to surprise, openness to being a fool, openness to self-construction or reconstruction and to construction or reconstruction of the "worlds" we inhabit playfully. Negatively, playfulness is characterized by uncertainty, lack of self-importance, absence of rules or a not taking rules as sacred, a not worrying about competence and a lack of abandonment or resignation to a particular construction of oneself, others, and one's relation to them. In attempting to take hold of oneself and of one's relation to others in a particular "world," one may study, examine and come to understand oneself. One may then see what the possibilities for play are for the being one is in that "world," one may study, examine and come to understand oneself. One may then see what the possibilities for play are for the being one is in that "world." One may even decide to inhabit that self fully in order to understand it better and find its creative possibilities. All of this is just self-reflection and it is quite different from resigning or abandoning oneself to the particular construction of oneself that one is attempting to take a hold of.

Conclusion

There are "worlds" we enter at our own risk, "worlds" that have agon, conquest, and arrogance as the main ingredients in their ethos. These are "worlds" that we enter out of necessity and which would be foolish to enter playfully.

But there are "worlds" that we can travel to lovingly and travelling to them is part of loving at least some of their inhabitants. The reason why I think that travelling to someone's "world" is a way of identifying with them is because by travelling to their "world" we can understand *what it is to be them and what it is to be ourselves in their eyes*. Only when we have travelled to each other's "worlds" are we fully subjects to each other.*

Knowing other women's "worlds" is part of knowing them and knowing them is part of loving them. The knowing can be done in greater or lesser depth, as can the loving. Travelling to another's "world" is not the same as becoming intimate with them. Intimacy is constituted in part by a very deep knowledge of the other self and "world"-travelling is only part of this knowledge. Some people, in particular those who are outsiders to the mainstream, can be known only to the extent that they are known in several "worlds" and as "world"-travellers.

---

*I agree with Hegel that self-recognition requires other subjects, but I disagree with his claim that it requires tension or hostility.

Without knowing the other's "world," one does not know the other, and without knowing the other one is really alone in the other's presence because the other is only dimly present to one.

Through travelling to other people's "worlds" we discover that there are "worlds" in which those who are the victims of arrogant perception are really subjects, lively beings, resistors, constructors of visions even though in the mainstream construction they are animated only by the arrogant perceiver and are pliable, foldable, file-awayable, classifiable. My mother was apparent to me mostly as a victim of arrogant perception. I was loyal to the arrogant perceiver's construction of her and thus disloyal to her in assuming that she was exhausted by that construction. I was unwilling to be like her and thought that identifying with her, seeing myself in her necessitated that I become like her. I was wrong. I came to realize through travelling to her "world" that she is not foldable and pliable, that she is not exhausted by the mainstream argentinian partriarchal construction of her. I came to realize that there are "worlds" in which she shines as a creative being. Seeing myself in her through travelling in her "world" has meant seeing how different from her I am in her "world." This is the form of identification that I consider incompatible with arrogant perception and constitutive of a new understanding of love.

From *Hypatia: A Journal of Feminist Philosophy* 2:2

Notes

1. Marilyn Frye, *The Politics of Reality: Essays in Feminist Theory* (Trumansburg, N.Y.: Crossing Press, 1983), 73.

2. Grafting the substance of another to oneself is partly constitutive of arrogant perception. See Frye, 66.

3. Frye, 53.

4. Frye, 75.

5. Frye, 73.

6. Frye, 77.

7. Frye, 75.

8. Johan Huizinga, *Homo Ludens* (Buenos Aires, Argentina: Emece Editores, 1968).

9. Hans-George Gadamer, *Truth and Method* (New York: Seabury Press, 1975).

About the Contributors

OPAL PALMER ADISA, Jamaican-born writer, is currently pursuing a doctorate degree in Ethnic Studies and English at UC Berkeley. Her published works are *traveling women*, a poetry collection with Devorah Major (Jukebox Press, 1989); *Bake-Face and Other Guava Stories* (Kelsey St. Press, 1986); and *Piña, The Many-Eyed Fruit* (Julian Richardson Associates, 1985).

NORMA ALARCON is an Assistant Professor of Chicano/Ethnic Studies at UC Berkeley. She is the editor and publisher of Third Woman Press, has published essays on the literature of Chicanas and has translated into Spanish *This Bridge Called My Back*.

PAULA GUNN ALLEN (Laguna/Sioux/Lebanese), born on the Cubero land grant in New Mexico, is a poet, writer and crictic. Her published works include *The Sacred Hoop: Recovering the Feminine in American Indian Traditions* (1986) and the edited collection *Studies in American Indian Literature: Critical Essays and Course Designs* (1983).

SIU WAI ANDERSON was born in Hong Kong in 1958 and grew up with a white family in many parts of the U.S. Publications include book reviews in *Sojourner* and the *Asian American Resource Workshop Newsletter*, and a short story in *The Forbidden Stitch: An Asian American Women's Anthology* (Calyx Press, 1989).

JUDITH FRANCISCA BACA is a native Angeleno, a visual artist, an arts activist, a community leader and a professor of visual arts. Currently, Ms. Baca is working on the *World Wall: A Vision of the Future Without Fear*; this 210-foot mural in seven parts addresses contemporary global issues: war, peace, cooperation, interdependence and spiritual growth.

BETH BRANT is a Bay of Quinte Mohawk from Theyindenaga Mohawk Territory in Ontario, Canada. She is the editor of *A Gathering of Spirit*, a collection by North American Indian women (Firebrand Books and The Women's Press) and is the author of *Mohawk Trail* (Firebrand Books).

ANNE MI OK BRUINING was born in Seoul, Korea and was adopted by a white U.S. family in 1966 at the age of five. A consultant and lecturer, she has published articles on racism and the international adoption industry, and is working on a book about the social, political, economic, racist and cultural implications of Korean adoptions in the U.S.

ANDREA R. CANAAN is a Black Southern Lesbian feminist, mother and writer. Originally from Louisiana, she currently lives in San Francisco.

LYNN WEBER CANNON is Professor of Sociology and Director of the Center for Research on Women at Memphis State University. She is the co-author (with Reeve Vannerman) of *The American Perception of Class* (Temple University Press, 1987).

LORNA DEE CERVANTES is currently a Ph.D. student in History of Consciousness at UC Santa Cruz and a creative writing teacher in Boulder, Colorado. Born in 1954 in San Francisco, her work has appeared in such publications as *Latin American Review*, *Revista Chicano-Riqueña* and the anthology *The Third Woman*.

SUCHENG CHAN is Professor of History and Chair of Asian American Studies at UC Santa Barbara. She received her Ph.D. from UC Berkeley where she taught for ten years and won a distinguished teaching award. She is the author of *This Bittersweet Soil: The Chinese in California Agriculture, 1869-1910* and six other books.

BARBARA CHRISTIAN is Full Professor of Afro-American Studies at UC Berkeley. She is the author of *Black Women Novelists: The Development of A Tradition, 1892-1976* (Greenwood Press, 1980); *Teaching Guide to Black Foremothers* (Feminist Press, 1980); *Black Feminist Criticism: Perspectives on Black Women Writers* (Pergamon Press, 1985); and an editor at *Feminist Studies* and *Black American Literature Forum*.

CHRYSTOS, of Menominee and Alsace-Lorraine/Lithuanian heritage, is a political activist for land and treaty rights, the release of Leonard Peltier and lesbian issues. She is the author of *Not Vanishing* (Press Gang, 1988), the winner of a 1990 NEA fellowship for literature, and has been published in many anthologies.

SANDRA CISNEROS is a migrant professor and permanent transient orignally from Chicago. She has won several writing awards including two NEA fellowships in Poetry (1982) and Fiction (1988). Her forthcoming collection of short stories will be published by Random House.

MICHELLE CLIFF is the author of several books; the most recent is a collection of short stories entitled *Bodies of Water*.

NORA COBB grew up in Honolulu, Hawaii, and is currently studying American Literature at UC Santa Cruz. She would like to return to Hawaii to teach at the university, to give something back to the Islands.

JUDITH ORTIZ COFER was born in Puerto Rico in 1952, moving as a child with her family to New Jersey. She is the author of *Terms of Survival*, poetry; *Line of the Sun*, a novel; and *Silent Dancing: A Partial Remembrance of a Puerto Rican Childhood*, personal essays. She is an NEA fellow and a Working Scholar at the Bread Loaf Writers' Conference. She lives in Georgia.

ELENA TAJIMA CREEF is a half-Japanese Gemini feminist Ph.D. candidate in History of Consciousness at UC Santa Cruz who is interested in unpopular culture, World War II, Asian American women's history and literature, Russian Blue cats, crested canaries and creative writing.

JULIA DE BURGOS (1914-1958) grew up without formal education in the Puerto Rican Carolina farmlands. She wrote newspaper articles advocating Puerto Rican independence and defending workers, women and blacks. She published two collections of poems, *Poema en siete surcos* (1938) and *Canción de la verdad* (1939). From 1942 to her death she led a miserable life in New York City. Her posthumous *Obra poética* contains all her poetry.

BONNIE THORNTON DILL was Founding Director of the Center for Research on Women at Memphis State University from 1982 until 1988. Currently, she is Research Professor at the Center and Associate Professor of Sociology, and is completing a book on women of color in the U.S. with Maxine Baca Zinn.

EDNA ESCAMILL lives in the Santa Cruz area where she is a social worker with the primarily Chicano/Mexican community in Watsonville. Her upcoming novel *Daughter of the Mountain* will be published by the Aunt Lute Foundation, and she is at work on a play.

GISELE FONG is a third generation Chinese American student activist born in San Francisco and raised on rice. Her goal is to research and teach in Asian American and Ethnic Studies in order to empower people of color as well as provide all people with a more complete sense of history and the present.

JEWELLE L. GOMEZ is a critic, poet and fiction writer. Her work has appeared in the *New York Times*, the *Village Voice*, *The Women's Review of Books*, *The Nation*, and *Black Scholar*. She is the author of two collections of poetry, the most recent *Flamingoes and Bears*, and a forthcoming novel, *The Gilda Stories* (Firebrand Books, 1991).

JANICE GOULD is a mixed-blood Maidu writer, student and musician who lives in Albuquerque, New Mexico. She won an NEA fellowship in 1989 for poetry, and awaits publication of her book *Beneath My Heart* by Firebrand Books.

JOY HARJO was born in Tulsa, Oklahoma in 1951, a member of the Creek tribe. She is the author of four books of poetry, the most recent *In Mad Love and War* (Wesleyan Press, 1990). She is currently an Associate Professor of English at the University of Arizona at Tucson.

VIRGINIA R. HARRIS is an African American writer, healer, facilitator, mediator and lecturer who works with individuals and groups in transition. She has published essays and short stories in *Broomstick*, *Common Lives/Lesbian Lives*, *Feminary*, *Plexus* and *Lesbian Contradiction*. She is presently working on a novel.

ELIZABETH HIGGINBOTHAM is an Associate Professor of Sociology and on the research faculty of the Center for Research on Women at Memphis State University. She has several publications on Afro-American women and is currently completing *Too Much To Ask: The Costs of Black Female Success*.

BELL HOOKS is a writer and teacher who speaks widely on issues of race, class and gender. Her books include *Ain't I A Woman: Black Women and Feminism*, and *Feminist Theory: From Margin to Center*. Her column "Sisters of the Yam" appears monthly in *Zeta* magazine.

CANÉLA JARAMILLO, a Chicana feminist from San Diego, now teaches at the University of Colorado, Boulder, where she has developed a pilot program in multicultural writing. She writes fiction, poetry, plays and criticism. Her most recent work appears in *Multiethnic Literature of the United States*, edited by Cordelia Candelaria.

JUNE JORDAN was born in Harlem and raised in Bedford-Stuyvesant. She is the author of over fifteen books, a political activist and teacher at UC Berkeley. Her most recent book of poems is *Naming Our Destiny* (Thunder's Mouth Press, 1989).

ROSEMARY CHO LEYSON is an immigrant from the Philippines and Korea, now living in San Francisco. She is proud to be a union carpenter and she thanks her buddies for their friendship and understanding.

AUDRE LORDE, Black, Lesbian, mother and cancer survivor, was born in New York City in 1934. She is the author of more than twelve books, both non-fiction and poetry. For many years she has taught English at Hunter College in New York.

MARÍA C. LUGONES is an Argentinian philosopher, grassroots educator and organizer who considers New Mexico her adoptive home. María has lived in the USA since 1967. She is elaborating a feminist theory that she calls pluralist feminism that honors women's many voices, many selves.

LYNDA MARÍN was born in 1947 and grew up in numerous households, mostly on the West Coast. For the last nineteen years she has taught writing and literature in junior high, high school and college. She currently lives with her family and is doing graduate work in feminist theory, pedagogy and literature at UC Santa Cruz.

TRINH T. MINH-HA, Associate Professor of Cinema at San Francisco State University, is a writer, filmmaker and composer. Her works include the books *Un Art sans oeuvre*, *En miniscules* (poetry) and *African Spaces: Designs for Living in Upper Volta* (a collaboration with Jean-Paul Bourdier), and the films *Reassemblage*; *Naked Spaces— Living Is Round*; and *Surname Viet Given Name Nam*.

JANICE MIRIKITANI, a Sansei who lives and works in San Francisco, is a poet, choreographer, editor and community activist. She has authored two books of poetry and prose: *Shedding Silence* (Celestial Arts, 1987) and *Awake In the River* (Isthmus Press, 1978). She has edited several anthologies and been published extensively in numerous magazines and journals.

PAPUSA MOLINA is a Mexican living in Iowa City where the landscape has started to look familiar but she still cannot find the ocean. Her work with the Women Against Racism Committee has informed her life in the U.S. Her friends and *compañeras* in the struggle have provided her with reasons to stay. She still believes that a radical change is possible.

PAT MORA, a Latina, is a native of El Paso, Texas now living in Cincinnati, Ohio. Her two poetry collections, *Chants* and *Borders*, were published by Arte Público Press. Pat has completed a third collection, *Journeys*. She also writes essays and children's books.

CHERRÍE MORAGA, born in California, is a poet, playwright and editor. She co-edited *This Bridge Called My Back* (1981) and *Cuentos: Stories by Latinas* (1983). Her own works include *Loving in the War Years: Lo que nunca pasó por sus labios* (1983) and *Giving Up the Ghost* (1986). She teaches Chicana/o Studies at UC Berkeley.

CARMEN MORONES lives in Santa Cruz with her husband, Andrew Baum, who assisted her with this story on the word processor. She is currently at work on a manuscript of short stories.

LAURA MUNTER-ORABONA, Puerto Rican/Swedish, was born in Puerto Rico and moved to Michigan at two years old. She is beginning to write again at 37, and is trying to heal the bi-racial ache.

EKUA OMOSUPE is a graduate student in American Literature at UC Santa Cruz. She is the mother for three children and says they are a crucial part of her support network. Ekua writes poetry and has recently begun to write short fiction. Her goal is to teach literature and writing at university and college levels.

TRINITY A. ORDOÑA is a Filipino American from an immigrant family of thirteen children. Trinity has a long history of civil rights activism in the Filipino community and recently in the gay people of color communities. She is a photographer and is especially known for her slideshow "Asian Pacific Lesbians: Coming Out and Coming Together."

PAT PARKER, Black lesbian poet, feminist medical administrator, mother of two daughters, lover of women, softball devotee and general progressive troublemaker, died of breast cancer on June 17, 1989 at the age of 45. Her 1978 work *Movement In Black* has recently been republished by Firebrand Books.

KIT YUEN QUAN is a F.O.B. who after twenty years is finally putting both feet on shore to go on her Learning To Learn adventures. One of her remedies for symptoms of internalized oppression is the Chinese B.L.T. (Bakery, Library, Tai Chi). Currently she is the office manager and bookkeeper at Spinsters/Aunt Lute Book Company.

TEY DIANA REBOLLEDO is an Associate Professor of Spanish at the University of New Mexico. She has written numerous articles about Chicana literature. Currently she is working on a critical anthology of Chicana writers.

CATALINA RÍOS is an educator and poet. She teaches Spanish as a second language in a Quaker school. Through her poems and teaching she wants to share the many voices often ignored or undermined: the immigrant, the fighter, the person who works for change; also the struggle, the pride and pain that contribute to our lives in a confused and confusing world.

BARBARA RUTH still believes in propoganda by the deed, revolution in the revolution, and that global patriarchy, in all its incarnations and variations, is not healthy for children and other living things.

ELBA ROSARIO SÁNCHEZ was born in Guadalajara, México, and grew up in San Francisco's Mission District. She teaches in the Spanish for Spanish Speakers Program at UC Santa Cruz, where she is also co-editor of *Revista Mujeres*, a bilingual publication by and for Chicanas and Latinas.

CHELA SANDOVAL is a writer, thinker, teacher, student and a UC Santa Cruz History of Consciousness scholar. Her primary interests are in the area of Cultural Criticism where her studies are of the forms of oppositional consciousness which emerge in response to social hierarchy.

BARBARA SMITH is co-founder of Kitchen Table: Women of Color Press. She speaks frequently for women's rights, for Lesbians and especially for Black women. Her work has been published, amongst other places, in *All The Women Are White, All The Blacks Are Men, But Some of Us Are Brave: Black Women's Studies* (1982), which she co-edited, and *Home Girls, A Black Feminist Anthology* (1983), which she edited.

ALETÍCIA TIJERINA, 36, lives in Flagstaff, Arizona with her *familia*: Alan Ray, Azaanabah "Xó," and Ché Tigre (five months). They live between the four sacred mountains of her husband's people, the Diné (Navajo). She is a ceremonial dancer (Sun Dance), and she carries a sacred pipe for the people, given to her through the Lakotas. Once she finishes school, she wants to build a school based on non-violence principles and teach culture, language and the arts.

LYNET UTTAL is the daughter of a Japanese American woman who grew up in Japan and the U.S. and a Russian American Jewish man. She is also a sociology graduate student studying the racial/ethnic and class relationship between mothers and child care providers. She is able to write thanks to Dan, Mary and Alison who take turns caring for David while she works.

HELENA MARÍA VIRAMONTES was born in East Los Angeles in 1954. She is the author of *The Moths and Other Stories* and a 1989 NEA recipient. She is working on a new collection of short stories entitled *Paris Rats in L.A.* and a novel titled *Woman Succumbing to the Pull of the Sea.*

ALICE WALKER, born in Eatonton, Georgia, now lives in northern California. Her novels include *The Third Life of Grange Copeland, Meridian, The Color Purple* and *The Temple of My Familiar.* She has also published collections of short stories, poetry and essays.

ANNE WATERS, of American Indian heritage, is currently finishing her dissertation in philosophy while attending law school. She has taught Women's Studies and Philosophy at six universities, received a National Dissertation Scholarship from NWSA in 1988 and was recently published in *For Lesbians Only* (Onlywomen Press, London, 1989).

SHIRLEY HILL WITT (Akwesasne Mohawk), who holds a Ph.D. in anthropology, has devoted her career to tribal, civil and human rights. She is known for her essays on Native American women and for her books, *The Tuscaroras* and *The Way: An Anthology of American Indian Life and Literature* (with Stan Steiner).

MITSUYE YAMADA, poet and writer, is the founder of Multi-Cultural Women Writers of Orange County; author of *Camp Notes and Other Poems* and *Desert Run: Poems and Stories*; and co-editor of *Sowing Ti Leaves: Writings by Multicultural Women*, now in progress. She is also National Board Member of Amnesty International.

GLORIA JENNIFER JACKSON YAMATO is a Black, single head-of-household mother of two sons, a facilitator, writing when she needs to, though not as often as she'd like. Her goal is to change whatever it is that makes the world seem that some of us were born to have it "our" way and others of us were born to have it "their" way.

BERNICE ZAMORA lives in Santa Clara and teaches for the English Department at Santa Clara University. She is the co-author of *Restless Serpents*, a book of poems. The book is co-authored with Jose Antonio Burciaga, muralist, journalist and poet.

MAXINE BACA ZINN is Professor of Sociology at the University of Michigan-Flint. She is the co-author (with D. Stanley Eitzen) of *Diversity in Families* (Harper and Row, 1990) and *The Reshaping of America* (Prentice Hall, 1990) with Bonnie Thornton Dill. She is co-editing a collection of social science works about women of color (Temple of University Press).

KRISTAL BRENT ZOOK is a light skinned-ded, somewhat nappy-headed Black African American writer working toward her Ph.D. in the History of Consciousness Program at UC Santa Cruz.

photo: Margaret Randall

Gloria E. Anzaldúa is a Chicana tejana lesbian-feminist poet and fiction writer from south Texas now living in Santa Cruz. She is co-editor of *This Bridge Called My Back: Writings by Radical Women of Color* (Kitchen Table: Women of Color Press, 1983), winner of the Before Columbus Foundation American Book Award. Her book *Borderlands/La Frontera: The New Mestiza* (Spinsters/Aunt Lute Book Co., 1987) was picked as one of the 38 Best Books of 1987 by *Library Journal.* She is also the author of a bilingual children's picture book, *Prietita Has A Friend/Prietita tiene un amigo* (Childrens Book Press, 1991). Presently she is working on *Entreguerras, entremundos/Civil Wars Among the Worlds,* a book of autobiographical and fictitious narratives, and on a collection of emerging Chicana/mexicana feminist theory.

Gloria has taught creative writing, Chicano Studies and Feminist Studies at University of Texas, San Francisco State University, Vermont College of Norwich University, University of California at Santa Cruz. She has been a contributing editor of Sinister Wisdom since 1984.

The Aunt Lute Foundation is a non-profit corporation that grew out of the work of the Spinsters/Aunt Lute Book Company. Its purpose is to publish and distribute books that have the educational potential to change and expand social realities.

We seek manuscripts, both fiction and non-fiction, by women from a variety of cultures, ethnic backgrounds and subcultures; women who are self-aware and who, in the face of all contradictory evidence, are still hopeful that the world can reserve a place of respect for each woman in it.

Please write or phone for a free catalogue of the other fine books we have published or if you wish to be on our mailing list for future titles. You can buy books directly from us by phoning in a credit card order or mailing a check with the order form that comes with our catalogue.

Aunt Lute Foundation Books
P.O. Box 410687
San Francisco, CA 94141
415-558-9655